Bridging the Social Gap

Bridging the Social Gap

PERSPECTIVES ON DALIT EMPOWERMENT

EDITED BY

SUKHADEO THORAT
NIDHI SADANA SABHARWAL

⑤SAGE www.sagepublications.com
Los Angeles • London • New Delhi • Singapore • Washington DC

First published in 2014 by

 SAGE Publications India Pvt Ltd
B1/I-1 Mohan Cooperative Industrial Area
Mathura Road, New Delhi 110 044, India
www.sagepub.in

SAGE Publications Inc
2455 Teller Road
Thousand Oaks, California 91320, USA

SAGE Publications Ltd
1 Oliver's Yard, 55 City Road
London EC1Y 1SP, United Kingdom

SAGE Publications Asia-Pacific Pte Ltd
3 Church Street
#10-04 Samsung Hub
Singapore 049483

Published by Vivek Mehra for SAGE Publications India Pvt Ltd, Phototypeset in 10.5/12.5pt Aldine401 BT by Diligent Typesetter, Delhi and printed at Saurabh Printers Pvt Ltd, New Delhi.

Library of Congress Cataloging-in-Publication Data Available

ISBN: 978-81-321-1311-9 (HB)

The SAGE Team: Shambhu Sahu, Alekha Chandra Jena, Nand Kumar Jha and Dally Verghese

To those who struggle to bring change at the grass-roots level

Paul Diwakar, Martin Macwan, Bejwara Wilson, Vimal Thorat, S. Prasad,
Henry Thiagaraj, Sudha Varghese, Manjula Pradeep, Jai Singh, Ruth Manorama,
Ram Kumar, Eknath Awad, P. L. Mimroth, Grace Nirmala and Gagan Sethi

CONTENTS

LIST OF TABLES

LIST OF FIGURES

LIST OF TEMPLATES

LIST OF ABBREVIATIONS

ANC	Antenatal Care
BMI	Body Mass Index
CMR	Child Mortality Rate
CSSM	Child Survival and Safe Motherhood
CPRs	Common Property Resources
GER	Gross Enrolment Rate
GMHPs	Government Maternal Health Programmes
HCR	Head Count Ratio
HDI	Human Development Index/Human Deprivation/Poverty Index
HDRs	Human Development Reports
IMR	Infant Mortality Rate
IRDP	Integrated Rural Development Programme
ILO	International Labour Organisation
MPCE	Monthly Per Capita Consumption Expenditure
NFHSs	National Family Health Surveys
NHDR	National Human Development Report
NIEPA	National Institute of Educational Planning and Administration
NSS	National Sample Survey
NSSO	National Sample Survey Organisation
NGOs	Non-Governmental Organisations
OBCs	Other Backward Classes
PCR	Protection of Civil Rights
PCTE	Per Capita Total (Household Consumer) Expenditure
PHC	Primary Health Centre
PNC	Post Natal Care
POA	Prevention of Atrocities
PPS	Probability Proportion to Size
PSUs	Public Sector Undertakings
RCH	Reproductive and Child Health
SAR	School Attendance Rate
SCs	Scheduled Castes
SEA	Self-Employed in Agriculture
SENA	Self-Employed in Non-Agriculture
SSA	Sarva Shiksha Abhiyan
SCP	Special Component Plann
SRS	Sample Registration System
STs	Scheduled Tribes
UIP	Universal Immunisation Programme
U-5MR	Under Five Mortality Rate
UNDP	United Nations Development Programme
UTs	Union Territories

PREFACE

This study was initially conceived as an alternative report on Human Development to be designated as a Dalit Development Report. However, the completion took more time. To disaggregate the human development indicators by caste and ethnic groups of Scheduled Castes and Scheduled Tribes and the rest is a difficult exercise. Difficulties arise primarily because of the lack of group-wise data, although the same data are available at the aggregate level. Therefore, the researchers had to find out and use alternative variables. This was particularly the case for the indicators which are required to construct Human Development and Human Poverty indices. Equally important challenge is the conceptual framework to study issues related to the excluded and indigenous groups of Scheduled Castes and Scheduled Tribes.

This book has attempted three things: (a) it has developed a conceptual framework to study the causes of low human development of excluded and indigenous groups and estimated the inter-groups disparities in Human Development Index and Human Poverty Index; (b) it constructed the Human Development Index and Human Poverty Index at aggregate level, and disaggregated by groups; and (c) it presents the situation of scheduled castes and scheduled tribes in comparison with others, with regard to each individual indicators. With respect to these three aspects, the book does make a contribution, although some of the data are somewhat dated.

ACKNOWLEDGEMENTS

We thank the authors for undertaking special efforts to collect the data and analyse them for the groups. We thank Martin Macwan, the member of the Governing Board and the former Chairman of Indian Institute of Dalit Studies for providing supplementary funding for the project. Thanks to Swiss Development Agency, New Delhi, for supporting this project.

We thank Tathagata Mandal for editing the draft report and helping with proofs. We thank Narendra Kumar for formatting and designing. Finally, we thank SAGE Publications for publishing this book on a priority basis.

INTRODUCTION

Sukhadeo Thorat and Nidhi Sadana Sabharwal

HUMAN DEVELOPMENT AND SOCIAL INEQUALITY

The preparation of Human Development Reports (HDRs) has brought about a significant shift in the notion of human development, insofar as now the emphasis is placed on 'outcomes of development' in terms of expansion of income and achievement in the quality of well-being of the people. This perspective recognises that though high per capita income is a prerequisite for human development, a rise in income alone may not necessarily guarantee that people receive what they need the most for their development. Therefore, the focus is centred not only on the generation of higher income but simultaneously how it has improved the quality of people's lives. In order to articulate this shift in perspective, Mahbub-ul-Haq observed:

> For long, the recurrent question was how much was a nation producing? Increasingly, the question now being asked is, 'how are its people faring?' Income is only one of the options—and an extremely important one—but it is not the sum total of human life. Health, education, physical environment and freedom may be just as important. (Mahbub-ul-Haq, 1995)

Within this perspective, the emphasis is on the expansion of the capacities of people—their capability to lead a healthy and creative life; to be well-nourished, secured, well-informed, educated, free and treated as equals. With this shift, human development has begun to be measured in terms of new evaluative criteria which are related to three essential elements of human life—longevity, knowledge and decent standard of living. These three elements are estimated using human development index (HDI) and human deprivation/poverty index (HPI).

In the course of this development, however, the notion of human development itself has been further widened in terms of its dimensions. Among other conceptual issues which have engaged researchers in the course of widening the dimensions of the concept of human development are those which relate to group inequalities, particularly inequality in human development across groups and its causes. It has been recognised that a common shortcoming in the measure of human development is its failure to capture the distributional dimensions in human development. The latter represent averages that conceal wide disparities in overall population. Therefore, efforts are made to make the analysis of human development more distribution-sensitive. The incorporation of the distributive aspects necessitated, first, a disaggregation of HDI and HPI by various groups such as class, ethnicity, religion, caste and other disadvantaged groups, and secondly, analysis of causal factors associated with a lower level of human development among certain disadvantaged groups.

Among other factors, the deprivation of marginalised groups like women, and ethnic, social, religious and other minorities generally occurs through the process of exclusion and discrimination. Efforts are, thus, directed towards understanding the societal interrelations and the institutions of exclusion, the prevalent forms of exclusion and discrimination, and their consequences on deprivation of these groups.

Limited instances of disaggregating indicators of human development by social groups are to be found in the HDRs of some countries. The countries which have disaggregated the individual indicators of HDI by groups are Malaysia, Gabon, Nepal, the United States, Canada, Guatemala and India. In Malaysia, for instance, the HDI has been worked out separately for the Chinese, the Indian and the Malaya ethnic groups. Similar exercises have been initiated in the United States for the African-Americans, native Americans and American whites (Halis Akder, 1994). In Nepal too, HDI has been worked out for the low-caste and the high-caste groups.

The attempts made to develop the concepts and methodologies to assess the impact of social exclusion on human deprivation are, however, limited in number. The efforts to develop the indicators of exclusion and to capture them in indices are even fewer. The HDRs of 2000 and 2004 prepared by the United Nations Development Programme (UNDP) made some headway with respect to dimensions of exclusion as well as indicators of exclusion.

At the conceptual level, the HDR 2000 brought to the fore a close link between equal human rights and human development, and emphasised the role of equal opportunity and choices as one of the pillars of human development. Exclusion and discrimination lead to restriction and denial of human rights. It is recognised that the deprivation of disadvantaged groups works through the societal process of exclusion which involves differential treatment and unequal access which in turn hinders human development. Therefore, liberation from discrimination becomes a necessary pre-condition for human development. The HDR 2004 extended the focus to cultural liberty and asserted that cultural liberty is central to the advancement of the capabilities of people. In the context of minorities in multi-ethnic states and indigenous people, it recognised two forms of cultural exclusions, namely (*a*) living mode exclusion which denies recognition to and accommodation of a lifestyle that a particular group would choose to have, and (*b*) participation exclusion which involves denial of social, political and economic opportunities for development to lower-caste groups who are discriminated against. Living mode exclusion often overlaps and intertwines with social, economic and political exclusion by fostering discrimination and disadvantages in terms of access to resources, employment, housing, schooling and political representation.

INDIA'S HUMAN DEVELOPMENT REPORT AND SOCIALLY DISADVANTAGED GROUPS

Following the release of HDRs, the Indian government also initiated the preparation of the National Human Development Report (NHDR) and similar reports for individual states. The first NHDR was prepared in 2001 and so far about 14 State Human Development Reports (SHDRs) have been prepared by the individual states.

Given the iniquitous and hierarchal character of Indian society and exclusion-linked deprivation of a large section of excluded groups and groups which are discriminated against, namely the Scheduled Castes (SCs), the Scheduled Tribes (STs) and Other Backward Classes (OBCs), which constitute more than half of India's population and have specific constitutional provisions, legal safeguards and reservation policies, the NHDRs and SHDRs specifically deal with dimensions of human development in relation to these disadvantaged groups. Hitherto, such exercises have been confined to the disaggregation of the individual indicators of human development and human poverty in a selective manner, without estimating the composite index of human development or human poverty of the social groups. The indicators used to disaggregate data by social groups vary from state to state. The Indian NHDR 2001 disaggregated consumption expenditure, access to toilet facilities, safe drinking water, electricity and literacy levels at the all-India level and observed that the attainment levels for SCs and STs seemed to be lower than for the others (non-SCs/STs) (Planning Commission, 2002: 11).

Similar methods to assess the attainment levels of social groups by employing selective indicators have been followed by a number of SHDRs. Most of the SHDRs employ indicators of literacy and only a few states supplement the literacy level by using poverty ratio, land ownership and health indicators. For instance, the SHDRs of Karnataka, Maharashtra, Tamil Nadu, Madhya Pradesh, West Bengal, Sikkim, Himachal Pradesh, Rajasthan, Assam and Punjab provide attainment rates for literacy among SCs, STs and others (the Himachal Pradesh SHDR also reports the enrolment ratio by social groups). Among these states, Maharashtra and Tamil Nadu also indicate the poverty level by social groups. The SHDRs of Madhya Pradesh, Sikkim and West Bengal further disaggregate land ownership and share of land and beneficiary of land reform by social groups. Some states like Madhya Pradesh and West Bengal include work participation rate, unemployment rate, sex ratio and urbanisation rate by social groups. The Punjab SHDR provides disaggregated results by social groups for literacy rate, employment pattern which includes employment under reservation, and child mortality rates.

The data provided in SHDRs related to SCs and STs is selective and limited in terms of the choice of indicators. Nevertheless, it clearly shows that any simple disaggregation by social groups for education (like literacy rate, enrolment ratios, etc.), healthcare (child mortality), access to resources (land ownership, employment rate) and urbanisation, among other indicators, reveal that SCs and STs lag quite far behind the other sections of Indian society.

This review indicates that despite the group-focus or approach in the development policies of central and state governments (in terms of due recognition of their specific problems, provision of legal safeguards, reservation and various other affirmative action policies, with stipulated objectives to reduce gaps in human development and human poverty between them and other sections of the Indian population), SHDRs generally avoid dealing with issues of inter-social group disparity in human development and human poverty in a focused manner, namely either by using a coherent set of indicators of human development (for example, life expectancy, literacy rate, enrolment ratio and some measures of access to resources), and human poverty (for example, illiteracy, dropout rate and lack of access to safe drinking water, public health services and electricity) or through estimation of a composite index of human development and human poverty by social groups. In addition, there is inadequate discourse on conceptualising caste- and ethnicity-based exclusion and discrimination, and its linkages with human deprivation faced by disadvantaged groups. Similarly, there has been no attempt to develop indicators which capture exclusion, discrimination and impact variables. In this context, the observations of Madhya Pradesh SHDR are relevant as it recognised the need to address such an issue.

> There is a need to look inward, within the country to identify groups that fare poorly in human development as against spatially, in terms of how districts fare or sectors fare. Deprivation in India has an obvious face of exclusion, the SCs due to social exclusion, and the STs due to geographical and cultural exclusion. The SCs suffer from deprivation on account of the residual power of a discriminatory caste system which though made illegal, continues to sway as a social force, whereas the STs see their predicament as victims of the state which denies them property rights to their habitat. An SC and ST development index needs to be developed by professionals to capture their deprivations so as to goad the state policy to address them. A broad attainment index, does not effectively address the roots of these very important deprivations in the Indian context. The process of democracy is at work to draw these people in the mainstream and seek to address their specific concerns. How well this is being done needs to be assessed through the development of SC/ST development index. (Madhya Pradesh State Human Development Report, 2002: 9)

APPROACH OF THE PRESENT BOOK

This book focuses on the issues of inter-social group inequalities in human development and exclusion-linked human deprivation of socially disadvantaged groups in Indian society. It attempts to address four interrelated issues which are mentioned below.

First, drawing from the prevailing theoretical literature, it conceptualises exclusion-linked deprivation of socially disadvantaged groups in Indian society; and elaborates the concept and meaning of social exclusion, in general, and of caste, untouchability and ethnicity-based exclusion, in particular. Second, it presents the status of disadvantaged groups, namely SCs and STs, and captures the inter-social group inequalities with respect to attainment in human development and human poverty by constructing HDI and HPI and also by analysing the individual indicators of well-being. Third, it analyses the economic factors associated with high level of deprivation among socially disadvantaged groups in terms of lower access to resources, employment, education and social needs. Fourth, it examines the role of caste discrimination in economic, civil, social and political spheres which involves denial of or selective restrictions on the right to development or equal opportunities for socially disadvantaged groups.

Chapter 1

EXCLUSION, DEPRIVATION AND HUMAN DEVELOPMENT: CONCEPTUAL FRAMEWORK TO STUDY EXCLUDED GROUPS

Sukhadeo Thorat, Arjan de Haan and Nidhi Sadana Sabharwal

The central purpose of this book is to highlight the status of socially marginalised groups such as Scheduled Castes (SCs) and Scheduled Tribes (STs) with respect to disparities in attainment of human development. Since the deprivation of these groups is closely linked to processes of caste- and ethnicity-based exclusions and discrimination, we shall discuss the concept of social exclusion in general, and caste- and untouchability-based exclusions and discrimination in particular which are seen as causative factors for deprivation faced by these groups.

CONCEPT OF SOCIAL EXCLUSION

In social science literature, there is a general agreement on the core features of social exclusion, its principal indicators and the manner in which it relates to poverty and inequality (Buvinic, 2005). Social exclusion implies the denial of equal opportunities imposed by certain groups on others which prevents an individual's participation in basic political, economic and social functioning of a society.

The following two defining characteristics of exclusion are particularly relevant. First, deprivation is caused through exclusion (or denial of equal opportunity) in multiple spheres which in turn reveal its multidimensionality. Second, it is embedded in societal relations and societal institutions, that is, the processes through which individuals or groups are wholly or partially excluded from full participation in the society in which they live (Haan, 1997). It recognises the diverse ways in which social exclusion can cause deprivation and poverty. The consequences of exclusion, thus, depend crucially on the functioning of social institutions and the degree to which they are exclusionary and discriminatory. Social exclusion has a sizable impact on an individual's access to equal opportunity, if social interactions occur between groups in a power subordinate relationship. The focus on groups, therefore, recognises the importance of social relations in the analysis of poverty and inequality (Buvinic, 2005).

Amartya Sen draws our attention to various meanings and dimensions of the concept of social exclusion (Sen, 2000). He draws a distinction between the situations wherein some people are being kept out (at least left out) and wherein some people are being included (perhaps even being forcibly included) in greatly unfavourable terms. He described these two situations as 'unfavourable exclusion' and 'unfavourable inclusion', respectively. 'Unfavourable inclusion' with unequal treatment may carry the same adverse effects as 'unfavourable exclusion'. Sen also differentiates between 'active' and 'passive' exclusions. For the causal analysis and policy response, Sen argues that

> it is important to distinguish between 'active exclusion'—fostering of exclusion through deliberate policy interventions by the government or by any other wilful agents (to exclude some people from some opportunities)—and 'passive exclusion' which works through the social process in which there are no deliberate attempts to exclude, but nevertheless, may result in exclusion from a set of circumstances.

Furthermore, Sen distinguishes between the 'constitutive relevance' of exclusion and its 'instrumental importance'. In the former, exclusion and deprivation have an intrinsic importance of their own. For example, not being able to relate to others or take part in community life can directly impoverish a person's life, in addition to causing further deprivation. This is different from social exclusion of 'instrumental importance' in which exclusion in itself does not lead to an impoverishment of human life.

Further elaborations of the concepts of exclusion or discrimination have emerged from mainstream economics in the context of race and gender. The mainstream economic literature throws light on discrimination that works through markets and develops the concept of market discrimination with some analytical clarity. In the market discrimination framework, exclusion may operate through restrictions on entry to markets and/or through 'selective inclusion', but with unequal treatment in market and non-market transactions. (This is close to Sen's concept of unfavourable inclusion.)

These developments in social science literature enable us to comprehend the meanings and manifestations of the concept of social exclusion and its applicability to caste- and ethnicity-based exclusion in India. From the manner in which it has been developed in social science literature, the concept of social exclusion, thus, essentially refers to the processes through which groups are wholly or partially excluded from full participation in the society in which they live.

It emphasises two crucial dimensions which involve the notion of exclusion, namely 'societal institutions' (of exclusion) and their 'outcomes' (in terms of deprivation). In order to understand the dimensions of exclusion, it is necessary to understand the societal interrelations and institutions which lead to exclusion of certain groups and deprivation in multiple spheres—civil, cultural, political and economic. Thus, to acquire a broader understanding of exclusion, it is important to gain insights into the societal processes and institutions of exclusion apart from understanding the outcome in terms of deprivation of certain groups. Exclusion could also manifest itself in diverse ways in terms of 'causes and outcomes'. Sen, therefore, refers to various meanings and manifestations of social exclusion particularly with respect to causes or processes of discrimination and deprivation in a given society. Exclusion could occur through direct exclusion, by violating fair norms of exclusion (i.e. unfavourable exclusion) or through inclusion, but under unfavourable conditions, again by violating fair norms of inclusion (i.e. unfavourable inclusion).

CONCEPT OF CASTE-BASED EXCLUSION AND DISCRIMINATION

In India, exclusion revolves around the societal interrelations and institutions that exclude, discriminate against, isolate and deprive some groups on the basis of their group identity, particularly caste. The nature of exclusion revolving around the caste system, thus, needs to be understood within a conceptual framework. It is caste-based exclusion which has formed the basis for the implementation of various anti-discriminatory policies in India. Historically, the caste system has regulated the social and economic life of the people of India. The organisational scheme of the caste system is based on the division of people into social groups (or castes), in which the civil, cultural and economic rights of each caste are pre-determined or ascribed by birth and heredity. The assignment of civil, cultural and economic rights is, therefore, unequal, graded and hierarchical. The most critical feature of caste system, however, is that it provides for a regulatory mechanism to enforce social and economic organisation through the instruments of social ostracism (or social and economic penalties), and reinforces this ostracism further by citing the justification and support from philosophical elements in Hindu religion (Ambedkar, 1936, first published in 1987; Lal, 1988).

The fundamental characteristics of caste system are fixed civil, cultural and economic rights for each caste with restrictions on change which implies the 'forced exclusion' of one caste from the rights of another caste or from undertaking the occupations of other castes. Exclusion and discrimination in the civil, cultural and particularly the economic spheres such as occupation labour and employment are, therefore, integral to the system and a necessary outcome of its governing principles. In the market economy framework, occupational immobility would operate through restrictions in various markets such as those of land, labour, credit, other inputs and services which are necessary for the pursuance of any economic activity. Since labour is an integral part of the production process of any economic activity, it would also obviously become a part of market discrimination. This theorisation implies that caste system involves negation of not only equality and freedom, but also of basic human rights, particularly of the lower caste or 'untouchables', which become impediments in their development. The principles of equality and freedom are not the governing principles of caste system, because the underlying principles of the latter assume particular notions of 'human rights'. Unlike in many other societies, caste system in India does not recognise individual in terms of her/his unique identity and distinctiveness as the centre of a social purpose. In fact, as regards the determination of rights and duties, the unit of Hindu society is not an individual (even the family is not considered as a unit in Hindu society, except for the purposes of marriage and inheritance). The primary unit in Hindu society is caste and hence rights and privileges (or the lack of those) accrue to an individual on account of her/his being a member of a particular caste (Ambedkar, first published in 1987). In addition, due to differential ranking and hierarchical nature of caste system, the entitlements to various rights narrow down as one goes down the hierarchical ladder of caste system. Various castes are interlinked and coupled with each other (in their rights and duties) in a manner such that the rights and privileges of higher castes become causative reasons for disadvantages and disabilities of the lower castes, particularly the untouchables. In this sense, as Ambedkar observed, caste does not exist in a single number, but only in plural. Castes exist as a system of endogenous groups which are interlinked with each other in an unequal measure of rights and relations in all walks of life. Members of castes at the topmost social order enjoy more rights at the expense of those at the bottom. Therefore, the 'untouchables' at the bottom of the caste hierarchy has the least economic and social rights.

Since the civil, cultural and economic rights (particularly with respect to occupation and property rights) of each caste are ascribed and compulsory, the institution of caste necessarily involves forced exclusion of one caste from the rights of another. The unequal and hierarchical assignment of economic and social rights by ascription, thus, obviously restricts freedom of occupation and human development.

FORMS OF EXCLUSION AND DISCRIMINATION

The practice of caste-based exclusion and discrimination necessarily entails lack of access and entitlements, not only to economic rights but also to civil, cultural and political rights. It involves 'living mode exclusion', exclusion in political participation, and exclusion and disadvantage in social and economic opportunities (UNDP HDR, 2004).

Exclusion based on caste, untouchability and ethnicity thus reflects the inability of individuals and groups like the former 'untouchables', Adivasis and similar groups to interact freely and productively with others and to participate fully in economic, social and political community life (Bhalla and Lapeyere, 1997). It is this accordance of partial citizenship or the denial of civil rights (freedom of expression, rule of law, right to justice), political rights (rights and means to participate in exercise of political power) and socio-economic rights (economic security and equality of opportunities) that constitutes the key to impoverished lives (Zoninsein, 2001).

Caste-based Exclusion

In the light of the above discussion, it follows that caste- and untouchability-based exclusion and discrimination can be categorised into economic, civil, cultural and political spheres.

Exclusion and Discrimination in Economic Spheres: Exclusion and denial of equal opportunity in the economic spheres would necessarily operate through markets and non-market transactions and exchange. First, exclusion may be practised in labour market through denial in hiring for jobs; in capital market through denial of access to capital; in agricultural land market through denial of sale and purchase of factor inputs and in consumer market through denial of sale and purchase of commodities and consumer goods. Second, discrimination can occur through what Amartya Sen describes as 'unfavourable inclusion', namely through differential treatment in terms and conditions of a contract, or may be reflected in discrimination in terms of prices charged to and received by the discriminated groups. This can be inclusive of the prices of factor inputs and consumer goods, prices of factors of production such as wages for labour, price of land or rent on land, interest on capital, rent on residential houses, charges or fees on services such as water and electricity. Discriminated groups may get lower prices for goods they sell and may be asked to pay higher prices for goods they buy as compared to the market price paid by other groups. Third, exclusion and discrimination can occur in terms of access to social needs supplied by the government or public institutions or by private institutions in areas of education, housing and healthcare which include common property resources (CPRs) like water bodies, grazing land and other lands of common use. Fourth, a group (particularly the 'untouchables') may face exclusion and discrimination from participation in certain categories of jobs (such as sweepers being excluded from performing jobs inside the house) because of the notion of purity and pollution associated with certain 'unclean' occupations. Members of high castes may not like to associate with persons engaged in these categories of jobs or to perform these jobs on account of their being 'unclean' or 'degrading', which is why such jobs may be relegated to the 'untouchables' (Dalits).

Exclusion and Discrimination in Civil and Cultural Spheres: In civil and cultural spheres, the 'untouchables' may face discrimination and exclusion in the use of public services like public roads, temples, water bodies and institutions which deliver services like education, healthcare and other public services.

Exclusion and Discrimination in Political Spheres: In political spheres, the Dalits could face discrimination in use of political rights and in participation in decision-making processes.

Exclusion and Discrimination in General Spheres: Dalit households being residentially (or physically) segmented or segregated face social exclusion on account of the notion of untouchability. Since societal mechanism is used to regulate and enforce customary norms and rules of the caste system, Dalits generally face opposition in the forms of social and economic boycotts, and the perpetration of violence and even atrocities. Such discriminatory and oppressive forms of social exclusion act as deterrents in their right to development.

Ethnic Identity-based Exclusion

Historically, ethnic social groups like Adivasis (or STs) have suffered from isolation, exclusion and underdevelopment due to their being culturally different from the mainstream Indian society. These groups have a distinct culture, language, social organisation and economy (they generally practise hunting, food gathering and shifting cultivation, and inhabit river valleys and forest regions). The historical nature of their isolation has resulted in considerable deprivation. In their case, exclusion can assume several forms, such as denial of right to resources that can be accessed in areas around which they live, unintended and intended consequences of government policies and societal processes, what Amartya Sen calls 'active and passive exclusions' (the 'active' fostering of exclusion through deliberate policy interventions by the government, or by any other wilful agents to exclude some people from availing opportunities), and 'passive exclusion' and deprivation which operates through social processes wherein there is no deliberate attempt to exclude the persons concerned, but which may nevertheless result in the exclusion of a particular social group from a set of circumstances. The Adivasis may further suffer from what Amartya Sen calls the 'constitutive relevance' of exclusion which arises due to their inability to relate to others, to take part in the life of the community, and thus could directly impoverish the members of these groups.

SUMMING UP

This overview of the development of the concept of 'exclusion', in general and that of caste-based untouchability and ethnicity-based exclusion and discrimination in particular brings out various dimensions of the concept in terms of its nature, forms and consequences. Caste- and untouchability-based exclusion and discrimination are essentially 'structural in nature', comprehensive and multiple in coverage, and involve denial of equal opportunities especially to excluded groups like former 'untouchables'. In the case of the Adivasis, however, such discrimination is not systemic or structural in nature and, therefore, the process of exclusion is different in nature though its outcomes are similar to those faced by former 'untouchables' in many respects, if not all.

Chapter 2

GOVERNMENT POLICY AGAINST DISCRIMINATION AND FOR EMPOWERMENT

Nidhi Sadana Sabharwal

The Indian government has recognised the problems of Scheduled Castes (SCs) and Scheduled Tribes (STs) which arise out of exclusion and discrimination and developed policies to overcome the problems. The government's approach towards SCs/STs draws primarily from the provision in the Constitution. The Constitution guarantees equality before the law (Article 14) (overturning the customary rules of the caste system); makes provisions to promote the political, educational and economic interests of SCs/STs, and protect them from social injustice and all forms of exploitation (Article 46); provides for special measures through reservation in government services and seats in democratic political institutions (Articles 330 and 335). The Constitution of Indian abolished the practice of untouchability and discrimination which arise out of untouchability (Article 17). It also provides for the establishment of a permanent body to investigate and monitor the social and economic progress of SCs and STs on an annual basis and to setting up a monitoring mechanism at the central and state levels.

OFFICIAL STRATEGY

In general, the approach and strategy of the government towards SCs/STs have been influenced by the following main considerations:

1. First, to provide safeguards against continuing exclusion and discrimination in civil, cultural, political and economic spheres in society through legal protection.
2. Second, to undertake specific measures to overcome the deprivation faced by certain groups due to denial of equal opportunities in the past and to improve their levels of access and participation in social, economic and

political processes in the country through development of inclusive policies and to bring them at par with other sections of Indian society to the maximum extent possible.

Towards this end, the government has adopted a twofold strategy. They are:

1. Remedial measures and safeguards against discrimination in various spheres.
2. Developmental and empowering measures particularly in economic sphere.

Remedial Measures

Remedial measures against discrimination include enactment of Anti-untouchability Act of 1955 (renamed as Protection of Civil Rights Act in 1979) and the Scheduled Castes and Scheduled Tribes (Prevention of Atrocities) Act, 1989. Under these Acts, the practice of untouchability and discrimination in public places and community life is treated as an offence. The second Act provides legal protection to SCs and STs against violence and atrocities perpetrated by members of higher castes.

Safeguards

The government policy, however, does not end with providing legal protection against discrimination but goes beyond, to develop measures to provide equal opportunity and fair participation in economic and political spheres. The reservation policy, under which a specific quota is reserved in proportion to the population in government services, public sector undertakings, insurance and government banking institutions, state-run and state-supported educational institutions, public housing, other public spheres, and in various political democratic bodies including the parliament, state assemblies, and panchayat institutions at the district, taluk and village levels, falls under measures aimed to ensure fair and equal participation for SCs/STs. The safeguards against discrimination have been used by the government to ensure proportional participation of SCs/STs in various public spheres which otherwise may not have been possible due to residual effects of exclusion and discrimination related to caste and untouchability, particularly for SCs.

The measures and safeguards against discrimination in the form of reservation policy are, however, confined to state-run and state-supported sectors, while the private sector comprising agriculture, private industry and cooperative sector, wherein the bulk of SC/ST workers (or population) are engaged, does not come under the umbrella of the reservation policy. In the absence of legal safeguards and a more comprehensive reservation policy that also covers the private sector, the state resorts to the implementation of general programmes to ensure economic, educational and social empowerment of SCs/STs.

Developmental and Empowering Measures

The focus has been to improve private ownership of fixed capital assets like agricultural land, non-land capital assets, education and skill development, and access to social and basic services like housing, healthcare, drinking water, electricity and others. The strategy to improve private ownership of capital assets or building human resource capabilities has been undertaken primarily as part of anti-poverty and other economic and social programmes for the poor by targeting or fixing specific informal quotas for SC/ST households in the case of divisible schemes. These measures in the private economic domain are, in a way, akin to informal affirmative action measures.

The above-mentioned measures have been developed to improve ownership of capital assets, land and non-land assets, and enhance business capabilities and skills of SC/ST persons to enable them to undertake self-employment activities. The distribution of surplus land from the ceiling and government land to landless households, with supportive schemes of supply of credit and inputs at subsided rates to SC/ST households in rural areas is expected to increase the ownership of agricultural land and productivity of land assets among these households. The schemes to provide financial capital, training and information to SCs/STs to assist them to initiate new businesses or improve the existing ones include measures to improve ownership of capital and business, and to strengthen their capacity to undertake entrepreneurial activities. The Integrated Rural Development Programme (IRDP) was the first self-employment programme launched to enable certain identified rural poor families to enhance their income through acquisition of credit-based productive assets. Wage employment is also provided to wage labour households under various wage employment schemes.

The social needs include provision of education, drinking water, housing, electricity, and sanitation, among other amenities. Educational development also constitutes to be part of a major programme of the government (about half of the Central Government spending on programmes for SCs/STs is in the area of education). The educational schemes being implemented by the government include measures to:

1. improve educational infrastructure, including scholarship/fellowship, hostel and remedial coaching for SCs/STs;
2. increase admission in educational institutions through reservation of seats and other measures;

3. provide financial support at various levels of education, including scholar-ships/fellowships (national and international);
4. provide remedial coaching to improve quality of education and capabilities;
5. provide special hostels for boys and girls.

In all these schemes, there is a special focus on girls' education.

The government has also developed schemes to improve the access of SC/ST households to civic amenities like drinking water, housing, sanitation, electric-ity and roads. Since the settlements of SCs in rural areas are mostly segregated, the civic amenities often fail to reach them. Therefore, special assistance is pro-vided to the state (under the special central assistance to Special Component Plan [SCP] for SCs and Tribal Sub-plan) to ensure supply of these amenities.

The problems faced by SC and ST women occupy special place in various government programmes. These women not only face gender discrimination like their upper-caste counterparts, but they simultaneously suffer the problems spe-cifically related to their caste and ethnic backgrounds, which include extremely low levels of literacy and education; dependence on wage labour, discrimination in employment and wages; heavy concentration in unskilled, low-paid and some-times hazardous manual jobs; violence and sexual exploitation; and victimisation due to the prevalence of religious and social superstitions like the *Devdasi* system. Therefore, in each of the programmes aimed at economic empowerment, educa-tional development and gender-related issues, there is a special focus on SC/ST women. Legislations have been enacted and schemes developed to overcome their specific problems.

About one-third of the total funds of the central government are allocated for economic empowerment; about half for education and the remaining one-fifth for social services like housing (Ministry of Social Justice and Empowerment Annual Report, 2005; Ministry of Tribal Affairs Manual, 2005).

ADMINISTRATIVE SET-UP FOR IMPLEMENTATION AND MONITORING

An elaborate administrative machinery has been developed at the Centre and in the states/Union Territories (UTs) to implement programmes for SCs/STs. The nodal ministries at the Centre are the Ministry of Social Justice and Empowerment, and the Tribal Ministry which support and supplement the financial efforts of the other Union ministries, state governments, UTs and non-governmental organisa-tions (NGOs) in this sphere. These ministries are entrusted with the task of policy framing, and monitoring and evaluation of central government programmes which are mainly implemented by individual states. The ministries work closely with the Planning Commission (under the Ministry of Planning) to formulate

SCP for SCs and Tribal Sub-plans for STs. At the Centre, most of the ministries have division or section which looks after specific schemes meant for SCs/STs. The ministries also conduct research and training programmes to evaluate the efficacy of ongoing programmes in order to improve their implementation.

The other important independent administrative institutions which supervise, monitor and offer suggestions for effective implementation of laws and schemes for SCs/STs are the National Commission for SCs and STs, Commission for Safai Karamcharis and Standing Committee of Parliamentarians on SCs and STs. The National Commission for SCs/STs is a statutory body which oversees the development of these groups and has been preparing annual reports since 1950, to document their progress. These reports are also discussed in the Parliament every year.

A similar administrative set-up also exists at the state level, though there are considerable variations across the states. Generally, most of the states have separate ministries for SCs/STs, whose function is to formulate policies, as well as implement, monitor and evaluate programmes for SCs/STs. These programmes are generally implemented through special departments at the state, division and district levels, and in many cases even at the taluk level. Further, many states have Commissions for SCs and STs, like the corresponding commission at the Centre.

FINANCIAL MECHANISM—SPECIAL COMPONENT PLAN AND TRIBAL SUB-PLAN

Over a period of time, the central and the state governments have developed a specific mechanism for allocation of funds for schemes intended for SCs/STs. Till the end of the Fourth Plan (1979–1980), the only funds available for the development of SCs/STs were under the general head of 'Backward Class Sectors'. From the Sixth Plan onwards, a new mechanism was introduced for the allocation of funds from the general sectors for the development of SCs and STs, such as the SCP for SCs and the Tribal Sub-plan for STs. The present mechanism or strategy of financial allocation has been operationalised through these special plans.

The SCP for SCs and Tribal Sub-plan for STs is designed to channelise the flow of funds (and the consequent benefits) from the general sectors in the plans of the state and central ministries for the development of SCs and STs in both physical and financial terms. These plans aim to identify schemes that would benefit SCs/STs, to quantify funds from all divisible programmes under each sector, and to determine specific targets in terms of the number of families that need to be covered for benefits offered under the programmes implemented for each sector. The practice that has been followed so far is to finalise sectoral outlays at the time of finalisation of the annual plan of a particular state, and the share under the SCP and Tribal Sub-plan for each sector is determined thereafter. The Special Central

Assistance to SCP is designed to supplement the efforts of the states towards ensuring the speedy development of SCs by providing additional support to SC families so as to enable them enhance their productivity and incomes to facilitate occupational diversification.

The central government and most of the state governments have also established financial institutions like the Scheduled Caste Finance Corporation, to provide SC entrepreneurs capital to undertake businesses and other economic activities. The main function of the Scheduled Caste Development Corporations in the states is to mobilise institutional credit for economic development schemes for the benefit of SC entrepreneurs by functioning as catalysts, promoters and guarantors. These corporations provide credit to SC/ST persons for business purposes and also encourage financial institutions, particularly the commercial banks, to give credit to SCs/STs. Under the priority sector guidelines, nationalised banks are also required to provide a specified 10 per cent of their total advances to the weaker sections which include SC/ST borrowers. The guidelines also prioritise bank advances for SCs/STs.

Chapter 3

EXCLUSION AND DISCRIMINATION: THE CONTEMPORARY SCENARIO

Sukhadeo Thorat and Prashant Negi

The disparities which stem from discriminatory societal attitudes constitute a stumbling block in furthering human development and human rights. The Constitution of India lays down elaborate and unequivocal ideals and legal instruments for justice, equality and prohibition of discrimination. Despite constitutional provisions, it is an unfortunate and visible social reality that Dalits in India continue to be subjected to injustice, social prejudice and exploitation. Since the focus of this book is to capture the incidences of 'exclusion-linked deprivation', this chapter focuses on the magnitude of discrimination and untouchability in multiple spheres which include civil rights violations and perpetration of atrocities against Dalits by using both official statistics and evidence from multiple micro-level studies. The evidence presented in support of this endeavour is characterised by both macro- and micro-level characteristics.

CASTE SYSTEM AND SOCIAL OSTRACISM

In a traditional and formal sense, caste system is characterised by three interrelated and highly intertwined principles. These are: first, the ascription of social, cultural, religious and economic rights for each caste; second, the unequal and hierarchical (graded) division of these rights between the castes and third, the provision of strong social ostracism mechanisms supported by social and religious ideologies. While the first two principles define and describe the framework of caste system, the third principle designates social mechanisms for its enforcement.

The incidences of social ostracism against Dalits are normally characterised by and enforced in the form of numerous penalties against violation of customary rules, norms and boundaries of caste system. The forms of social ostracism vary from social, cultural, political and economic boycott to various types of physical punishments. Apparently, those who initiate change and display some sort of upward social and financial mobility or those who attempt to extricate themselves from the traditional rules of caste behaviour are at the receiving end. Since the customary rules of caste derive support from some elements of the Hindu social philosophy, any deviation from the moral code of conduct laid down in the caste system invites social ostracism and various forms of atrocities against Dalits, all of which are considered to be socially just and morally right.

NATURE OF ATROCITIES AND VIOLATION OF CIVIL RIGHTS

Chapter 2 has outlined the government strategy to ameliorate the problems and to improve the status of Dalits and Adivasis in India, and also to provide them social, economic, educational, cultural and political safeguards. In order to ensure the provision of legal safeguards, the government has introduced two Acts: the Protection of Civil Rights (PCR) Act 1955, and the Scheduled Castes and Scheduled Tribes (Prevention of Atrocities) (POA) Act 1989. The objectives of these Acts are to deliver social justice and enable SCs/STs to live with dignity without the fear of violence and atrocities. Unfortunately, even the presence of such elaborate statutes does not seem to be a sufficient deterrent as the perpetuation of crimes against SCs and incidences of discrimination against them in secular public spheres continue unabated. The incidences of the violation of the civil, social, economic, political and cultural rights of Dalits, and also crimes committed against SC/ST women are given in Tables 3.1 to 3.6. The extent, magnitude and nature of various crimes committed against SCs and STs, as evident from these tables, indicate that both exclusion of and discrimination against SCs/STs continue to be practised and that the traditional mechanisms of their enforcement are still prevalent.

Macro Evidence

The official statistics for the decadal period 1992–2001 indicate that a total of about 285,871 cases of various crimes were registered countrywide by SCs of which 14,030 were registered under the PCR Act, and 81,796 under the POA Act (Annexure I Table 3A.1). This implies that an average of 28,587 cases of caste discrimination and atrocities against SCs were registered every year during the 1990s. An analysis of the types of civil rights violations and atrocities indicates that on an average (for the 10-year period 1992–2001), 561 murders, 3,262 cases of injury, 982 rapes, 266 cases of kidnapping/abduction, 64 dacoities, 181 robberies, 399 cases of arson, 1,403 incidences of caste discrimination and 8,179 cases of atrocities were registered by SCs.

The average incidence of crime during the period 1999–2001 shows that the three states, Uttar Pradesh, Rajasthan and Madhya Pradesh, together account for

Table 3.1
Civil Rights Violations

	Date and Place	Nature of Incidence/Atrocities
1.	22 September 1999, Pedakalikri village, Andhra Pradesh	Traffic delayed temporarily by a Dalit *Vinayaka* procession. One upper-caste youth named Venu Naidu disembarked from the bus, abused Dalits and later attacked the Dalit community and chopped off the hands of a Dalit named Mogili Eswar.
2.	5 March 2005, Bhavnagar, Gujarat	A Dalit named Lakhabhai Nathubhai was attacked and his hands and legs were broken because he sought the help of state authorities to recover land that was illegally taken from him by an upper-caste individual.
3.	28 March 2007, Perambalur, Tamil Nadu	Eviction, dumping of waste on the road to block the path of Dalits to their homes, physical abuse and molestation, arbitrary arrest in Arunagirimangalam village.
4.	6 August 2006, Bhojpur, Bihar	Four *Nats* beaten to death by a mob in Ara village for allegedly stealing a buffalo.
5.	6 March 2004, Shinde, Maharashtra	Dalits attempted to assert their rights and mobilise themselves to secure them. The higher-caste mob attacked the Dalits and brutally injured 20 Dalits. Even children and women were not spared. The Dalit dwellings were burnt.
6.	18 August 2004, Samastipur, Bihar	A Dalit named Subai Mahto of Hansa village was shot dead by a police officer named Rajesh Kumar Roy for protesting against the kidnapping and brutal murder of his son Amarnath. Enjoying the support of the police authorities and district administration, Rajesh Kumar Roy roughed up Subai; arrested, jailed and tortured him; and eventually killed him in custody.
7.	18 February 2004, Hissar, Haryana	Dalits were protesting against the kidnapping and murder of a Dalit named Vijay Kumar of Ambedkar Colony as the alleged murderer and his accomplices were given protection by members of the upper castes and the police.
8.	20 July 2004, Barabanki, Uttar Pradesh	A Dalit resident named Salikram of Dhanayi village in Siddhaur filed a petition before the Chief Minister to save his land from being acquired for the construction of a road. For filing his petition, Salikram was locked up in jail by the police in collusion with the local politicians. They also implicated him in a false case.
9.	23 February 2004, Muzzafarnagar, Uttar Pradesh	A Dalit was killed and others were injured after protesting at an event, for which they were attacked.
10.	15 March 2005, Moga, Punjab	Upper-caste Hindus, with police aid, have been refusing to allow Dalits to build toilets in the panchayat even though they have nowhere else to build the facilities.

Source: As reported in media.

Table 3.2
Social Rights Violations

	Date and Place	Nature of Incidence/Atrocities
1.	10 January 2007, Raipur, Chhattisgarh	A locality inhabited by Dalits in Tundra village was devastated on account of a caste conflict which arose from tensions over the fact that Dalit women cooked food in the mid-day meal scheme which the children from the upper castes refused to eat.
2.	14 December 2001, Jaipur, Rajasthan	Harassment and torture of Dalits by members of dominant caste for bathing in a public pond in Chakwara village.
3.	20 December 2004, Cuddapah, Andhra Pradesh	Members of upper castes in Kotha Cheruvu village, attempted to thwart government plans to provide adequate water supplies to Dalits. The latter were also subjected to physical assault and discrimination for trying to expose the actions of the upper caste members.
4.	20 December 2006, Supaul, Bihar	Dalits threatened with death after an inter-caste marriage took place between a Dalit girl and a youth from a dominant caste in Ithamanikpur village. The police refused to offer any protection to the Dalits or even file an FIR against those who issued the threats.
5.	10 March 2004, Kozhikode, Kerala	Educational benefits being offered to SC/ST students in the self-financing colleges were stopped and Dalit students were told to discontinue their studies if they could not remit the fees.
6.	11 March 2004, Jaunpur, Uttar Pradesh	Upper-caste teachers at a school in Pandeypur village in Machal-ishar subdivision dictated that only the upper caste and Yadav girls would take the practical test of Home Science (cookery) examination while Dalits were disallowed from taking the examination.
7.	14 January 2004, Nathdwara, Rajasthan	At Shrinathji Temple in Nathdwara, about 25 members of a Dalit human rights group were denied entry into the temple by upper-caste Hindus, while the police present there did not offer any help to Dalits.
8.	24 February 2004, Jalna, Maharashtra	Forty Dalit families of Babultara village were living in terror following a dispute regarding a common water pump. They were forced to hide at the police station after upper-caste men issued grave threats and badly beat up one member of their community.

Source: As reported in media.

63.6 per cent of the total crimes committed against SCs (Annexure I Table 3A.2). These three states are also among the top three in terms of crime rate (number of crimes committed against SCs in relation to their population). The other states where crime rate is close to all-India average of 2.7 per cent are Andhra Pradesh, Gujarat, Karnataka, Orissa and Tamil Nadu. In addition to high crime rate, the conviction rate for the perpetrators of atrocities is very low which reflects that the traditional customary rules associated with caste and the institution of

Table 3.3
Economic Rights Violations

	Date and Place	Nature of Incidence/Atrocities
1.	2002, Mahboobnagar, Andhra Pradesh	Upper-caste men resorted to interference with cultivation at a farm owned by a Dalit in Chilver village in Medjil *mandal*. The upper-caste farmers forcibly laid a borewell on Dalit agricultural land by digging a 3-km long pipeline till their own field. The stoppage of irrigation water supply to the Dalit farmer led to drying up of his crops. He was also beaten up and abused when he demanded his right.
2.	August 2004–October 2004, Krishna and Hyderabad, Andhra Pradesh	Land assigned to Dalits for housing was forcefully taken away by the upper-caste members.
3.	20 December 2006, Sagar, Madhya Pradesh	Dalits took a land area on lease near the Beela dam from the MP irrigation department for cultivation. Individuals from dominant caste illegally reaped the produce and physically assaulted the lessee, chopping off his ears and breaking his left femur.
4.	12 July 2006, Guntur, Andhra Pradesh	Dalits faced seizure of their lands, physical assault and abuse after they protested against the obstruction of the flow of irrigation water to their lands by members of upper castes in Kantepudi village.
5.	20 January 2007, Coimbatore, Tamil Nadu	Dalits were subjected to bonded labour in Muthunagar village.
6.	6 March 2004, Jabalpur, Madhya Pradesh	Twenty-five Adivasis and Dalits of Maihar were kept as bonded labourers at a brick factory for five months.
7.	2 January 2004, *The Times of India*	In a bid to control agricultural land, many tehsil officials openly joined hands with members of upper castes to usurp the lands of rightful owners who are mostly tribals, backward caste members or Dalits.
8.	Starting from 1974 till the present day in Ghazipur, Uttar Pradesh	A Dalit working as a *safai karamchari* in a government-aided senior basic school since 1974 has till date been facing monetary exploitation by way of gross under-payment of wages which are substantially below the stipulated minimum wage.

Source: As reported in media.

untouchability continue to exercise an influence in Indian society. All over India, out of about 9,000 cases brought to courts (as in 2002) under the PCR Act, in one year, the trial was completed in only 15 per cent of the cases and nearly 7,750 cases were still pending by the end of the year (Annexure I Table 3A.3). In about 87 per cent cases in which the trials were completed, no conviction was made.

Table 3.4
Political Rights Violations

	Date and Place	Nature of Incidence/Atrocities
1.	22 October 2003, *The Hindu*	Dalits faced the denial of their right to contest elections, as the Tamil Nadu government refused to support efforts to allow reserved political seats in the state to be filled by those for whom they had been reserved.
2.	13 January 2004, *Indian Express*	There was fear amongst Dalits in Patna, Bihar, with the elections drawing near, as the Ranvir Sena continued to operate without being labelled as a terrorist organisation, despite indulging in numerous massacres of Dalits.
3.	14 October 2006, Cuddalore, Tamil Nadu	Dalits were denied political participation during the local government election in 2006 in Pathirakottai village. Upper-caste members unleashed violence against Dalits, damaged their property and attacked them with weapons after the Dalits refused to withdraw their candidature in the elections.
4.	8 December 2006, East Godavari, Andhra Pradesh	The Sarpanch of Kovvuru village, who was an elected representative at the grassroot level, was restrained from discharging her duties on account of her Dalit status. She also faced physical assault and abuse because of her caste.
5.	22 November 2006, Thoothukudi, Tamil Nadu	A Dalit was killed due to assertion of his right of political participation in the panchayat in Nakkalamuthapati village.
6.	2 April 2004, NDTV	Dalits in a village in Kaithal, Haryana, suffered boycotts and threats for over a year and were forced to flee their village after they refused to support the local Jats in elections.
7.	18 March 2004, *The Hindu*	Dalits in Kollam, Kerala, alleged that they were not being given even the bare minimum of concessions that should be provided under the Constitution in terms of political appointments and opportunities.
8.	18 February 2004, *Navbharat Times*	A woman panchayat president of Mahijakancheri village in Tripur district, Tamil Nadu, was subjected to social boycott because she questioned leaders of upper caste who illegally felled a tree.

Source: As reported in media.

In fact, out of a total of 150 cases in which the accused was punished, 137 cases were from a single state, Tamil Nadu. The record of states like Madhya Pradesh, Maharashtra and Karnataka, wherein large numbers of cases were registered under the PCR ACT, is also very poor in terms of speedy provision of justice. Besides the cases under the PCR Act, the number of other pending cases of crime and atrocities against SCs is also very high. In all, 100,891 cases were still pending in courts by the end of the year 2000 countrywide. Uttar Pradesh topped the list with 74,303 pending cases, followed by Maharashtra (8,212), Rajasthan (5,836),

Table 3.5
Cultural Rights Violations

	Date and Place	Nature of Atrocities/Incidence
1.	9 March 2004, Meerut, Uttar Pradesh	In Mahalawala village under the Kitaur police station limits, a Dalit youth was hacked to death with a sword while 10 others were grievously injured during a caste clash that took place when they were playing Holi.
2.	February 2007 Angul, Orissa	There were reports of discriminatory practices against Dalit children in schools, as the latter were made to sit outside on the verandah while higher caste children sat inside classrooms.
3.	4 March 2007 Khurda, Orissa	Dalits in Chanagiri village were beaten up by non-Dalits when the former refused to beat drums on the occasion of Holi.
4.	22 November 2006, Chhattarpur, Madhya Pradesh	Members of upper caste beat up some Dalits, painted their faces black, festooned slippers around their necks and paraded them on donkeys on the suspicion that these Dalits practised witchcraft against upper castes.
5.	29 January 2004, *Dainik Jyoti*	The village panchayat president in Raythal village of Rajasthan forcibly stopped a wedding procession of Dalits and threatened to kill them if they continued with the procession.
6.	31 March 2004, *Indian Express*	Dalits in Raigad village of Maharashtra suffered a total social boycott by the rest of the community for an entire year after they drew water from a common well.
7.	26 March 2004, *The Tribune*	A Dalit youth in Panipat, Haryana, was shot dead and his body was cut into pieces for his alleged affair with an upper-caste girl.

Source: As reported in media

Table 3.6
Abuse and Crime against SC Women

	Date and Place	Nature of Incidence/Atrocities
1.	12 February 2004, Shivpuri, Madhya Pradesh	A Dalit woman was allegedly raped by her landlord and his friend and then set her on fire when she threatened to complain about it.
2.	29 September 2006, Bhandara, Maharashtra	A Dalit mother and her daughter were paraded naked in Tah Mohadi village over a land dispute and allegations of an illicit relationship.
3.	7 December 2006, Jaisalmer, Rajasthan	A Dalit woman was sexually assaulted and her house was ransacked and destroyed in a bid by upper castes to usurp a piece of panchayat land given to the Dalit family in Bhaniyana village.
4.	30 January 2003, Puri, Orissa	A local women's organisation in Nuagaon village forced a Dalit woman to sign for a loan and turned violent with her when she refused to do so.

(Table 3.6 Contd.)

(Table 3.6 Contd.)

	Date and Place	Nature of Incidence/Atrocities
5.	December 2006–February 2007, Patiala, Punjab	A Dalit woman was subjected to rape and atrocities for three months after being lured for a job in the city.
6.	10 November 2003, *The Tribune*	A Dalit woman in Haryana was allegedly stripped and abused in front of her son after another son of her's allegedly eloped with the daughter of one of the persons who attacked her.
7.	22 February 2004, *Indian Express*	In Mumbai, about 1,000 members of the Air Corporation SC/ST Employees' Association demonstrated at the Air India Colony after the officials of the Corporation reportedly stated that 'untouchables' could not become air hostesses.
8.	8 February 2004, *Amar Ujala*	A 14-year-old Dalit girl in Banda, Uttar Pradesh was kidnapped by youth and raped for two days before being drugged and dropped outside the forest. The police refused to offer any help in the incident.

Source: As reported in media.

Orissa (5,669), Andhra Pradesh (1,845), Tamil Nadu (1,810), Karnataka (1,794) and Kerala (1,768).

The reported incidence and rate of crime against STs is lower than against SCs (see Annexure I Tables 3A.1 and 3A.4). The total number of registered cases during the period 1999–2001 was about 47,000, out of which 8 per cent cases pertained to rape and 16 per cent were registered under the POA Act. As regards STs, across the states, as seen in the case of crimes against SCs, the states of Rajasthan and Madhya Pradesh are the top two states in terms of crime rate recorded against STs. These two states account for 57 per cent of the cases registered at the all-India level regarding the perpetration of atrocities against STs. The ranking of the states based on the crime rate is identical for both SCs and STs which indicate that in certain states, the roots of discrimination based on caste and ethnicity are equally deep.

Micro Evidence

The studies based on primary surveys capture the qualitative nature and pattern of caste discrimination and atrocities, and also suggest that in actual practice, the incidences of atrocities are much greater in number than seen in the official statistics reported to the police. On the basis of primary studies and media reports, some such incidences and the nature of discrimination and atrocities are outlined below that highlight the extent and nature of the civil, social, cultural, political, economic and gender-related atrocities perpetrated against SCs and STs in the country.

DISCRIMINATORY PRACTICES

The widespread prevalence of discriminatory practices in various spheres of public life, like access to water resources, public thoroughfares, modes of public (but not state-owned) transport and other village-level services and amenities like tea shops, and services of barbers or washermen and so on speak volumes about the status of the scheduled social groups in India, particularly the SCs. The ActionAid Study (2001) which was carried out in about 550 villages in 11 states throws light on umpteen discriminatory practices which prevail in the countryside. Some of them are reproduced below.

Residential Segregation

Caste-segregated neighbourhoods tend to be the rule rather than exception in Indian villages and the dwellings are usually clustered on caste basis. The treatment of SC *wada* or *cheri* or *basti* (colonies) as outcastes (or 'outcasting' them, as the practice is commonly known as) is a common feature found all over the country. There are often explicit customs about the particular direction (relative to the 'main' village) that SC settlements can or cannot occupy (see Template I).

Template I
Residential Segregation in Punjab

Traditionally, in Punjab, SC settlements have to be located on the west side (of the main village). Although in several villages it was found that SC houses were not located on the western side of the main village, yet at the same time, in almost all the villages surveyed, the SC dwellings were constructed outside the village and were, therefore, residentially segregated. Over the years, however, population growth and a continuous urban expansion to the peripheral areas have, to some extent, diluted the old settlement structure of the village. As the upper castes build new and big houses outside the village, SC settlements begin to look less isolated than before. Nevertheless, segregation with regard to playing of children seems to be strictly and openly enforced in several villages.

Government programmes for SC housing are also unable to escape the spatial segregation dictated by upper-caste 'tradition'. Government schemes such as the Indira Awaas Yojana for SCs are obviously welcomed by SCs because of the financial aid they offer, but since most of them are located at a distance from the village and only SC families are allotted houses in these schemes, they end up reinforcing the segregation of SCs from the main village.

Denial of Access and Discriminatory Treatment in Basic Public Services

Drinking Water: In rural areas, discrimination against SCs in terms of access to drinking water is quite common. This is generally manifested in SCs who have to wait for higher castes to fill water first, move away from the well if a higher-caste person arrives to fill water, or wait on one side of the water source, and ensure that their vessels do not touch those of the upper-caste persons who are drawing water or waiting for their turn, among other such practices. Sometimes SCs are also completely denied access to a particular water source in the village such as a well, tank or tubewell (see Template II).

Template II
Friction over Access to Drinking Water Sources

In Lon Khurd village of Parbhani district (in Marathwada region of Maharashtra), there are separate sources of drinking water for SC and non-SC/ST persons. If an SC draws water from public source, there are protests. If SC and non-SC/ST persons draw water at the same time, the SCs are made to wait till non-SCs/STs have finished their turn. There are seven handpumps in the village, out of which only three are located in SC colony. During their visit to the village, the ActionAid researchers saw that Sopan Jandhale, an SC, was drawing water when Shankar Jogdand, a Maratha, came there and told the former to move his vessels away. Jogdand then filled his own vessels and went away. When anyone belonging to the Maratha or Laud castes is at the handpump, the SCs who may be there at the same time are made to wait until the higher-caste persons have finished. If the water vessels of the SCs touch those of the higher-caste members, then the latter wash and refill their vessels. Many fights have broken out whenever any SC has refused to be subservient to the *savarna* (higher caste) person. Villagers also narrated an incident related to filling of water that led to a big brawl in 1994. This resulted in a police case that went on in the local courts for about two to three years.

In Itwakhas village of Panna district (in Bundelkhand region of Madhya Pradesh), SC women said that they always have to wait at a common well in the village. They are forced to stand at a distance with their vessels so that they do not touch those of non-SCs/STs. The *savarna* women also take long time to fill their vessels while they leisurely chat with their friends. At times, this leads to quarrels, and *savarna* women hurl casteist (abusive) names at SC women. At times, such delays in filling of water cause SC women to be late for their daily work, which, in turn, adversely affects their chances of earning labour wages for that particular day.

Village Shops: At several places, SCs are made to wait outside or at some distance from the shops. The shopkeepers often place the things to be sold on the ground for SC buyers to pick them up. Similarly, money is not directly accepted from SC customers who have to leave it somewhere so that they do not come into physical contact with higher-caste shopkeepers. Incidences of discrimination are also observed at teashops, wherein SC customers are asked to sit separately from their non-SC/ST counterparts, and are served in separate utensils which are usually washed by SC customers themselves. Apart from the cases mentioned in Template III, there are several reports about the widespread prevalence of 'two-glass system' in Indian villages which suggest that discriminatory treatment in matters of food and drink is among the most pervasive aspects of the practice of untouchability in the country.

Template III
Teacups in Bihar and Rajasthan

In Rusundo of Damoh (in Mahakoshal region of Bihar) village, the researchers of ActionAid came face-to-face with the practice of untouchability in a village teashop. The shopkeeper, a non-SC/ST and member of Lodhi caste told the researchers that tea glasses for *Chamars* and *Basods*, two prominent SC castes in the area, were kept separately. He added that he does not wash those glasses after use, regardless of caste the customers belong to. When the researchers too refused to wash the glasses they had used, they had to pay for the new glasses and the used glasses were given to local SCs. Such incidents of separate utensils being kept for SC customers were also reported from villages in western Madhya Pradesh and Bundelkhand region.

Dayal, a 25-year-old SC, lived in a Suroth village in Karauli district of eastern Rajasthan. Once when his friend from the same community visited him, he took the former to the nearest hotel owned by a non-SC/ST called Roshanlal for tea. When he saw that the tea did not contain the requisite quantity of milk, Dayal asked Roshanlal's son the reason. Annoyed at being so questioned, Roshanlal's son insulted Dayal and his friend using derogatory language. Dayal was insulted again the next day when he came to buy something from the hotel. Angry, at these public insults, Dayal and his two friends beat up Roshanlal's son. Previously, Dayal had also complained against the village sarpanch for not solving the problems faced by SC residents of the village. Seeing this as an opportunity to take revenge, the non-SC/ST sarpanch, in collusion with Roshanlal, set Roshanlal's hotel on fire and lodged an FIR against Dayal in the police station accusing him of arson. False witnesses were tutored against Dayal and his father, and the latter were made to apologise in front of the entire village besides being directed to pay a fine of ₹3,000.

Subsequently, though Dayal's father went to Roshanlal with the money, the latter refused to take it. Eventually, police arrested Dayal for a crime that he had not committed. He was subjected to ruthless torture and abuses in police station and later released on bail. Dayal's travails did not stop there. Later, when he started a bicycle repairing shop, a non-SC/ST customer brought a cycle for repair to his shop and refused to pay for the service. He told Dayal to sell the bicycle and take the money for repairing. The very next day another person came to his shop and accused him of stealing his bicycle. He even lodged a complaint against Dayal at the police station. He was again arrested and subjected to torture and abuses. Presently, he has to appear in court every month for two cases that have been falsely registered against him.

Apart from the restrictions on sharing of food and drink between Dalits and non-SCs/STs, there is a much wider prevalence of discrimination in more 'traditional' spheres as is evident from Template IV.

Template IV
Discrimination by Hairdressers in Tamil Nadu

SC men generally get their hair cut by their own family members or members of their castes as the village barbers refuse to serve them. Many young SC men now prefer not to get their hair styled by their fathers (or other kinsmen), calling them old-fashioned. Hence, they visit nearby towns for haircuts where anonymity allows them to avail the service from barbers. However, a few young SC men narrate instances whereby even in towns, the barbers ask them to wait and let the upper-caste members from their own village be served before them. One SC youth revealed that when he visited a barber shop for a haircut, he was invited to occupy the saloon chair by the barber. However, just as he was about to sit in the chair, he noticed some upper-caste members of his village enter the shop. Fearing that they would settle scores with him in the village later if he got his haircut done before them, he offered them his turn and decided to wait. Unfortunately for him, it turned out to be a never-ending wait as two more upper-caste members turned up at the same shop before he could get his haircut done.

Discriminatory Restrictions on Public Behaviour

Some of the most prominent forms of sanctions on public behaviour of SCs include ban on marriage and festival processions on public roads, imposition of a dress code and an unambiguous display of signs of their subordination. The instance of chopping off of hands of an SC member due to delay caused in traffic by a religious procession taken out by the SCs has been mentioned in an earlier section.

ECONOMIC AND MARKET DISCRIMINATION

Under the traditional economic framework of caste system, the occupation and economic rights (including property rights) of each caste are fixed and compulsory and therefore, involve forced exclusion of one caste from the occupations (and rights) of another. SCs are particularly excluded from access to all sources of livelihood, except manual labour and rendering of service to other castes. Economic exclusion and discrimination involves:

1. Denial in hiring of SCs for jobs in sale and purchase of factors of production (like agricultural land, non-land capital assets and various factor inputs),

consumer goods and social services like education, housing and healthcare, including common property resources (CPRs) such as water bodies and grazing land.

2. Restrictions on any change in caste-based occupations signify a form of exclusion which may operate through discriminatory working of capital markets. In modern economic terms, SCs may not also be allowed to invest and participate in the occupations of other castes.

3. Differences in prices received or charged from SC customers in the markets depend on whether they are sellers or buyers. This may relate to the price of factor inputs, and consumer goods such as wages for labour, price of land or rent on land, interest on capital, rent on residential houses, and charges or fees for services such as housing, water and electricity.

4. Restrictions on participation of SCs in certain categories of jobs and the sale and purchase of certain consumer goods.

Labour Market Discrimination

Empirical evidence from the ActionAid study indicates that in about 36 per cent villages surveyed, SCs were denied wage-paid employment in agriculture. In about 25 per cent villages, SCs faced discrimination in wage payments. The wage discrimination also assumes various forms and includes payment of lower wages to SC labourers as compared to non-SC/ST labourers, or of lower market wage rates as compared to the number of hours of work put in by SC labourers, extraction of more work from them, extra economic coercion and practice of untouchability or to avoid physical contact with SC workers when paying them wages in kind or cash (see Template V).

Template V
Appalling Working Conditions of SCs in Bihar

In Birkheni village in Bihar, women are paid ₹20–25 or 1.25 kg rice or flour as daily wages, whereas men are paid ₹30–40 and 1.25 kg flour or rice. Only men are involved in extraction of *patua* which is used to make ropes. Out of the total *patua* extracted, the landowner takes 20–25 bundles and the workers get about four bundles. In this work, the labourer has to remain in water for the whole day to extract about 15–20 bundles. The nature of work mutilates workers' toes, and causes their skin to break, and it takes many months for the victims to recover. The ActionAid researchers even saw a worker (Anandi Paswan) who worked despite blood oozing from his toes.

It has been observed that payment of lower wages, and to force SC workers to over-work and coercion intertwined with caste obligations were not just confined to the agrarian situation associated with semi-feudal relations in Bihar, but also assumed new and oppressive forms in capitalist agrarian relations in the communalised agriculture of Punjab. The Punjab study found that SC labourers were also being physically assaulted by their employers. Cases of the use of abusive language against SC labourers and invoke their caste identity were also commonly observed (see Template VI).

Template VI
Evidences from Punjab

> *Physical Assault:* This refers to a case of death/murder reported from Urdhan village in Amritsar district. A young boy of around 16 to 17 years of age died while he was working on the farm. According to his employer, the boy died because he had a sudden epileptic fit. However, the members of his family and other SCs in the village contest this version and claim that the boy died because he was beaten up mercilessly by his employer and that he succumbed to his injuries while he was still at the farm. Apparently, the farmer tried to cremate the body without reporting the matter to police. However, the local SCs protested and demanded that police be called and a post-mortem be conducted on the body. The farmer agreed to pay ₹45,000 to the family of the deceased and the case eventually went unreported.
>
> ### Exploitation and Torture of Labourers
>
> In yet another case reported from Majha region in Wadala Bhittewad village in Amritsar district, an SC boy, who worked as an attached labourer with a Jat farmer, reportedly died because of being physically beaten by his employer. This boy, aged 14 to 15 years, had started working as an attached labourer only a few years back. One day while he was resting after having completed some work, the farmer asked him to get up and perform some other job. The labourer told him that he was too tired to start working again immediately. This offended the farmer and he hit him with a wooden stick. The strike injured the boy's head and he fell unconscious. He was reportedly in coma for several months before he passed away.

Another aspect that emerges quite clearly from the micro-level survey is related to the practice of untouchability among SC and non-SC/ST labourers themselves (see Template VII). As far back as in 1936, Ambedkar had argued that occupational division across castes is not a division of labour alone, but also a division of the labourer itself. The SC and non-SC/ST wage labourers, who work together and constitute the same economic class, also organise themselves into socially separate modes while they eat and drink after doing the same work.

A study carried out by the International Labour Organisation (ILO) further substantiates the existence of profound labour market discrimination. The study found the prevalence of inter-caste differences in terms of access to employment for farm labourers and wages received. In 2005, at overall level, the casual labourer was found to work for about 108 days in an annual agricultural year. Surprisingly,

Template VII
Untouchability among Labour Classes

> It has been observed that both SC and non-SC/ST workers are employed by higher-caste employers, but they do not work side by side. The SC workers either work on separate fields or a little away from non-SC/ST. The SC labourers are also given wages from a distance. Although there is no discrimination in wage rates when the wages are paid in cash, yet when the wages are paid in kind, the SC workers are generally given lesser amounts of paddy than their non-SC/ST counterparts—while non-SCs/STs get 1 *mana* (3 kg) of paddy per day, the SCs get only about 2 kg per day. While discrimination in hiring SCs for agricultural work was observed in 31 per cent of the surveyed villages, discrimination in payment of wages was a common practice and was observed in 52 per cent of the sample villages.

higher-caste casual labourers managed to receive employment for about 154 days which was about 50 per cent higher than the corresponding figure for SC casual labourers who were employed for 100 days. The ST labourers, on the other hand, managed to get employment for about 109 days. Similarly, the overall wage rate in 2005 was about ₹33 per day but SC and ST workers received only about ₹30 per day. Such discrimination is prevalent in non-farm work also. In the non-farm sector, higher-caste casual labourers managed to secure employment for about 290 days which again was higher than the corresponding figures for SC (189 days) and ST (81 days) workers. As regards the wages received in non-farm sector in 2005, higher-caste casual labourers received ₹77 as compared to ₹58 and ₹37 received by SC and ST workers, respectively.

The study concluded that non-economic factors or caste-related attributes characteristically contribute towards the differentials in wages and employment in both farm and non-farm sectors. It also claimed that hiring and wage payment seems marred by restrictive or discriminatory practices, as over one-fifth of the respondents reported the incidence of preferential hiring by higher caste employers.

Discrimination in Factor Markets

The discriminatory treatment accorded to SC workers is not confined to the labour market alone, but is equally operative in other factor markets as well. These include markets which pertain to agricultural land and irrigation on both public and private lands. In case of agricultural land, selective evidence from some states highlights hostile and aggressive attitude of higher castes towards SCs who try to acquire land and cultivate land for agricultural purposes (see Template VIII).

The ILO study quantitatively measured the practice of land market discrimination by assessing it in terms of variables such as sale and purchase, rental markets

Template VIII
SCs Denied Right to Cultivate Their Own Lands—A Case from Bihar

In Ganiari Khurd village in Garhwa district of Bihar, in 1982–1983, the government distributed land of sizes 1 acre, 48 decimals, and 1 acre to Sarju Bhuyian, Ganesh Bhuyian, and Shyam Sunder Bhuyian, respectively. However, though they were legal owners of the land given by the government, they still could not cultivate the land due to opposition from higher castes in the village. The land in question is still being controlled and cultivated by Devnarayan Singh, Desai Singh, and Prabhu Singh who are members of the higher castes. Thus, though the Bhuyians have the official allotment letters for the land, due to the power wielded by higher castes, they cannot cultivate their own land.

Landlords Capture Even the *Gairmazarua* Lands in Birkheni— A Case from Bihar

Birkheni village in Bihar is replete with incidences of forcible land grabbing. The lands allocated by the government to SC residents of the village including Satyanarayan Ram (four *katthas*), Ishwar Bhuyian (two *katthas*), and Jagannath Ram, Gauri Ram, Bhawan Ram, Jethu Ram, Vridha Ram and Bhagra Ram, among others, were forcibly taken away by landlords. Ishwar, who had been cultivating the land for over 50 years, claimed that their protests were of no avail and that the landlords resorted to violence and coercion to usurp the lands of the SCs.

Encroachment on SC Lands under the Aegis of the Police— A Case from Andhra Pradesh

In a bizarre incident, a few members of upper caste including Mopidevi Marnemaiah, Vaddi Sankar Rao and Peethala Narasaiah, who belong to *agni kula kshatriya*, occupied 130 acres of the SC lands. When the owners protested, they were assaulted by the landlords. The police, who were hand in glove with the culprits, refused to register a case and went to the extent of advising SC victims not to take up the matter further. They then ostensibly mediated between higher caste members and SCs, and pushed the latter to sell their lands to higher castes for as low as ₹800 per acre, from which amount they also reportedly charged ₹200 per acre as commission from the SCs. Thus, the state apparatus first supported encroachments on SC lands by higher castes and then forced the rightful SC owners to part with their lands at throwaway prices.

SCs Attacked and Killed for Land—A Case from Andhra Pradesh

In 1980, about 100 SC families and 108 Yanadi families put up their settlement at a vacant public land on the roadside in a village in Nellore district of Andhra Pradesh. The upper castes opposed this occupation by SCs. They then dragged both SCs and Yanadis and beat them mercilessly. Even women and children were not spared. Four SC/Yanadi women and children died in the attack. Most of the men were grievously injured and were admitted to hospitals. Some even ran away from the village fearing a backlash.

SCs Discriminated against in the Leasing of Land— A Case from Andhra Pradesh

The normal lease for acreage of land in Bodapadu village is about ₹10,000 per annum. But the money has to be paid in advance by the tenant. A case came to the fore wherein discriminatory lease practices were being followed. When SC landlords leased out their lands, they were asked to pay advance rent of the land whereas in identical situations, non-SC/ST landlords were not asked to pay the advance rent.

for residential purposes, and lease of lands. In the case of sale and purchase of land, it was observed, first, that the participation of SCs was initially limited; second, wherever evident, SC participation was limited to transactions either with STs or Other Backward Classes (OBCs); third, SCs were also subjected to price discrimination and had to pay prices that were higher than the prevailing market prices for the purchase of land; fourth, SCs were generally given land, which was either at the periphery, lacked access to irrigational facilities or was of poor quality; and fifth, SCs were denied purchase of land that had a common border with the land belonging to members of the higher castes.

Discriminatory Access to Common Property Resources

CPRs like grazing land, fishing ponds and other resources provide an important source of livelihood and a subsistence base to SCs/STs. The ActionAid study indicates that in most of the cases, the upper castes have developed a strong hold on CPRs. In some cases, CPRs in SC/ST-dominated settlements had been encroached upon by non-SCs/STs. Efforts to regain such lands or to gain access to the village CPRs by scheduled groups resulted in the implementation of severe punitive measures against SCs/STs by higher castes.

Discrimination in Sale and Purchase of Goods

The nature and forms of exclusion/discrimination as well as the notions behind discriminatory and irrational economic behaviour of higher-caste persons towards SCs in the market spheres assumes various forms and does not necessarily follow a uniform pattern. For instance, in a case in Orissa, discrimination in the purchase of milk by SCs was relatively higher than in the sale of milk. This was because of the prevalence of a specific cultural taboo. The Orissa report observed that people in Orissa believe that if anyone sells milk to an SC customer, his/her cattle would die, or would stop giving milk. Further, discrimination in the case of food products manufactured in bakeries owned by SCs was also quite prominent and was reported from a number of states like Orissa and Tamil Nadu (see Template IX). Other cases of discrimination were observed in the market in terms of denial of space to SC entrepreneurs, which was especially manifested in cases wherein SC shopkeepers happened to sell the same product as the one sold by their non-SC/ST counterparts.

The imposition of restrictions on the sale of number of consumer items in the village markets by sellers who could be easily identified in terms of their castes compelled SC shopkeepers to look for markets in small towns and other places

Template IX
Ostracisation of SC Bakers in Orissa

In Malmunda village in Orissa, Sanjukta, Padma Suna and a few other SC women run a bakery and sell their products in local markets. However, they claim that non-SC/ST customers do not purchase bread made in their factory. Similarly, they are not allowed to sell milk and milk products, either to non-SC/ST customers or to the milk co-operative society.

Boycott of an SC Teashop in Tamil Nadu

In Tamil Nadu, 67-year-old Ammavan runs a teashop. His teashop is, however, boycotted by non-SCs/STs and only SC customers come to buy tea and snacks from him though he keeps his shop fairly clean.

where their caste identity would not be so obvious and could remain hidden. The SCs, thus, chose to move out of their villages to access markets outside or in nearby villages even though this entailed additional time and effort, and multiplied the operational costs.

Further, SCs have also reported instances of discrimination in the inputs market ranging from delayed supply of agricultural implements to a complete refusal to supply the same to them because of their caste. SCs are also denied access to formal and informal agencies of credit. While access to formal credit agencies is denied more on grounds of lack of security rather than caste prejudices, in the informal markets, on the other hand, the ILO has observed caste to be a causative factor.

CONCLUSION

It is evident that even elaborate protective arrangements made to eliminate iniquitous customs, practices and institutional arrangements, which include provisions in law, seem to act as deterrents to caste-based discrimination only in a limited way. The numerous punitive measures in this sphere also apparently fail to discourage members of upper castes from perpetrating atrocities on lower castes. Violence and exploitation inflicted on SCs is rooted in the social structure and societal relations, which condemns them to a life of indignity, subordination, servility and humiliation. Further, the attempts of lower-caste untouchables to seek equal rights are genuinely met with violent opposition from higher castes. This effectively reduces the lower caste to assert their rights to development and seek equitable treatment and share in the progress in the country.

ANNEXURE I

Table 3A.1

Nature and Pattern of Atrocities against SCs and STs

Year	1992	1993	1994	1995	1996	1997	1998	1999	2000	2001	Total
Types of cases											
					Crimes against SCs						
Murder	616	510	546	571	543	513	516	506	526	763	5,610
Rape	849	798	992	873	949	1,037	923	1,000	1,083	1,316	9,820
Kidnapping and abduction	213	246	251	276	281	243	253	228	268	400	2,659
Dacoity	81	102	78	70	90	58	49	36	38	41	643
Robbery	265	197	259	218	213	162	150	109	108	133	1,814
Arson	406	369	533	500	464	389	346	337	290	354	3,988
Hurt	N.A.	N.A.	4,542	4,544	4,585	3,860	3,809	3,241	3,497	4,547	32,625
Cases registered under the Prevention of Civil Rights Act, 1955	2,900	2,531	1,731	1,528	1,417	1,216	724	678	672	633	14,030
Cases registered under the Prevention of Atrocity (SC/ST) Act, 1989	N.A.	N.A.	14,938	13,925	9,620	8,070	7,443	7,301	7,386	13,113	81,796
Other Offences	19,592	20,220	10,038	10,492	13,278	12,396	11,425	11,657	11,587	12,201	1,32,886
Total	**24,922**	**24,973**	**33,908**	**32,997**	**31,440**	**27,944**	**25,638**	**25,093**	**25,455**	**33,501**	**2,85,871**

Types of cases

Crimes against STs

Types of cases											
Murder	103	105	105	75	94	95	66	80	59	167	949
Rape	334	328	385	369	314	315	331	384	447	573	3,780
Kidnapping and abduction	62	44	64	74	50	41	56	59	403	67	920
Dacoity	8	9	8	18	32	3	5	3	48	16	150
Robbery	19	21	8	27	21	8	15	8	5	73	205
Arson	47	26	36	40	51	29	38	43	2	108	420
Hurt	N.A.	N.A.	699	688	694	706	638	646	32	756	4,859
Cases registered under the Prevention of Civil Rights Act, 1955	248	150	63	71	72	88	50	45	31	58	876
Cases registered under the Prevention of Atrocity (SC/ST) Act, 1989	N.A.	N.A.	1,316	1,480	754	643	709	574	502	1,667	7,645
Other offences	3,485	2,969	2,335	2,656	2,891	2,716	2,368	2,608	2,661	2,732	27,421
Total	**4,306**	**3,652**	**5,019**	**5,498**	**4,973**	**4,644**	**4,276**	**4,450**	**4,190**	**6,217**	**47,225**

Source: Reports on Crime in India, National Crime Records Bureau, Ministry of Home Affairs, Government of India, New Delhi.
Note: N.A. means not available.

Table 3A.2
State-wise Incidence of Violation of Civil Rights and Atrocities against SCs in India

S. No.	State	Incidence of Total Crime				Percentage of Crime to All-India Figure	Rate Per Lakh	Rank
		1999	*2000*	*2001*	*Average of Three Years*			
1.	Andhra Pradesh	1,749	1,582	2,933	2,088	7.5	2.8	06
2.	Assam	07	11	06	08	0.0	0.0	15
3.	Bihar	820	741	1,303	955	3.4	1.2	11
4.	Gujarat	1,781	1,332	1,242	1,452	5.2	2.9	05
5.	Haryana	121	117	229	156	0.6	0.7	12
6.	Himachal Pradesh	54	52	110	72	0.3	1.2	10
7.	Karnataka	1,277	1,329	1,621	1,409	5.0	2.7	07
8.	Kerala	514	467	499	493	1.8	1.5	09
9.	Madhya Pradesh	4,667	4,631	4,212	4,503	16.1	7.5	02
10.	Maharashtra	605	489	625	573	2.0	0.6	13
11.	Orissa	772	793	1734	1100	3.9	3.0	04
12.	Punjab	39	34	134	69	0.2	0.3	14
13.	Rajasthan	5,623	5,190	4,892	5,235	18.7	9.3	01
14.	Tamil Nadu	883	1296	2,336	1,505	5.4	2.4	08
15.	Uttar Pradesh	6,122	7,330	10,732	8,061	28.8	4.9	03
16.	West Bengal	00	00	10	03	0.0	0.0	16
	India	**25,093**	**25,455**	**33,501**	**28,016**	**100**	**2.7**	

Source: Crime in India 1999–2001, National Crime Records Bureau, Ministry of Home Affairs, Government of India, New Delhi.
Note: All figures represent the number of cases registered under the PCR Act (1955) and Scheduled Castes and Scheduled Tribes (Prevention of Atrocities) Act (1989).

Table 3A.3
Statement Showing Cases with Courts under the PCR Act and Their Disposal during 2002

S. No.	State/UT	No. of Cases in Courts Including Those Brought Forward in 2002	No. of Cases Withdrawn by the Government	No. of Cases Compounded or Withdrawn	No. of Cases in Which Trials Have Been Completed		No. of Cases Pending in Courts at the End of 2002
					Persons Convicted	Persons Acquitted or Discharged	
1.	Andhra Pradesh	506	0	0	5	207	294
2.	Bihar	131	0	0	0	0	131
3.	Chhattisgarh	2	0	0	0	0	2
4.	Gujarat	133	0	0	0	48	85
5.	Haryana	6	0	0	0	2	4
6.	Himachal Pradesh	12	0	0	1	3	8
7.	Karnataka	2,038	0	70	2	49	1,917
8.	Kerala	6	0	0	0	3	3
9.	Maharashtra	1,630	12	0	2	115	1,501
10.	Madhya Pradesh	1,637	0	0	0	6	1,631
11.	Orissa	132	0	0	0	2	130
12.	Punjab	5	0	0	0	1	4
13.	Rajasthan	1	0	0	0	0	1
14.	Tamil Nadu	2,716	0	0	137	582	1,997
15.	Uttar Pradesh	4	0	0	2	2	0
16.	Delhi	20	1	0	0	2	17
17.	Pondicherry	32	0	0	1	9	22
	Total	**9,011**	**13**	**70**	**150**	**1,031**	**7,747**

Source: Annual Report on the Protection of Civil Rights Act, 1955 for the year 2002 (22nd Report), Government of India, Ministry of Social Justice and Empowerment, New Delhi, 2002.
Note: Nil data reported by 18 states/UTs, viz. Assam, Arunachal Pradesh, Goa, Jammu and Kashmir, Jharkhand, Manipur, Meghalaya, Mizoram, Nagaland, Sikkim, Tripura, Uttarakhand, West Bengal, Andaman and Nicobar Islands, Chandigarh, Dadra and Nagar Haveli, Daman and Diu, and Lakshadweep.

Table 3A.4
State-wise Incidence of Violation of Civil Rights and Atrocities against STs in India

S. No.	State	Incidence of Total Crime				Percentage of Crime to All India	Rate Per Lakh	Rank
		1999	2000	2001	Average of Three Years			
1.	Andhra Pradesh	178	202	512	297	6.0	0.4	6
2.	Assam	2	0	0	1	0.0	0.0	15
3.	Bihar	67	61	47	58	1.2	0.1	11
4.	Gujarat	367	315	309	330	6.7	0.7	5
5.	Haryana	0	0	0	0	0.0	0.0	12
6.	Himachal Pradesh	19	11	4	11	0.2	0.2	10
7.	Karnataka	60	64	276	133	2.7	0.3	7
8.	Kerala	81	63	83	76	1.5	0.2	9
9.	Madhya Pradesh	1,756	1,845	1,535	1,712	34.6	2.8	2
10.	Maharashtra	171	142	238	184	3.7	0.2	13
11.	Orissa	335	228	734	432	8.7	1.2	4
12.	Punjab	5	6	0	4	0.1	0.0	14
13.	Rajasthan	1,221	1,130	1,023	1,125	22.7	2.0	1
14.	Tamil Nadu	105	9	9	41	0.8	0.1	8
15.	Uttar Pradesh	58	78	254	130	2.6	0.1	3
16.	West Bengal	0	0	2	1	0.0	0.0	16
	India	**4,450**	**4,190**	**6,217**	**4,952**	**100.0**	**0.5**	

Source: Crime in India 1999–2001, National Crime Records Bureau, Ministry of Home Affairs, Government of India, New Delhi.
Note: All figures represent the number of cases registered under the PCR Act (1955) and SC/ST POA Act (1989).

Chapter 4

HUMAN DEVELOPMENT AND HUMAN POVERTY BY SOCIAL GROUPS

Sukhadeo Thorat and S. Venkatesan

This chapter assesses the progress of Scheduled Castes (SCs) and Scheduled Tribes (STs) in comparison to their non-SC/ST counterparts in terms of human development, human poverty and other indicators of well-being through the development of a composite index of human development and human poverty across social groups at all-India and state levels. Further, an analysis of improvement in individual indicators used in human development framework has also been carried out.

The individual indicators of attainments and composite indices attempt to capture human development from two perspectives—achievement and deprivation. The achievement perspective captures advances made by society as a whole while the deprivational perspective assesses the level of deprivation. The achievements in human development by different social groups are presented in terms of human development index (HDI) through the use of three indicators, namely infant mortality rate (IMR[1] as a substitute variable for life expectancy); literacy rate and inflation adjusted as per the monthly per capita consumption expenditure (MPCE) (as a substitute variable for income).

The human poverty index (HPI) measures deprivation in basic human development dimensions, such as health, education and income. Deprivation in these three dimensions is captured by the following indicators: IMR (as a substitute of probability at birth of not surviving the age of 40 years); percentage of adults who are illiterate; and a composite variable of overall economic dimension in terms of head count ratio of poverty, percentage of non-institutional deliveries, percentage of non-vaccinated children and percentage of children underweight-for-age (as a substitute of unweighted average of population without sustainable access to an

---

[1] IMR generally captures deprivational aspects, but here the same variable is used to capture the achievement aspects by using reciprocal values of IMR.

improved water supply and children underweight-for-age).[2] For HDI, the higher the value, the higher would be the achievement and vice versa whereas for HPI, the higher the value, the higher would be the deprivation and vice versa. In order to estimate the disparities in human development, human poverty and other related variables between SCs and non-SCs on one hand and STs and non-STs on the other hand a simple method called 'disparity ratio' has been used. This ratio measures the attainments of Group A (such as SCs/STs) relative to Group B (such as non-SCs/STs) or the achievements of Group A/achievements of Group B. In case of HDI, values lower than one would show lower achievement for Group A and vice versa. However, in case of HPI, the values lower than one indicate lower level of deprivation among members of Group A and vice versa. This is because the indicators of HDI are inverse to those of HPI.

DATABASE

The construction of HDI and HPI first involved the preparation of an extensive database which covers several indicators in terms of social groups. The entire data sets have been compiled for three time points, namely 1980s, 1990s and 2000s at all-India and state levels from various sources such as the Census of India; the National Sample Survey (NSS); the National Family Health Survey, Report on Differential in Mortality in India (vital statistics); Report on Crime in India and other official surveys; and some independent sources. The Human Development Indices have been prepared for the 1980s and 2000s, while the Human Poverty Indices have been prepared for the 1990s and the 2000s.[3]

STATUS OF HUMAN DEVELOPMENT: SOCIAL GROUPS, 2000

The achievement by different sections of the population in different spheres of life is summarised in terms of HDI values between 0 and 1. Higher development for a social group means a value closer to 1. In this case, it would imply that the entire population of the group has achieved minimal attainment on each of the dimensions considered. The HDI has been calculated for the time periods 1980 and 2000 for all major states, excluding Jammu and Kashmir and the north-eastern states. The values of HDI estimated in this book would vary with the values calculated by United Nations development Programme (UNDP) for the paper submitted to Twelfth Finance Commission ("Human Development Indices in

---

[2] For details, see Annexure II.
[3] For details, see Annexure II.

India—Trends and Analysis"), due to difference in the use of different indicators.[4] However, though the analysis here employs differing variables, the ranking of states in both estimates seems to be more or less similar.

The level of human development is analysed at all-India as well as state levels for the year 2000. The exclusion of the disadvantaged groups is analysed using the disparity ratio across the states between SCs and non-SCs/STs, on one hand, and STs and non-SCs/STs, on the other hand. This is followed by an analysis of temporal changes in HDI (2000 over 1980) again for all-India and state levels with respect to disparities.

All Groups

All-India HDI was estimated to be 0.366 and showed a variation across the states, with values ranging from 0.279 for Bihar to 0.715 for Kerala. Further, seven states, including Assam (0.360) and Bihar (0.279), had HDI values that were lower than all-India average. The states with higher HDI values[5] were Kerala, Himachal Pradesh, Maharashtra, Tamil Nadu, Punjab, Haryana, West Bengal, Gujarat and Karnataka. Besides Assam and Bihar, the other states with low HDI values were Andhra Pradesh, Rajasthan, Madhya Pradesh, Orissa and Uttar Pradesh (Table 4.1).

Table 4.1
High- and Low-HDI States

	SC	*ST*	*Non-SC/ST*	*All Groups*
High-HDI States	Kerala	Kerala	Kerala	Kerala
	Himachal Pradesh	Assam	Himachal Pradesh	Himachal Pradesh
	Maharashtra	Tamil Nadu	Maharashtra	Maharashtra
	Tamil Nadu	Gujarat	Tamil Nadu	Tamil Nadu
	Gujarat	Maharashtra	West Bengal	Punjab
	Assam	Karnataka	Punjab	Haryana
	West Bengal	**India**	Gujarat	West Bengal
	Punjab	Rajasthan	Haryana	Gujarat
	Haryana	West Bengal	Karnataka	Karnataka
	Karnataka	Uttar Pradesh	**India**	**India**
	India	Madhya Pradesh	Andhra Pradesh	Assam

(Table 4.1 Contd.)

[4] See Annexure II for details.
[5] Here, higher HDI values always refer to values greater than all-India level and vice versa.

(Table 4.1 Contd.)

	SC	ST	Non-SC/ST	All Groups
Low-HDI States	Madhya Pradesh	Andhra Pradesh	Madhya Pradesh	Andhra Pradesh
	Rajas than	Orissa	Rajasthan	Rajasthan
	Orissa	Bihar	Orissa	Madhya Pradesh
	Andhra Pradesh		Assam	Orissa
	Uttar Pradesh		Uttar Pradesh	Uttar Pradesh
	Bihar		Bihar	Bihar

Source: Thorat, Sukhadeo, M. Mahamallik and S. Venkatesan. 2007. 'Human Poverty and Socially Disadvantaged Groups in India', *UNDP Discussion Paper Series 18*, p. 18. New Delhi: Human Development Resource Centre.

Scheduled Castes

The HDI for SCs at all-India level was estimated to be 0.303 which was lower than that for non-SCs/STs (0.393). The states with higher HDI values for SCs included Kerala (0.661), Himachal Pradesh (0.450), Maharashtra (0.416), Tamil Nadu (0.411), Assam (0.407), Gujarat (0.371), West Bengal (0.359), Punjab (0.343), Haryana (0.343) and Karnataka (0.308). The rest of the six states had HDI values lower than all-India average. Among them, the values for HDI were particularly the lowest for the states of Madhya Pradesh (0.294) and Bihar (0.195) (Figure 4.1).

Figure 4.1
Human Development Index for SCs—Regional Variations, 2000

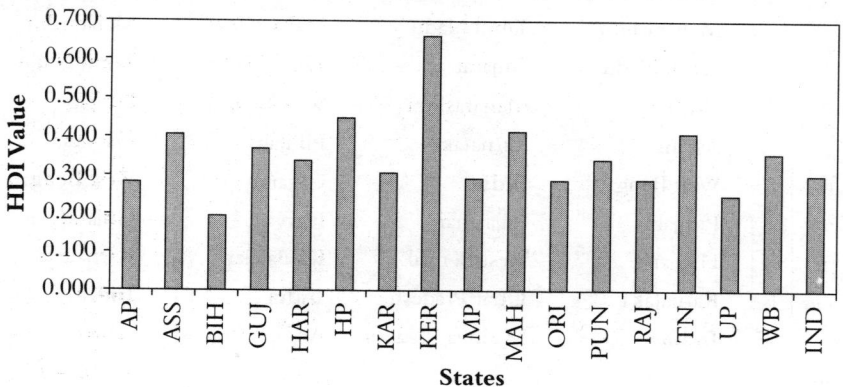

Source: Thorat, Sukhadeo, M. Mahamallik and S. Venkatesan. 2007. 'Human Poverty and Socially Disadvantaged Groups in India', *UNDP Discussion Paper Series 18*, p. 19. New Delhi: Human Development Resource Centre.

Scheduled Tribes

The HDI for STs was estimated for 13 major states. The values for HDI at all-India level were estimated to be 0.270 which were significantly lower than those for non-SCs/STs (0.393). Among the 13 states, the values for HDI for STs were relatively higher in Kerala (0.613), followed by Assam (0.361). Significantly, the gap between the first and the second ranking states, that is, Kerala and Assam, was quite large. The performance of Kerala in terms of better HDI values could possibly be attributed to its enhanced position with respect to the three constitutive components of the composite of HDI. The literacy rate for STs in Kerala was 64.35 per cent followed by Assam at 62.52 per cent. However, this gap when compared to that for other states was found to be high. In addition, the values for MPCE for Kerala were high at ₹456 as compared to ₹400 for all the other states. The variable which made a significant contribution towards the transition of Kerala to the highest position was perhaps the IMR which was as low as 21 as compared to 59 for Assam (Figure 4.2).

Non-SCs/STs

The HDI at all-India level for non-SCs/STs was estimated to be 0.393, which was higher than those for SCs, STs and all groups. At the state levels, the HDI values showed a variation ranging from 0.755 for Kerala to 0.301 for Bihar. Interestingly, the inter-state variations were quite similar to those for SCs and STs.

Figure 4.2
Human Development Index for STs—Regional Variations, 2000

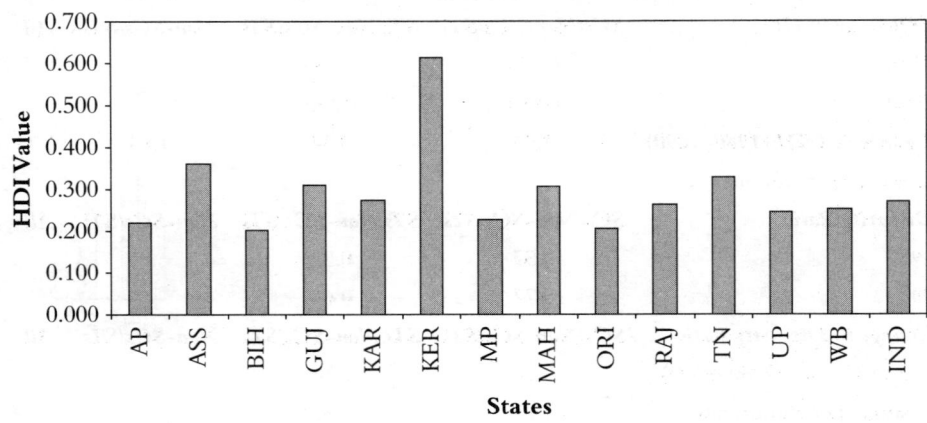

Source: Thorat, Sukhadeo, M. Mahamallik and S. Venkatesan. 2007. 'Human Poverty and Socially Disadvantaged Groups in India', *UNDP Discussion Paper Series 18*, p. 19. New Delhi: Human Development Resource Centre.

Inter-social Group Variations

The regional pattern of HDI by social groups indicated the emergence of a common group of states (Bihar, Uttar Pradesh, Orissa and Madhya Pradesh in that order), wherein HDI was relatively lower for all the social groups. There is also a group of states comprising Kerala, Himachal Pradesh, Maharashtra and Tamil Nadu which showed a high level of human development. This section attempts to delineate the disparities in the levels in human development across social groups (Table 4.2).

In 2000, at all-India level, HDI for SCs was about 0.303, as compared to 0.393 for non-SCs/STs. Therefore, the disparity ratio between the two social groups was about 0.77, indicating that the attainments in human development for SCs were less than 23 per cent of that of non-SCs/STs. At the state level, HDI values were lower for SCs as compared to those for non-SCs/STs. The disparity levels were relatively higher in Bihar (0.65), Andhra Pradesh (0.74), Karnataka (0.74), Punjab (0.77) and Uttar Pradesh (0.77). The attainment level of human development was about 35 per cent less among SCs as compared to non-SCs/STs in Bihar and about 26 per cent less in Andhra Pradesh and Karnataka. The disparity levels were relatively lower for the states of Kerala (0.89), Tamil Nadu (0.88),

Table 4.2
Human Development Index—Levels and Disparity, 1980–2000

Index	*Social Groups*			
HDI Levels	*SCs*	*STs*	*Non-SCs/STs*	*All*
1980	0.162	0.150	0.285	0.241
2000	0.303	0.270	0.393	0.366
Difference in HDI	*SCs/Non-SCs/STs*	*STs/Non-SCs/STs*	*Non-SCs/STs*	*All*
1980	0.124	0.136		
2000	0.091	0.123		
Change in HDI (1980–2000)	3.55	3.34	1.80	2.35
(Per cent per annum)				
Disparity Ratio	*SCs/Non-SCs/STs*	*STs/Non-SCs/STs*	*Non-SCs/STs*	*All*
1980	0.57	0.52		
2000	0.77	0.69		
Change in Disparity Ratio	*SCs/Non-SCs/STs*	*STs/Non-SCs/STs*	*Non-SCs/STs*	*All*
Net difference (1980–2000)	0.20	0.16		
Change (per annum rate)	1.72	1.52		

Source: Authors' estimates. Data taken from different years of Census of India, National Sample Surveys and National Family Health Surveys.

Maharashtra (0.87), Gujarat and Himachal Pradesh (0.86)—the values of the disparity ratio tended to be closer to 1 in all these states. These states with lower disparity ratios also happen to be the regions of high human development. Lower disparity levels seem to go hand in hand with high level of human development. In other words, it could well be ascertained that states with low disparity ratios and proportionally higher HDIs have succeeded in reducing the gaps between the marginalised and the dominant social groups.

In case of STs, the gap between them and non-SCs/STs was higher as compared to the corresponding gap for SCs. A comparison of HDIs at the national level in the year 2000 indicates that the HDI for STs was 0.270 as compared to 0.393 for non-SCs/STs. The disparity ratio in this case worked out to be 0.69 indicating that the attainment levels for STs were 31 per cent of those for non-SCs/STs. The state level analysis suggested that the disparity ratio was less than 1 in all the states, except Assam. Further, the disparity level was relatively higher in seven states (West Bengal, Orissa, Andhra Pradesh, Madhya Pradesh, Maharashtra, Karnataka and Bihar) ranging from 0.56 to 0.67. In all these states, as compared to non-SCs/STs, HDI was less by a margin of about 44–33 per cent for STs (Figure 4.3).

Figure 4.3
Disparity in HDI Levels during 1980–2000, All India

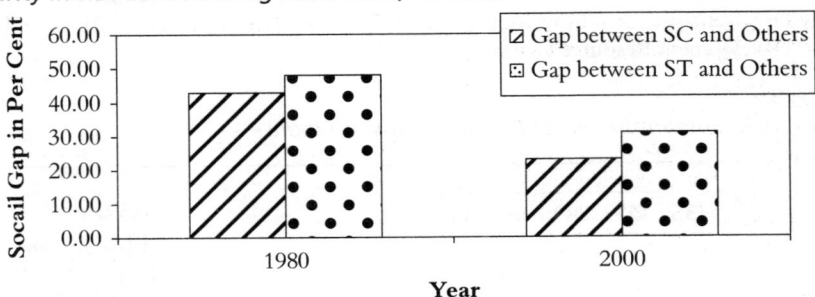

Source: Thorat, Sukhadeo, M. Mahamallik and S. Venkatesan. 2007. 'Human Poverty and Socially Disadvantaged Groups in India', *UNDP Discussion Paper Series 18*, p. 19. New Delhi: Human Development Resource Centre.

CHANGES IN THE LEVEL OF HUMAN DEVELOPMENT INDEX BY SOCIAL GROUPS

Between 1980 and 2000, HDI had improved for all the social groups, but there are significant differences in terms of the rate of change. Also, given the lower base of human development for SCs and STs, the per annum rate was evidently higher for them as compared to non-SCs/STs. The annual rates of growth were 3.55 per cent, 3.34 per cent and 1.80 per cent for SCs, STs and non-SCs/STs, respectively. The state level analysis too indicates a differential rate of change between various social groups for the individual states (Figures 4.4 and 4.5).

Figure 4.4
Disparities between SCs and Non-SCs/STs in HDI, 2000

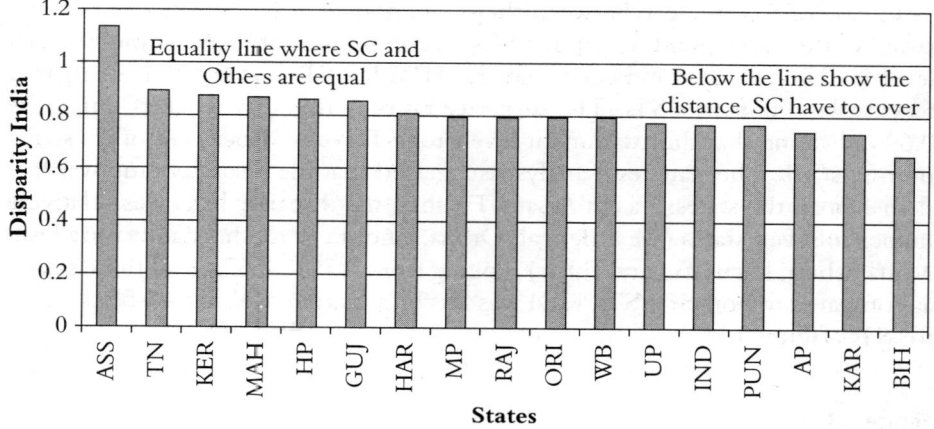

Source: Thorat, Sukhadeo, M. Mahamallik and S. Venkatesan. 2007. 'Human Poverty and Socially Disadvantaged Groups in India', *UNDP Discussion Paper Series 18*, p. 21. New Delhi: Human Development Resource Centre.

Figure 4.5
Human Development Index for Social Groups, All India

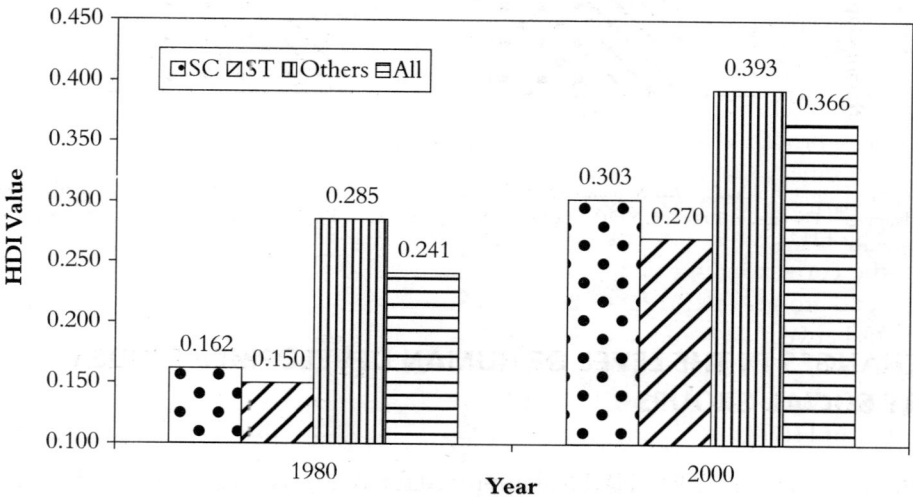

Source: Thorat, Sukhadeo, M. Mahamallik and S. Venkatesan. 2007. 'Human Poverty and Socially Disadvantaged Groups in India', *UNDP Discussion Paper Series 18*, p. 20. New Delhi: Human Development Resource Centre.

In case of SCs in eight states, the rates of change in HDI values were found to be higher than all-India average with HDI values ranging from 7.15 per cent in Assam to 3.70 per cent in Madhya Pradesh. The states which fall under this range included Assam, Tamil Nadu, Uttar Pradesh, Rajasthan, Orissa, Himachal Pradesh, West Bengal and Madhya Pradesh. However, in states like Haryana, Maharashtra, Andhra Pradesh, Karnataka, Bihar, Kerala, Punjab and Gujarat, HDI values were found to be less than all-India average, with the rate of change varying from 2.17 in Gujarat to 3.51 in Haryana. With the exception of Bihar, the rate of change was found to have improved in all the states where the values for HDI during the base year were low as compared to those where the values for HDI during the base year were high.

At all-India level, in case of STs, the value of HDI was found to have increased at the per annum rate of 3.34 per cent. The rate of increase was higher than all-India average in the four states of Assam, Gujarat, Maharashtra and Rajasthan. In the rest of the nine states, HDI values were found to have increased at a lower rate than all-India average.

Lastly, in the case of non-SCs/STs, the HDI values had increased by 1.8 per cent per annum at all-India level. The rate of increase was lower in Punjab, Kerala and Karnataka. In the remaining states, the annual rate of increase was higher than all-India average. In case of non-SCs/STs also, the rate of change in HDI is found to be low for high-HDI states as compared to low-HDI states.

Changes in Disparity (1980–2000)

The preceding discussion on the rates of change in HDI values during the periods 1980–2000 indicated an improvement in the levels of HDI values for all social groups in all the states. Given the low base of HDI values in 1980 for SCs and STs, the rate of change among them was higher as compared to non-SCs/STs. Since HDI improved at a faster rate between SCs and STs, it is expected that such an improvement would be concomitantly accompanied by a reduction in the levels of disparity between SCs, STs and non-SCs/STs.

The HDI values for SCs stood at 0.162 in 1980 which was lower as compared to the corresponding figure of 0.285 for non-SCs/STs. Thus, the gap between the two groups was 0.124. In 2000, this difference reduced to 0.09. The disparity ratios between SCs and non-SCs/STs were found to have improved from 0.57 in 1980 to 0.77 in 2000, thereby approximating more closely to the equality value of 1. However, since the base level of HDI values for SCs itself were low, the disparity in HDI between them and the non-SCs/STs remained at a higher level. In 2000, as compared to the HDI values for non-SCs/STs, those for SCs continued to be less by a margin of 23 per cent.

The decline in disparity in HDI values between SCs and non-SCs/STs was fairly widespread across the states. Although similar trends were visible for STs, they were also accompanied by certain differences. In 1980, the HDI values for STs and non-SCs/STs stood at 0.150 and 0.285, respectively, with the net difference being 0.135. However, the disparity ratio between STs and non-SCs/STs improved from 0.52 in 1983 to 0.69 in 2000 reaching closer to the equality value of 1, but not being adequate enough to reduce the net difference by a reasonable margin. In 2000, the HDI value for STs was lower by about one-third.

STATUS OF HUMAN POVERTY: SOCIAL GROUPS, 2000

The HPI not only measures the deprivation in basic human development dimensions, which are included in the HDI, but also includes additional aspects related to social needs. Such additional aspects include access to healthcare and nutritional status.

All Social Groups

The value of HPI was estimated to be 33.63 for all the social groups taken together at all-India level. There are six states, namely Bihar, Uttar Pradesh, Orissa, Assam, Madhya Pradesh and Rajasthan where HPI values are more than the corresponding all-India value which implies greater deprivation as compared to all-India average. States where the level of deprivation is lower as compared to all-India level are West Bengal, Andhra Pradesh, Himachal Pradesh, Haryana, Karnataka, Gujarat, Maharashtra, Punjab, Tamil Nadu and Kerala. Among the more deprived states, the HPI value varies from 37.79 in Rajasthan to 46.4 in Bihar, and among the less deprived states, it varies from 11.77 in Kerala to 32.44 in West Bengal.

Scheduled Castes

The HPI for SCs was estimated to be 41.47 at all-India level, which was much higher as compared to the corresponding figure of 31.34 for non-SCs/STs. The HPI values for SCs revealed significant variations across the states with values ranging from 18.62 to 59.36. The level of deprivation was the highest in Bihar (59.36) followed by Uttar Pradesh (50.03), Orissa (47.66), Rajasthan (43.78) and Madhya Pradesh (43.68). In these states, the rate of deprivation exceeded that for all-India level (41.47). In the rest of the 11 states under consideration, the rate of deprivation was less than the corresponding all-India values. The deprivation values were the lowest for Kerala (18.62) (see Figure 4.6).

Figure 4.6
Human Poverty Index for SCs—Regional Variation, 2000

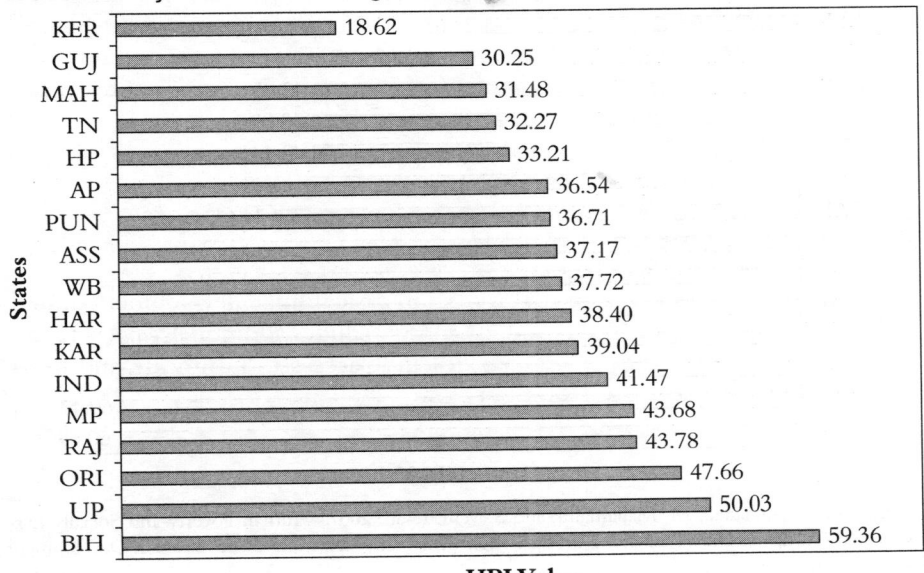

Source: Thorat, Sukhadeo, M. Mahamallik and S. Venkatesan. 2007. 'Human Poverty and Socially Disadvantaged Groups in India', *UNDP Discussion Paper Series 18*, p. 24. New Delhi: Human Development Resource Centre.

Scheduled Tribes

In case of STs, the HPI was calculated for 13 states. The value of HPI at all-India level stood at 47.79, and ranged from 27.65 in Kerala to 60.69 in Orissa. The states with higher HPI values were Orissa, Bihar, Uttar Pradesh, Madhya Pradesh and Rajasthan. Conversely, eight other states had HPI values that were less than all-India average which implies that the level of deprivation among these states was less in consideration to that observed for the former group of five states. The states where the values of HPI were low included Kerala and West Bengal whereas HPI values varied between 27.65 and 47.72 in that order. For both SCs and STs, the illiteracy rate was closely associated with high level of deprivation (Figure 4.7).

Non-SCs/STs

It is important to note that the deprivation among non-SCs/STs was lower as compared to SCs and STs at both all-India level as well as in the states. The HPI

Figure 4.7
Human Poverty Index for STs—Regional Variation, 2000

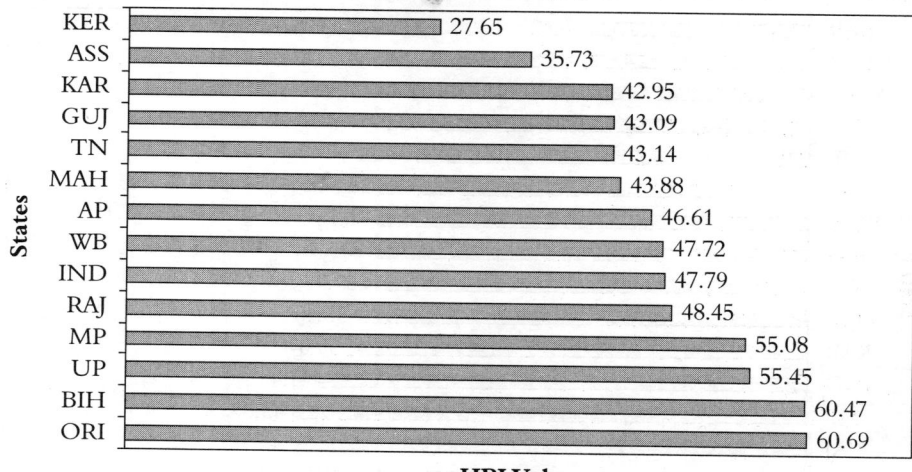

Source: Thorat, Sukhadeo, M Mahamallik and S. Venkatesan. 2007. 'Human Poverty and Socially Disadvantaged Groups in India', *UNDP Discussion Paper Series 18*, p. 24. New Delhi: Human Development Resource Centre.

values for non-SCs/STs were higher than the corresponding all-India values in the eight states, namely Bihar, Uttar Pradesh, Assam, Rajasthan, Madhya Pradesh, Orissa, Haryana and Punjab. The HPI values in these states varied from 31.47 in Punjab to 43.2 in Bihar. In the rest of the states, the HPI values were less than all-India average which indicates a lower level of deprivation.

Inter-social Group Variations

Having examined the inter-state variations, we now examine the inter-social group variations in HPI. In 2000, at all-India level, the HPI values stood at 33.63, but the value varied across three social groups. The HPI was higher for SCs and STs as compared to non-SCs/STs (Table 4.3).

The above inter-social group differences are reflected in the disparity ratio. The net difference in HPI values between SCs and non-SCs/STs was about 10 percentage points with disparity ratio about 1.32 in 2000 which indicate that among the SCs the HPI values or the deprivational aspects were higher by about 32 percentage points as compared to non-SCs/STs. The disparity ratio for the SCs as compared to non-SCs/STs at state level was greater than 1 for all states, except Assam.

Table 4.3
Human Poverty Index—Level, Disparity and Changes, 1990–2000, All India

Index	SCs	STs	Non-SCs/STs	All
1990	54.36	60.32	42.09	43.65
2000	41.47	47.79	31.34	33.63
Net Difference in HPI	*SCs/Non-SCs/STs*	*STs/Non-SCs/STs*	*Non-SCs/STs*	*All*
1990	−12.27	−18.23		
2000	−10.13	−16.45		
Disparity Ratio	*SCs/Non-SCs/STs*	*STs/Non-SCs/STs*	*Non-SCs/STs*	*All*
1990	1.29	1.43		
2000	1.32	1.52		
Change in HPI (1990–2000 per annum)	−3.79	−3.27	−4.13	−3.66
Change in Disparity Ratio	*SCs/Non-SCs/STs*	*STs/Non-SCs/STs*	*Non-SCs/STs*	*All*
Net change	0.03	0.09		
Percentage change per annum	0.34	0.89		

Source: Authors' estimates. Data taken from different years of Census of India, National Sample Surveys and National Family Health Surveys.

Similarly, the HPI values for STs (47.79) were higher as compared to non-SCs/STs, with the disparity ratio being 1.52. The HPI among STs was about 50 per cent higher than non-SCs/STs. A common group of states comprising Bihar, Uttar Pradesh, Assam, Madhya Pradesh and Rajasthan indicated the prevalence of high levels of HPI for SCs, STs and non-SCs/STs.

Andhra Pradesh was the only state where both HDI and HPI values were lower than all-India average. This means that it had both low attainment and low deprivation levels, whereas the indices for other states indicated a different relationship, wherein low HDI was matched with high HPI. This was true for Bihar, Uttar Pradesh, Orissa, Himachal Pradesh and Rajasthan.

CHANGES IN THE LEVEL OF HPI BY SOCIAL GROUPS (1990–2000)

Unlike HDI, the analysis of deprivational quotient is limited by the availability of comparable data for 1980. Therefore, the changes in the levels of HPI were analysed for the time periods 1990 and 2000. During the period 1990–2000, the levels

Figure 4.8
Human Poverty among Social Groups in India, 1990–2000

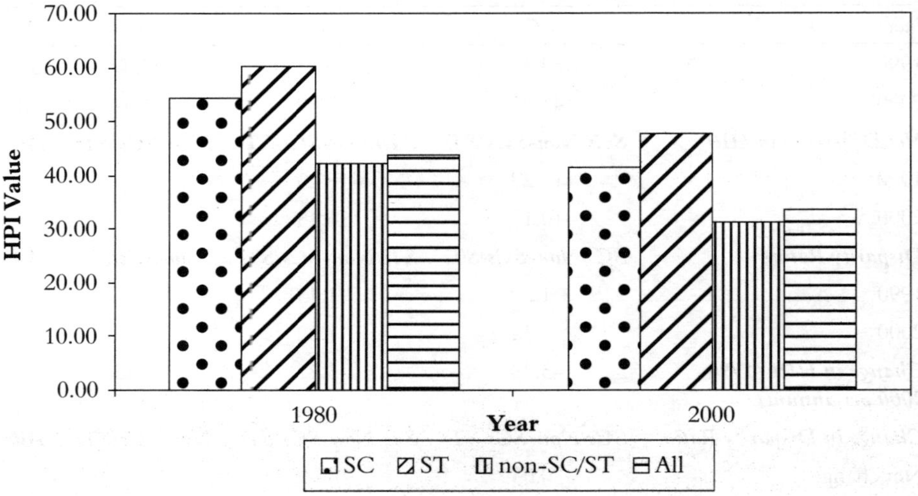

Source: Thorat, Sukhadeo, M. Mahamallik and S. Venkatesan. 2007. 'Human Poverty and Socially Dis-advantaged Groups in India', *UNDP Discussion Paper Series 18*, p. 26. New Delhi: Human Development Resource Centre.

of HPI declined for all social groups. In 1990s, the HPI declined from 54.36, 60.32 and 42.09 to 41.47, 47.79 and 31.34 for SCs, STs and non-SCs/STs, respectively.

At the aggregate level, the HPI values declined at per annum rate of 3.66 per cent for all the social groups but the decline took place at a lower per annum rate for SCs (3.79 per cent) and STs (3.27 per cent), as compared to non-SCs/STs (4.13 per cent) (Figure 4.8).

At the state level, the HPI values declined at higher rates than the national average of 3.27 per cent per annum for SCs. This rate of decline was evident in the states of Andhra Pradesh, Maharashtra, Rajasthan and Tamil Nadu. Conversely, the HPI values declined at much lower rates in Bihar, Uttar Pradesh and Gujarat. For STs, apparently, the relatively higher rate of decline was confined to the two states of Maharashtra and Andhra Pradesh. The rate of decline was also quite slow in Uttar Pradesh, Orissa, Madhya Pradesh, Gujarat and Bihar, which incidentally also happen to be high human poverty regions.

Changes in Disparity (1990–2000)

The decrease in HPI values between SCs, STs and non-SCs/STs, both in terms of net change and percentage change, during the time period 1990–2000 was minimal. In 1990, the gap in terms of the net difference in the HPI values between

Figure 4.9
Disparity in Human Poverty Index

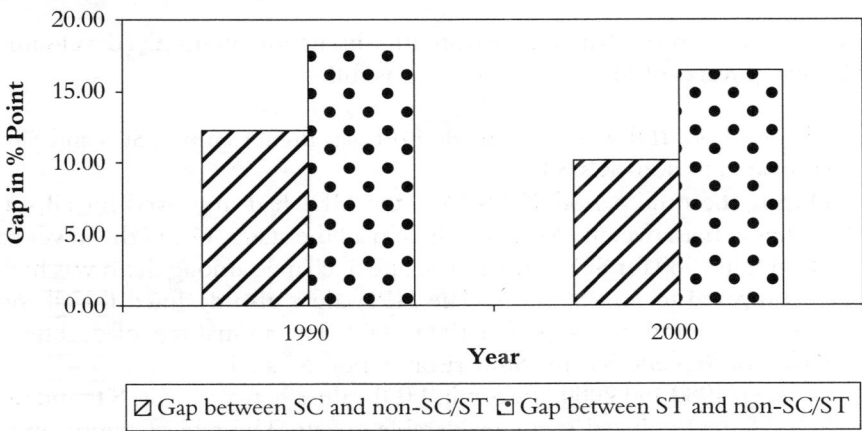

Source: Thorat, Sukhadeo, M. Mahamallik and S. Venkatesan. 2007. 'Human Poverty and Socially Disadvantaged Groups in India', *UNDP Discussion Paper Series 18*, p. 26. New Delhi: Human Development Resource Centre.

SCs and non-SCs/STs, on one hand, and between STs and non-SCs/STs, on the other hand, stood at 12.27 and 18.23, respectively. In 2000, this gap had reduced marginally to 10.13 for SCs as compared to non-SCs/STs, and 16.45 for STs as compared to non-SCs/STs (Figure 4.9).

Similarly, the poverty ratio for SCs as compared to non-SCs/STs increased from 1.29 in 1990 to 1.32 in 2000 at per annum rate of 0.34 per cent. Correspondingly, the poverty ratio for STs as compared to non-SCs/STs increased from 1.43 in 1990 to 1.52 in 2000 at per annum rate of 0.89. The analysis also established an increase in the disparity ratio of HPI for the time period 1990–2000 between SCs and non-SCs/STs, on one hand, and between STs and non-SCs/STs, on the other hand, which was closely associated with a slower decline in the levels of HPI during the same time period.

The disparity figures vary across states not only in terms of intensity (magnitude) of change but also direction of change. Here, it is important to recognise that the decline in the disparity between SCs and non-SCs/STs at overall levels during the period 1990–2000 was limited to the states of Gujarat, Haryana, Himachal Pradesh, Madhya Pradesh, Maharashtra, Orissa, Punjab, Rajasthan and West Bengal, which indicate an overall improvement in the situation. In the remaining states, namely Andhra Pradesh, Assam, Bihar, Karnataka, Kerala, Tamil Nadu and Uttar Pradesh the disparity ratios were found to have increased.

The disparity ratios in case of STs and non-SCs/STs were also found to have increased in all the states, except Kerala and Maharashtra, wherein the ratios were seen to have declined.

SUMMING UP

The distinctive features that emerge from this discussion on human development and human poverty of the social groups are as follows:

1. The level of HDI was lower while HPI was higher among SCs and STs as compared to non-SCs/STs.
2. During the time period 1980–2000, the HDI had improved for all social groups at both overall levels as well as in all the states. Given the lower base of HDI in 1980 for SCs and STs, the rate of change among them was higher as compared to non-SCs/STs. The HPI values also declined for all social groups during the time period 1990–2000. The annual rate of decline was lower for SCs and STs in comparison to non-SCs/STs.
3. Between 1980 and 2000, the gap in HDI values between SCs, STs and non-SCs/STs had reduced to a considerable extent. The rate of improvement, nevertheless, was much lower for STs. In general, the rate of improvement in HDI values for SCs and STs was marginal and therefore, could not make a considerable difference to reduce the gaps between them and non-SCs/STs. It is evident that in 2000 the levels of HDI for SCs and STs were lower by a margin of about 25 per cent and 30 per cent, respectively.
4. In case of HPI, the disparity between SCs/STs and non-SCs/STs in terms of net difference declined only marginally. Due to a minimal decline in the net difference of the HPI values in 2000, the disparity ratios indicated no improvements to reduce the gaps in HPI values between SCs/STs and non-SCs/STs in 2000 from its level in 1990. On the contrary, the gap widened.
5. There is a set of states, where human development was found to be relatively low for all three groups. This group includes the states of Bihar, Uttar Pradesh, Orissa and Madhya Pradesh. On the other hand, HDI was high for all the three social groups in Kerala, Himachal Pradesh, Maharashtra and Tamil Nadu. As regards the HPI, at the state level, with an exception of one or two states, a common group of states comprising Bihar, Uttar Pradesh, Assam, Madhya Pradesh and Rajasthan indicated higher levels of HPI values for SCs, STs and non-SCs/STs.

ANNEXURE II

Human Development and Human Poverty Index

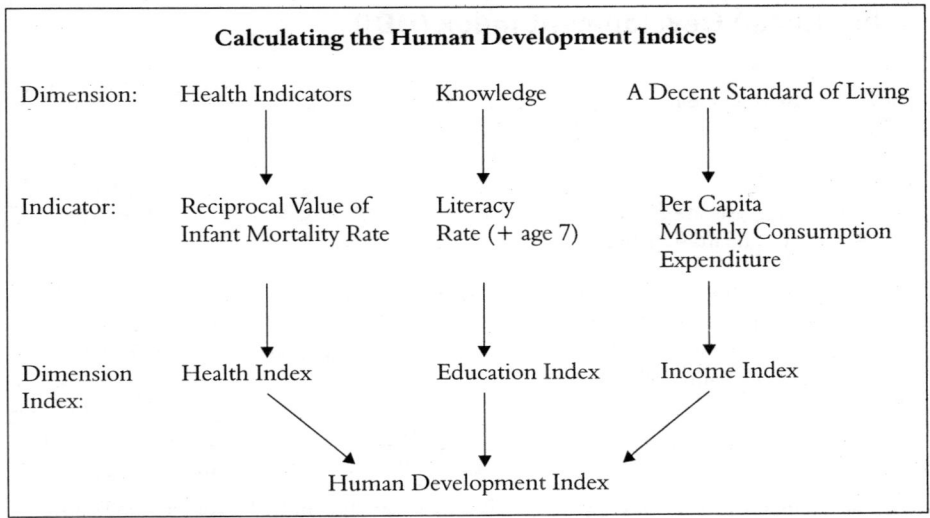

Calculating the Human Development Indices

Dimension:	Health Indicators	Knowledge	A Decent Standard of Living
Indicator:	Reciprocal Value of Infant Mortality Rate	Literacy Rate (+ age 7)	Per Capita Monthly Consumption Expenditure
Dimension Index:	Health Index	Education Index	Income Index

Human Development Index

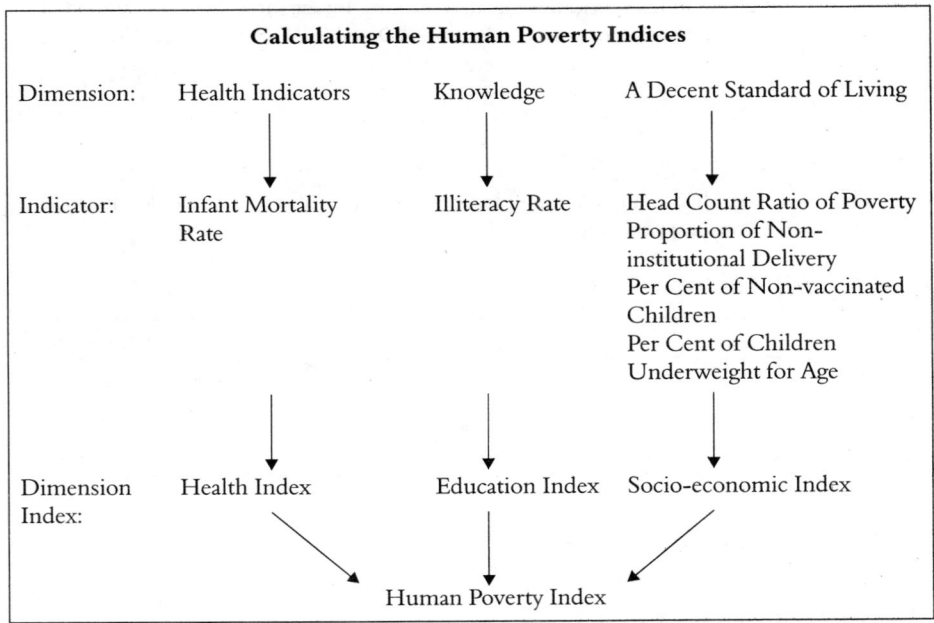

Calculating the Human Poverty Indices

Dimension:	Health Indicators	Knowledge	A Decent Standard of Living
Indicator:	Infant Mortality Rate	Illiteracy Rate	Head Count Ratio of Poverty Proportion of Non-institutional Delivery Per Cent of Non-vaccinated Children Per Cent of Children Underweight for Age
Dimension Index:	Health Index	Education Index	Socio-economic Index

Human Poverty Index

Source: Thorat, Sukhadeo, M. Mahamallik and S. Venkatesan. 2007. 'Human Poverty and Socially Disadvantaged Groups in India', *UNDP Discussion Paper Series 18*, p. 89. New Delhi: Human Development Resource Centre.

TECHNICAL NOTE I

The Human Development Index (HDI)

HDI is a quantitative measure of the achievement level of human well-being. It generally covers three basic aspects of human subsistence:

1. Health,
2. Knowledge/education and
3. A decent standard of living.

To calculate HDI, a separate index is needed to be calculated for each dimension like Health, Knowledge and Decent standard of living. To calculate these dimension indices, minimum and maximum values are chosen for each indicator separately. The formula used for the calculation of these indices is

$$\text{Dimension Index} = \frac{(\text{Actual Value} - \text{Minimum Value})}{(\text{Maximum Value} - \text{Minimum Value})}$$

Here the performance is expressed as a value between 0 and 1 by applying the above formula. The HDI is then calculated as a simple average of the dimension indices. To construct composite indices for different social groups, for example, SCs, STs and other communities separately, the formula can be: the HDI value of the jth group (Ij) for the ith variable is defined as the average of these variables.

$$Ij = \sum Iij/3, \qquad i = 1, 2, 3$$

j = SCs, STs and others

Therefore, the HDI value, for example, for SCs = (health index value + education index value + consumption index value)/3.

Scaling Norm for HDI

Indicators	Minimum	Maximum
IMR	20 per 1,000	—
Literacy rate for 7+ years	0	100
Average consumption expenditure (per capita per month)	₹125	₹1,500

Steps to Calculate the HDI

(A) Calculating the Health Index

The Health Index of a group of individuals measures the relative achievement in health status of that group vis-à-vis other groups and across states. The variable we have chosen here to measure the health achievement is 'Infant Mortality Rate'. As the chosen variable reflects the deprivation aspect of the situation, to measure the achievement aspect we have used the reciprocal value of this variable. (This is because of the unavailability of the other reliable health variable across social groups to measure the achievement aspect of the Health Index.)

(A.1) Calculating the Reciprocal Value of Infant Mortality Rate

Identify the lowest value of the domain (here in this case lowest 'Infant Mortality Rate' in the caste state matrix). Then divide each value (of Infant Mortality Rate) with that 'lowest single value'—the lowest value of the domain. The values in different shells of the new matrix will be the reciprocal figure of the respective shell of the original matrix.

$$\text{Reciprocal Health Index (Infant Mortality Index)} = \frac{\text{Lowest Single Value}}{\text{Original Respective Value}}$$

In this way we will get values for all the states across all social groups. From these reciprocal values the real reciprocal health index can be calculated using the formula:

$$\text{Reciprocal Health Index (Reciprocal Infant Mortality Index)} = \frac{\text{Actual Value} - \text{Minimum Value}}{\text{Maximum Value} - \text{Minimum Value}}$$

(B) Calculating the Education Index

In UNDP reports, Education Index is calculated with the help of two variables—Adult literacy rate and Gross enrolment rate with 2/3 and 1/3 weight, respectively. In the present book, the Education Index measures the relative achievement in literacy level alone by social groups across states as we realise that the available enrolment data across social group is misleading.

$$\text{Education Index} = \frac{\text{Actual Value} - \text{Minimum Value}}{\text{Maximum Value} - \text{Minimum Value}}$$

(C) Calculating MPCE Index

In the present book instead of Gross Domestic Product per capita (GDP/GSDP as taken by UNDP reports), Average MPCE (at 1993 prices) is used for calculation of HDI. It captures the relative achievement of opportunities/capabilities in terms of purchasing power in their hand. The MPCE index can be calculated as follows:

$$\text{MPCE Index} = \frac{\text{Actual Value} - \text{Minimum Value}}{\text{Maximum Value} - \text{Minimum Value}}$$

(D) Calculating the HDI

The HDI value can be obtained by a simple average of the above individual dimension indices.

$$\text{HDI} = \frac{(\text{Reciprocal Health Index } + \text{ Education Index} + \text{MPCE Index})}{3}$$

Calculating HPI

While HDI measures average *achievement,* the HPI measures *deprivations* in the three basic dimensions as in HDI. Calculating the HPI is more straightforward than calculating the HDI. The indicators used to measure the deprivations are already normalised between 0 and 100 (because they are expressed as percentages), so there is no need to create dimension indices as for the HDI. Infant mortality rate, illiteracy rate, poverty (head count ratio), lack of access to healthcare and under nutrition are the key indicators which have been used to estimate the HPI.

The formula for calculating the HPI is as follows:

$$\text{HPI} = \left[\frac{1}{\alpha}\left(P_1^{\alpha} + P_2^{\alpha} + P_3^{\alpha} + P_4^{\alpha}\right)\right]^{\frac{1}{\alpha}}$$

where
P_1 = infant mortality rate in per cent
P_2 = illiteracy rate (for age 7 years and above population)
P_3 = head count ratio of poverty
P_4 = composite indicator on health-related variables (this is an unweighted average of P_{41} and P_{42}) where
P_{41} = percentage of households not having access to public health facilities (this is an unweighted average of percent of non-vaccinated children and percent of non-institutional deliveries)
P_{42} = percentage of children underweight for age

Why α = 4 in Calculating the HPI

The value of α has an important impact on the value of the HPI. If $\alpha = 1$, the HPI is the average of its dimensions. As α rises, greater weight is given to the dimension in which there is the most deprivation. Thus as α increases towards infinity, the HPI will tend towards the value of the dimension in which deprivation is greatest.

Source: Thorat, Sukhadeo, M. Mahamallik and S. Venkatesan. 2007. 'Human Poverty and Socially Disadvantaged Groups in India', *UNDP Discussion Paper Series 18*, pp. 91–92. New Delhi: Human Development Resource Centre.

TECHNICAL NOTE II

For the composite index of human development, we use infant mortality rate (reciprocal value has been used to get the achievement value), literacy rate and average monthly per capita expenditure (at 1993–1994 prices). The infant mortality indicators have been developed from two sets of sources, namely Mortality Differentials in India, Vital Statistics for the early 1980s and the National Family Health Survey I and II for the early 1990s and for recent period, that is, 1999–2000. In the case of literacy rate, population census has been used for all the three time periods. The literacy rate is measured as the proportion of literate population in the age group of seven years and above to the total population of the same age group for 1991 and 2001, whereas for 1981, the literacy rate is for the population aged of five years and above. The third indicator used for the composite index is average monthly per capita expenditure (at 1993–1994 prices). This has been drawn from the unit level data on consumption expenditure survey obtained from the National Sample Survey for 1983 and 1999–2000. Deprivation indicators (a detailed list is given in Chapter 5, Annexure) have been used to estimate the HPI. The IMR has been used to capture the deprivation in the health dimension, illiteracy rate to capture educational deprivation and proportion of people living below the poverty line to capture economic deprivation. Other dimensions of human poverty include lack of access to public provisions, viz. health and nutrition, proportion of non-institutional deliveries, proportion of non-vaccinated children and proportion of children who are underweight for age. These indicators are derived from the National Family Health Survey I and II.

The data on other human development related indicators such as access to land and capital, status of employment and unemployment, wage earnings and human rights violations are collected from various sources. These include population census, NSS employment surveys, NSS decennial land holding surveys, NSS consumption expenditure surveys, Rural Labour Enquiry Reports, and Reports on Crime in India, National Commission for SC/ST and National Human Rights Commission Report. In the case of non-SC/ST groups, some variables like employment/unemployment rate, percentage of self-employed in agriculture and self-employed in non-agriculture, variables related to ownership of land are given separately for non-SCs/STs (designated as Others in NSS terminology). For other variables like urban population, non-farm and farm worker, cultivator, literate and those under different level of education are not given separately for non-SCs/STs and hence had to be worked out by deducting the number of SCs/STs from general figures to arrive at non-SC/ST category. In the case of some variables, this method could not be used as the data is available in ratio form (and not in absolute numbers). Hence we had no choice but to use them in their general form for non-SCs/STs. These variables, however, are only few in number and relate to farm and non-farm wages in rural areas, rural wage labour and agricultural wage labour.

Source: Thorat, Sukhadeo, M. Mahamallik and S. Venkatesan. 2007. 'Human Poverty and Socially Disadvantaged Groups in India', *UNDP Discussion Paper Series 18*, pp. 93–94. New Delhi: Human Development Resource Centre.

Data Sources

Main Index	Time Period	Minor Index	Variable Used	Universe	Time Period	Sources
HDI	1980s and 2000s	(1) Health index	Infant mortality rate (reciprocal value)	SCs, STs, non-SCs/STs and all groups	1984, 1992–1993 and 1998–1999	Vital statistics and NFHS
		(2) Education index	Literacy rate (+age 7)	- For SCs calculated for 16 major states and all-India level	1981 and 2001	Census of India
		(3) Income index	Average monthly per capita consumption expenditure	- For STs calculated for 13 major states and all-India level	1983 and 1999–2000	NSSO
				- For non-SCs/STs and all groups calculated for 16 major states and all-India level		
HPI	1990s and 2000s	(1) Health index	Infant mortality rate (reciprocal value)	SCs, STs, non-SCs/STs, All Groups	1984, 1992–1993 and 1998–1999	NSSO
		(2) Education index	Illiteracy rate (age 7+)	- For SCs calculated for 16 major states and all-India level	1991 and 2001	Vital Statistics and NFHS
		(3) Socio-economic index	Head count ratio of poverty	- For STs calculated for 13 major states and all-India level	1993–1994 and 1999–2000	Census of India
			Percentage of non-vaccinated children	- For non-SCs/STs and All Groups calculated for 16 major states and all-India level	1992–1993 and 1998–1999	NSSO
			Percentage of non-institutional delivery		1992–1993 and 1998–1999	NFHS
			Percentage of children underweight for age		1992–1993 and 1998–1999	NFHS
					1992–1993 and 1998–1999	NFHS
Social Justice Index	2000		Incidence of total crime	SCs, STs, non-SCs/STs and all Groups For SCs and STs calculated for 16 major states and all-India level	1999, 2000 and 2001	Crime in India

Source: Thorat, Sukhadeo, M. Mahamallik and S. Venkatesan. 2007. 'Human Poverty and Socially Disadvantaged Groups in India', *UNDP Discussion Paper Series 18*, p. 96. New Delhi: Human Development Resource Centre.

HUMAN DEVELOPMENT INDEX: IIDS AND UNDP COMPARISON

The Human Development Values calculated in this book for the all social groups are comparatively lower compared to the UNDP values at all-India level as well as state level. The reason for the lower value of HDI estimated by IIDS is due to the choice of variables.[6] However, with a few exceptions the ranking of the states in both estimates is more or less similar (see table below).

In both estimates a definite set of states have higher HDI value and another definite set of states have lower HDI value. There are, however, differences in the ordering of the states. This may possibly be due to two reasons, namely

1. the choice of variables in the construction of HDI used by IIDS and UNDP,
2. inclusion of some newly formed states.[7]

	States with HDI Value Higher than All-India Value	States with HDI Value Lower than All-India Value
Based on IIDS Estimates	(1) Kerala (2) Himachal Pradesh (3) Maharashtra (4) Tamil Nadu (5) Punjab (6) Haryana (7) West Bengal (8) Gujarat (9) Karnataka	(10) Assam (11) Andhra Pradesh (12) Rajasthan (13) Jharkhand (14) Madhya Pradesh (15) Orissa (16) Uttar Pradesh (16) Bihar
Based on UNDP Estimates	(1) Goa (2) Kerala (3) Maharashtra (4) Tamil Nadu (5) Nagaland (6) Punjab (7) Gujarat (8) Sikkim (9) Manipur (10) Himachal Pradesh (11) Karnataka (12) Tripura (13) West Bengal (14) Haryana (15) Arunachal Pradesh (16) Meghalaya	(17) Andhra Pradesh (18) Jammu and Kashmir (19) Chhattisgarh (20) Rajasthan (21) Jharkhand (22) Assam (23) Madhya Pradesh (24) Orissa (25) Uttar Pradesh (27) Bihar

Source: Thorat, Sukhadeo, M. Mahamallik and S. Venkatesan. 2007. 'Human Poverty and Socially Disadvantaged Groups in India', *UNDP Discussion Paper Series 18*, p. 97. New Delhi: Human Development Resource Centre.

[6] A detailed description of variables used at both the levels (IIDS and UNDP) is given in the Technical Note II.

[7] In case of the inclusion of some newly emerged states like Jharkhand and Chhattisgarh, the values of prime variables (MPCE, IMR, Literacy Rate) may get disturbed. In IIDS analysis, these states are parts of some other states but here these are independent states. So it affects the ordering of the states in both ways, that is, the original states as well as the newly emerged states.

	Indian Institute of Dalit Studies	*UNDP Reports (this data is from 2004 Report)*
Human Development Index	1. Reciprocal value of infant mortality rate 2. Literacy rate (age 7+) 3. Average monthly per capita expenditure	1. Life expectancy at birth 2. Adult literacy rate and gross enrolment rate 3. GDP per capita
Human Poverty Index	1. Infant mortality rate 2. Illiteracy rate 3. Head count ratio of poverty 4. Percentage of non-institutional deliveries 5. Percentage of non-vaccinated children 6. Percentage of children underweight for age	1. Probability at birth of not surviving the age of 40 years 2. Adult illiteracy rate 3. Unweighted average of population Without sustainable access to an improved water source and children underweight for age

Source: Thorat, Sukhadeo, M. Mahamallik and S. Venkatesan. 2007. 'Human Poverty and Socially Disadvantaged Groups in India', *UNDP Discussion Paper Series 18*, p. 95. New Delhi: Human Development Resource Centre.

Chapter 5

LEVELS AND PATTERNS OF CONSUMPTION EXPENDITURE OF SOCIAL GROUPS

Ashwini Deshpande

This chapter examines the various levels and patterns of income by using consumption expenditure as a proxy indicator for Scheduled Castes (SCs) and Scheduled Tribes (STs). The consumption expenditure is used as a proxy variable to assess the material standards of living in the absence of reliable data on income. There is a great deal of correspondence between income and consumption expenditure, particularly at low levels of income when savings are negligible. Thus, an analysis of the consumption patterns of different social groups provides a good insight into their material standard of living. Besides, consumption expenditure is the basis of poverty measurement in India.

DATABASE

The analysis is based on data from the consumption expenditure surveys of four large sample rounds of the National Sample Survey (NSS), such as the 38th, 43rd, 50th and 55th rounds, corresponding to the years 1983, 1987–1988, 1993–1994 and 1999–2000, respectively. In view of the issues relating to compatibility of the 55th round with earlier rounds (Sen and Himanshu, 2004), an attempt has been made to ensure consistency of the concepts and data used across all the rounds, but some contentious issues remain. To calculate the monthly per capita consumption expenditure (MPCE), the 30–365 day estimates have been used for all the four rounds utilised for analysis. For the 38th and 43rd rounds, 30-day estimates have been used for all the items, except for three items, such as durables, clothing and footwear, for which the 365-day estimate has been used. The 50th round allows the calculation of total MPCE in two ways. One estimate is obtained by excluding the 365-day institutional medical expenditures and certain educational expenditures, but including the 365-day estimates for durables, clothing and footwear: this estimate is comparable to 38th and 43rd rounds. The second estimate is obtained by including the aforementioned medical and educational expenditures and the 365-day estimates for durables, clothing and footwear. This estimate is comparable to 55th round. Thus, in order to make all the rounds comparable, the ratio between two estimates (with and without medical and educational expenditures) for the 50th round was taken and that ratio was used to deflate the estimate for the 55th round. This was done for each social group and in each state.

The other issue pertains to categorisation of population into social groups. The 38th, 43rd and 50th rounds divide the population into three broad categories: SCs, STs and non-SCs/STs. The 55th round further divides non-SC/ST category into Other Backward Classes (OBCs) and the remaining non-SCs/STs. In order to make all these rounds comparable, in this study, the 55th round estimates have been calculated in such a way that non-SC/ST category includes OBCs. While these categories are broad and do not allow us to isolate the upper castes, it needs to be noted that the gaps based on this three-way classification of social groups would under-estimate the disparities between SCs and STs, and the groups at the top end of the caste spectrum.

The NSS rounds give us the MPCE at nominal prices. In order to assess the real changes in the MPCE, this study uses the official poverty lines as deflators because these are used in official policy-related calculations. However, these are available only for the big states. For smaller states, the deflator for geographically the nearest big state is used. For calculating the real increase, 1983 has been taken as the base year.

LEVEL OF MPCE BY SOCIAL GROUPS (1999–2000)

This section examines all-India and state-wise real MPCE (with the base year as 1983) for SCs, STs, non-SCs/STs and all, separately for rural and the urban areas, on the basis of estimates from the 55th round of the NSS, to bring out the inter-state variations in consumption expenditure across social groups. Table 5A.1 (Annexure III) provides the values of MPCE at constant prices for each social groups for both all-India level and across states.

Scheduled Castes

In 1999–2000, all-India average MPCE for SCs in rural and urban areas was ₹114 and ₹159, respectively. Across the states, the highest absolute real MPCE levels for SCs in rural areas were for the states Kerala (₹157) followed by Punjab (₹144), Himachal Pradesh (₹143), Tamil Nadu and Haryana (₹133). At the lower end of the spectrum (rural and the urban MPCE levels) were the states like Bihar, Madhya Pradesh and Uttar Pradesh. The other two states with the lowest MPCE levels for rural SCs were Andhra Pradesh (₹105) and Assam (₹111). Similarly, for the urban SCs, the states of Orissa (₹124) and Haryana (₹149) had the lowest MPCE levels (Figure 5.1).

Figure 5.1
Real MPCE (Base Year 1983) across Social Groups: 1999–2000

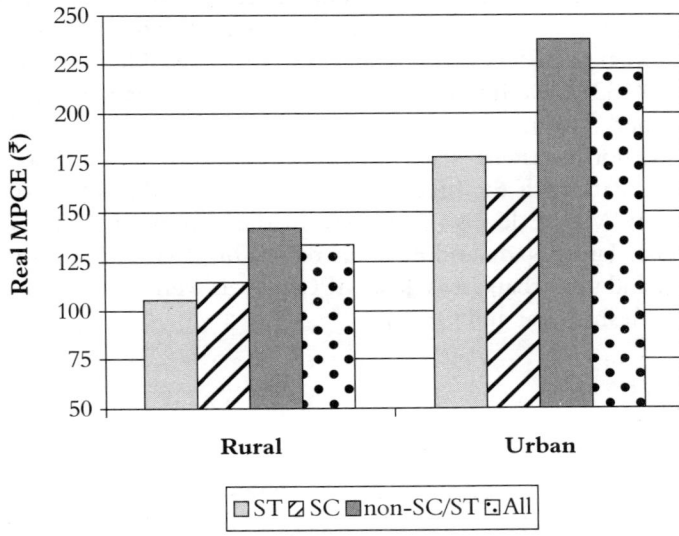

Source: NSSO, 55th round, Consumer Expenditure Survey, 1999–2000.

Scheduled Tribes

At the outset, for analysing STs, it is pertinent to distinguish between those who inhabit the north-eastern states (where they constitute a majority) and those in the other states (where they constitute a minority). The all-India average rural MPCE level for STs was ₹106. Among the north-eastern states, the top three states for STs were Nagaland (₹250), Mizoram (₹195) and Arunachal Pradesh (₹178). At the other end of the continuum were the states like Assam (₹117), Tripura (₹126) and Manipur (₹142). Interestingly, all the ST states mentioned above have average MPCE levels that are higher than all-India average.

Elsewhere in the country, the states which exhibit a high MPCE level for the rural STs were Kerala (₹180), Himachal Pradesh (₹157), Punjab (₹132), Haryana (₹124) and Tamil Nadu (₹119). On the other hand, the bottom five states were Madhya Pradesh (₹87), Orissa (₹94), Bihar (₹99) and Andhra Pradesh, Maharashtra and Uttar Pradesh (all at ₹107). However, not all states (for example, Punjab and Haryana) have a significant representation of ST population and hence the presence of these states in the list of top five states ought to be interpreted with caution.

The all-India average MPCE level for urban STs was ₹178. Among the north-eastern states, the top three were Nagaland, Tripura and Sikkim with MPCE levels of ₹379, ₹327, and ₹302, respectively. At the other end were the states of Manipur, Assam and Arunachal Pradesh with MPCE levels of ₹193, ₹224 and ₹248, respectively. Elsewhere in the country, the top five states were Himachal Pradesh (₹287), Tamil Nadu (₹276), Kerala (₹266), Uttar Pradesh (₹234) and Haryana (₹232). The aforementioned disclaimer applies to the latter two states, since the proportion of STs in these states is very low. The bottom five states were Orissa (₹132), Madhya Pradesh (₹147), West Bengal (₹148), Karnataka (₹149) and Bihar (₹160).

Among the north-eastern states in both rural and urban areas, Nagaland emerges as the state with the highest MPCE level for STs, while Manipur and Assam have low MPCE levels. Elsewhere in the country, the states Himachal Pradesh, Kerala, Tamil Nadu and Haryana record high MPCE levels for STs. For both the rural and the urban areas, low MPCE levels were recorded for the states of Madhya Pradesh, Bihar and Orissa.

Non-SCs/STs

The all-India average for non-SCs/STs was ₹143 which was higher than the MPCE levels for SCs and STs. The top five states with higher rural MPCE levels for non-SCs/STs (excluding the Union Territories and the north-eastern states) were Goa (₹240), Punjab (₹208), Kerala (₹207) and Haryana (₹188), followed by Himachal Pradesh and Tamil Nadu (both at ₹174). The bottom five states were Assam (₹114), Bihar (₹119), Madhya Pradesh (₹119), Uttar Pradesh (₹122) and Andhra Pradesh (₹134).

The all-India average for non-SCs/STs in the urban areas was ₹236. The top five states in this category were Delhi (₹401), Himachal Pradesh (₹316), Tamil Nadu (₹272), Goa (₹270) and Punjab (₹261). The bottom five states were Orissa (₹183), Madhya Pradesh (₹190), Uttar Pradesh (₹191), Bihar (₹193) and Andhra Pradesh (₹196).

For non-SCs/STs, the common states with high MPCE levels were Punjab, Goa, Himachal Pradesh and Tamil Nadu. On the other hand, low MPCE levels were recorded in Bihar, Uttar Pradesh, Madhya Pradesh and Andhra Pradesh.

All Categories

The all-India average rural MPCE level for all categories was ₹133. The top five states for all categories were Goa (₹241), Kerala (₹202), Punjab (₹182), Haryana (₹175) and Himachal Pradesh (₹166). The bottom five states were Madhya Pradesh (₹107), Bihar (₹112), Assam (₹114), Uttar Pradesh (₹116) and Orissa (₹127).

The all-India urban average for all categories was ₹223. The top five states in this category were Delhi (₹364), Himachal Pradesh (₹296), Goa (₹270), Tamil Nadu (₹256) and Kerala (₹251). The bottom five states were Orissa (₹167), Madhya Pradesh (₹180), Bihar (₹183), Uttar Pradesh (₹185) and Andhra Pradesh (₹189).

Thus, it emerges from the above results that the states with higher state domestic product (SDP) also have higher MPCE levels for the social groups and the opposite holds true for the states with low MPCE levels, as they tend to be in the lower half of SDP distribution. Except a few changes in ranking for individual social groups, there is a great deal of overlap in the ranking of individual states for different social groups. The states in the Hindi belt continue to register low consumption levels for different social groups, thereby reflecting low levels of SDP. Similarly, the states of Himachal Pradesh and Punjab can be seen in the top five lists for all social groups. Thus, the ranking of states broadly follows the distribution of states by the SDP, though this inference is marked by variations. For instance, the state of Maharashtra, which ranks high in terms of SDP is not amongst the top five states in terms of MPCE.

DISPARITIES IN MPCE (1999–2000)

The extent of disparities in MPCE levels with regard to SCs versus non-SCs/STs, STs versus non-SCs/STs, and SCs versus STs have been examined through the ratio of their respective MPCE levels (see Annexure III Table 5A.2).

SCs versus Non-SCs/STs

At all-India level, this ratio was 0.8 for rural areas and 0.67 for urban areas, which suggest that disparity in consumption levels between SCs and non-SCs/STs in urban India was higher than that in rural India. This pattern was seen in most of the states except Andhra Pradesh, Punjab (where rural and urban ratio was more or less the same) and Kerala (where urban ratio was higher than that of the rural). In addition, the ratio was less than 1 in all the states of India, except for Goa and the north-eastern states where the SC population is insignificant. It thereby reflects the persistence of caste disparities. As suggested in the previous sections, these disparities are marked by regional variations. In rural India, the states with disparity ratios above all-India average (a ratio of less than 0.8) were Andhra Pradesh, Gujarat, Haryana, Karnataka, Kerala, Maharashtra, Punjab and Tamil Nadu, in that order. The states that were close to all-India average (ratios ranging between 0.80 and 0.82) were Bihar, Himachal Pradesh and Uttar Pradesh. The remaining states had disparity levels that were lower than all-India average.

A similar inspection for urban India indicates that states with disparity ratios above all-India average (a ratio of less than 0.67) were Assam, Haryana, Himachal Pradesh, Karnataka, Tamil Nadu, Tripura, Uttar Pradesh, West Bengal and Delhi. The states that were close to all-India average (with ratios ranging between 0.67 and 0.69) were Bihar, Gujarat, Maharashtra, Orissa, Punjab and Rajasthan. The remaining states had disparity levels that were lower than all-India average.

Thus, the analysis indicates that there is not only regional variation but also that this variation is not uniform across rural and urban India.

STs versus Non-SCs/STs

The ratio of STs versus non-SCs/STs was similar for rural and urban India. For the former it was 0.74 while for the latter it stood at 0.75. However, herein too, a great deal of regional variation is observed. For rural India, the states which have higher than average disparity ratio (less than 0.74) were Gujarat, Haryana, Madhya Pradesh, Maharashtra, Orissa, Punjab and Tamil Nadu. On the other hand, the state with disparity ratio that was closer to all-India average (ratio between 0.74 and 0.76) was Karnataka, with all the other states having disparity ratio lower than all-India average. For urban India, the states with higher than average disparity ratio (less than 0.75) were Goa, Gujarat, Karnataka, Maharashtra, Orissa, Punjab and West Bengal. The state with a disparity that was closer to all-India average (ratio between 0.75 and 0.77) was Madhya Pradesh.

CHANGES IN THE LEVEL OF MPCE (1983–2000)

The changes in the levels of MPCE are captured through the growth rate of real MPCE over the larger period of 1983–2000 (Table 5.1), and for smaller sub-periods, that is, 1983–1993 (first phase) and 1993–2000 (second phase) for SCs, STs and non-SCs/STs, respectively (see Annexure III Tables 5A.3, 5A.4 and

Table 5.1
Rate of Growth in Real MPCE: All India

Social Groups	Rural			Urban		
	1983–2000	1983–1993	1993–2000	1983–2000	1983–1993	1993–2000
SCs	0.2	0.1	0.1	0.3	0.1	0.1
STs	0.2	0.2	0.0	0.3	0.2	0.1
Non-SCs/STs	0.2	0.1	0.1	0.4	0.2	0.1

Source: Computed from various rounds of NSSO consumer expenditure surveys.

5A.5) for the rural and urban areas. These years correspond to the 38th, 50th and 55th rounds of the NSS in that order.

SCs

For SCs, the rural MPCE has grown over a 20-year period, but the increase has been greater during the first phase than the second phase. The increase in urban MPCE follows exactly the same pattern. Thus, for SCs, the liberalisation decade saw a sharp reduction in the rate of growth of MPCE, for both rural and urban areas. Across the states, for rural SCs, the states that have seen greater than all-India increase for the entire period include some rich as well as poor states such as Maharashtra, Kerala, Tamil Nadu, Goa, Orissa and Bihar. The states that have seen a reduction in growth rate during the liberalisation decade were Andhra Pradesh, Assam, Bihar, Karnataka, Madhya Pradesh, Maharashtra, Orissa, Tamil Nadu, Tripura and West Bengal. The states that have recorded a stagnated rate of growth were Gujarat, Punjab and Rajasthan. Thus, as all-India figures suggest, most of the states in India experienced either stagnation or a sharp reduction in the rate of growth of MPCE during the liberalisation period.

The picture is more or less similar for urban India. What is striking about urban India is the fact that several states like Assam, Goa, Haryana and West Bengal experienced a negative rate of growth of the real MPCE for SCs during the liberalisation decade, which means that the real MPCE actually fell as compared to that recorded during the previous decade.

STs

For rural India, the rate of growth for STs was similar to that for SCs, while for urban India, it was higher. However, as in the case of SCs, STs too experienced a sharp decline in the rate of growth of real MPCE during the liberalisation decade. In fact, for both rural and urban areas, the rate of growth of real MPCE during the liberalisation decade (second phase) was much lower than that for SCs with the rates being so low that they virtually stagnated. Among the north-eastern states, Meghalaya and Tripura in the rural areas, and Assam in the urban areas have seen a negative rate of growth of real MPCE for STs during the liberalisation decade. Elsewhere in the country, the states of Andhra Pradesh, Gujarat, Madhya Pradesh, Orissa, Punjab, Rajasthan, Tamil Nadu, Uttar Pradesh and West Bengal have seen a negative rate of growth of real MPCE in the rural areas. In the urban areas, the states of Goa, Gujarat, Himachal Pradesh, Kerala, Punjab, Rajasthan and West Bengal have seen a negative rate of growth, which effectively means that large parts of the country have seen a sharp reduction or decline in the rate of growth of consumption levels for STs. If the experiences of SCs and STs are combined, it becomes clear that the liberalisation decade has seen a further marginalisation in the standards of living of the marginalised social groups.

Non-SCs/STs

Interestingly, the pattern for the decadal changes in consumption levels for non-SCs/STs was similar, that is, there was a deceleration in the rate of growth during the liberalisation decade. However, if this trend is disregarded, it can be seen that there were clear inter-caste disparities within the social groups with none of the major states witnessing a negative rate of growth for non-SCs/STs. Thus, while the overall rate of growth declined during the second phase, the outcomes have been better for non-SCs/STs than for SCs and STs. It is useful to remember that given the heterogeneous nature of non-SCs/STs, the top end of non-SCs/STs as a socially heterogeneous group must have actually experienced an improvement in living standards. Conversely, we can suppose that lower end of the non-SC/ST group must have experienced outcomes similar to those experienced by SCs and STs.

CHANGES IN DISPARITIES (1983–2000)

Given the differential rate of change in MPCE for the three social groups, the extents of disparities have also changed over the time. The ratios of MPCE for the three social groups for the years 1983, 1993 and 1999–2000, presented in Annexure III Tables 5A.3, 5A.4 and 5A.5 are used to interpret the changes in disparities in the rural and the urban areas (see Annexure III Tables 5A.6 and 5A.7).

SCs versus Non-SCs/STs

For rural India, there was a marginal improvement in the ratio of MPCE between SCs and non-SCs/STs over the period 1983–2000, though the increase was very small. However, the opposite trend was observed in some states such as Andhra Pradesh, Gujarat, Haryana, Punjab and Uttar Pradesh. It should be noted that barring Uttar Pradesh, these states lie in the upper half of the SDP distribution. For urban India, as noted earlier, this ratio was lower than that for the rural areas, and actually worsened over the period for all-India figure and the figures for most of the states except Goa, Kerala, Maharashtra, Tamil Nadu and Tripura. Thus, SC versus non-SC/ST disparity in urban India was not only higher than rural areas but worsened over the last two decades over large parts of the country.

STs versus Non-SCs/STs

For rural India, as was the case with SCs, there was a marginal improvement in MPCE ratio between STs and non-SCs/STs. However, a number of states, except north-eastern states, which include Haryana, Himachal Pradesh, Kerala, Maharashtra, Orissa, Tripura and West Bengal saw decline in this ratio. For urban India, there has been a decline in this ratio at all-India level which signifies an increase in disparities. This pattern was also evident in the states of Assam, Bihar, Goa, Haryana, Himachal Pradesh, Karnataka, Madhya Pradesh, Sikkim and West Bengal.

ASSOCIATION BETWEEN THE LEVELS OF MPCE AND DISPARITY

Some notable aspects are discernible from the evidence which pertains to the level of MPCE and changes in disparities. Several states with high absolute levels of MPCE have seen an increase in the levels of disparity. For example, as regards the urban MPCE, in rural Punjab and in almost all the top five states, the disparities between SCs and non-SCs/STs have accentuated further. Thus, high absolute levels of MPCE reflect high income levels for a respective state and such levels of MPCE can be related to both incidences of high disparity and disparities that have been worsening over time. Similarly, for STs, it can be observed that high absolute levels of MPCE do not automatically ensure low disparities. The states with high absolute levels of MPCE for STs such as Kerala, Himachal Pradesh and Haryana have seen a worsening of disparities for the rural areas. Similarly, in urban areas, Himachal Pradesh has seen a worsening of disparities. However, it is important to note that this is not a causal relationship. The states with low levels of MPCE have also seen a worsening of disparities. The important conclusion that emerges is that disparities can go hand in hand with both high and low levels of MPCE. Thus, this is an independent problem and needs to be treated as such.

SUMMING UP

The MPCE is the highest for non-SCs/STs among all social groups, in both rural and urban India, followed by SCs in rural areas and STs in urban areas. The disparity in consumption levels between SCs and non-SCs/STs in urban India was higher (disparity ratio 0.67) than that in rural India (disparity ratio 0.8). However, as regards STs versus non-SCs/STs, the ratio was similar for rural and urban India.

Over the period 1983–2000, the MPCE increased for all the three social groups, but the rate of growth was higher during 1983–1993 as compared to 1993–2000, in general, and for the urban areas, in particular. During this period, the inter-social group disparities between SCs and non-SCs/STs, on one hand, and between STs and non-SCs/STs, on the other hand, improved in rural areas but worsened in urban areas.

The above discussion makes it apparent that there are marked disparities in material standards of living between scheduled and non-scheduled groups throughout the country and that this pattern has more or less persisted over the last 20 years, a period associated with the opening up and liberalisation of the economy. The limitations in data did not permit us to isolate the status of upper castes, but it is reasonable to assume that inter-caste disparities between SCs/STs and the upper castes are even starker.

It is often argued that the focus of economic policies should be on growth, such that there would be a bigger pie to be divided among the social groups. However, the regional pattern of inter-group disparities presents a picture that defies a simple causative relationship between growth, levels of SDP, absolute standards of living of the marginalised social groups, and disparities. We have seen that disparities are high in both high-SDP and high-growth states, on one hand, as well as in low-SDP and low-growth states, on the other hand. Thus, growth by itself offers no guarantee of reduction of inter-group disparities, and indeed lack of growth is not a solution either. This suggests that the problem of inter-group disparities needs to be tackled independently through special policies such as affirmative action.

ANNEXURE III

Table 5A.1
State Variations in MPCE by Social Groups, 1999–2000

	Rural				Urban			
	MPCE at Constant Prices (1983 = 100)				*MPCE at Constant Prices (1983 = 100)*			
			Non-SCs/				*Non-SCs/*	
States	*STs*	*SCs*	*STs*	*All*	*STs*	*SCs*	*STs*	*All*
Andhra Pradesh	107.4	105.0	134.3	125.8	160.8	152.1	196.3	189.3
Arunachal Pradesh	178.4	500.4	156.2	175.3	247.6	238.6	224.3	235.0
Assam	117.3	110.8	114.2	114.3	223.8	167.4	256.8	245.6
Bihar	98.7	96.4	118.5	112.5	159.5	133.8	192.6	183.4

(Table 5A.1 Contd.)

(Table 5A.1 Contd.)

	Rural				Urban			
	MPCE at Constant Prices (1983 = 100)				*MPCE at Constant Prices (1983 = 100)*			
			Non-SCs/				*Non-SCs/*	
States	*STs*	*SCs*	*STs*	*All*	*STs*	*SCs*	*STs*	*All*
Goa	540.1	409.6	240.1	241.2	167.2	247.4	270.0	270.2
Gujarat	114.1	118.3	156.0	143.7	173.2	174.4	250.5	236.2
Haryana	124.4	133.8	188.4	175.0	231.5	148.5	244.3	223.0
Himachal Pradesh	157.0	142.7	174.2	166.0	287.2	205.3	316.3	295.6
Jammu and Kashmir	N.A.	N.A.	N.A.	N.A.	N.A.	N.A.	N.A.	N.A.
Karnataka	108.3	112.9	142.3	133.8	148.8	139.4	227.3	214.2
Kerala	179.9	156.6	207.8	202.2	266.4	215.7	253.6	251.1
Madhya Pradesh	87.1	100.7	119.4	107.6	147.1	135.1	190.6	179.7
Maharashtra	106.7	119.0	148.9	138.0	168.4	167.0	243.7	230.2
Manipur	142.2	149.5	147.6	145.3	192.7	231.0	212.0	211.3
Meghalaya	150.8	220.7	149.6	150.9	285.4	248.1	307.8	290.7
Mizoram	194.7	810.3	164.7	193.3	317.3	316.6	340.8	317.4
Nagaland	250.5	N.A.	244.1	249.9	378.6	309.0	341.9	371.4
Orissa	94.1	116.2	142.4	123.7	132.0	124.3	183.4	167.4
Punjab	132.2	143.6	208.6	182.9	168.3	180.6	261.5	237.6
Rajasthan	108.4	117.3	136.2	127.6	170.8	150.2	215.8	202.0
Sikkim	153.5	129.1	139.4	142.3	301.5	207.7	272.7	271.1
Tamil Nadu	119.1	133.7	174.2	161.2	276.7	156.3	271.6	256.0
Tripura	125.9	146.4	148.9	146.1	327.5	207.7	275.7	264.5
Uttar Pradesh	107.3	99.2	122.4	116.5	234.6	148.0	191.0	184.7
West Bengal	113.3	132.4	141.6	137.2	148.3	152.7	241.8	224.1
Andaman and Nicobar Islands	213.8	253.3	250.1	243.0	288.4	194.1	292.4	289.7
Chandigarh	435.9	175.5	249.0	246.8	451.3	229.9	402.9	380.9
Dadra and Nagar Haveli	127.3	156.2	311.8	154.7	170.0	435.9	319.6	283.8
Daman and Diu	177.8	N.A.	312.3	254.7	193.3	N.A.	237.0	229.8

(Table 5A.1 Contd.)

(Table 5A.1 Contd.)

	Rural				Urban			
	MPCE at Constant Prices (1983 = 100)				*MPCE at Constant Prices (1983 = 100)*			
			Non-SCs/				*Non-SCs/*	
States	*STs*	*SCs*	*STs*	*All*	*STs*	*SCs*	*STs*	*All*
Delhi	N.A.	N.A.	N.A.	N.A.	234.2	194.1	401.0	363.5
Lakshadweep	225.2	0.0	551.4	233.4	265.8	N.A.	496.1	274.3
Pondicherry	243.5	140.9	205.0	186.0	244.5	179.0	206.4	204.6
All India	**105.9**	**114.4**	**142.6**	**132.9**	**177.8**	**159.0**	**236.3**	**223.1**

Source: NSSO, 55th round, Consumer Expenditure Survey, 1999–2000.
Note: N.A. means not available.

Table 5A.2
Inter-group Disparities in MPCE, 1999–2000 (Based on Ratios)

	Rural		Urban	
States	*STs/Non-SCs/STs*	*SCs/Non-SCs/STs*	*STs/Non-SCs/STs*	*SCs/Non-SCs/STs*
Andhra Pradesh	0.8	0.8	0.8	0.8
Arunachal Pradesh	1.1	3.2	1.1	1.1
Assam	1.0	1.0	0.9	0.7
Bihar	0.8	0.8	0.8	0.7
Goa	2.2	1.7	0.6	0.9
Gujarat	0.7	0.8	0.7	0.7
Haryana	0.7	0.7	0.9	0.6
Himachal Pradesh	0.9	0.8	0.9	0.6
Jammu and Kashmir	N.A.	N.A.	N.A.	N.A.
Karnataka	0.8	0.8	0.7	0.6
Kerala	0.9	0.8	1.1	0.9
Madhya Pradesh	0.7	0.8	0.8	0.7
Maharashtra	0.7	0.8	0.7	0.7
Manipur	1.0	1.0	0.9	1.1
Meghalaya	1.0	1.5	0.9	0.8
Mizoram	1.2	4.9	0.9	0.9
Nagaland	1.0	N.A.	1.1	0.9
Orissa	0.7	0.8	0.7	0.7
Punjab	0.6	0.7	0.6	0.7

(Table 5A.2 Contd.)

(Table 5A.2 Contd.)

	Rural		Urban	
States	STs/Non-SCs/STs	SCs/Non-SCs/STs	STs/Non-SCs/STs	SCs/Non-SCs/STs
Rajasthan	0.8	0.9	0.8	0.7
Sikkim	1.1	0.9	1.1	0.8
Tamil Nadu	0.7	0.8	1.0	0.6
Tripura	0.8	1.0	1.2	0.8
Uttar Pradesh	0.9	0.8	1.2	0.8
West Bengal	0.8	0.9	0.6	0.6
Andaman and Nicobar Islands	0.9	1.0	1.0	0.7
Chandigarh	1.8	0.7	1.1	0.6
Dadra and Nagar Haveli	0.4	0.5	0.5	1.4
Daman and Diu	0.6	N.A.	0.8	N.A.
Delhi	N.A.	N.A.	0.6	0.5
Lakshadweep	0.4	0.0	0.5	N.A.
Pondicherry	1.2	0.7	1.2	0.9
All India	**0.7**	**0.8**	**0.8**	**0.7**

Source: NSSO, 55th round, Consumer Expenditure Survey, 1999–2000.
Note: N.A. means not available.

Table 5A.3
Changes in MPCE Level—Rural and Urban SCs

	Rural			Urban		
States	Rate of Growth, 1983–2000	Rate of Growth, 1983–1993	Rate of Growth, 1993–2000	Rate of Growth, 1983–2000	Rate of Growth, 1983–1993	Rate of Growth, 1993–2000
Andhra Pradesh	0.1	0.1	0.0	0.2	0.1	0.1
Arunachal Pradesh	N.A.	N.A.	2.3	N.A.	N.A.	0.2
Assam	0.0	0.0	0.0	0.4	0.5	−0.1
Bihar	0.3	0.2	0.1	0.2	0.2	0.0
Goa	2.0	0.6	0.8	0.4	0.6	−0.1
Gujarat	0.1	0.0	0.0	0.2	0.0	0.1
Haryana	0.1	−0.1	0.2	0.1	0.1	0.0
Himachal Pradesh	0.1	−0.1	0.2	0.2	0.1	0.1

(Table 5A.3 Contd.)

(*Table 5A.3 Contd.*)

	Rural			Urban		
States	*Rate of Growth, 1983–2000*	*Rate of Growth, 1983–1993*	*Rate of Growth, 1993–2000*	*Rate of Growth, 1983–2000*	*Rate of Growth, 1983–1993*	*Rate of Growth, 1993–2000*
Jammu and Kashmir	N.A.	N.A.	N.A.	N.A.	N.A.	N.A.
Karnataka	0.2	0.1	0.1	0.1	–0.1	0.2
Kerala	0.5	0.2	0.3	0.5	0.1	0.3
Madhya Pradesh	0.1	0.2	0.0	0.2	0.1	0.0
Maharashtra	0.3	0.2	0.1	0.3	0.2	0.1
Manipur	0.0	–0.1	0.1	0.6	0.2	0.4
Meghalaya	1.6	1.0	0.3	0.7	0.8	0.0
Mizoram	4.3	0.7	2.1	1.0	1.4	–0.2
Nagaland	N.A.	N.A.	N.A.	0.9	1.1	–0.1
Orissa	0.3	0.3	0.0	0.1	0.4	–0.2
Punjab	0.1	0.0	0.1	0.2	0.1	0.1
Rajasthan	0.1	0.0	0.1	0.1	0.0	0.0
Sikkim	17.0	18.4	–0.1	0.1	0.3	–0.1
Tamil Nadu	0.6	0.4	0.1	0.4	0.2	0.2
Tripura	9.2	8.7	0.0	0.7	0.5	0.1
Uttar Pradesh	0.1	0.0	0.1	0.3	0.1	0.2
West Bengal	0.4	0.3	0.1	0.1	0.2	0.0
Andaman and Nicobar Islands	1.1	1.1	0.0	0.2	0.5	–0.2
Chandigarh	0.2	0.0	0.2	0.6	0.6	0.0
Dadra and Nagar Haveli	0.1	0.3	–0.1	N.A.	N.A.	0.9
Daman and Diu	N.A.	N.A.	N.A.	N.A.	N.A.	N.A.
Delhi	N.A.	N.A.	N.A.	0.4	0.1	0.2
Lakshadweep	N.A.	N.A.	–1.0	N.A.	N.A.	N.A.
Pondicherry	0.8	0.6	0.1	1.0	0.2	0.6
All India	**0.2**	**0.1**	**0.1**	**0.3**	**0.1**	**0.1**

Source: Computed from various rounds of NSSO consumer expenditure surveys.
Note: N.A. means not available.

Table 5A.4
Changes in MPCE Level—Rural and Urban STs

States	Rural			Urban		
	Rate of Growth, 1983–2000	*Rate of Growth, 1983–1993*	*Rate of Growth, 1993–2000*	*Rate of Growth, 1983–2000*	*Rate of Growth, 1983–1993*	*Rate of Growth, 1993–2000*
Andhra Pradesh	0.2	0.2	0.0	0.4	0.2	0.1
Arunachal Pradesh	N.A.	N.A.	0.4	1.0	0.7	0.2
Assam	0.1	0.0	0.0	0.3	0.4	0.0
Bihar	0.2	0.2	0.0	0.2	0.2	0.0
Goa	3.2	0.7	1.5	0.1	0.5	−0.3
Gujarat	0.2	0.2	0.0	0.5	0.5	0.0
Haryana	0.1	−0.1	0.2	0.1	0.1	0.0
Himachal Pradesh	0.0	−0.3	0.5	0.0	0.0	0.0
Jammu and Kashmir	N.A.	N.A.	N.A.	N.A.	N.A.	N.A.
Karnataka	0.3	0.2	0.0	0.1	0.0	0.1
Kerala	0.3	0.1	0.2	0.6	1.5	−0.4
Madhya Pradesh	0.1	0.1	0.0	0.1	−0.1	0.1
Maharashtra	0.2	0.2	0.0	0.3	0.1	0.2
Manipur	0.2	0.1	0.1	0.5	0.3	0.2
Meghalaya	0.2	0.2	−0.1	0.5	0.4	0.1
Mizoram	0.6	0.4	0.1	0.6	0.5	0.1
Nagaland	N.A.	N.A.	0.2	1.0	0.5	0.3
Orissa	0.3	0.3	0.0	0.2	0.2	0.0
Punjab	0.0	0.1	−0.1	0.2	0.4	−0.1
Rajasthan	0.3	0.3	0.0	0.1	0.2	−0.1
Sikkim	8.1	7.0	0.1	0.2	0.1	0.1
Tamil Nadu	0.2	0.2	0.0	1.6	1.1	0.2
Tripura	4.8	5.0	0.0	0.7	0.5	0.2
Uttar Pradesh	0.1	0.2	0.0	0.6	0.1	0.5
West Bengal	0.3	0.3	0.0	0.2	0.6	−0.3

(Table 5A.4 Contd.)

(*Table 5A.4 Contd.*)

	Rural			Urban		
States	*Rate of Growth, 1983–2000*	*Rate of Growth, 1983–1993*	*Rate of Growth, 1993–2000*	*Rate of Growth, 1983–2000*	*Rate of Growth, 1983–1993*	*Rate of Growth, 1993–2000*
Andaman and Nicobar Islands	0.7	0.6	0.0	0.9	0.6	0.2
Chandigarh	N.A.	N.A.	2.4	0.1	–1.0	N.A.
Dadra and Nagar Haveli	0.4	0.2	0.2	N.A.	N.A.	0.5
Daman and Diu	N.A.	N.A.	0.2	N.A.	N.A.	0.3
Delhi	N.A.	N.A.	N.A.	0.4	0.2	0.1
Lakshadweep	N.A.	N.A.	0.1	0.6	0.4	0.1
Pondicherry	N.A.	N.A.	0.4	N.A.	N.A.	1.3
All India	**0.2**	**0.2**	**0.0**	**0.3**	**0.2**	**0.1**

Source: Computed from various rounds of NSSO consumer expenditure surveys.
Note: N.A. means not available.

Table 5A.5
Changes in MPCE Level—Rural and Urban Non-SCs/STs

	Rural			Urban		
States	*Rate of Growth, 1983–2000*	*Rate of Growth, 1983–1993*	*Rate of Growth, 1993–2000*	*Rate of Growth, 1983–2000*	*Rate of Growth, 1983–1993*	*Rate of Growth, 1993–2000*
Andhra Pradesh	0.2	0.2	0.0	0.3	0.1	0.2
Arunachal Pradesh	N.A.	N.A.	0.0	0.1	0.2	–0.1
Assam	0.0	0.0	0.0	0.6	0.5	0.1
Bihar	0.2	0.1	0.1	0.4	0.3	0.0
Goa	0.3	0.2	0.1	0.2	–0.1	0.3
Gujarat	0.2	0.0	0.1	0.4	0.2	0.2
Haryana	0.2	0.0	0.2	0.2	0.0	0.2
Himachal Pradesh	0.1	–0.1	0.2	0.2	0.0	0.2
Jammu and Kashmir	N.A.	N.A.	N.A.	N.A.	N.A.	N.A.

(*Table 5A.5 Contd.*)

(Table 5A.5 Contd.)

States	Rural			Urban		
	Rate of Growth, 1983–2000	Rate of Growth, 1983–1993	Rate of Growth, 1993–2000	Rate of Growth, 1983–2000	Rate of Growth, 1983–1993	Rate of Growth, 1993–2000
Karnataka	0.2	0.1	0.1	0.3	0.1	0.2
Kerala	0.4	0.1	0.3	0.4	0.3	0.1
Madhya Pradesh	0.0	0.1	−0.1	0.2	0.1	0.1
Maharashtra	0.3	0.2	0.1	0.2	0.1	0.1
Manipur	0.1	0.0	0.1	0.5	0.2	0.3
Meghalaya	0.4	0.6	−0.2	0.2	0.2	0.0
Mizoram	0.2	0.2	−0.1	0.1	0.0	0.0
Nagaland	N.A.	N.A.	0.1	0.6	0.2	0.3
Orissa	0.3	0.2	0.1	0.2	0.2	0.0
Punjab	0.2	0.0	0.1	0.3	0.1	0.2
Rajasthan	0.0	0.0	0.1	0.3	0.2	0.1
Sikkim	5.8	6.0	0.0	0.3	0.3	0.0
Tamil Nadu	0.4	0.2	0.1	0.6	0.2	0.4
Tripura	3.9	4.2	−0.1	0.5	0.3	0.1
Uttar Pradesh	0.2	0.1	0.1	0.4	0.3	0.1
West Bengal	0.3	0.3	0.0	0.4	0.2	0.1
Andaman and Nicobar Islands	1.0	1.2	−0.1	0.2	0.5	−0.2
Chandigarh	0.1	−0.1	0.3	0.4	0.3	0.1
Dadra and Nagar Haveli	0.6	0.4	0.1	N.A.	N.A.	0.2
Daman and Diu	N.A.	N.A.	0.3	N.A.	N.A.	0.2
Delhi	N.A.	N.A.	N.A.	0.6	0.4	0.1
Lakshadweep	N.A.	N.A.	0.4	0.4	−0.3	1.1
Pondicherry	0.7	0.6	0.0	0.4	0.2	0.2
All India	**0.2**	**0.1**	**0.1**	**0.4**	**0.2**	**0.1**

Source: Computed from various rounds of NSSO consumer expenditure surveys.
Note: N.A. means not available.

Table 5A.6

Changes in Disparities—Rural Areas

	Rural Areas								
	SCs/Non-SCs/STs			*STs/Non-SCs/STs*			*SCs/STs*		
States	*1983*	*1993*	*2000*	*1983*	*1993*	*2000*	*1983*	*1993*	*2000*
Andhra Pradesh	0.8	0.8	0.8	0.8	0.8	0.8	1.0	0.9	1.0
Arunachal Pradesh	N.A.	0.9	3.2	N.A.	0.8	1.1	N.A.	1.2	2.8
Assam	1.0	1.0	1.0	1.0	1.0	1.0	1.0	1.0	0.9
Bihar	0.8	0.8	0.8	0.8	0.9	0.8	0.9	1.0	1.0
Goa	0.7	1.0	1.7	0.7	1.0	2.2	1.0	1.0	0.8
Gujarat	0.8	0.8	0.8	0.7	0.8	0.7	1.1	1.0	1.0
Haryana	0.7	0.7	0.7	0.7	0.6	0.7	1.0	1.1	1.1
Himachal Pradesh	0.8	0.8	0.8	1.0	0.7	0.9	0.8	1.1	0.9
Jammu and Kashmir	0.9	N.A.	N.A.	0.9	N.A.	N.A.	1.0	N.A.	N.A.
Karnataka	0.8	0.8	0.8	0.7	0.8	0.8	1.1	1.0	1.0
Kerala	0.7	0.7	0.8	1.0	0.9	0.9	0.8	0.8	0.9
Madhya Pradesh	0.8	0.8	0.8	0.7	0.7	0.7	1.1	1.2	1.2
Maharashtra	0.8	0.8	0.8	0.8	0.8	0.7	1.0	1.0	1.1
Manipur	1.1	1.0	1.0	0.9	1.0	1.0	1.2	1.1	1.1
Meghalaya	0.8	0.9	1.5	1.2	0.9	1.0	0.6	1.1	1.5
Mizoram	1.1	1.5	4.9	0.9	1.0	1.2	1.3	1.5	4.2
Nagaland	N.A.	0.0	N.A.	N.A.	0.9	1.0	N.A.	0.0	N.A.
Orissa	0.8	0.9	0.8	0.7	0.7	0.7	1.2	1.2	1.2
Punjab	0.7	0.7	0.7	0.8	0.8	0.6	0.9	0.9	1.1
Rajasthan	0.8	0.8	0.9	0.7	0.9	0.8	1.2	1.0	1.1
Sikkim	0.4	1.0	0.9	0.8	0.9	1.1	0.4	1.0	0.8
Tamil Nadu	0.7	0.8	0.8	0.8	0.8	0.7	0.8	0.9	1.1
Tripura	0.5	0.9	1.0	0.7	0.8	0.8	0.7	1.1	1.2
Uttar Pradesh	0.8	0.8	0.8	0.9	1.0	0.9	0.9	0.8	0.9
West Bengal	0.8	0.8	0.9	0.8	0.8	0.8	1.1	1.1	1.2

(Table 5A.6 Contd.)

(Table 5A.6 Contd.)

	Rural Areas								
	SCs/Non-SCs/STs			STs/Non-SCs/STs			SCs/STs		
States	*1983*	*1993*	*2000*	*1983*	*1993*	*2000*	*1983*	*1993*	*2000*
Andaman and Nicobar Islands	1.0	0.9	1.0	1.0	0.8	0.9	0.9	1.2	1.2
Chandigarh	0.7	0.7	0.7	0.0	0.7	1.8	N.A.	1.1	0.4
Dadra and Nagar Haveli	0.7	0.6	0.5	0.4	0.4	0.4	1.6	1.7	1.2
Daman and Diu	N.A.	0.0	N.A.	N.A.	0.6	0.6	N.A.	0.0	N.A.
Delhi	1.0	N.A.	N.A.	0.6	N.A.	N.A.	1.6	N.A.	N.A.
Lakshad-weep	N.A.	0.5	0.0	N.A.	0.5	0.4	N.A.	1.0	0.0
Pondicherry	0.7	0.6	0.7	0.0	0.9	1.2	N.A.	0.7	0.6
All India	**0.8**	**0.8**	**0.8**	**0.7**	**0.8**	**0.7**	**1.1**	**1.0**	**1.1**

Source: Computed from 38th, 49th and 55th rounds of NSSO consumer expenditure surveys for the years 1983, 1993 and 1999–2000, respectively.
Note: N.A. means not available.

Table 5A.7
Changes in Disparities—Urban Areas

	Urban Areas								
	SCs/Non-SCs/STs			STs/Non-SCs/STs			SCs/STs		
States	*1983*	*1993*	*2000*	*1983*	*1993*	*2000*	*1983*	*1993*	*2000*
Andhra Pradesh	0.8	0.8	0.8	0.8	0.8	0.8	1.1	1.0	0.9
Arunachal Pradesh	0.0	0.8	1.1	0.6	0.9	1.1	0.0	0.9	1.0
Assam	0.7	0.8	0.7	1.0	1.0	0.9	0.7	0.8	0.7
Bihar	0.8	0.7	0.7	1.0	0.8	0.8	0.8	0.8	0.8
Goa	0.8	1.3	0.9	0.6	1.1	0.6	1.2	1.2	1.5
Gujarat	0.8	0.7	0.7	0.6	0.8	0.7	1.3	0.9	1.0
Haryana	0.7	0.7	0.6	1.1	1.2	0.9	0.7	0.6	0.6
Himachal Pradesh	0.7	0.7	0.6	1.1	1.1	0.9	0.6	0.6	0.7

(Table 5A.7 Contd.)

(*Table 5A.7 Contd.*)

		Urban Areas							
	SCs/Non-SCs/STs			STs/Non-SCs/STs			SCs/STs		
States	1983	1993	2000	1983	1993	2000	1983	1993	2000
Jammu and Kashmir	0.9	N.A.	N.A.	1.2	N.A.	N.A.	0.8	N.A.	N.A.
Karnataka	0.8	0.6	0.6	0.8	0.7	0.7	0.9	0.9	0.9
Kerala	0.8	0.7	0.9	1.0	1.9	1.1	0.8	0.4	0.8
Madhya Pradesh	0.8	0.8	0.7	0.9	0.8	0.8	0.9	1.0	0.9
Maharashtra	0.6	0.6	0.7	0.6	0.6	0.7	1.0	1.0	1.0
Manipur	1.0	1.0	1.1	0.9	1.0	0.9	1.1	1.0	1.2
Meghalaya	0.6	0.8	0.8	0.7	0.9	0.9	0.8	0.9	0.9
Mizoram	0.5	1.2	0.9	0.6	0.9	0.9	0.8	1.4	1.0
Nagaland	0.8	1.3	0.9	0.9	1.1	1.1	0.9	1.2	0.8
Orissa	0.7	0.8	0.7	0.7	0.7	0.7	1.0	1.1	0.9
Punjab	0.7	0.8	0.7	0.7	0.9	0.6	1.0	0.9	1.1
Rajasthan	0.9	0.8	0.7	1.0	1.0	0.8	0.9	0.7	0.9
Sikkim	0.9	0.9	0.8	1.2	1.0	1.1	0.7	0.8	0.7
Tamil Nadu	0.7	0.7	0.6	0.6	1.1	1.0	1.1	0.6	0.6
Tripura	0.7	0.7	0.8	1.0	1.1	1.2	0.6	0.7	0.6
Uttar Pradesh	0.8	0.7	0.8	1.0	0.9	1.2	0.8	0.8	0.6
West Bengal	0.7	0.7	0.6	0.7	0.9	0.6	1.1	0.8	1.0
Andaman and Nicobar Islands	0.7	0.7	0.7	0.6	0.7	1.0	1.1	1.0	0.7
Chandigarh	0.5	0.6	0.6	1.4	0.0	1.1	0.4	N.A.	0.5
Dadra and Nagar Haveli	N.A.	0.8	1.4	N.A.	0.4	0.5	N.A.	2.1	2.6
Daman and Diu	N.A.	0.0	N.A.	N.A.	0.8	0.8	N.A.	0.0	N.A.
Delhi	0.5	0.4	0.5	0.7	0.6	0.6	0.8	0.8	0.8
Lakshadweep	0.0	0.0	N.A.	0.5	1.0	0.5	0.0	0.0	N.A.
Pondicherry	0.6	0.6	0.9	0.0	0.6	1.2	N.A.	1.0	0.7
All India	**0.7**	**0.7**	**0.7**	**0.8**	**0.8**	**0.8**	**1.0**	**0.9**	**0.9**

Source: Computed from 38th, 49th and 55th rounds of NSSO consumer expenditure surveys for the years 1983, 1993 and 1999–2000, respectively.
Note: N.A. means not available.

Chapter 6

LEVELS AND DISPARITIES IN POVERTY

Arjan de Haan and Amaresh Dubey

This chapter assesses the extent of disparities in the incidence of poverty that are prevalent among different social groups in India and brings out the inter-state and regional variations in the levels of disparity among various social groups in India. The analysis aligns itself to determine change in the incidence of poverty at both all-India and state levels over a given period under consideration. The ensuing sections delineate the methodological issues involved in using the household survey data for analysing inter-social group disparities, present the results of the analysis, and summarise the discussions for policy implications.

DATA AND METHODOLOGICAL ISSUES

The quantitative assessment of the disparities required a set of comparable data across various social and religious groups. Therefore, the household level data collected by National Sample Survey (NSS) was used to investigate the levels of disparities in consumption and to demarcate the incidence of poverty among social and religious groups. The sampling design of NSS is such that the households are selected on the basis of probability proportion to size (PPS) of the population in each state. Thus, the population size of the states has an obvious bearing on the number of households selected for survey by the NSS. For example, in Uttar Pradesh, the number of households selected for the survey was over 10,000, whereas in Lakshadweep and other smaller states, it was limited to just 250. Clearly, the smaller sample size restricts the analytical abilities of the analysis by precluding reliable estimates of any characteristics. Also, the distribution of Scheduled Tribe (ST) and Scheduled Caste (SC) population was not uniform over the states, as several Indian states have predominantly tribal populations, while many others have a mix of non-SC/ST and SC population.

The analysis at the state level, therefore, has to take into account these factors and has to align itself methodologically before it can embark on a delineation of the characteristics of consumption and poverty. Hence, the states and Union Territories were categorised into two groups, and the analysis was carried out thereupon. For the first group of states, the analysis was carried out separately for all the social groups. The second group, wherein SCs and STs are grouped together, includes 21 states and Union Territories—needless to say, the figures would reflect the conditions of the dominant group, irrespective of whether it is constituted by STs or SCs, in a respective state or Union Territory.

INCIDENCE OF POVERTY AMONG SOCIAL GROUPS

In this section, the incidence of poverty across social groups at the national and sub-national levels is discussed by using 1999–2000 data of the 55th round of NSS. Poverty is measured in terms of simple head count ratio (HCR) which is defined as the proportion of population that is poor out of the total population.

All-India Level

The incidence of poverty across social groups during 1999–2000 shows that rural poverty ratios were higher than those for urban poverty except for SCs (Table 6.1). It is also apparent from this table that STs in rural areas were the most vulnerable to poverty. In 1999–2000, 44 per cent STs lived below poverty line. For SCs, the incidence of poverty was 35 per cent, while for non-SCs/STs it was about 21 per cent. In urban areas, SCs had the highest HCR of 39 per cent followed by STs at about 37 per cent. Non-SCs/STs recorded the least poverty ratio of about 21 per cent. Thus, there are clear variations in the incidence of poverty across social groups.

The organisation of Indian society into different castes, tribes and religious denominations necessitates a two-way classification of the incidence of poverty across religious and social groups in rural and urban sectors. Such a classification establishes that the deprived Hindu social groups face higher degree of

Table 6.1
Incidences of Poverty (HCR) across Social Groups, 1999–2000

Sector/Social Groups	STs	SCs	Non-SCs/STs	All
Rural	44.33	35.43	21.14	26.50
Urban	37.44	39.09	20.78	23.98
Total	**43.65**	**36.13**	**21.04**	**25.87**

Source: NSSO, 55th round, Consumer Expenditure Survey, 1999–2000.

vulnerability in terms of incidence of poverty by HCR (see Annexure IV Table 6A.1). Also, it distinctly emerges from Annexure IV Table 6A.1 that the incidence of poverty among SCs and STs was higher than that for non-SCs/STs irrespective of their religion. At the same time, it is evident that these social groups are relatively better off in other religious denominations as compared to those among the Hindus and Muslims.

State Level

Rural Areas: In 1999–2000, for majority of the states the incidence of poverty for SCs in rural areas was the highest in Jharkhand (62.16 per cent) followed by Bihar (58.66 per cent), Orissa (52.30 per cent) and Chhattisgarh (46.19 per cent). Andhra Pradesh (16.47 per cent) had the lowest HCR in this group. In nine out of the 14 states, STs appeared to be the most vulnerable to poverty. Orissa recorded the highest HCR for STs at about 73.10 per cent. The other states wherein the incidence of poverty was high for STs were Jharkhand (60.62 per cent), Madhya Pradesh (57.19 per cent) and Chhattisgarh (57.05 per cent).

The incidence of poverty was high for non-SCs/STs in Jharkhand (41.15 per cent), Assam (39.66 per cent), Chhattisgarh (38.83 per cent) and Bihar (37.60 per cent), respectively. It can be deduced from the figures that the incidence of poverty among non-SCs/STs was lower than that for both SCs and STs (see Annexure IV Table 6A.2).

In 1999–2000, there were large inter-state variations in the level of rural poverty in smaller states (see Annexure IV Table 6A.3). The HCRs for SC and ST rural population in smaller states ranged from almost nil in Goa, Nagaland and several Union Territories to above 20 per cent in Arunachal Pradesh, Tamil Nadu and Uttarakhand. Clearly, in these states, the incidence of poverty was much lower than that in the major states. In general, in most of the states and Union Territories, the incidence of poverty was higher for STs and SCs as compared to non-SCs/STs, except in Meghalaya, Nagaland, Sikkim and Chandigarh. The population structures of these states are self-explanatory to arrive at the above inference.

Urban Areas: In 1999–2000, large inter-state variations in levels of poverty are discernible in urban areas of major states. The incidence of poverty by HCR for SCs was the highest in Orissa (72.03 per cent) followed by Bihar (60.73 per cent), Madhya Pradesh (56.41 per cent) and Chhattisgarh (54.32 per cent). On the other hand, in the north-eastern state of Tripura, less than 10 per cent urban SC population was below poverty line.

Similarly, the incidence of poverty by HCR for the major states was the highest for STs in Orissa (59.38 per cent), Madhya Pradesh (58.73 per cent), Karnataka (51.68 per cent) and Andhra Pradesh (47.53 per cent). In the north-eastern states of Assam and Tripura, less than 3 per cent population lived below poverty line.

Again, for non-SCs/STs the incidence of poverty in the major states in 1999–2000 was the highest in Chhattisgarh, Orissa, Madhya Pradesh and Bihar (see Annexure IV Table 6A.4).

In 1999–2000, the incidence of poverty in the urban areas for smaller states too demonstrates a picture similar to that observed in the major states. Although the poverty ratios vary greatly, in general the incidence of poverty was higher among SCs and STs than non-SCs/STs (see Annexure IV Table 6A.5).

DISPARITIES IN INCIDENCE OF POVERTY AMONG SOCIAL GROUPS

The above discussion on the levels of rural and urban poverty across various social groups for major and smaller states clearly indicates the existence of disparities among these social groups. While we take up the issue of disparity further, in this section, an attempt has been made to quantify the extent of disparities at both all-India and state levels.

All-India Level

The difference in HCR between SCs and STs on one hand and non-SCs/STs on the other hand indicates that the highest amount of disparity exists between STs and non-SCs/STs in rural areas (see Table 6.2). Further, the analysis also reiterates the fact that in rural areas, STs constituted the most deprived group as compared to SCs and non-SCs/STs, while in urban areas SCs were the most vulnerable.

The dimensions of disparities among social groups are apparent from the distribution of population across consumption expenditure. The available literature in this context suggests that historically deprived groups have lower living standards which would be quantitatively reflected in their per capita total (household consumer) expenditure (PCTE). In other words, this implies that different social groups register different distribution of expenditure.

Table 6.2
Disparities in Incidence of Poverty across Social Groups in 1999–2000 (Percentage Points)

Sectors	STs and Non-SCs/STs	SCs and Non-SCs/STs
Rural	23.19	14.28
Urban	16.65	18.31
Total	**22.61**	**15.09**

Source: NSSO, 55th round, Consumer Expenditure Survey, 1999–2000.

A plotting of the monthly PCTE classes against the proportion of population in each class for each of the three social groups brings out the fact that there are significant differences in the levels of expenditure distribution for the different social groups (see Figures 6.1 and 6.2). While SCs appear to be marginally better off than STs, the consumption distribution for both the groups seems to be lesser than that for non-SCs/STs. The analysis also establishes the fact that a relatively

Figure 6.1
Distribution of Social Groups by Expenditure Classes in 1999–2000 in Rural Areas

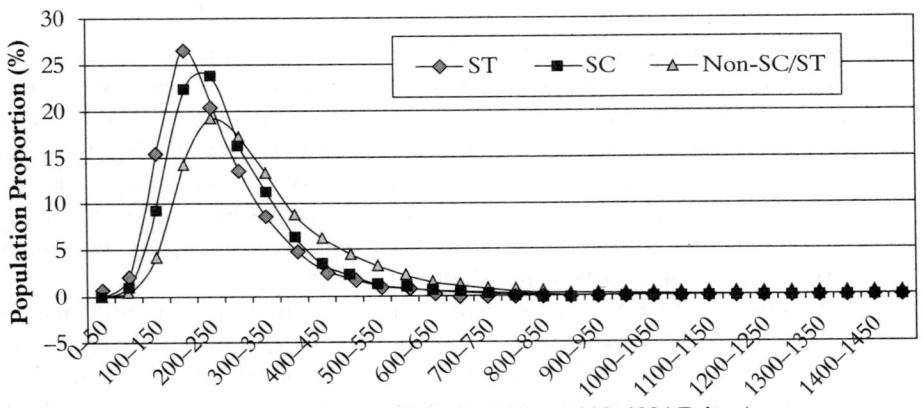

Source: NSSO, 55th round, Consumer Expenditure Survey, 1999–2000.

Figure 6.2
Distribution of Social Groups by Expenditure Classes in 1999–2000 in Urban Areas

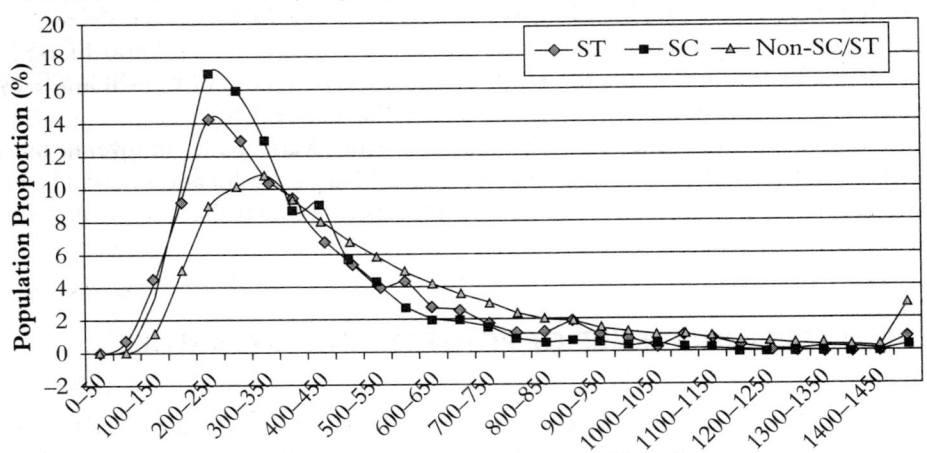

Source: NSSO, 55th round, Consumer Expenditure Survey, 1999–2000.

higher proportion of SCs and STs were concentrated at the lower end of distributional spectrum. Clearly, there seems to be a proportional relationship between consumption expenditure and the standard of living of a particular social group.

State Level

A similar analysis at the state level brings out the regional dimensions of the extent of disparities.

Rural Areas: An analysis of disparities in rural areas across major states shows that there were substantial and glaring inter-group disparities, especially between STs and non-SCs/STs in a number of major states (see Annexure IV Table 6A.6). In rural areas of Orissa, the HCR of STs exceeded that of non-SCs/STs by about 40 percentage points. The difference between HCR of the two groups was also sizable, at about 35 percentage points, in Madhya Pradesh. On the other hand, the disparities between SCs and non-SCs/STs in rural areas across major states were high in Bihar, Jharkhand, Orissa and Madhya Pradesh.

The analysis in rural areas across smaller states indicated a much lower magnitude of disparities as compared to major states. The states and Union Territories in which HCRs of SCs and STs exceeded those of non-SCs/STs by more than 10 percentage points were Haryana, Jammu and Kashmir, Manipur, Tamil Nadu, Dadra and Nagar Haveli, and Pondicherry. The pattern was reversed in Meghalaya, Mizoram, Nagaland, Sikkim and Chandigarh where non-SCs/STs had higher poverty ratios than SCs and STs (see Annexure IV Table 6A.7).

Urban Areas: In 1999–2000, in urban areas of major states, STs seemed to be better off than SCs in seven out of 14 states. Consequently, the highest level of disparity to the tune of 38 percentage points was observed between SCs and non-SCs/STs in Orissa. Except in Tripura, the HCR of SCs exceeded those of non-SCs/STs by more than 15 percentage points (see Annexure IV Table 6A.6).

In the urban areas of smaller states, the disparities were greater in several states and Union Territories like Goa, Haryana, Tamil Nadu, Dadra and Nagar Haveli and Daman and Diu. In few states, the difference between the two groups was marginal (see Annexure IV Table 6A.7).

CHANGES IN INCIDENCE OF POVERTY AND DISPARITIES

Hitherto the discussion was concentrated on the contemporaneous situation of the incidence of poverty and levels of disparities prevalent among various social groups. It would, therefore, be interesting to delve into the changes in the incidence of poverty and disparities for social groups over the four time point surveys, that is, the years 1983, 1987–1988, 1993–1994 and 1999–2000.

Changes in Incidence of Poverty

Rural Areas: The incidence of poverty in rural areas has declined over the years for all social groups. In 1983, close to 64 per cent STs lived below poverty line in rural areas. However, the situation was marginally better for the period 1999–2000. For SCs, the incidence of poverty was 58.96 per cent in 1983 and 35.43 per cent in 1999–2000. The incidence of poverty for non-SCs/STs, on the other hand, was about 41 per cent in 1983 and 21.14 per cent in 1999–2000. Between 1983 and 1999–2000, the poverty head count index declined by about 20 percentage points for STs; by over 25 percentage points for SCs; and by about 20 percentage points for non-SCs/STs (see Figure 6.3). The consistent decline in poverty during the period 1983 to 1999–2000 among the three social groups occurred irrespective of their religion. Within ST group the magnitude of decline by religious denomination was the highest for ST Muslims, while among SCs, the Christians showed maximum improvement in terms of the incidence of poverty (see Annexure IV Table 6A.8).

The highest decline in poverty occurred during 1993–1994 to 1999–2000 (see Table 6.3). However, at all-India level, despite a significant decline in incidence

Figure 6.3
Incidence of Poverty across Social Groups in Rural India

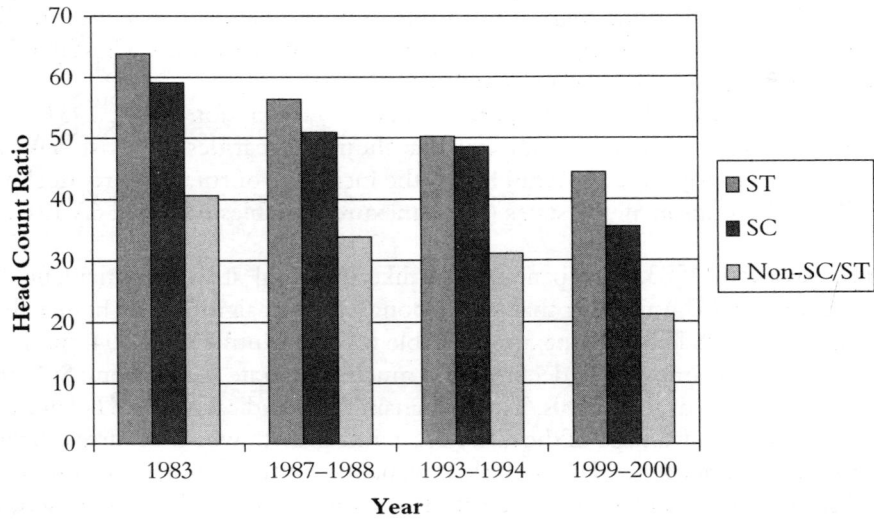

Source: NSSO, 55th round, Consumer Expenditure Survey, 1999–2000.

Table 6.3

Average Annual Percentage Change in Head Count Ratio by Social Groups in Rural Areas

Social Groups/Years	STs	SCs	Non-SCs/STs	All
1983 to 1999–2000	–1.91	–2.49	–3.01	–2.69
1983 to 1987–1988	–2.97	--3.40	–4.36	–3.85
1987–1988 to 1993–1994	–1.80	–0.85	–1.21	–1.05
1993–1994 to 1999–2000	–1.96	–4.45	–5.37	–4.69

Source: Computed from various rounds of NSSO consumer expenditure surveys.

of poverty, the relative position of the social groups did not improve. The analysis herein aligns only with the official poverty line. The HCR calculated by using other poverty lines did not show different results as far as the ranking of the social groups was concerned—it instead indicated almost similar numerical gaps in the incidence of poverty (Haan and Dubey, 2003; Dubey, 2003). Despite the controversy related to change in the survey design and recall period, among other indicators, the fact that the incidence of poverty declined during the 1990s was robust and independent of the poverty line used.

Across the states, the changes in incidence of poverty and disparities in rural areas for social groups have been ascertained for the years 1983, 1987–1988 and 1993–1994. In general, the HCRs for rural areas among all social groups were higher during the initial period under consideration. In 1983, the HCR for SCs ranged from 83 per cent in Bihar to about 37 per cent in Andhra Pradesh. As regards the STs, Andhra Pradesh had the lowest incidence of poverty at 35.7 per cent while Orissa had the highest incidence of poverty at over 87 per cent. The incidence of poverty for non-SCs/STs, on the other hand, was the highest in Bihar (60.42 per cent) and the lowest in Gujarat (19.96 per cent).

An analysis of the data for the periods under consideration (1983, 1987–1988 and 1993–1994) sufficiently establishes that though disparities did exist between various social groups, yet at overall levels, the incidence of rural poverty declined for all social groups in all the states (see Annexure IV Tables 6A.9 and 6A.10).

Urban Areas: In 1983, in urban areas, unlike the rural areas, the incidence of poverty among STs was lower than that among SCs, but significantly higher than among non-SCs/STs (see Annexure IV Table 6A.12). Until 1993–1994, the incidence of poverty among STs declined at a much faster rate than among SCs and non-SCs/STs, but during 1990s, it was stagnant. This indicates that STs have not been able to take advantage of the faster economic growth which occurred during the post-liberalisation era. The possible explanation for this could be that the share of STs in urban population was stagnant. It is quite likely that the recent increase in urban population has been more in favour of non-SCs/STs than SCs and STs.

Figure 6.4
Incidence of Poverty across Social Groups in Urban India

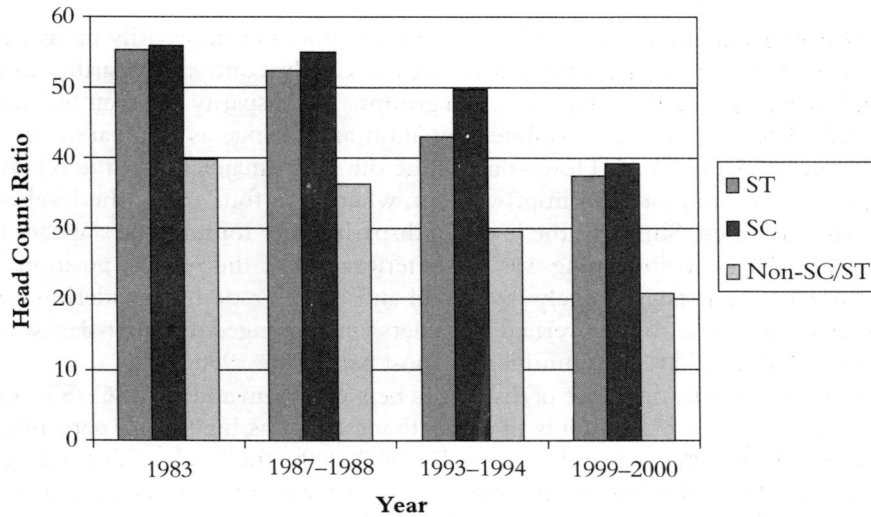

Source: Computed from various rounds of NSSO consumer expenditure surveys.

Since economic growth during the post-reform period has shown an urban bias, the marginalised social groups appear to have been bypassed by the boom in the economy or rather they could not take advantage of the same (see Figure 6.4).

An examination of the changes in incidence of urban poverty across social groups cross-classified by religious denominations indicated that the decline during the period 1983 to 1999–2000 was the sharpest among the Sikhs followed by Christians (Table 6.4). Similarly, a decline in the incidence of poverty was also seen among the Hindu and Muslim SCs and STs, though in a lesser magnitude (see Annexure IV Table 6A.11).

Table 6.4
Average Annual Percentage Change in Head Count Ratio by Social Groups in Urban Areas

Social Groups	STs	SCs	Non-SCs/STs	All
1983 to 1999–2000	–2.02	–1.87	–2.99	–2.71
1983 to 1987–1988	–1.37	–0.39	–2.25	–1.86
1987–1988 to 1993–1994	–2.99	–1.58	–3.08	–2.72
1993–1994 to 1999–2000	–2.12	–3.56	–4.95	–4.47

Source: Computed from various rounds of NSSO consumer expenditure surveys.

Changes in Disparities

Rural Areas: The decline in incidence of poverty does not necessarily imply that disparities between social groups ceased to exist. On the contrary, disparities were found to exist in HCR among the social groups. The disparity between SCs and non-SCs/STs in rural areas exhibited variation and change as is apparent from Annexure IV Table 6A.15. However, in nine out of 14 major states, the relative position of SCs indicated an improvement, whereas in four states, the levels of disparity increased. Similarly, the levels of disparity were found to be stagnant in one state. What was intriguing was the deterioration of the relative position of SCs in two major states, namely Jharkhand and Uttar Pradesh, considering that these two states have been governed by leaders who belonged to Other Backward Classes (OBC) and SC communities for most part of the 1990s.

In the case of STs, the range of disparities between them and non-SCs/STs was as low as 5.69 percentage points in Uttar Pradesh but as high as 37 percentage points in Madhya Pradesh and Gujarat. By 1999–2000, the levels of disparity for STs increased in Uttar Pradesh by about 9 percentage points. On the other hand, the levels of disparity in Gujarat declined by about 20 percentage points. In all the 14 major states, the relative position of STs vis-à-vis non-SCs/STs improved only in six states, while the remaining eight states witnessed a relative deterioration (see Annexure IV Table 6A.17).

For the smaller states, the analysis of temporal variation in disparities is limited to 1990s only due to the fact that the survey was not carried out in a number of states in the 1980s. However, the poverty ratios do not preclude the time period mentioned above. The analysis also brings out the striking fact that if there were wide variations among the major states, the variations were even wider and more perceptible in the smaller states (see Annexure IV Table 6A.18).

In 1993–1994, HCR for SCs/STs in rural areas of smaller states and Union Territories ranged from less than 3 per cent in Goa, Nagaland, Andaman and Nicobar Islands, and Lakshadweep to 45 per cent in Tamil Nadu and 53 per cent in Dadra and Nagar Haveli. An analysis of the degree of disparity between SCs, STs and non-SCs/STs brought to the fore the fact that disparity had declined for most of the states from 1993–1994 to 1999–2000, which implicitly translated into the fact that the conditions for SCs and STs had generally improved. In Meghalaya, Sikkim and Nagaland and the Union Territory of Chandigarh, the relative position of SCs and STs had particularly improved in 1999–2000. In Pondicherry, however, the condition of SCs and STs had deteriorated. Other states wherein the disparity widened between the social groups were Jammu and Kashmir and Pondicherry.

Urban Areas: The inferences arrived at for the rural areas as discussed above are also apparent for the urban areas—the disparity in the urban areas indicates a large variation in poverty ratios across the states. Such an inference also holds true for the social groups. While one delves into the statistics for the incidence of poverty in urban areas of the major states, one should remember that the share of both SCs and STs in urban population is relatively lower than non-SCs/STs (see Annexure IV Table 6A.13). Therefore, one should proceed with caution while she/he undertakes an analysis for the same, considering the fact that the sample methodology of the NSS is based on PPS—the number of sampled households may not be sufficient to provide robust estimates. Therefore, these are to be considered as indicative only.

The disparities between SCs and non-SCs/STs indicate a large-scale variation during two time points under consideration, that is, 1983 and 1999–2000. The relative situation of SCs in 12 major states, indeed, worsened while that in Assam and Tripura improved (see Annexure IV Table 6A.16).

The disparities between STs and non-SCs/STs too present a picture that is similar to that for SCs. For instance, in Gujarat, the disparity in the incidence of poverty for the year 1983 stood at 44 percentage points. The relative condition of STs was better than non-SCs/STs in Assam, Bihar, Uttar Pradesh and Tripura. Correspondingly, the extent of disparities between STs and non-SCs/STs showed an increasing trend by 1999–2000.

An analysis of the average annual change in HCR between 1983 and 1999–2000 for SCs, STs and non-SCs/STs indicates that non-SCs/STs have experienced a faster average rate of decline than SCs and STs during the given period. However, during the two time points under consideration, the statistics suggest that the overall situation of all the social groups has improved.

Between the years 1993–1994 and 1999–2000, the incidence of poverty in urban areas declined in almost all the smaller states and for all the social groups. However, the incidence of poverty increased for SCs/STs in Goa, Haryana, Sikkim, and Jammu and Kashmir. The non-SCs/STs, on the other hand, experienced an increase in the incidence of poverty in Sikkim.

In 1993–1994, the states and Union Territories of Tamil Nadu, Dadra and Nagar Haveli, Daman and Diu and Pondicherry exhibited a very high incidence of poverty for SCs and STs, with HCR in these states being above 50 per cent. On the other hand, six states out of 21 states showed HCR levels of less than 10 per cent for SCs and STs (see Annexure IV Table 6A.14). The relative position of the social groups can also be observed in Annexure IV Table 6A.14. The states with high incidence of poverty among SCs/STs also showed a high degree of disparity between them and non-SCs/STs. The figures also indicate that disparity had increased in Goa, Haryana, Jammu and Kashmir, Kerala, Tamil Nadu and Chandigarh.

The above analysis clearly suggests that the decline in incidence of poverty was not uniform across all states and for all social groups. In some cases, the extent of decline was substantial, while for the others it was marginal.

SUMMARY

The above analysis of poverty across different social groups in India over the periods 1983 to 1999–2000 predominantly asserts that the deprived social groups were principally rural-based. The analysis further re-confirms the existence of disparities among the three social groups. On an average, STs seem to have the highest HCR. In both rural and urban areas, SCs seem to be more or less inter-woven between non-SCs/STs and STs. This ranking is independent of time. In other words, during the 1980s and 1990s, STs were the most disadvantaged social groups in both rural and the urban areas.

During the 1980s and the 1990s, there has been decline in vulnerability to poverty among all social groups in India. However, disparities across social groups were substantial and continued to be significant. Moreover, the recent surge in economic growth seemed to have bypassed the deprived social groups. The analysis also suggests that the relative position of the socially deprived groups has not changed at all.

ANNEXURE IV

Table 6A.1
Incidence of Poverty by HCR among Social Groups and Religions, 1999–2000

Social Groups → *Religions* ↓	*STs*	*SCs*	*Non-SCs/STs*	*All*
		Rural Areas		
Hindu	46.24	36.40	20.06	26.63
Muslim	34.54	33.07	30.20	30.31
Christian	28.20	15.82	11.45	18.17
Sikh	17.75	13.21	1.69	5.65
Others	34.27	37.54	18.57	31.52
Total	**44.33**	**35.43**	**21.14**	**26.50**
		Urban Areas		
Hindu	43.32	38.93	17.53	22.00
Muslim	29.82	45.06	36.72	36.76
Christian	12.00	36.35	9.71	12.34
Sikh	22.92	10.23	3.78	4.97
Others	32.82	51.82	4.31	22.62
Total	**37.44**	**39.09**	**20.78**	**23.98**

Source: NSSO, 55th round, Consumer Expenditure Survey, 1999–2000.

Table 6A.2
Incidence of Poverty by HCR in Rural Areas for Major States, 1999–2000

States	STs	SCs	Non-SC/ST	All
Andhra Pradesh	23.07	16.47	7.39	10.54
Assam	39.16	44.97	39.66	40.17
Bihar	52.33	58.66	37.60	42.46
Jharkhand	60.62	62.16	41.15	50.15
Gujarat	27.50	15.57	7.65	12.36
Karnataka	24.86	25.67	13.59	16.85
Madhya Pradesh	57.19	39.22	22.22	33.74
Chhattisgarh	57.05	46.19	38.83	45.94
Maharashtra	44.20	31.64	16.72	23.24
Orissa	73.10	52.30	33.29	48.05
Rajasthan	24.83	19.52	8.41	13.47
Tripura	29.11	14.21	15.95	16.67
Uttar Pradesh	36.58	43.60	27.50	31.66
West Bengal	50.05	34.91	28.42	31.65

Source: NSSO, 55th round, Consumer Expenditure Survey, 1999–2000.

Table 6A.3
Incidence of Poverty by HCR in Rural Areas for Smaller States, 1999–2000

States	STs/SCs	Non-SCs/STs	All
Arunachal Pradesh	23.56	19.13	22.55
Goa	0.00	0.00	0.00
Haryana	16.71	4.38	7.41
Himachal Pradesh	12.09	6.27	7.87
Jammu and Kashmir	13.19	3.00	3.94
Kerala	17.00	8.38	9.37
Manipur	19.24	8.95	14.11
Meghalaya	5.83	7.82	5.96
Mizoram	3.00	0.00	2.85
Nagaland	0.00	4.29	0.21
Punjab	12.01	2.11	6.00
Sikkim	17.96	23.33	21.61

(Table 6A.3 Contd.)

(Table 6A.3 Contd.)

States	STs/SCs	Non-SCs/STs	All
Tamil Nadu	32.22	14.40	20.08
Uttarakhand	28.69	12.69	15.42
Andaman and Nicobar Islands	1.31	0.00	0.26
Chandigarh	0.57	9.93	7.74
Dadra and Nagar Haveli	18.81	3.77	16.58
Daman and Diu	0.00	0.00	0.00
Delhi	5.56	0.00	0.73
Lakshadweep	0.00	0.00	0.00
Pondicherry	19.13	7.96	11.47

Source: NSSO, 55th round, Consumer Expenditure Survey, 1999–2000.

Table 6A.4
Incidence of Poverty by HCR in Urban Areas for Major States, 1999–2000

States	STs	SCs	Non-SCs/STs	All
Andhra Pradesh	47.53	42.10	24.15	27.17
Assam	2.92	21.14	5.85	7.23
Bihar	33.53	60.73	32.75	35.65
Jharkhand	46.78	39.52	24.10	29.28
Gujarat	38.44	26.83	11.44	14.78
Karnataka	51.68	46.67	20.37	24.62
Madhya Pradesh	58.73	56.41	33.74	38.71
Chhattisgarh	35.55	54.32	35.43	37.53
Maharashtra	42.75	40.71	23.90	26.71
Orissa	59.38	72.03	34.18	43.59
Rajasthan	21.80	43.25	13.68	19.43
Tripura	0.00	9.03	0.35	2.16
Uttar Pradesh	10.42	47.15	28.94	31.62
West Bengal	33.69	28.27	11.23	14.71

Source: NSSO, 55th round, Consumer Expenditure Survey, 1999–2000.

Table 6A.5
Incidence of Poverty by HCR in Urban Areas for Smaller States, 1999–2000

States	STs/SCs	Non-SCs/STs	All
Arunachal Pradesh	5.65	4.62	5.06
Goa	29.15	5.70	6.20
Haryana	25.62	4.71	9.34
Himachal Pradesh	5.42	4.38	4.58
Jammu and Kashmir	9.15	1.25	1.93
Kerala	25.85	19.42	19.87
Manipur	0.00	0.55	0.53
Meghalaya	0.00	0.00	0.00
Mizoram	0.00	0.00	0.00
Nagaland	0.00	0.00	0.00
Punjab	11.53	2.99	5.48
Sikkim	8.02	3.49	4.90
Tamil Nadu	43.24	19.29	22.54
Uttarakhand	9.19	16.12	14.07
Andaman and Nicobar Islands	0.00	0.57	0.54
Chhattisgarh	14.73	0.85	3.06
Dadra Nagar Haveli	38.55	0.00	12.28
Daman and Diu	38.74	7.44	10.89
Delhi	21.34	6.70	9.22
Lakshadweep	3.31	2.96	3.30
Pondicherry	35.86	21.12	22.35

Source: NSSO, 55th round, Consumer Expenditure Survey, 1999–2000.

Table 6A.6
Disparities in Incidence of Poverty for Major States, 1999–2000 (in Percentage Points)

States	Rural Areas		Urban Areas	
	STs versus Non-SCs/STs	SCs versus Non-SCs/STs	STs versus Non-SCs/STs	SCs versus Non-SCs/STs
Andhra Pradesh	15.68	9.08	23.38	17.95
Assam	–0.50	5.32	–2.92	15.30
Bihar	14.73	21.06	0.77	27.97

(Table 6A.6 Contd.)

(Table 6A.6 Contd.)

	Rural Areas		Urban Areas	
States	STs versus Non-SCs/STs	SCs versus Non-SCs/STs	STs versus Non-SCs/STs	SCs versus Non-SCs/STs
Jharkhand	19.47	21.01	22.68	15.42
Gujarat	19.85	7.92	27.00	15.39
Karnataka	11.27	12.08	31.32	26.30
Madhya Pradesh	34.98	17.00	24.99	22.67
Chhattisgarh	18.22	7.36	0.11	18.88
Maharashtra	27.48	14.92	18.85	16.81
Orissa	39.81	19.00	25.20	37.85
Rajasthan	16.42	11.11	8.12	29.57
Tripura	13.16	−1.73	−0.35	8.68
Uttar Pradesh	9.08	16.10	−18.52	18.21
West Bengal	21.63	6.49	22.46	17.04

Source: NSSO, 55th round, Consumer Expenditure Survey, 1999–2000.

Table 6A.7
Disparities in Incidence of Poverty between SCs/STs and Non-SCs/STs in Smaller States, 1999–2000 (in Percentage Points)

States	Rural Areas	Urban Areas
Arunachal Pradesh	4.43	1.03
Goa	0.00	23.45
Haryana	12.34	20.90
Himachal Pradesh	5.82	1.04
Jammu and Kashmir	10.20	7.90
Kerala	8.62	6.43
Manipur	10.29	−0.55
Meghalaya	−1.99	0.00
Mizoram	3.00	0.00
Nagaland	−4.29	0.00
Punjab	9.90	8.54
Sikkim	−5.37	4.53
Tamil Nadu	17.82	23.95

(Table 6A.7 Contd.)

(Table 6A.7 Contd.)

States	Rural Areas	Urban Areas
Uttarakhand	15.99	−6.93
Andaman and Nicobar Islands	1.31	−0.57
Chandigarh	−9.35	13.88
Dadra and Nagar Haveli	15.04	38.55
Daman and Diu	0.00	31.30
Delhi	5.56	14.64
Lakshadweep	0.00	0.36
Pondicherry	11.17	14.75

Source: NSSO, 55th round, Consumer Expenditure Survey, 1999–2000.

Table 6A.8
Poverty Head Count Index by Social Groups and Religion in Rural Sector

Social Groups→ Religions ↓	STs	SCs	Non-SCs/STs	All
		1983		
Hindu	65.83	59.94	40.17	46.99
Muslim	57.65	47.67	51.13	51.19
Christian	43.93	54.42	33.77	37.72
Sikh	22.47	24.91	8.10	11.94
Others	44.91	58.95	25.44	47.93
		1987–1988		
Hindu	57.89	51.88	32.84	39.62
Muslim	51.84	54.56	43.91	44.19
Christian	42.51	37.80	26.27	32.35
Sikh	5.60	16.49	3.77	7.14
Others	46.01	57.11	16.93	45.38
		1993–1994		
Hindu	51.72	48.81	29.55	36.51
Muslim	55.05	31.70	45.04	44.99
Christian	35.96	42.76	27.11	31.40
Sikh	0.00	28.38	4.40	11.47
Others	39.54	55.32	17.99	45.52

(Table 6A.8 Contd.)

(Table 6A.8 Contd.)

Social Groups→ Religions ↓	STs	SCs	Non–SCs/STs	All
		1999–2000		
Hindu	46.24	36.40	20.06	26.63
Muslim	34.54	33.07	30.20	30.31
Christian	28.20	15.82	11.45	18.17
Sikh	17.75	13.21	1.69	5.65
Others	34.94	37.88	17.58	31.71
	Average Annual Percentage Change 1983 to 1999–2000			
Hindu	–1.86	–2.45	–3.13	–2.71
Muslim	–2.51	–1.91	–2.56	–2.55
Christian	–2.24	–4.43	–4.13	–3.24
Sikh	–1.31	–2.94	–4.94	–3.29
Others	–1.39	–2.23	–1.93	–2.11

Source: Computed from various rounds of NSSO consumer expenditure surveys.

Table 6A.9

Social Group-wise Incidence of Poverty (HCR) for Major States in Rural Areas

States	1983				1987–1988				1993–1994			
	STs	SCs	Non-SCs/STs	All	STs	SCs	Non-SCs/STs	All	STs	SCs	Non-SCs/STs	All
Andhra Pradesh	35.73	36.63	23.54	26.78	39.56	28.50	17.67	21.07	26.90	25.95	11.78	15.93
Assam	48.60	43.51	42.02	43.30	46.17	34.84	39.01	39.75	41.97	45.73	45.82	45.26
Bihar	72.98	83.00	60.42	64.72	69.17	71.89	49.96	54.15	59.37	69.94	52.17	56.51
Jharkhand	74.73	74.83	57.48	65.60	60.51	62.45	43.53	52.70	70.87	72.84	54.35	62.25
Gujarat	56.69	37.07	19.96	29.44	43.52	35.91	22.85	28.48	30.83	32.85	17.26	22.23
Karnataka	56.93	54.30	31.03	36.23	39.63	57.27	29.82	34.77	38.08	45.73	24.49	30.08
Madhya Pradesh	72.19	62.21	35.16	49.25	65.50	48.28	27.67	40.13	59.62	47.93	27.37	39.23
Chhattisgarh	58.98	50.35	41.69	50.66	56.94	46.05	35.81	46.72	53.50	38.56	38.44	44.36
Maharashtra	62.55	60.57	39.53	45.95	54.22	57.53	35.28	40.91	51.72	51.49	32.46	38.11
Orissa	87.08	75.99	58.52	68.43	83.82	65.75	47.31	58.62	71.31	49.79	40.16	49.78
Rajasthan	63.46	44.86	31.74	38.63	57.10	35.84	26.52	33.30	45.51	38.19	18.14	26.36
Tripura	47.06	60.20	31.74	39.28	37.04	35.30	16.49	23.73	39.30	26.80	18.92	23.64
Uttar Pradesh	50.71	58.48	45.02	48.11	54.25	58.10	38.95	43.87	37.94	60.36	37.62	43.10
West Bengal	76.71	73.21	58.24	63.76	63.21	57.19	42.94	48.80	62.09	46.30	35.55	41.18

Source: Computed from various rounds of NSSO consumer expenditure surveys.

Table 6A.10

Social Group-wise Incidence of Poverty (HCR) for Smaller States in Rural Areas

States	1983			1987–1988			1993–1994		
	STs/SCs	Non-SCs/STs	All	STs/SCs	Non-SCs/STs	All	STs/SCs	Non-SCs/STs	All
Arunachal Pradesh	N.A.	N.A.	N.A.	28.83	17.29	26.43	43.04	30.77	41.29
Goa	3.00	9.76	9.53	25.28	14.94	15.53	0.00	5.43	5.00
Haryana	36.56	17.62	22.42	25.46	8.79	13.15	46.02	20.68	27.99
Himachal Pradesh	26.25	14.33	17.79	13.32	9.91	10.98	41.22	26.14	30.37
Jammu and Kashmir	43.59	25.50	27.36	37.97	24.01	25.85	22.23	16.22	18.24
Kerala	59.90	36.56	39.76	41.23	30.09	31.64	37.60	23.80	25.39
Manipur	37.48	16.60	25.61	25.65	8.99	15.81	27.10	13.50	18.94
Meghalaya	37.18	54.26	38.52	36.58	28.56	36.18	24.43	22.84	24.35
Mizoram	28.26	4.38	27.67	3.75	16.11	3.93	6.32	0.00	6.22
Nagaland	N.A.	N.A.	N.A.	N.A.	N.A.	N.A.	2.43	0.00	2.30
Punjab	26.98	9.08	14.45	18.77	3.65	8.94	22.08	4.80	11.49
Sikkim	22.33	32.70	28.42	46.46	37.79	41.00	38.06	29.42	31.70
Tamil Nadu	69.17	52.79	56.73	62.78	40.73	46.38	44.73	28.49	32.98
Uttarakhand	33.01	23.62	25.11	15.78	12.69	13.38	34.31	21.26	24.83
Andaman and Nicobar Islands	33.54	24.91	27.05	4.67	5.45	5.20	1.07	1.06	1.06
Chandigarh	6.01	5.04	5.26	17.43	18.97	18.65	17.54	8.71	11.79
Dadra and Nagar Haveli	72.88	10.50	67.36	72.45	34.59	69.40	53.27	0.00	51.67
Daman and Diu	N.A.	N.A.	N.A.	N.A.	N.A.	N.A.	24.12	0.00	4.71
Delhi	7.20	6.68	6.93	0.00	11.19	9.11	10.83	0.00	2.00
Lakshadweep	N.A.	N.A.	N.A.	24.59	57.23	26.94	0.00	0.00	0.00
Pondicherry	74.87	52.32	60.52	59.05	39.11	44.07	17.70	21.20	19.99

Source: Computed from various rounds of NSSO consumer expenditure surveys.

Note: N.A. means not available.

Table 6A.11
Average Annual Rate of Decline of HCR between 1983 and 1999–2000 (in Percentage Points)

States	Rural			Urban			Total		
	STs	SCs	Non-SCs/STs	STs	SCs	Non-SCs/STs	STs	SCs	Non-SCs/STs
Andhra Pradesh	-2.21	-3.44	-4.29	0.67	-1.16	-2.10	-1.66	-2.78	-3.24
Assam	-1.21	0.21	-0.35	-5.27	-3.22	-4.33	-1.39	-0.11	-0.64
Bihar	-1.77	-1.83	-2.36	-1.11	-1.08	-2.66	-1.93	-1.79	-2.40
Jharkhand	-1.18	-1.06	-1.78	-0.67	-1.86	-1.57	-1.20	-1.09	-1.64
Gujarat	-3.22	-3.62	-3.86	-3.36	-2.42	-4.43	-3.21	-3.09	-4.13
Karnataka	-3.52	-3.29	-3.51	0.00	-0.50	-3.20	-2.95	-2.81	-3.38
Madhya Pradesh	-1.30	-2.31	-2.30	0.23	-1.37	-2.15	-1.24	-2.04	-2.18
Chhattisgarh	-0.20	-0.52	-0.43	-1.94	0.57	-1.72	-0.29	-0.39	-0.75
Maharashtra	-1.83	-2.98	-3.61	-2.26	-2.12	-2.18	-1.89	-2.64	-3.04
Orissa	-1.00	-1.95	-2.69	-1.22	0.22	-1.15	-1.02	-1.68	-2.52
Rajasthan	-3.80	-3.53	-4.59	-3.56	-0.71	-3.90	-3.80	-2.78	-4.39
Tripura	-2.38	-4.77	-3.11		-4.62	-6.15	-2.63	-4.79	-3.43
Uttar Pradesh	-1.74	-1.59	-2.43	-4.36	-1.33	-2.74	-2.01	-1.55	-2.49
West Bengal	-2.17	-3.27	-3.20	-1.29	-2.60	-3.97	-2.12	-3.21	-3.25

Source: Computed from various rounds of NSSO consumer expenditure surveys.

Table 6A.12
Poverty Head Count Index by Social Groups and Religion in Urban Areas

Social Groups→ Religions ↓	STs	SCs	Non-SCs/STs	All
		1983		
Hindu	60.53	55.97	36.79	40.33
Muslim	42.84	68.14	57.21	57.24
Christian	27.10	65.08	28.94	30.86
Sikh	97.13	36.82	16.24	19.25
Others	36.82	53.43	27.07	35.36
		1987–1988		
Hindu	57.65	54.97	32.82	36.95
Muslim	51.52	56.61	54.73	54.70
Christian	20.28	55.93	25.88	27.25
Sikh	20.34	16.84	9.15	10.62
Others	41.16	64.48	27.20	38.89
		1993–1994		
Hindu	47.87	50.04	26.24	30.64
Muslim	40.00	48.00	47.73	47.66
Christian	11.36	56.23	20.73	22.55
Sikh	0.00	28.95	7.57	10.78
Others	40.48	49.79	11.90	31.57
		1999–2000		
Hindu	43.32	38.93	17.53	22.00
Muslim	29.82	45.06	36.72	36.76
Christian	12.00	36.35	9.71	12.34
Sikh	22.92	10.23	3.78	4.97
Others	32.18	52.90	4.09	22.65
	Average Annual Percentage Change 1983 to 1999–2000			
Hindu	−1.78	−1.90	−3.27	−2.84
Muslim	−1.90	−2.12	−2.24	−2.24
Christian	−3.48	−2.76	−4.15	−3.75
Sikh	−4.78	−4.51	−4.79	−4.64
Others	−0.79	−0.06	−5.31	−2.25

Source: Computed from various rounds of NSSO consumer expenditure surveys.

Table 6A.13
Social Group-wise Incidence of Poverty (HCR) for Major States in Urban Areas

States	1983				1987–1988				1993–1994			
	STs	SCs	Non-SCs/STs	All	STs	SCs	Non-SCs/STs	All	STs	SCs	Non-SCs/STs	All
Andhra Pradesh	42.96	51.74	36.40	37.97	51.83	49.75	39.80	41.19	45.63	45.74	37.92	38.80
Assam	18.67	43.54	19.01	22.14	7.61	20.91	10.15	11.45	8.35	16.48	7.26	7.93
Bihar	40.77	73.44	56.94	58.72	55.40	78.93	61.55	63.81	43.06	66.23	37.90	40.77
Jharkhand	52.36	56.23	32.16	37.20	54.55	34.31	31.83	34.65	34.45	49.21	19.88	26.53
Gujarat	83.22	43.76	39.21	41.37	64.01	49.72	34.92	38.52	35.64	45.91	25.59	28.28
Karnataka	51.65	50.71	41.79	43.04	69.94	62.92	46.91	49.19	62.40	62.76	35.50	39.73
Madhya Pradesh	56.64	72.27	51.42	54.81	77.18	68.03	44.80	49.85	72.98	64.28	43.10	48.97
Chhattisgarh	51.60	49.80	48.84	49.26	44.96	71.37	29.82	35.99	43.84	61.60	41.21	44.25
Maharashtra	66.99	61.62	36.73	40.97	64.10	66.40	35.58	40.52	60.58	53.84	30.48	34.97
Orissa	73.73	69.53	41.86	49.66	61.37	59.52	37.87	42.58	62.81	45.46	36.26	40.64
Rajasthan	50.64	48.83	36.46	38.55	27.94	53.76	34.83	37.89	8.40	49.69	27.91	31.05
Tripura	0.00	34.62	21.76	21.99	0.00	21.24	10.87	11.22	0.00	8.84	5.72	6.04
Uttar Pradesh	34.44	59.91	51.50	52.44	51.13	57.56	44.84	46.43	25.56	50.74	33.45	35.64
West Bengal	42.41	48.35	30.72	33.44	43.27	49.47	31.11	33.74	23.49	38.74	19.70	22.95

Source: Computed from various rounds of NSSO consumer expenditure surveys.

Table 6A.14
Social Group-wise Incidence of Poverty (HCR) for Smaller States in Urban Areas

States	1983			1987–1988			1993–1994		
	STs/SCs	Non-SCs/STs	All	STs/SCs	Non-SCs/STs	All	STs/SCs	Non-SCs/STs	All
Arunachal Pradesh	37.32	7.30	14.53	9.03	19.47	16.22	11.89	3.66	6.05
Goa	23.02	36.06	35.44	25.41	36.68	36.08	10.30	29.33	28.26
Haryana	45.51	24.74	28.13	39.52	13.35	18.57	24.72	14.64	16.47
Himachal Pradesh	23.17	9.36	12.63	14.87	3.43	7.20	18.19	6.86	9.26
Jammu and Kashmir	19.42	17.42	17.47	29.45	13.67	14.98	6.00	4.97	5.13
Kerala	59.84	44.54	45.70	53.23	37.54	38.69	29.83	23.92	24.31
Manipur	21.97	13.56	14.74	12.68	5.25	6.52	11.15	6.04	6.89
Meghalaya	13.57	0.74	7.67	2.94	0.23	2.04	0.77	4.01	1.81
Mizoram	2.47	0.00	2.44	0.63	0.00	0.62	0.00	0.00	0.00
Nagaland	3.49	2.28	2.97	0.00	0.00	0.00	0.00	0.00	0.00
Punjab	37.24	19.56	23.47	25.69	10.59	13.71	26.07	6.29	10.89
Sikkim	3.75	10.59	8.83	5.04	8.80	7.72	3.67	0.00	0.96
Tamil Nadu	70.21	48.43	50.84	61.99	37.25	40.27	57.84	36.62	39.95
Uttarakhand	24.52	22.75	23.06	46.94	16.56	20.36	34.42	14.69	17.85
Andaman and Nicobar Islands	34.35	15.24	17.05	16.61	5.97	6.86	14.75	4.32	5.22
Chandigarh	34.08	9.38	14.21	19.39	1.81	5.36	0.00	2.59	2.08
Dadra and Nagar Haveli	N.A.	N.A.	N.A.	N.A.	N.A.	N.A.	65.42	11.62	38.83
Daman and Diu	N.A.	N.A.	N.A.	N.A.	N.A.	N.A.	54.55	20.80	21.66
Delhi	50.64	21.19	28.61	42.29	10.32	16.74	44.47	8.37	16.11
Lakshadweep	58.22	0.00	41.09	40.39	20.58	38.31	16.41	0.00	15.93
Pondicherry	91.13	59.51	62.90	75.44	50.71	56.06	57.45	34.50	36.47

Source: Computed from various rounds of NSSO consumer expenditure surveys.
Note: N.A. means not available.

Table 6A.15

Average Annual Rate of Decline of HCR between 1993–1994 and 1999–2000 (in Percentage Points)

States	Rural Areas			Urban Areas			Total		
	STs/SCs	Non-SCs/STs	All	STs/SCs	Non-SCs/STs	All	STs/SCs	Non-SCs/STs	All
Arunachal Pradesh	-7.54	-6.31	-7.56	-8.74	4.37	-2.72	-7.58	-2.84	-7.17
Goa		-16.67	-16.67	30.51	-13.43	-13.01	77.85	-13.80	-13.34
Haryana	-10.61	-13.14	-12.25	0.60	-11.30	-7.22	-9.18	-12.73	-11.38
Himachal Pradesh	-11.78	-12.67	-12.35	-11.70	-6.04	-8.43	-11.77	-12.50	-12.25
Jammu and Kashmir	-6.77	-13.59	-13.06	8.75	-12.47	-10.40	-5.68	-12.79	-12.25
Kerala	-9.13	-10.80	-10.51	-2.23	-3.14	-3.05	-8.16	-8.71	-8.62
Manipur	-4.84	-5.63	-4.25	-16.67	-15.14	-15.39	-4.20	-7.97	-5.21
Meghalaya	-12.69	-10.96	-12.59	-16.67	-16.67	-16.67	-12.88	-11.10	-12.78
Mizoram	-8.76	N.A.	-9.04	N.A.	N.A.	N.A.	-9.78	N.A.	-9.95
Nagaland	-16.67	N.A.	-15.18	N.A.	N.A.	N.A.	-16.67	N.A.	-15.25
Punjab	-7.60	-9.35	-7.96	-9.30	-8.74	-8.28	-8.00	-9.08	-8.07
Sikkim	-8.80	-3.45	-5.30	19.74		68.33	-8.65	-3.53	-5.30
Tamil Nadu	-4.66	-8.24	-6.52	-4.21	-7.89	-7.27	-4.73	-8.04	-6.82
Uttarakhand	-2.73	-6.71	-6.31	-12.22	1.62	-3.53	-6.28	-5.30	-5.93
Andaman and Nicobar Islands	3.65	-16.67	-12.64	-16.67	-14.45	-14.94	-8.36	-15.28	-14.15
Chandigarh	-16.12	2.33	-5.73	N.A.	-11.21	7.82	38.11	-6.51	1.72
Dadra and Nagar Haveli	-10.78	N.A.	-11.32	-6.84	-16.67	-11.39	-10.59	-10.35	-11.36
Daman and Diu	-16.67	N.A.	-16.67	-4.83	-10.70	-8.28	-13.24	-9.14	-9.98
Delhi	-8.10	N.A.	-10.62	-8.67	-3.32	-7.13	-9.35	-5.59	-8.59
Lakshadweep	N.A.	N.A.	N.A.	-13.30		-13.21	-12.51		-12.43
Pondicherry	1.35	-10.41	-7.10	-6.26	-6.47	-6.45	-3.02	-7.47	-6.72

Source: Computed from various rounds of NSSO consumer expenditure surveys.

Note: N.A. means not available.

Table 6A.16
Disparities in Incidence of Poverty in Rural Areas for Major States (in Percentage Points)

	1983		1999–2000	
States	*STs versus Non-SCs/STs*	*SCs versus Non-SCs/STs*	*STs versus Non-SCs/STs*	*SCs versus Non-SCs/STs*
Andhra Pradesh	12.19	13.10	15.68	9.08
Assam	6.58	1.49	−0.50	5.32
Bihar	12.56	22.58	14.73	21.06
Jharkhand	17.25	17.35	19.47	21.01
Gujarat	36.73	17.11	19.85	7.92
Karnataka	25.89	23.26	11.27	12.08
Madhya Pradesh	37.03	27.05	34.98	17.00
Chhattisgarh	17.28	8.66	18.22	7.36
Maharashtra	23.02	21.04	27.48	14.92
Orissa	28.56	17.47	39.81	19.00
Rajasthan	31.72	13.12	16.42	11.11
Tripura	15.32	28.46	13.16	−1.73
Uttar Pradesh	5.69	13.46	9.08	16.10
West Bengal	18.47	14.96	21.60	6.46

Source: Computed from various rounds of NSSO consumer expenditure surveys.

Table 6A.17
Disparities in Incidence of Poverty for Major States in Urban Areas (in Percentage Points)

	1983		1999–2000	
States	*STs versus Non-SCs/STs*	*SCs versus Non-SCs/STs*	*STs versus Non-SCs/STs*	*SCs versus Non-SCs/STs*
Andhra Pradesh	6.56	15.34	23.38	17.95
Assam	−0.34	24.53	−2.92	15.30
Bihar	−16.18	16.50	0.77	27.97
Jharkhand	20.20	24.07	22.68	15.42
Gujarat	44.01	4.56	27.00	15.39
Karnataka	9.85	8.92	31.32	26.30
Madhya Pradesh	5.22	20.85	24.99	22.67
Chhattisgarh	2.76	0.96	0.11	18.88
Maharashtra	30.26	24.90	18.85	16.81
Orissa	31.87	27.67	25.20	37.85

(Table 6A.17 Contd.)

(Table 6A.17 Contd.)

| States | 1983 | | 1999–2000 | |
	STs versus Non-SCs/STs	SCs versus Non-SCs/STs	STs versus Non-SCs/STs	SCs versus Non-SCs/STs
Rajasthan	14.19	12.38	8.12	29.57
Tripura	–21.76	12.86	–0.35	8.68
Uttar Pradesh	–17.06	8.40	–18.52	18.21
West Bengal	11.70	17.63	22.46	17.04

Source: Computed from various rounds of NSSO consumer expenditure surveys.

Table 6A.18
Disparities in Incidence of Poverty in Smaller States (in Percentage Points)

| States | Rural Areas | | Urban Areas | | All | |
| | 1993–1994 | 1999–2000 | 1993–1994 | 1999–2000 | 1993–1994 | 1999–2000 |
	STs/SCs versus Non-SCs/STs		STs/SCs versus Non-SCs/STs		STs/SCs versus Non-SCs/STs	
Arunachal Pradesh	12.26	4.43	8.23	1.03	21.78	6.22
Goa	–5.43	0.00	–19.03	23.45	–12.15	17.37
Haryana	25.34	12.34	10.08	20.90	23.25	14.49
Himachal Pradesh	15.08	5.82	11.32	1.04	15.35	5.58
Jammu and Kashmir	6.00	10.20	1.03	7.90	7.51	9.78
Kerala	13.81	8.62	5.91	6.43	12.55	7.19
Manipur	13.60	10.29	5.12	–0.55	13.99	12.94
Meghalaya	1.59	–1.99	–3.24	0.00	8.60	0.52
Mizoram	6.32	3.00	0.00	0.00	4.32	1.78
Nagaland	2.43	–4.29	0.00	0.00	1.93	–1.87
Punjab	17.28	9.90	19.78	8.54	17.56	9.48
Sikkim	8.64	–5.37	3.67	4.53	8.27	–4.34
Tamil Nadu	16.24	17.82	21.23	23.95	16.18	17.88
Uttarakhand	13.05	15.99	19.73	–6.93	14.58	7.93
Andaman and Nicobar Islands	0.02	1.31	10.43	–0.57	0.16	0.99
Chandigarh	8.83	–9.35	–2.59	13.88	0.42	10.09
Dadra and Nagar Haveli	53.27	15.04	53.80	38.55	47.19	17.13
Daman and Diu	24.12	0.00	33.75	31.30	17.32	1.30
Delhi	10.83	5.56	36.11	14.64	33.85	13.18
Lakshadweep	0.00	0.00	16.41	0.36	8.20	–0.03
Pondicherry	–3.50	11.17	22.95	14.75	–1.16	7.18

Source: Computed from various rounds of NSSO consumer expenditure surveys.

Chapter 7

LITERACY AND EDUCATIONAL LEVELS

Sachidanand Sinha

This chapter presents an account of the current literacy levels and educational scenario among Scheduled Castes (SCs) and Scheduled Tribes (STs) with respect to progress made therein with special reference to social, gender and inter-state inequities vis-à-vis non-SC/ST population. The chapter is thematically divided into four parts. The first part takes stock of social and economic dynamics of literacy among SCs and STs while tracing growth trends of the literate population during the last few decades. The second part examines the levels and patterns of school enrolment, whereas the third part presents a profile of the participation of SCs and STs in higher education. The final part pertains to policy recommendations and future prospects with regard to educational attainments of SCs and STs.

LITERACY

According to the Census of India, 'literacy' is defined as an ability to read and write with an understanding in any language and is applicable to the population aged seven years and above. A literate population, therefore, includes all those persons who have acquired literacy through means of formal education or otherwise, irrespective of the stage of education.

All-India Level

Current Status: In 2001, there were over 300 million illiterate persons in India. Of these, the illiterate SCs accounted for about 62 million or 20 per cent of the total illiterate population, while the comparable figures for ST stood at 36 million or 12 per cent of the total illiterate population. The two segments of SCs and STs, therefore, carry nearly one-third of the total burden of illiteracy in the country, which by far exceeds their share in the population.

The National Sample Survey (NSS) 55th round (1999–2000) reports that over 41 per cent and 48 per cent SC and ST households, respectively, in rural areas did not have a single literate member aged 15 years and above. The magnitude of illiteracy among SC and ST females is even more alarming with the survey reporting that nearly three-fourths of rural SC and ST households did not have a single literate female.

Decadal Changes: Table 7.1 presents the decadal change in literacy rates for SCs and STs, on one hand, and non-SCs/STs, on the other hand. In 2001, reportedly over one-half of the SC and ST population was literate, which was significantly higher than the corresponding figure of one-tenth of SC and ST population in 1961. The figures underline the fact that the growth of literacy in India has been rather slow. The growth pattern for non-SCs/STs too was not very different, but for the initial difference in the level of literacy, which was higher by nearly 18 and 19 percentage points than the corresponding figure for SCs and STs in 1961.

Literacy Gap across Social Groups: During 1961–1991, the growth in literacy rates for non-SCs/STs remained higher than SCs and STs which resulted in increasing wide literacy gaps between these two segments of India's population. This trend, however, registered a reversal as the literacy rates for SCs and STs during the 1990s rose by over 17 and 19 percentage points, respectively, while the comparable rise for non-SCs/STs was reported to be a little over 11 percentage points. This was largely due to the prevalence of low levels of literacy among the former two social groups. Consequently, the literacy gaps between non-SCs/STs and SCs, on one hand, as well as between non-SCs/STs and STs, on the other hand, began

Table 7.1
Trends in Literacy Rates and Literacy Gaps by Social Groups, 1961–2001

| | Literacy Rates | | | Literacy Gap★ | |
Years	Non-SC/ST	SC	ST	Non-SC/ST versus SC	Non-SC/ST versus ST
1961	27.91	10.27	8.54	17.64	19.37
1971	33.80	14.67	11.30	19.13	22.50
1981	41.30	21.38	16.35	19.92	24.95
1991	57.69	37.41	29.60	20.28	28.09
2001	68.81	54.70	47.10	14.11	21.71

Source: Census of India, 1961–2001.
★ Percentage point difference.

to narrow down, perhaps for the first time in the history of independent India. However, the differences between the social groups still remain significantly large.

By Gender and Place of Residence: Another important development during the 1990s pertains to relatively higher growth rate of female literacy both among SCs and STs as well as non-SCs/STs. In 1991, the male literacy rate for SCs was 49.9 per cent which increased to 66.6 per cent in 2001. In the case of SC and ST females, the literacy rates increased from 23.8 per cent to 41.9 per cent, and 18.1 per cent to 34.7 per cent, respectively, during the same period. Correspondingly, non-SC/ST females registered a rise from 44.8 per cent to 58.2 per cent. The growth in female literacy among SCs was, thus, observed to be higher than that of their tribal and non-scheduled counterparts.

The gender gap among ST and SC population, however, remains significantly higher than non-SCs/STs, especially in urban areas, largely due to their lower base. The urban ST females appear to be doing better than their SC counterparts, while their rural counterparts are worse off than them, which indicates the prevalence of poor accessibility to schools in tribal inhabited areas of India. Although the tribes constitute the most educationally disadvantaged social segment, their level of deprivation would in all likelihood increase further if one were to exclude the tribes of the north-east from the aggregate ST population in the country.

The ever-persistent rural–urban divide in male literacy rates has begun to wane for both SC and non-scheduled populations, though the gender gap within the two communities in both urban and rural areas remains significantly large. This reinforces the fact that it is the rural females, in general, and SCs and STs among them, in particular, who constitute the most disadvantaged base of the illiteracy pyramid (see Annexure V Table 7A.1).

Inter-state Variations

The coefficient of variation in literacy rates for SCs and STs shows wide inter-state variations (see Annexure V Tables 7A.2 and 7A.3). This variation is far greater than that observed for non-SCs/STs for whom the coefficient of variation in the case of males was marginal. The variation in literacy rates was seen to decline for all social groups during the 1990s. This suggests that while non-SCs/STs have done well in terms of attaining greater literacy almost everywhere, the gains remain inequitably distributed across the states for SCs and STs as they continue to register very high inter-state variations. The higher level of decadal change in literacy rates observed among these disadvantaged groups is largely due to a low base of literacy (see Annexure V Table 7A.4).

As regards SCs, one observes the highest literacy rates among them for both males and females in Kerala, followed by Tripura, Maharashtra, Gujarat and

Himachal Pradesh where the rates were above 70 per cent in 2001. On the other hand, the lowest literacy rates among SCs were observed in Bihar, Uttar Pradesh, Rajasthan, Karnataka and Andhra Pradesh. Bihar, which was at the bottom of the literacy pyramid, recorded a little over a quarter of its SC population as literates, while only 15.6 per cent of SC females in the state were literate. The other states which recorded a significant growth in literacy were Rajasthan, Madhya Pradesh and Andhra Pradesh. Rajasthan, which held the second last rank in 1991, owing largely to a very poor female literacy rate, improved its position significantly in 2001. The state recorded fourfold growth in female literacy during this period, while male literacy in the state reportedly increased from 42.4 per cent in 1991 to 69 per cent in 2001, a figure that was incidentally far better than those for Karnataka, Haryana and Punjab. However, with regard to gender gap in Rajasthan, there is a status quo with the 1991 figures, though this gap showed significant magnitudes of decline in other states with the sole exception of Bihar.

As regards the literacy levels among ST, Mizoram stands out as the only Indian state where nearly 90 per cent of the tribes were reportedly literate. Although the states of Sikkim, Manipur, Nagaland, Kerala, Assam and Himachal Pradesh have attained nearly two-thirds literacy among the tribes, yet they are still way behind Mizoram. On the other hand, the states which reported literacy rates lower than all-India average for tribes were Orissa, Andhra Pradesh, Bihar, Jammu and Kashmir, Tamil Nadu and West Bengal. The prevalence of poor literacy rates among the Indian tribes, both in the mid-Indian tribal belt as well as in the northeast (Mizoram being the only exception) may help encapsulate the twin impacts of physical and socio-economic isolation and the process of socio-economic marginalisation which the tribes have been subjected to for long.

In terms of the literacy gaps between non-SCs/STs and SCs, it has been observed that barring most of the north-eastern states, the gap remains fairly pronounced in several states of India. Assam emerged as the only state to have negligible level of inequality between the social groups, where SCs and STs appeared to be doing far better than their counterparts elsewhere in the country. The states which registered a remarkable decline in the magnitude of literacy gaps include Maharashtra, Himachal Pradesh and West Bengal. Even in Kerala, the position of SCs vis-à-vis non-SCs/STs remains very weak. Among all the states surveyed, Bihar was the worst-off and registered the highest literacy gaps between SCs, on one hand, and non-SCs/STs, on the other hand. As a matter of fact, there has been an increase in social inequality between SCs and non-SCs/STs in the context of female literacy. Interestingly, while the magnitude of literacy gap between SCs and non-SCs/STs is the same in Punjab and Orissa, the two states are poles apart in terms of economic development. In this context, Orissa seems to have done well to attain identical levels of literacy as that of Punjab for various social groups in spite of its poor resources and much slower trajectory of economic development.

EDUCATIONAL ATTAINMENT

The degree of educational attainment by age and levels of education culled from the 2001 Census for SCs, STs and non-SCs/STs is presented in Annexure V Table 7A.5. The figures in the table show the stock of educated population for the three social segments which is irrepressibly poor across the board. The SCs and STs, however, lag significantly behind their non-scheduled counterparts, which is an indication of the fact that education has generally remained the prerogative of the non-scheduled segment in India. The higher attainment rates for SCs and STs up to primary level of education and a gradual drop in these rates thereafter shows that a majority of SC and ST children have to terminate their school education after completion of or before primary classes, whereas non-SC/ST children continue their higher level education. Among all the literate SCs, only 16.3 per cent attained education up to middle or upper primary level and another 15 per cent received education up to secondary and higher secondary levels. Only 3.1 per cent were fortunate enough to acquire college level education. On the other hand, over 22 per cent non-SC/ST children could attain high school education and another 7.64 per cent acquired graduate and post-graduate degrees. The latest Census figures also revealed that during the initial stages of school education corresponding to the age group of seven to nine years, little difference was observed between the two communities. The disparity, however, widened among the subsequent age groups and stages of education. Among SCs, there was a very sharp decline in literacy rates from 68 per cent for the age group of seven to nine years to 39.6 per cent for the age group of 25 years and above, as opposed to the corresponding decline from 73.2 per cent to 62.7 per cent for non-SCs/STs which speaks volumes about the limited educational opportunities available for the scheduled groups even after 50 years of planned interventions in the area of educational development. The picture was almost similar as far as ST was concerned.

The current stock of educated manpower among SCs and STs is characterised not only by low levels of educational attainment, but also by poor diversification into skill- and job-oriented technical and professional courses. Annexure V Table 7A.6 presents the distribution of population aged 15 years and above by sex and social groups for those who have attained graduate degrees and above. In 2001, those who hold technical degrees in engineering and technology among SC males accounted for a little above 5 per cent of the educated population, while that for SC females was 3.6 per cent. The corresponding figures for non-SCs/STs were 8.6 per cent and four per cent, respectively. Although the inter-community difference for graduates in medicine was not as glaring as that seen in the field of engineering and technology, non-SCs/STs had a definite edge in this sphere too. The teaching stream has emerged as an attractive course where the attainment levels for SCs and STs was a little better than that for non-SCs/STs. These figures must, however, be seen in relation to the fact that a much smaller number of SC and ST students are enrolled in higher education than non-SC/ST students.

SCHOOL ENROLMENT

This section on school enrolment and related attributes is largely based on the Census and NSS figures. The information from the Department of Education on enrolment tends to overstate the actual enrolment rates because it refers to students actually enrolled in school registers at the beginning of the academic year and does not take into consideration the fact as to whether those enrolled actually attend school or not. For example, the administrative data presented by the Department of Education puts the gross enrolment rate (GER) for SC children in primary and upper primary classes, that is, I–V and VI–VIII, respectively, for 2001–2002 at 93 per cent and 86 per cent, respectively, which implies that only a small proportion of children in the relevant school-going age (six to 14 years) are currently out of school. On the other hand, according to the Census of India 2001, about 74 per cent SC children in the seven to 11 years age group and 68 per cent in 12–14 years age group attended schools. While one may also note that the GER is a gross measure that does not discount for the presence of over-aged and under-aged children among those enrolled, the discrepancies between the two sources are instructive to arrive at any meaningful inference on the state of school education among SC and ST children. Therefore, instead of using GER we have used school/college attendance figures culled out from NSS household level sample surveys and the Census sources for 2001.

All India

The NSS 1999–2000 (see Annexure V Table 7A.7) puts the school attendance rate (SAR) for SC children aged 5–14 years at 70.1 per cent for rural males and fewer than 80 per cent for urban males. The corresponding figures for rural and urban females were 58.6 per cent and 73.9 per cent, respectively. There has been a steady increase in SAR since 1983. In 1983, SAR for male SC children stood at 48.9 per cent for rural areas and 66.7 per cent for urban areas, whereas SARs for rural and urban SC females were 25.5 per cent and 52.3 per cent, respectively. The increase in school attendance figures has been more impressive in rural areas during 1983 to 1993–1994 (see Annexure V Table 7A.8). It became sluggish during the late 1990s and more so in urban areas with respect to SC males. The SARs for ST males in the 5–14 years age group for rural areas stood at 63.2 per cent, whereas for ST females they were about 10 percentage points lower at 53 per cent in 1999–2000. The ST children, including both males and females, did better than their SC counterparts in urban areas.

The Census data presents nearly identical attendance rates for SCs and STs and somewhat lower rates for non-SC/ST population. If one were to accept that the figures obtained from the two sources could be different primarily because one is based on sample surveys, whereas the other is a Census, one would naturally have a greater inclination to place more confidence in the latter. However, if the earlier rounds of the NSS estimates are any indication of the state of school education, then it becomes apparent that while SAR for SCs and STs in both rural and urban areas did increase, those for non-SCs/STs remained nearly stagnant during 1990s. What needs to be underlined here is that in spite of the growth in enrolment rates at various stages of school education experienced by SCs and STs, a large proportion of SC and ST children are still not covered under school education.

According to the NSS (1993–1994), 75 per cent and 61 per cent boys and girls, respectively, who belong to non-SC/ST population in the five to 14 years age group attended educational institutions. The comparable figures stood at 64.3 per cent and 46.2 per cent, respectively, for SC boys and girls, and at 58 per cent and 41 per cent, respectively, for ST boys and girls. This implies that over 25 per cent boys and nearly 40 per cent girls in the relevant age groups among non-SCs/STs did not attend school, while the comparable figures for SCs and STs were over two-fifths and one-half of the total population of boys and girls, respectively.

In 2001, the Census reported the prevalence of a more or less similar situation in the rural areas. The percentage of non-SC/ST boys and girls who attended educational institutions was 70 per cent and 64 per cent, respectively; whereas for SCs, the corresponding attendance rates showed some improvements with over two-thirds boys and 50 per cent girls reporting school attendance. In the case of ST boys and girls, SARs were 59 per cent and 47 per cent, respectively. If one compares the NSS (1993–1994) and the Census figures, then one can observe that SAR for SC girls increased by nearly 10 percentage points while those for non-SCs/STs and STs increased by 3 percentage points and 6 percentage points, respectively. Although the gaps between the social groups declined in 2001 in comparison to 1993–1994 figures, this could largely be attributed to a decline in the attendance rates among non-SCs/STs (see Annexure V Table 7A.9).

State Level

The inference that the gains of educational development have been socially inequitable is, thus, beyond doubt. However, significantly, the gains have been disparate across the various states of India.

In 2001, the magnitude of out-of-school children acquired serious proportions in Bihar (including Jharkhand) where over two-thirds of the boys and nearly four-fifths of the girls among SCs remained deprived of school education. In Uttar Pradesh, the comparable figures stood at two-fifths and one-half for the boys and girls, respectively. The other states where the proportion of SC children who attended schools in the age group of five to 14 years was either below or around the national average included Orissa, West Bengal, Arunachal Pradesh, Karnataka, Punjab and Rajasthan. Except Arunachal Pradesh and Meghalaya, ST registered better SAR in the north-eastern states, Maharashtra, Himachal Pradesh and Kerala. Elsewhere in the country, the proportion of out-of-school children among them was found to be significantly higher at nearly two-fifths among the boys and one-half among the girls. The highest figure over one-half among the boys and two-thirds among the girls was recorded in Bihar.

One must also take note of the fact that disparity between non-SC/ST and SC children with respect to SAR in elementary education has shrunk significantly in Assam, Himachal Pradesh, Gujarat, Jammu and Kashmir, Kerala, Maharashtra, Tripura and West Bengal. In spite of their higher level of economic development, Punjab and Haryana continue to have large social and gender gaps in school education which indicate that the advantages of economic development have remained confined to non-SCs/STs while SC females are particularly excluded.

With every successive stage of higher education and age cohort, the enrolment rates among SC children tend to decline more sharply than among non-SC/ST children. This is not to suggest that the progress in enrolment to high and higher secondary classes has been unimpressive. As a matter of fact, the number of SC children enrolled in high/higher secondary classes has registered an impressive growth from 2.5 million in 1990–1991 to 4.3 million in 2001–2002 which indicate an increase in their participation rate from 11 per cent to 14 per cent, respectively. However, in spite of their increasing participation in school education, the enrolment of SC children aged 15–19 years, as per the 2001 Census, was only one-third of the total population, while the corresponding figure for non-scheduled population who attend high/higher secondary classes stood at about 40 per cent.

DROPOUT RATES

One of the major impediments to the achievement of universal elementary education among SCs is the high level of school dropout rates which set in no sooner than the child is enrolled in Class I. According to the departmental statistics, nearly 45 per cent children enrolled in Class I tend to dropout by the time they reach Class V. Only 39 per cent of those enrolled in Class I are able to complete Class VIII, while about 28 per cent complete their high school examination. In 1980–1981, there was little difference in the dropout rates of SCs and all children in elementary classes (see Table 7.2). In spite of the decline registered during the last two decades the gaps in dropout rates have widened between SCs and STs on one hand, and non-SCs/STs on the other hand. This indicates that the impact of school retention measures has been differently allocated or experienced by scheduled and non-scheduled populations. One may also venture to suggest that a qualitative change may have affected the dropout rates during the last two decades. The absence of any difference in the dropout rates for SCs and all communities in the early 1980s was largely due to low level of SC enrolment in schools by those who had the necessary resources or propensity to educate their children, after they have overcome social stigma or exclusion forced on them for

Table 7.2

School Dropout Rates for Boys and Girls by Stages of Education and Social Groups

Years	All Communities			Scheduled Castes			Scheduled Tribes		
	I–V	I–VIII	I–X	I–V	I–VIII	I–X	I–V	I–VIII	I–X
1980–1981	58.7	72.7	82.5	60.2	76.8	86.9	75.7	86.7	91.2
1985–1986	47.6	64.4	77.6	52.5	72.5	81.4	65.6	81.9	88.8
1990–1991	42.6	60.9	71.3	49.4	67.8	77.7	62.5	78.6	85.0
1995–1996	42.1	58.8	69.6	45.7	67.0	77.7	56.6	66.0	84.2
2000–2001	39.0	54.6	66.0	45.2	60.7	72.1	52.3	69.5	81.2

Source: Selected Educational Statistics, MHRD.

generations. Therefore, a majority of those among the SCs who went to school were relatively non-poor. They did not dropout owing largely to their poor economic condition but significantly because of the adverse social climate and maltreatment by peers and teachers alike within the school setting. On the other hand, the base of enrolment for non-scheduled population was larger as among them, education was seen as socially and culturally desirable attainment to enable them maintain their superior social position. Since the social and income profiles of children who attend schools have become more variegated and access to education had increased, such tendencies supposedly sustain high dropout rates among socially and economically poorer sections of the society.

Another aspect which pertains to the issue of dropouts can be gauged by the transition rates. Transition rate refers to the percentage of children enrolled in the subsequent class during the current year to the total children enrolled in the previous class during the previous year. The transition rate from primary stage to middle or upper primary stage was about 76 per cent for SCs during the latter half of the 1990s. This implies that only three-fourths of those who have completed Class V could enrol themselves in Class VI.

The inter-state pattern of school dropout rates varies significantly among boys and girls for elementary classes (see Annexure V Table 7A.10). The highest dropout rates in 2001–2002 for SC boys and girls in primary classes were observed in Rajasthan followed by Bihar and Uttar Pradesh. The dropout rate was the highest in Bihar for upper primary classes as well. Some states such as Karnataka and Maharashtra have done very well by bringing down the levels of dropout rates in primary classes below 10 per cent. Other states wherein the dropout rates were lower than 30 per cent were Himachal Pradesh and Madhya Pradesh. Haryana and Punjab have also registered higher retention rates in the primary stage but the latter continues to show higher dropout rates in upper primary classes. The states where the magnitude of female dropouts in the upper primary stage was significantly higher than the national average include Andhra Pradesh, Assam, Bihar, Gujarat, Orissa, Uttar Pradesh, Rajasthan and Tripura. This picture suggests that a lot needs to be done in order to achieve the sustained enrolment and retention of children, especially girls in elementary classes.

PARTICIPATION IN HIGHER EDUCATION

It is rather well known that fewer men and women from SCs and STs are fortunate enough to be able to seek and acquire higher education.

All India

According to the 2001 Census, a little more than 5 per cent SCs aged 20–24 years reportedly acquired post-higher secondary education. Their presence in vocational courses was also found to be rather miniscule. On the other hand, over 10 per cent non-SC/ST men and women attended colleges. The ST was the worst placed as far as their participation in higher education was concerned. While it is not desirable to work out the enrolment ratios for higher education, the participation rates in relation to the share of SCs and STs in the total population can serve as a good index of equality (Table 7.3).

The participation rate of SC males in 2001 was up by over 2 percentage points as it stood at 11.1 per cent of the total enrolment in higher education. The increase for SC females was even more spectacular which registered over twofold growth from 4.5 per cent in 1991 to 8.8 per cent in 2001. The increase in participation rate evidently took place in all the streams, courses and stages of higher education for SCs, but more significantly in graduation (both humanities and sciences) and BEd courses. Although their participation in technical and professional courses such as engineering and medicine improved, it still remains less in proportion to their share in the total population. There has been a marginal improvement in their participation in post-matriculation technical diploma courses as they continue to be under represented in polytechnics, and in technical and industrial crafts. The STs are even less represented in higher education and the growth in their participation among both males and females, remained poor during 1991–2001. The improved level of participation of SCs and STs in BEd, MBBS and post-matriculation teacher training courses is largely a product of the reservation policy, though the impact of this policy is less visible in other professional courses.

The traditional divide between high-caste Hindus and SCs, insofar as the choice of educational courses was concerned, has begun to wilt. There used to be fewer SC students enrolled in science and commerce courses of the three-year bachelor programme in the past. Presently, SCs have improved their presence in BSc course from 6.6 per cent to 11 per cent. Commerce too, has emerged as an attractive proposition for SCs. It must, however, be noted that much of

Table 7.3

Participation of Scheduled Castes and Scheduled Tribes in Higher Education in India between 1991 and 2001

	Scheduled Castes				Scheduled Tribes			
	1991		2001		1991		2001	
Stages of Higher Education	Male	Female	Male	Female	Male	Female	Male	Female
Total Higher Education	9.0	4.5	11.1	8.8	2.4	1.5	3.8	3.2
Research and Postgraduate	8.9	2.2	13.4	9.3	2.6	0.6	3.3	2.3
Graduate General/ Non-Technical Degree	9.4	4.9	14.0	8.2	2.5	1.7	4.2	2.8
BA/BA Hons.	13.6	5.6	16.6	9.4	4.1	2.5	6.1	3.9
BSc/BSc Hons.	6.6	4.6	11.0	8.6	1.1	0.6	2.2	1.7
BCom/BCom Hons.	5.8	3.6	11.5	4.9	1.4	0.8	2.1	1.2
BEd/BT	11.0	5.0	15.2	11.0	2.8	1.6	5.5	3.8
Graduate Technical/ Professional Degree	6.4	6.9	7.4	13.6	1.5	1.4	4.8	4.6
BE/BSc Engg./BArch	5.7	5.5	7.4	7.5	1.1	0.6	4.2	1.6
MBBS	8.9	8.1	11.0	10.8	2.9	2.1	11.6	11.4
Others	N.A.	N.A.	16.1	16.1	N.A.	N.A.	8.7	7.8
Post Matriculation Diploma	10.9	3.8	10.6	12.2	4.2	1.6	4.2	4.5
Polytechnic	8.7	8.5	10.2	11.4	2.1	1.5	3.6	3.8
Teachers Training Schools	14.3	1.4	17.0	14.2	2.5	10.5	8.8	6.2
Technical and Industrial Crafts	12.0	12.5	10.2	11.7	4.1	5.1	4.1	4.6

Source: Selected Educational Statistics, 1991 and 2001.
Note: N.A. means not available.

this increase could be due to overwhelming presence of SC men and women in pass courses as fewer get admitted to honours courses because of the high cut-off marks in the latter. The significant growth of SCs and STs in short-term job-oriented professional degree courses such as BEd is a pointer to the possibility of attracting more SCs and STs to higher education if the current graduation courses are further diversified and made more job-oriented.

State Level

The pattern of participation of SCs and STs in higher education varies enormously across the states. As shown in Annexure V Tables 7A.11 and 7A.12 in 2001, the highest participation of SCs was observed in Tamil Nadu followed by Tripura,

Gujarat and Uttar Pradesh. Tamil Nadu, Tripura, Kerala and Maharashtra nearly achieved equality between the two segments, insofar as enrolment to higher education was concerned. Gujarat stood out as the only state where the coefficient of equality for SCs was over two times the share of their population in the state. This means that SCs have made significant inroads into college education in Gujarat. It may be noted that higher education has not been a priority among the land-owning classes in the state for very long. After attaining school education, non-SC/ST communities ventured into businesses, be they on farm or non-farm activities, either within the family enterprise or outside it. While this has certainly provided greater access to SCs in higher education, professional and technical education for them has remained relatively inaccessible, though the situation in Gujarat is much better than elsewhere in the country except Assam, Rajasthan and Uttar Pradesh. The coefficient of equality for technical education in Gujarat was 0.76, a shade better than that in 1991. The higher participation of SCs in technical education in Rajasthan and Uttar Pradesh, especially as these states are far behind the equality mark, presents an interesting picture that needs to be examined further. One of the probable reasons for greater participation of SCs in higher education in Gujarat may be the high repetition rate for SCs in technical courses that may have increased their enrolment over and above the reserved seats in the quota system. States such as Bihar, Haryana, Punjab, Orissa, Madhya Pradesh and West Bengal have performed poorly in terms of giving greater access to their SC and ST population in higher education. As a matter of fact, the participation rate of SCs in technical education registered a significant decline in 2001 in comparison to 1991 figures for the states of Punjab, Haryana and Himachal Pradesh.

EXPLAINING EDUCATIONAL DEPRIVATION

Deprivation of education among SCs and STs, and the resultant social inequities have largely and rightly been attributed to historical and cumulative socio-economic and structural deprivation suffered by them for centuries. Like economic resources, access to educational resources for SCs has also remained a forbidden territory. Various studies have indicated several causes of educational deprivation among SCs. The main reasons for this are the practice of social discrimination within and outside the educational institutions; poverty; poor availability of educational infrastructure, especially in SC-dominant habitations; declining quality of education and forbidding cost of education.

The prevalence of poverty among SC and ST households has largely been attributed as one of the causative factors for the occurrence of poor enrolment rates among them. Studies have amply established that one of the main causes of high magnitude of 'never enroled, currently out-of-school children' and high rate of school dropout is chronic poverty which forces children at a very early stage of their formative lives to look for livelihood options either for existential reasons or to augment their family incomes. The recent figures from the NSS 55th round (1999–2000) shows that the percentage of households with no literate member was over 40 per cent in lower monthly per capita consumption expenditure (MPCE) classes (< ₹380) for rural SCs, while it was over 50 per cent for ST (see Annexure V Table 7A.13). These households accounted for over two-thirds of all illiterate population for SCs and over one-half for ST. The percentage of such households among non-SCs/STs did not have the same magnitude of illiteracy. In fact, the percentage of non-SC/ST households with no literate member declines sharply in MPCE class above ₹300. The difference between the percentage of SC and non-SC/ST households with no literate members even in the lowest MPCE class was significant and indicative of the fact that caste-based segmentation in education has been in operation for long. Similarly, the proportion of never enrolled and currently non-attending children was found to be much larger among the lower 40 per cent MPCE classes than others (NSS, 1997). Several scholars also found the impact of poverty on enrolment or on SAR of SC children, more specifically the girls, to be greater than on other children.

Several factors including income insecurities, dependence on wage labour and agricultural activities, migration to alternative markets or places of work, illness and death of parents, among others, are known to influence enrolment and attendance rates, and the continuation of education for SC children. The proportion of dropouts was also found to be greater among SCs than among other social groups. While attempting to delineate the reasons for the prevalence of high dropout rates among SC children, the NSS (42nd round) found that 'economic reasons', 'inability to cope with studies or failure', 'lack of interest in studies' and 'attending household chores' (mainly for girl children) were the main reasons for SC children to discontinue their studies. In the 50th round, the NSS included 'unfriendly atmosphere in school' as one of the explanatory phrases to probe the reason for the prevalence of high dropout rates among SC children. Significantly, this phrase did not muster much support as the single most important reason for dropouts—responses such as 'not interested in studies' and 'inability to cope with failure' may override other experiences of discrimination or 'the unfriendly school environment'. Nevertheless, there are reports of children from SC households being made to sit separately from other children or even outside the classrooms when mid-day meals are being served. There have also been reports in several studies that teachers pay greater attention to non-SC/ST children (Anitha, 2000; Dreze and Gazdar, 1996; Nambissan, 2001).

The cost of schooling is also one of the critical factors that influence the process of educational attainments. Although school education up to the age of 14 years is free, studies have indicated that households spend a large proportion of their incomes to meet the cost of books, stationery and uniforms which signify a major financial constraint, especially for SC households (Tilak, 2002). The Sixth All India Educational Survey, 1993, reports that only half of the primary schools in the country were covered by the 'free textbooks' scheme and that only 10 per cent SC students could avail it.

While poverty continues to lead to educational deprivation among SCs and STs, the quantity and quality of education, especially in rural areas, is also one of the prominent causes. Therefore, the availability of adequate number of schools and teachers becomes the most important prerequisite for educational development. It is beyond doubt that there has been a significant growth in the number of schools in the country since independence. The All India Education Surveys report that SC habitations have fewer primary schools than those of the higher castes. The availability of schools within their habitations could be crucial to the educational development of SCs as schools located in non-SC/ST habitations may be less accessible to SC children for one reason or another. One may also note that the proportion of habitations that do not have a primary school is much higher for smaller habitations. This factor adversely affects the access to education among ST as their settlement sizes are generally smaller and more dispersed than those of other social groups.

It must also be noted that the settlement pattern in rural areas is constantly changing. The number of habitations has registered varying degrees of increase across states. Therefore, the allocation of new schools is both a social and political concern. Annexure V Table 7A.14 shows that the states where availability of primary schools (within the habitations) was poor recorded different levels of growth during 1993–2002. Himachal Pradesh, Uttar Pradesh, Maharashtra, Orissa and Rajasthan have done better than others in terms to improve the physical accessibility to primary education. Bihar stands out as the only state where accessibility to primary schools, in effect, declined during the same period. Gujarat and Haryana also experienced a decline in terms of the availability of schools within the habitations as they failed to cope with the growth in the number of habitations. As noted above, while a significantly large proportion of enrolled children tend to dropout before they reach Class V, another large chunk of children discontinues schooling after they attain primary education. While most of these children may dropout because of financial constraints or have to work to supplement their family incomes, and the girls particularly might be required to look after their younger siblings while their parents are away at work, a significantly large number of boys and girls have to discontinue education because of the absence of or poor physical accessibility to upper primary classes. Deficiencies in schooling infrastructure such as the existence of dilapidated buildings, inadequate and dingy classrooms, teacher absenteeism, overcrowded classrooms and lack of seating facilities, sanitation, blackboards, learning materials and other teaching aids, also adversely affect the educational process, as these factors compel children to dropout of schools, which, in turn, affects the enrolment and retention rates, and increases the number of out-of-school children. This process has aptly been referred to as the 'discouragement effect'. Empowering the village communities by enabling them to oversee the activities of the schools through Village Education Committees as part of the move to strengthen the Panchayati Raj Institutions (PRIs) is likely to go a long way towards improving the quality and quantity of education in village schools.

Although India has expanded its elementary education base to reach even the most inaccessible parts of the country, yet the country do not have adequate number of teachers especially in primary schools. Thus, availability of teachers is another supply side attribute with significant qualitative and quantitative ramifications without which no educational process could be of any consequence. For example, almost one-fifth of the schools in the country have either no teacher or merely a single teacher (see Annexure V Table 7A.15). The figure varies from a little below 10 per cent in Haryana, West Bengal and Tripura to nearly 30 per cent in Bihar. In contrast, the states of Delhi and Kerala had sufficient number of teachers in primary schools. The state level figures, however, conceal the fact that it is the medium- and small-sized SC habitations located in inaccessible areas which tend to have fewer than the stipulated number of teaching staff. An analysis of the district report cards prepared by National Institute of Educational Planning and Administration (NIEPA) reveals that the schools that had fewer than two teachers were mostly located in those districts which have for long remained neglected insofar as the development of social and economic infrastructure was concerned. A study of Bihar also shows a large discrepancy between the number of sanctioned posts in schools and the number of teachers actually appointed. A similar problem which arises out of a faulty transfer policy and political interference in Madhya Pradesh had to be corrected through rationalisation of teachers as per the current strength of students across schools. Such rationalisation enables to address the problem of teacher shortage without having to appoint new teachers, which, in turn, had a positive impact on enrolment and dropout rates. These steps finally converged as part of what is now known as the Education Guarantee Scheme which was first introduced on an experimental basis in Madhya Pradesh and later adopted by other states.

Teacher absenteeism, especially in schools located in rural areas, has also been a major cause of worry. While citing a study undertaken in Karnataka on the issue, Dreze and Sen (2003) pointed out that multi-teacher schools do better academically because of constant peer scrutiny which ensures that teachers are present in school, arrive on time and take classes regularly. On the other hand, single- or two-teacher schools have traditionally reported a very high degree of teacher absenteeism. During the last few years, the appointment of para-teachers to meet the additional requirement of teachers in schools has been seen as a cost-effective alternative to meet the educational needs in the rural areas. The NSS reports that private unaided and unrecognised schools have mushroomed all over the country, especially in rural areas during the last decade. There have been instances of children from deprived communities being enrolled in such schools. Since most of these schools are profit-oriented, they lack adequate facilities and pay low salaries to teachers who are also invariably untrained and inadequately qualified. This adversely affects the quality of education being imparted.

At the macro level, a close association between economic growth, public spending and school enrolments can be discerned. The administrative figures regarding the expenditure per child (in the age group of six to 14 years) on school education for the period 1998–1999 indicate differential spending on elementary education by various states. For example, Himachal Pradesh and a few north-eastern states spent over ₹3,000 per child on elementary education, while Bihar, Uttar Pradesh, West Bengal and Andhra Pradesh spent much smaller amounts, that is, less than ₹1,000 per child. Deolalikar (2005) found that states where enrolment or attendance of children in elementary classes was low, spent much smaller amounts per enrolled child. This study also concluded that in most of the states, there was an impressive rise in real growth in aggregate public spending on elementary education between 1980–1981 and 1999–2000. While exploring the relationship between inter-state changes in public spending on elementary education per child with changes in enrolments over time, Deolalikar found a positive association between GER for primary education and real public expenditure on elementary education. The ongoing Sarva Shiksha Abhiyan (SSA) which is designed to strengthen school infrastructure and improve the quality of education is expected to provide the much-needed fillip to development of school education in India and to ensure universal primary enrolment by 2007. The Mid-Day Meal Scheme also has an encouraging impact on elementary school enrolment in several states, particularly Tamil Nadu, especially among SCs and other vulnerable sections which include girls.

SUMMARY

There have been significant improvements in school enrolment and attendance rates during the last decade. The benefits of these gains have, however, been socially and spatially disparate and differential to some extent. While the enrolment rates of SC boys, in both rural and urban areas have increased, those of SC girls have not been equally impressive. The disparities between SCs and non-SCs/STs have begun to narrow down with respect to both school and college education. Further, the benefits of social and economic opportunities which include education have been confined to some numerically preponderant, politically articulate, and a few urban-based SC sub-castes. Among the states, Himachal Pradesh, Rajasthan, Madhya Pradesh, Tamil Nadu, Gujarat and Maharashtra have done well to ensure educational benefits for the deprived social sections in comparison to Bihar, Uttar Pradesh, Punjab and Haryana. However, the twin problems of a large magnitude of out-of-school children and high school dropout rates continue to deter the process of educational development among both SCs and STs.

ANNEXURE V

Table 7A.1
Literacy Rates for Social Groups by Sex and Place of Residence, 2001

Residence	Total	Male	Female	Gender Gap*
Non-scheduled Population				
Total	68.8	78.7	58.2	20.50
Rural	62.6	74.3	50.1	24.20
Urban	81.8	87.6	75.3	12.30
Urban–rural gap	19.2	13.3	25.2	
Scheduled Castes (SC)				
Total	54.7	66.6	41.9	24.70
Rural	51.2	63.7	37.8	25.90
Urban	68.1	77.9	57.5	20.40
Urban–rural gap	16.9	14.2	19.7	
Scheduled Tribes (ST)				
Total	47.1	59.2	34.8	24.4
Rural	45.0	57.4	32.4	25.0
Urban	69.1	77.8	59.9	17.9
Urban–rural gap	24.1	20.4	27.5	
Gap between Non-SC/ST and SC				
Total	14.1	12.1	16.3	
Rural	11.4	10.6	12.3	
Urban	13.7	9.7	17.8	
Gap between Non-SC/ST and ST				
Total	21.7	19.5	23.4	
Rural	17.6	16.9	17.7	
Urban	12.7	9.8	15.4	

Source: Census of India, 2001, Gaps indicated by percentage point difference.
Note: *Literacy rates for social groups by sex and place of residence, 2001.

Table 7A.2
Literacy Rates and Inter-group Gaps by Social Groups and Sex, 1991

States	Non-scheduled (NSD)			Scheduled Castes (SC)			Scheduled Tribes (ST)			Gap between NSD and SC			Gap between NSD and ST		
	Persons	Males	Females	Persons	Males	Females	Persons	Males	Females	Persons	Males	Females	Persons	Males	Females
All India	57.7	69.5	44.8	37.4	49.9	23.8	29.6	40.7	18.1	20.3	19.6	21.0	28.1	28.9	26.7
Andhra Pradesh	48.7	60.1	36.9	31.6	41.9	20.9	17.2	25.3	8.7	17.1	18.2	16.0	31.5	34.9	28.2
Arunachal Pradesh	53.7	61.4	40.6	57.3	66.3	41.4	34.5	44.0	24.9	-3.6	-4.9	-0.8	19.3	17.4	15.7
Assam	53.4	64.1	43.7	53.9	63.9	43.0	49.2	58.9	39.0	-0.5	0.2	0.7	4.2	5.2	4.7
Bihar	43.1	57.8	26.6	19.5	30.7	7.1	26.8	38.4	14.8	23.6	27.1	19.5	16.3	19.4	11.8
Goa	75.9	83.9	67.5	58.7	69.6	47.5	42.9	54.4	29.1	17.2	14.3	20.0	33.0	29.5	38.4
Gujarat	65.9	77.5	53.6	61.1	75.3	45.5	36.5	48.3	24.2	4.8	2.2	8.1	29.4	29.2	29.4
Haryana	59.8	73.2	44.3	39.2	52.1	24.2	NST	NST	NST	20.6	21.1	20.1	NST	NST	NST
Himachal Pradesh	68.6	79.8	57.2	53.2	65.0	41.0	47.1	62.7	31.2	15.4	14.8	16.2	21.5	17.1	26.0
Karnataka	60.6	71.7	49.1	38.1	49.7	26.0	36.0	48.0	23.6	22.5	22.0	23.1	24.6	23.8	25.5
Kerala	91.3	94.9	87.9	79.7	85.2	74.3	57.2	63.4	51.1	11.6	9.7	13.6	34.1	31.5	36.8
Madhya Pradesh	54.5	69.4	38.1	35.1	50.5	18.1	21.6	32.2	10.7	19.4	18.9	20.0	32.9	37.2	27.4
Maharashtra	63.4	80.4	57.0	35.1	50.5	18.1	36.8	49.1	24.0	28.3	29.9	38.9	26.6	31.3	33.0
Manipur	63.4	76.8	49.3	56.4	65.3	47.4	53.6	62.4	44.5	7.0	11.5	1.9	9.8	14.4	4.8
Meghalaya	62.9	69.3	53.8	44.3	54.5	31.2	46.7	49.8	43.6	18.6	14.8	22.6	16.2	19.5	10.2
Mizoram	75.2	75.4	73.9	77.9	77.5	81.3	82.7	86.7	78.7	-2.7	-2.1	-7.3	-7.5	-11.3	-4.8
Nagaland	69.0	74.8	57.1	NSC	NSC	NSC	60.6	66.3	54.5	NSC	NSC	NSC	8.4	8.5	2.6
Orissa	61.6	75.6	47.0	36.8	52.4	20.7	22.3	34.4	10.5	24.8	23.2	26.3	39.3	41.2	36.5
Punjab	65.1	71.7	57.7	41.1	49.8	31.0	NST	NST	NST	24.0	21.9	26.7	NST	NST	NST

(Table 7A.2 Contd.)

(Table 7A.2 Contd.)

States	Non-scheduled (NSD)			Scheduled Castes (SC)			Scheduled Tribes (ST)			Gap between NSD and SC			Gap between NSD and ST		
	Persons	Males	Females	Persons	Males	Females	Persons	Males	Females	Persons	Males	Females	Persons	Males	Females
Rajasthan	44.8	61.8	26.1	26.3	42.4	8.3	19.4	33.4	4.4	18.5	19.4	17.8	25.4	28.4	21.7
Sikkim	56.8	65.9	45.9	51	58.7	42.8	59.0	66.8	50.4	5.8	7.2	3.1	-2.2	-0.9	-4.5
Tamil Nadu	66.8	77.8	55.6	46.7	58.4	34.9	27.9	35.3	20.2	20.1	19.4	20.7	38.9	42.5	35.4
Tripura	72.8	81.3	63.7	56.7	67.3	45.5	40.4	52.9	27.3	16.1	14.0	18.2	32.4	28.4	36.4
Uttar Pradesh	45.5	59.7	29.1	26.8	40.8	10.7	35.7	50.0	19.9	18.7	18.9	18.4	9.8	9.7	9.2
West Bengal	65.0	74.1	54.9	42.2	54.6	25.9	27.8	40.1	15.0	22.8	19.5	29.0	37.2	34.0	39.9
CV	19.2	12.8	32.4	47.4	31.7	82.6	64.5	48.8	106.6						

Source: Census of India, 2001.

NSC/NST = Non-scheduled Castes/Non-scheduled Tribes enumerated in the state.

Table 7A.3
Literacy Rates and Inter-group Gaps by Social Groups and Sex, 2001

	Non-scheduled (NSD)			Scheduled Castes (SC)			Scheduled Tribes (ST)			Gap between NSD and SC			Gap between NSD and ST		
	Persons	Males	Females	Persons	Males	Females	Persons	Males	Females	Persons	Males	Females	Persons	Males	Females
All India	68.8	78.7	58.2	54.7	66.6	41.9	47.1	59.2	34.8	14.1	12.1	16.3	21.7	19.5	23.4
Andhra Pradesh	63.8	73.6	53.9	53.5	63.5	43.3	37.0	47.7	26.1	10.3	10.1	10.5	26.8	25.9	27.8
Arunachal Pradesh	62.5	71.2	49.9	67.6	76.3	55.0	49.6	58.8	40.6	-5.1	-5.2	-5.1	12.9	12.4	9.3
Assam	63.1	70.7	54.7	66.8	75.7	57.1	62.5	72.3	52.4	-3.7	-5.0	-2.4	0.5	-1.6	2.3
Bihar	52.8	65.8	38.6	30.3	42.5	17.0	39.5	52.6	26.1	22.5	23.4	21.6	13.4	13.3	12.4
Goa	82.2	88.5	75.6	71.9	81.6	62.1	55.9	63.5	47.3	10.3	7.0	13.6	26.3	25.1	28.3
Gujarat	72.9	83.0	61.9	70.5	82.6	57.6	47.7	59.2	36.0	2.4	0.5	4.3	25.2	23.8	25.9
Haryana	70.8	81.2	58.9	55.4	66.9	42.3	NST	NST	NST	15.4	14.3	16.6	NST	NST	NST
Himachal Pradesh	79.2	87.6	70.6	70.3	80.0	60.4	65.5	77.7	53.3	8.9	7.6	10.3	13.7	9.9	17.3
Jammu and Kashmir	57.5	68.7	44.8	59.0	69.6	47.5	37.5	48.2	25.5	-1.5	-0.9	-2.6	20.0	20.5	19.3
Karnataka	71.0	80.0	61.7	52.9	63.8	41.7	48.3	59.7	36.6	18.1	16.2	19.9	22.7	20.3	25.1
Kerala	92.1	95.2	89.2	82.7	88.1	77.6	64.4	70.8	58.1	9.4	7.2	11.6	27.8	24.4	31.1
Madhya Pradesh	71.6	83.4	58.8	59.7	73.6	44.6	45.1	57.6	32.4	11.9	9.8	14.2	26.5	25.8	26.3
Maharashtra	79.7	88.2	70.5	71.9	83.3	60.0	55.2	67.0	43.1	7.8	4.9	10.5	24.5	21.2	27.4
Manipur	73.0	84.2	61.6	72.3	81.8	63.0	65.9	73.2	58.4	0.7	2.4	-1.4	7.1	11.0	3.2
Meghalaya	70.0	75.7	62.9	56.3	65.9	45.2	61.3	63.5	59.2	13.7	9.8	17.7	8.7	12.2	3.7
Mizoram	80.2	80.2	80.2	89.2	88.4	92.2	89.3	91.7	86.9	-9.0	-8.2	-12.0	-9.2	-11.5	-6.8
Nagaland	71.9	77.1	62.6	NSC	NSC	NSC	65.9	70.3	61.3	NSC	NSC	NSC	5.9	6.9	1.3
Orissa	73.9	84.6	62.7	55.5	70.5	40.3	37.4	51.5	23.4	18.3	14.1	22.4	36.5	33.1	39.4

(Table 7A.3 Contd.)

(Table 7A.3 Contd.)

	Non-scheduled (NSD)			Scheduled Castes (SC)			Scheduled Tribes (ST)			Gap between NSD and SC			Gap between NSD and ST		
	Persons	Males	Females	Persons	Males	Females	Persons	Males	Females	Persons	Males	Females	Persons	Males	Females
Punjab	74.9	79.8	69.3	56.2	63.4	48.3	NST	NST	NST	18.7	16.4	21.1	NST	NST	NST
Rajasthan	65.0	79.6	49.2	52.2	69.0	33.9	44.7	62.1	26.2	12.8	10.6	15.4	20.4	17.5	23.1
Sikkim	69.7	77.0	60.8	63.0	70.2	55.7	67.1	73.8	60.2	6.6	6.8	5.1	2.5	3.2	0.7
Tamil Nadu	76.2	84.9	67.5	63.2	73.4	53.0	41.5	50.2	32.8	13.1	11.5	14.5	34.7	34.8	34.7
Tripura	82.3	88.1	76.0	74.7	81.8	67.2	56.5	68.0	44.6	7.6	6.2	8.8	25.8	20.1	31.4
Uttar Pradesh	59.7	71.7	46.2	47.0	61.0	31.3	55.3	68.4	41.4	12.7	10.7	14.9	4.4	3.3	4.9
West Bengal	73.6	80.5	66.0	59.0	70.5	46.9	43.4	57.4	29.2	14.5	9.9	19.1	30.2	23.1	36.9
CV	12.8	9.1	20.0	31.7	26.5	43.7	41.1	34.4	55.8						

Source: Census of India, 1991.

NSC/NST = Non-scheduled Castes/Non-scheduled Tribes enumerated in the state.

Note: In order to facilitate temporal comparisons, the figures for Bihar, Madhya Pradesh and Uttar Pradesh pertain to their respective boundaries as in 1991.

Table 7A.4
Decadal Change in Literacy Rates, 1991–2001

States	Non-SC/ST			Scheduled Castes (SC)			Scheduled Tribes (ST)		
	Persons	Males	Females	Persons	Males	Females	Persons	Males	Females
All India	11.1	9.2	13.4	17.3	16.7	18.1*	17.5	18.5	16.7
Andhra Pradesh	15.2	13.5	17.0	21.9	21.6	22.4	19.9	22.4	17.4
Arunachal Pradesh	8.8	9.8	9.3	10.3	10.0	13.6	15.2	14.8	15.7
Assam	9.7	6.6	11.0	12.9	11.8	14.1	13.3	13.4	13.4
Bihar	9.7	8.1	12.0	10.8	11.8	9.9	12.7	14.2	11.3
Goa	6.3	4.6	8.1	13.2	12.0	14.6	13.0	9.1	18.2
Gujarat	7.0	5.5	8.3	9.4	7.3	12.1	11.2	10.9	11.8
Haryana	11.0	8.0	14.6	16.2	14.8	18.1	NST	NST	NST
Himachal Pradesh	10.6	7.8	13.4	17.1	15.0	19.4	18.4	15.0	22.1
Karnataka	10.4	8.3	12.6	14.8	14.1	15.7	12.3	11.7	13.0
Kerala	0.8	0.3	1.3	3.0	2.9	3.3	7.2	7.4	7.0
Madhya Pradesh	17.1	14.0	20.7	24.6	23.1	26.5	23.5	25.4	21.7
Maharashtra	16.3	7.8	13.5	36.8	32.8	41.9	18.4	17.9	19.1
Manipur	9.6	7.4	12.3	15.9	16.5	15.6	12.3	10.8	13.9
Meghalaya	7.1	6.4	9.1	12.0	11.4	14.0	14.6	13.7	15.6
Mizoram	5.0	4.8	6.3	11.3	10.9	10.9	6.6	5.0	8.2
Nagaland	2.9	2.3	5.5	NSC	NSC	NSC	5.3	4.0	6.8
Orissa	12.3	9.0	15.7	18.7	18.1	19.6	15.1	17.1	12.9
Punjab	9.8	8.1	11.6	15.1	13.6	17.3	NST	NST	NST
Rajasthan	20.2	17.8	23.1	25.9	26.6	25.6	25.3	28.7	21.7
Sikkim	12.9	11.1	14.9	12.0	11.5	12.9	8.1	7.0	9.8
Tamil Nadu	9.4	7.1	11.9	16.5	15.0	18.1	13.6	14.9	12.6
Tripura	9.5	6.8	12.3	18.0	14.5	21.7	16.1	15.1	17.3
Uttar Pradesh	14.2	12.0	17.1	20.2	20.2	20.6	19.6	18.4	21.5
West Bengal	8.6	6.4	11.1	16.8	15.9	21.0	15.6	17.3	14.2

Source: Census of India, 1991 and 2001.
NSC/NST = Non-scheduled Castes/Non-scheduled Tribes enumerated in the state.
Note: In order to facilitate temporal comparisons, the figures for Bihar, Madhya Pradesh and Uttar Pradesh pertain to their boundaries as in 1991.

Table 7A.5
Educational Attainment by Age and Levels for Social Groups, 2001

Educational Levels	Age Groups					
	7–9 Years	*10–14 Years*	*15–19 Years*	*20–24 Years*	*25+ Years*	*All Ages*
Scheduled Castes (SC)						
Literate without formal education	1.2	1.1	2.5	4.1	7.0	4.10
Up to primary level	98.8	87.5	41.0	37.3	49.5	61.2
Middle level	0.0	10.4	30.2	22.4	17.2	16.3
Secondary level	0.0	0.0	20.8	17.0	13.5	10.4
Higher secondary level	0.0	0.0	5.2	12.5	5.9	4.5
Under-graduate	0.0	0.0	0.2	1.0	0.6	0.4
Technical diploma	0.0	0.0	0.0	0.1	0.0	0.0
Non-technical diploma	0.0	0.0	0.2	0.9	0.6	0.4
Graduate and above	0.0	0.0	0.0	5.7	6.3	3.1
All literate and educated	68.0	78.5	73.5	63.0	39.6	54.7
Scheduled Tribes (ST)						
Literate without formal education	1.3	1.5	3.4	5.6	9.9	5.5
Up to primary level	98.7	89.8	45.8	41.3	53.6	65.1
Middle level	0.0	8.7	28.7	20.7	14.2	14.1
Secondary level	0.0	0.0	17.9	15.9	11.7	8.9
Higher secondary level	0.0	0.0	3.9	11.4	5.1	3.8
Under-graduate	0.0	0.0	0.2	0.7	0.6	0.3
Technical diploma	0.0	0.0	0.2	0.7	0.5	0.3
Non-technical diploma	0.0	0.0	0.0	0.0	0.0	0.0
Graduate and above	0.0	0.0	0.0	4.3	5.0	2.4
All literate and educated	59.0	69.6	63.7	53.8	50.0	47.1
Non-SC/ST Population						
Literate without formal education	1.2	1.1	1.5	3.3	4.5	3.4
Up to primary level	98.8	84.1	30.0	27.2	36.6	49.5
Middle level	0.0	14.8	28.8	18.7	16.1	16.2
Secondary level	0.0	0.0	29.1	20.1	18.5	15.1
Higher secondary level	0.0	0.0	9.6	17.8	10.0	7.3
Under-graduate	0.0	0.0	0.4	1.5	1.2	0.8
Technical diploma	0.0	0.0	0.0	0.1	0.1	0.1
Non-technical diploma	0.0	0.0	0.4	1.4	1.1	0.7
Graduate and above	0.0	0.0	0.0	11.5	12.7	7.6
All literate and educated	73.2	83.9	82.1	77.2	62.7	68.8

Source: Census of India, 2001.

Table 7A.6
Educational Attainment for Population Aged 15+ Years by Social Groups and Sex, 2001

Educational Levels	Non-SC/ST		Scheduled Castes		Scheduled Tribes	
	Male	*Female*	*Male*	*Female*	*Male*	*Female*
1 Graduate and above	8.8	4.6	3.4	1.0	2.2	0.8
2 Graduate degree other than technical	68.2	67.5	69.6	70.0	71.4	72.2
3 Post-graduate degree other than technical	17.3	21.0	18.6	18.9	16.9	16.1
4 Technical degrees						
a) Engineering and technology	8.6	4.0	5.1	3.6	4.4	2.3
b) Medicine	2.2	1.9	1.4	2.1	1.6	2.0
c) Agriculture and dairying	0.4	0.1	0.3	0.1	0.5	0.2
d) Veterinary	0.1	0.1	0.1	0.0	0.1	0.1
5 Teaching	3.3	5.5	4.4	7.1	6.2	7.2
6 Others	0.1	0.1	0.1	0.2	0.1	0.1

Source: Census of India, 2001.

Table 7A.7
School Attendance Rates among Children Aged 5 to 14 Years by Social Groups (NSSO, Different Rounds)

Social Groups	School Attendance Rates				
	1983	*1987–1988*	*1993–1994*	*1999–2000*	*Census 2001*
			Male (Rural)		
SC	48.9	49.8	64.3	70.1	71.1
ST	39.5	44.5	57.9	63.2	64.1
Non-SC/ST	59.2	63.4	74.9	80.2	75.1
			Male (Urban)		
SC	66.7	68.2	77.5	79.2	77.9
ST	67.0	67.2	79.7	80.9	78.7
Non-SC/ST	76.5	78.0	86.8	88.0	83.0
			Female (Rural)		
SC	25.5	31.1	46.2	58.6	59.4
ST	20.4	26.2	40.9	52.7	50.5
Non-SC/ST	39.2	45.8	61.0	73.8	65.3
			Female (Urban)		
SC	52.3	53.8	68.6	73.9	73.8
ST	52.7	62.3	69.7	74.0	73.4
Non-SC/ST	69.1	72.6	83.0	85.4	81.2

Source: NSSO, Various Reports, Census of India, 2001.

Table 7A.8
School Attendance Rates among Children in Age Group of 5–14 Years in Rural Areas (NSSO, 1993–1994)

States	SC		ST		NSD		Gap between NSD and SC		Gap between NSD and ST	
	Boys	*Girls*	*Boys*	*Girls*	*Boys*	*Girls*	*Boys*	*Girls*	*Boys*	*Girls*
Andhra Pradesh	64.4	44.5	43.8	27.1	71.7	56.0	7.3	11.5	27.9	28.9
Assam	75.4	70.8	80.7	77.9	75.9	71.7	0.5	0.9	−4.8	−6.2
Bihar	46.0	22.5	50.8	29.8	63.5	44.1	17.5	21.6	12.7	14.3
Gujarat	77.5	65.3	70.3	57.3	78.6	62.6	1.1	−2.7	8.3	5.3
Haryana	76.6	56.6	£	£	85.0	71.7	8.4	15.1	£	£
Himachal	87.6	82.1	87.5	57.9	91.8	83.9	4.2	1.8	4.3	26.0
Jammu and Kashmir	87.5	63.9	34.3	16.6	85.0	75.7	−2.5	11.8	50.7	59.1
Karnataka	65.7	40.5	66.9	53.3	76.2	67.6	10.5	27.1	9.3	14.3
Kerala	96.0	88.5	65.2	67.7	92.9	94.0	−3.1	5.5	27.7	26.3
Madhya Pradesh	57.6	37.0	48.6	34.2	70.4	52.5	12.8	15.5	21.8	18.3
Maharashtra	83.8	72.8	67.1	56.8	86.4	76.7	2.6	3.9	19.3	19.9
Orissa	67.9	43.9	51.0	32.3	76.5	68.0	8.6	24.1	25.5	35.7
Punjab	68.6	59.2	£	£	88.4	83.6	19.8	24.4	£	£
Rajasthan	58.1	21.5	54.7	16.6	76.8	41.1	18.7	19.6	22.1	24.5
Tamil Nadu	76.9	71.2	76.9	72.1	85.6	76.6	8.7	5.4	8.7	4.5
Tripura	87.9	83.2	76.1	73.6	86.7	86.6	−1.2	3.4	10.6	13.0
Uttar Pradesh	59.7	31.5	66.2	34.5	69.9	49.4	10.2	17.9	3.7	14.9
West Bengal	67.9	56.9	47.1	38.7	71.1	65.9	3.2	9.0	24.0	27.2
CV	18.0	36.5	24.3	43.7	10.6	22.0				

Source: NSSO, 50th round (Report No. 425), Government of India.
£ = No ST enumerated in the state.

Table 7A.9

Age-specific Attendance Ratio by Social Groups, Census 2001

States	Age Group	Non-SC/ST		Scheduled Castes		Scheduled Tribes		Gap between Non-SC/ST and SC		Gap between Non-SC/ST and ST	
		Males	Females	Males	Females	Males	Females	Males	Females	Males	Females
All India	6–11	72.6	65.9	69.4	61.7	63.7	53.5	3.20	4.19	8.90	12.4
	12–14	77.6	64.6	72.7	57.1	64.5	47.5	4.86	7.53	13.06	17.1
Andhra Pradesh	6–11	85.0	80.6	84.1	78.2	73.8	61.8	0.87	2.43	11.16	18.8
	12–14	75.4	60.1	72.7	54.0	61.7	37.5	2.63	6.15	13.65	22.6
Assam	6–11	60.3	57.1	70.3	66.8	68.7	65.4	–9.99	–9.71	–8.39	–8.3
	12–14	64.0	61.8	71.1	66.0	75.9	70.6	–7.07	–4.15	–11.93	–8.8
Bihar	6–11	50.5	39.1	35.6	22.8	31.9	20.0	14.95	16.34	18.62	19.1
	12–14	62.9	45.6	45.9	25.3	43.4	22.6	16.95	20.25	19.51	23.0
Gujarat	6–11	82.7	74.1	86.0	81.2	67.6	59.2	–3.29	–7.13	15.08	14.9
	12–14	79.8	60.7	84.2	68.4	64.1	50.2	–4.41	–7.73	15.63	10.5
Haryana	6–11	80.3	74.6	73.1	67.0	£	£	7.22	7.62	£	£
	12–14	88.4	76.9	78.6	64.4	£	£	9.79	12.54	£	£
Himachal Pradesh	6–11	92.0	90.6	89.9	87.8	88.8	85.4	2.09	2.88	3.14	5.2
	12–14	96.1	93.6	93.6	89.0	93.3	84.9	2.44	4.62	2.79	8.7
Jammu and Kashmir	6–11	65.5	55.4	75.9	67.4	50.5	37.3	–10.37	–12.05	15.03	18.1
	12–14	77.2	60.8	82.1	69.0	60.9	39.8	–4.90	–8.14	16.30	21.0
Karnataka	6–11	80.9	77.8	75.0	68.0	71.1	63.6	5.86	9.80	9.79	14.1
	12–14	77.4	67.5	68.6	52.8	62.8	46.8	8.79	14.76	14.56	20.7
Kerala	6–11	93.9	94.1	93.4	93.7	82.0	82.2	0.48	0.40	11.94	11.9
	12–14	97.1	97.3	94.7	95.1	78.0	77.9	2.43	2.19	19.10	19.4

(Table 7A.9 Contd.)

(Table 7A.9 Contd.)

States	Age Group	Non-SC/ST		Scheduled Castes		Scheduled Tribes		Gap between Non-SC/ST and SC		Gap between Non-SC/ST and ST	
		Males	Females	Males	Females	Males	Females	Males	Females	Males	Females
Madhya Pradesh	6–11	78.9	71.2	74.2	65.4	56.9	45.7	4.78	5.86	21.99	25.6
	12–14	83.4	64.1	79.8	58.1	56.6	36.7	3.56	6.06	26.79	27.5
Maharashtra	6–11	88.3	86.6	87.0	85.2	76.4	70.9	1.23	1.44	11.89	15.7
	12–14	89.7	84.1	88.0	81.7	73.0	61.5	1.67	2.45	16.67	22.6
Orissa	6–11	81.0	76.4	72.3	63.3	57.2	42.9	8.67	13.09	23.80	33.5
	12–14	79.7	70.5	70.0	52.8	55.2	35.2	9.69	17.73	24.49	35.3
Punjab	6–11	84.3	82.2	74.3	71.0	£	£	9.97	11.20	£	£
	12–14	87.6	83.9	73.7	68.1	£	£	13.81	15.80	£	£
Rajasthan	6–11	80.9	65.5	73.4	55.3	70.0	48.8	7.53	10.17	10.89	16.7
	12–14	84.7	52.4	75.7	41.0	72.0	36.7	8.99	11.37	12.65	15.7
Tamil Nadu	6–11	91.0	89.9	90.7	89.5	70.5	64.6	0.31	0.46	20.50	25.3
	12–14	84.6	79.9	84.3	79.8	59.8	49.2	0.36	0.12	24.84	30.7
Uttar Pradesh	6–11	64.8	55.1	65.3	56.1	50.1	34.7	-0.52	-0.99	14.67	20.3
	12–14	75.2	57.0	73.5	53.7	55.9	31.1	1.66	3.28	19.28	25.9
West Bengal	6–11	70.9	70.0	72.4	67.0	61.5	51.8	-1.57	2.95	9.38	18.2
	12–14	71.5	71.2	70.2	60.6	62.4	45.4	1.29	10.65	9.07	25.8
CV	6–11	14.9	19.7	17.0	23.1	21.1	31.1				
	12–14	11.6	19.9	14.3	26.3	17.7	35.7				

Source: Census of India, 2001.

£ = No ST population enumerated in the state.

Table 7A.10
School Dropout Rates by Stages of Education and Social Groups, 2002

	I–V Boys			I–V Girls			I–VIII Boys			I–VIII Girls		
States	*All*	*SC*	*ST*	*All*	*SC*	*ST*	*All*	*SC*	*ST*	*All*	*SC*	*ST*
All India	38	44	51	40	47	54	53	59	67	57	64	73
Andhra Pradesh	43	47	66	43	50	72	61	67	68	65	74	65
Assam	47	49	63	51	49	57	68	67	71	71	67	75
Bihar	61	54	65	63	57	70	74	83	82	77	84	85
Gujarat	27	31	37	22	36	37	50	56	73	56	71	78
Haryana	30	32	★	31	33	★	8	35	★	17	49	★
Himachal Pradesh	15	24	27	18	27	30	21	35	28	23	38	37
Jammu and Kashmir	32	39	35	25	35	37	32	50	79	27	47	79
Karnataka	24	1	14	24	11	12	51	55	57	51	60	57
Kerala	0	0	13	0	0	12	0	0	21	0	0	27
Madhya Pradesh	29	25	37	30	23	41	46	45	60	55	57	66
Maharashtra	6	6	32	9	11	37	35	33	60	39	44	67
Orissa	39	47	58	40	57	62	62	66	51	60	74	66
Punjab	21	31	★	19	28		35	52	★	39	52	★
Rajasthan	55	64	64	74	84	81	47	49	53	65	71	73
Tamil Nadu	30	33	56	24	26	46	44	43	57	35	39	31
Tripura	50	45	63	51	46	67	69	65	80	69	69	81
Uttar Pradesh	46	53	30	55	64	28	56	68	39	67	80	37
West Bengal	39	49	54	40	55	58	68	63	83	74	64	81
Delhi	27	0	64	28	0	82	10	58	79	23	57	85

Source: Selected Educational Statistics, various years, MHRD, New Delhi, 2002.
★ No ST.

Table 7A.11
Participation and Coefficient of Equality in Higher Education for Scheduled Castes

	Participation in				Coefficient of Equality			
	Higher Education		Technical Education★		All Higher Education		Technical Education	
States	*1991*	*2001*	*1991*	*2001*	*1991*	*2001*	*1991*	*2001*
All India	7.43	10.29	6.47	7.23	0.45	0.64	0.40	0.45
Andhra Pradesh	11.29	13.90	10.08	12.13	0.71	0.86	0.63	0.75
Assam	7.45	8.80	5.46	10.72	1.01	1.28	0.74	1.55

(Table 7A.11 Contd.)

136   Sachidanand Sinha

(Table 7A.11 Contd.)

States	Participation in Higher Education 1991	2001	Technical Education* 1991	2001	CoE All Higher Education 1991	2001	CoE Technical Education 1991	2001
Bihar	N.A.	5.58	N.A.	3.42	N.A.	0.36	N.A.	0.22
Gujarat	7.24	15.23	5.26	5.38	0.98	2.14	0.71	0.76
Haryana	5.65	9.45	16.95	3.93	0.29	0.48	0.86	0.20
Himachal Pradesh	7.33	12.55	13.32	8.96	0.29	0.51	0.53	0.36
Jammu and Kashmir	N.A.	0.00	N.A.	0.00	N.A.	0.00	N.A.	0.00
Karnataka	N.A.	12.74	3.96	5.89	N.A.	0.79	0.24	0.36
Kerala	6.41	9.63	6.75	6.52	0.65	0.98	0.68	0.66
Madhya Pradesh	7.27	8.99	10.20	6.34	0.50	0.59	0.70	0.42
Maharashtra	8.25	9.85	5.73	1.72	0.74	0.97	0.52	0.17
Orissa	6.36	9.34	9.22	8.53	0.39	0.57	0.57	0.52
Punjab	11.75	12.07	18.55	7.80	0.42	0.42	0.66	0.27
Rajasthan	N.A.	10.34	N.A.	19.17	N.A.	0.60	N.A.	1.11
Tamil Nadu	12.93	18.62	10.01	10.98	0.67	0.98	0.52	0.58
Tripura	11.45	15.79	15.80	16.97	0.70	0.91	0.97	0.98
Uttar Pradesh	11.61	14.08	4.80	22.03	0.55	0.67	0.23	1.04
West Bengal	7.49	11.70	5.94	8.04	0.32	0.51	0.25	0.35
Delhi	5.76	10.28	11.27	8.74	0.30	0.61	0.59	0.52

Source: Census of India, 1991 and 2001.
* Degree courses only.
Note: N.A. means not available.

Table 7A.12
Participation and Coefficient of Equality in Higher Education for Scheduled Tribes

States Years	All Higher Education 1991	2001	Technical Education* 1991	2001	CoE All Higher Education 1991	2001	CoE Technical Education 1991	2001
All India	2.05	3.57	1.48	5.29	0.25	0.44	0.18	0.65
Andhra Pradesh	1.51	3.64	2.04	4.24	0.23	0.55	0.31	0.64
Assam	8.24	12.67	9.07	10.89	0.66	1.02	0.73	0.88
Bihar	N.A.	3.14	N.A.	4.84	N.A.	0.44	N.A.	0.68
Gujarat	7.41	7.27	2.64	6.03	0.50	0.49	0.18	0.41

(Table 7A.12 Contd.)

(Table 7A.12 Contd.)

| | Coefficient of Equality | | | | | | | |
| States | All Higher Education | | Technical Education* | | All Higher Education | | Technical Education | |
Years	1991	2001	1991	2001	1991	2001	1991	2001
Haryana	N.A.	N.A.	N.A.	N.A.	N.A.	N.A.	N.A.	N.A.
Himachal Pradesh	2.83	4.07	6.39	5.38	0.70	1.01	1.59	1.34
Jammu and Kashmir	N.A.	0.00	N.A.	0.00	N.A.	0.00	N.A.	0.00
Karnataka	N.A.	3.59	0.94	1.56	N.A.	0.55	0.14	0.24
Kerala	0.33	0.82	0.59	0.84	0.29	0.72	0.52	0.74
Madhya Pradesh	4.80	11.84	5.70	8.53	0.21	0.51	0.25	0.37
Maharashtra	1.69	3.00	1.20	0.77	0.19	0.34	0.14	0.09
Orissa	5.15	8.17	10.46	11.57	0.23	0.37	0.47	0.52
Punjab	0.00	0.00	0.00	0.00	N.A.	N.A.	N.A.	N.A.
Rajasthan	N.A.	7.18	N.A.	2.30	N.A.	0.57	N.A.	0.18
Tamil Nadu	0.25	1.67	0.72	11.61	0.24	1.60	0.69	11.12
Tripura	4.25	9.64	15.20	25.98	0.14	0.31	0.49	0.84
Uttar Pradesh	0.35	0.27	0.50	1.18	1.74	1.37	2.49	5.89
West Bengal	0.32	1.47	0.59	0.17	0.06	0.27	0.11	0.03
Delhi	0.51	1.95	1.45	3.56	N.A.	N.A.	N.A.	N.A.

Source: Census of India, 1991 and 2001.
* Degree courses only.
Note: N.A. means not available.

Table 7A.13
Rural Households with No Literate Member Aged 15+ Years by MPCE and Social Groups, NSS, 1999–2000

| MPCE Class (₹) | Households with No Literate Member | | | Households with No Literate Female Member | | | Per Cent Distribution of Persons in Households with No Literate Member | | |
	SC	ST	Non-SC/ST	SC	ST	Non-SC/ST	SC	ST	Non-SC/ST
< 225	53.9	64.2	43.8	82.2	87.5	64.7	16.6	25.9	12.1
225–255	49.9	59.9	43.0	79.9	82.4	66.2	9.9	14.3	9.1
255–300	46.8	51.8	29.1	78.4	77.5	59.8	15.6	13.6	11.6
300–340	44.3	47.5	24.5	75.9	76.0	54.7	14.2	12.1	11.5
340–380	41.4	47.7	24.7	73.5	77.9	49.4	11.6	10.3	11.7
380–420	39.3	44.8	22.2	70.3	74.2	49.7	8.5	7.1	9.9
420–470	38.1	39.2	20.5	71.1	68.6	45.7	7.8	6.0	10.8

(Table 7A.13 Contd.)

(Table 7A.13 Contd.)

MPCE Class (₹)	Households with No Literate Member			Households with No Literate Female Member			Per Cent Distribution of Persons in Households with No Literate Member		
	SC	ST	Non-SC/ST	SC	ST	Non-SC/ST	SC	ST	Non-SC/ST
470–525	35.9	40.6	17.3	65.9	69.3	41.5	5.8	4.2	7.1
525–615	36.0	37.3	14.4	66.8	61.2	38.3	5.0	3.8	6.6
615–775	32.7	28.4	14.0	62.6	51.8	36.2	3.3	1.8	5.6
775–950	28.5	35.3	10.8	57.5	60.8	33.7	1.2	0.8	2.1
950 and more	17.6	17.0	7.5	54.6	57.1	32.3	0.5	0.4	1.9
All	41.3	47.6	19.8	72.4	74.5	44.9	100.0	100.0	100.0

Source: NSSO, 55th round.

Table 7A.14
Availability of Primary Schools in Rural Habitations

States/Union Territories	Habitations Per Cent Change 1993–2002	Habitations with Primary Schools				Per Cent Increase in Schools	
		Within Per Cent		Up to 1 km		Within	Up to 1 km
		1993	2002	1993	2002	1993–2002	
All India	16.1	49.8	53.0	83.4	87.0	23.68	21.13
Andhra Pradesh	5.8	69.7	78.5	88.6	93.9	19.05	12.13
Assam	63.0	54.5	44.6	85.7	84.3	33.26	60.40
Bihar	12.7	58.2	56.7	92.3	88.9	9.83	8.54
Gujarat	29.2	90.4	77.9	95.8	93.6	11.3	26.28
Haryana	16.5	82.5	78.2	93.0	91.9	10.5	15.06
Himachal Pradesh	2.4	21.0	28.8	59.4	75.0	40.57	29.18
Jammu and Kashmir	37.6	59.8	50.6	80.5	78.6	16.47	34.35
Karnataka	6.2	60.4	67.4	83.8	88.4	18.69	12.14
Kerala	–23.8	61.6	60.7	82.2	79.5	–24.92	–26.37
Madhya Pradesh	19.6	58.3	69.0	81.1	89.2	41.53	31.51
Maharashtra	7.4	64.7	67.6	84.2	91.2	12.24	16.21
Orissa	22.6	49.0	51.5	82.4	82.9	29.07	23.36
Punjab	10.3	80.8	79.3	95.7	93.5	8.22	7.74
Rajasthan	26.6	51.1	53.4	74.6	79.8	32.34	35.56
Tamil Nadu	19.6	53.5	53.9	98.6	88.5	20.63	7.29

(Table 7A.14 Contd.)

(Table 7A.14 Contd.)

States/Union Territories	Habitations	Habitations with Primary Schools				Per Cent Increase in Schools	
	Per Cent Change	Within Per Cent		Up to 1 km		Within	Up to 1 km
	1993–2002	1993	2002	1993	2002	1993–2002	
Tripura	11.1	38.5	37.5	75.5	75.9	8.25	11.65
Uttar Pradesh	9.2	29.3	40.6	80.5	88.0	50.94	19.36
West Bengal	19.9	38.3	35.3	87.7	92.3	10.47	26.14
Delhi	–33.9	65.3	59.8	86.3	100.0	–39.55	–23.5

Source: All India Educational Survey, 2002.

Table 7A.15
Pupil–Teacher Ratio and Schools with Single or No Teacher, 2002

States/Union Territories	Primary Schools			Upper Primary Schools			Rural Primary Schools with Teachers		
	Rural	Urban	Total	Rural	Urban	Total	None	One	Less than Two
All India	44	36	42	35	32	34	1.28	16.41	64.28
Andhra Pradesh	32	35	33	31	27	30	0.59	19.87	65.52
Assam	30	23	30	16	18	16	1.08	18.79	60.80
Bihar	85	60	83	77	51	73	3.62	24.33	83.70
Gujarat	28	37	31	38	40	38	5.31	14.55	89.20
Haryana	42	35	41	27	22	26	2.12	7.71	36.18
Himachal Pradesh	22	23	22	15	13	15	0.81	13.58	62.09
Jammu and Kashmir	21	11	19	20	14	18	1.54	22.00	77.90
Karnataka	26	28	26	37	37	37	2.85	20.36	74.45
Kerala	28	28	28	28	26	28	0.27	0.65	2.69
Madhya Pradesh	38	29	36	31	22	28	1.81	16.08	69.42
Maharashtra	30	46	36	35	42	37	0.00	25.50	77.34
Orissa	41	36	40	40	30	38	1.32	23.17	70.38
Punjab	39	36	38	17	24	18	3.65	16.95	53.80
Rajasthan	42	33	41	34	25	31	0.25	13.52	65.67
Tamil Nadu	35	33	34	42	38	40	0.00	0.00	63.28
Tripura	23	21	23	20	16	20	0.80	8.47	37.68
Uttar Pradesh	61	36	55	37	29	35	0.61	11.58	51.38
West Bengal	55	43	53	52	39	50	0.52	8.06	44.88
Delhi	38	40	40	26	27	27	0.00	0.00	0.90

Source: All India Educational Survey, 2002.

Chapter 8

HOUSING AND HOUSEHOLD AMENITIES

Sachidanand Sinha

Housing or shelter is one of the essential prerequisites of human development and a significant factor to determine the quality of life. In addition, access to household amenities such as safe drinking water, sanitation facilities and electricity are basic ingredients that are strongly associated with health and working status, as well as income, productivity and quality of life of individuals in particular and the society in general.

This chapter is based on the Census of India data on housing and household amenities. It examines the quantity and quality of housing stock and its availability across the social groups in order to determine the magnitude and nature of inequality, insofar as the access to housing and household amenities are concerned. It also examines the incidence of crowding of living spaces by cross-tabulating the size of households in terms of availability of rooms in every house covered in the Census of India. The quality of shelter has been measured by the condition of the house and the material utilised for construction. However, it needs to be emphasised that in the light of the larger context of social segmentation and caste-based residential segregation (as highlighted in Chapter 3), the question of shelter and quality of housing are associated with a variety of intangible elements that are difficult to reveal through statistical data. Many of the constituting factors which demarcate the living experience of a Scheduled Caste (SC) household, therefore, have to be reconstructed by going beyond the confines of collated statistical data presented either by the Census of India or by sample surveys. Nevertheless, there is no denying the fact that a house is a physical entity whose availability, quality and ownership may throw up a variety of public policy issues.

HOUSING STOCK

It is important to familiarise oneself with the definitions and methods employed by the Census of India during the course of enumeration. The term 'Census house' pertains to houses used for residential, partly residential and non-residential purposes. A question on the use to which a Census house was put to facilitates the classification of the Census houses as residential, partly residential and non-residential or vacant. In this chapter, occupied residential and partly residential and vacant Census houses constitute the 'housing stock'. Table 8.1 presents the temporal profile of the housing stock in the country. In order to make the figures comparable with the earliest Census data, the housing stocks for Assam, Jammu and Kashmir, and Goa; and the Union Territory of Daman and Diu were excluded as the Census of India figures for these states were not available for certain Census years. It was also not possible to estimate the housing stock for the social groups, as data which pertain to ownership of vacant houses during the time of house-listing were unavailable.

In 2001, the housing stock in India increased by about two and a half times as compared to that in 1961. Currently, the total housing stock stands at about 187 million, out of which 52 million or 28 per cent is located in urban areas. This figure apparently compares well with rural–urban distribution of population. However, one may also observe that there has been a sharp decline in the growth of housing stock since 1991. During 1991–2001, the housing stock increased by about 26 per cent for all areas which was down by about 4 percentage points from that observed during 1980s. The decline was even sharper in urban areas as compared to rural areas. It may also be noted that decadal growth in the number of Census houses other than non-residential Census houses was much higher than that of residential houses. A similar pattern was also observed in the case of houses that were partly residential. Given the fact that a large number of SC households belong to artisan classes, who carry out specialised production and repair occupations, they are likely to have a larger share of such houses. However, in view of the increasing unemployment rates and paucity of jobs, in both rural and urban areas, the tendency to establish a small shop or business from home, which is run by both men and women, as also the aged family members to supplement household incomes has also gained momentum in recent decades.

The index of housing shortage expressed as number of residential and partly residential Census houses per 1,000 households[1] increased from 933 in 1961 to 974 in 2001 for all areas, and from 899 to 969 in urban areas during the same period. In effect, about 2.5–3.0 per cent households do not have any shelter. This implies that such households do not have access to any private or public land whatsoever, and have to live under the open sky. Understandably, the share

---

[1] A household is defined as a group of persons who normally live together and take their meals from a common kitchen unless the exigencies of work prevent any of them from doing so. The persons living in a household may be related or unrelated or a mix of both. However, if a group of unrelated persons inhabit a Census house, but do not take their meals from a common kitchen, then they are not considered to constitute a common household. Each such person is then treated as a separate household, with the common kitchen, therefore, being the important and the constituting link for definitional purposes of a household. Households could be one-member, two-member or multi-member households.

Table 8.1
Growth of Housing Stock and Index of Housing Shortage (in Millions), 1961–2001

Years	Total			Rural			Urban		
	Residential/Partial Residential Census Houses**	Per cent Decadal Change	Index*	Residential/Partial Residential Census Houses	Per cent Decadal Change	Index*	Residential/Partial Residential Census Houses	Per cent Decadal Change	Index*
1961	76.20		933	62.44		940	13.76		899
1971	89.18	17.03	952	71.13	13.92	901	18.05	31.18	963
1981	110.74	24.18	943	83.96	18.04	941	26.78	48.37	947
1991	143.19	29.30	974	105.02	25.08	971	38.17	42.53	980
2001	180.26	25.90	974	129.55	23.35	976	50.81	33.11	969
2001***	187.06		974	135.09		977	52.06		969

Source: Census of India.

Notes: *Defined as number of residential/partly residential Census houses per 1,000 households.
**Excluding Assam, Jammu and Kashmir, Goa and Daman and Diu.
***Including Assam, Jammu and Kashmir, Goa and Daman and Diu.

of such households in metropolitan cities is likely to be higher than in other categories of towns and cities. However, what is intriguing is the fact that the number of homeless households in rural areas has remained virtually stagnant for over two decades in spite of several interventions made by the state to enhance access to housing through various rural housing projects such as the Indira Awaas Yojana (IAY) or the Pradhan Mantri Gramin Awaas Yojana (PMGAY) among others

CONDITION OF SHELTER

Access to housing is understood not only in terms of physical availability of shelter, but also with reference to quality of housing and the condition or the 'state of shelter'. The enquiry which relate to the condition of Census house was made only if the Census house was used for residential or partly residential purposes. Again, the condition of the Census house was ascertained only if a normal household occupied the Census house. Since the local conditions vary from place to place, even in rural and urban areas, it was not considered feasible to provide any single comprehensive definition for the terms used to determine the condition of a Census house. The condition of the Census houses was recorded as 'good', 'livable' and 'dilapidated' on the basis of perceptions and responses of the respondents. While this question was added as an additional feature in the Census operation during 2001, the earlier practice of enlisting houses on the basis of construction material was also continued. The classification of houses by materials from which roofs and walls are constructed allows them to be categorised as *pucca*, *kutcha* and semi-*pucca*. If both, walls and roof are made of *pucca* materials such as tiles, burnt bricks, corrugated sheets, stone and RBC/RCC or concrete, a house is categorised as *pucca*. On the other hand, if walls and roof of a house are made of materials such as grass, leaves, sunburnt bricks, bamboo, mud, wood, reeds or thatch, then the house is classified as *kutcha*. In all other cases, a house is classified as semi-*pucca*. For instance, the walls of a house may be made of burnt bricks, while the roof could be a mix of thatch overlaid by potters tiles or bamboo. Annexure VI Table 8A.1 provides the distribution of the condition of houses by social groups as perceived by inmates. It is clear that the percentage of SC households who live in dilapidated houses was the highest among the three social groups. The gap between SC and non-SC/ST households was larger by about 16 percentage points in favour of non-SC/ST households. Not more than 3 per cent non-SC/ST households lived in dilapidated houses in urban areas as compared to 6.4 per cent among SCs. The proportion of dilapidated houses was higher in rural areas. It must be emphasised here that the perceptions regarding the condition of house are governed and influenced by local conditions.

The inter-state variations in conditions of houses were no less significant. They varied from nearly 17 per cent SC households reported to be living in 'good' houses in Orissa, followed by Bihar and Assam, where nearly a quarter of SC households felt that they were living in 'good' houses, while the corresponding figure was 85 per cent in Tamil Nadu. As a matter of fact, most states have reported figures that are closer to all-India average with Tamil Nadu standing out as an exceptional case. The highest proportion of SC households who reported 'dilapidated' conditions of their homes were from Orissa, Bihar, Assam, Kerala and Delhi. The per capita state domestic product (SDP) does not seem to have any relationship with the condition of 'good' housing, though it may have some association with the magnitude of 'dilapidated' houses. More than a half of non-SC/ST households lived in 'good' houses. Their proportion was reported to be the highest in Tamil Nadu. In most of the relatively developed states, the proportion of non-SC/ST households who reported 'good' housing conditions was found to be higher. However, it needs to be ascertained as to whether the gap between SC and non-SC/ST households who live in 'good' houses bears any relationship with per capita SDP. If it does, then one may suggest that besides the income effect on housing, the benefits of special schemes for housing the poor such as schemes for the Economically Weaker Section (EWS) scheme floated by most developmental authorities could have gradually slipped into the hands of non-SC/ST and non-poor households.

QUALITY OF SHELTER

The perception of housing condition bears little relationship with the materials used for the construction of a house. The materials used for construction could be a good indicator of the durability of the house and the kind of security it provides to the residents. A *pucca* house is more durable and strong than a *kutcha* house, and may not require frequent maintenance. However, it is the combination of materials used for the construction of roof and walls that is of crucial importance in the context of housing. There are many options to cover the roofs and *pucca* materials used for this purpose may range from stone slabs, tiles, GI metal or asbestos sheets to concrete. Generally, the use of *pucca* materials is preferred to cover the roof, irrespective of the material used for the construction of walls. According to Annexure VI Table 8A.2 the percentage of Census houses that used *pucca* materials for the construction of roof far exceeded the comparable figure for walls. Most of the non-SC/ST households live in houses made of *pucca* roofs in urban areas, while the corresponding figure stands at nearly three-fourths in rural areas. On the other hand, about 65 per cent SC households in rural areas used *pucca* materials for the construction of roof while the corresponding figure for urban areas stood at 86.5 per cent. The percentage of houses having *pucca* walls, however, was much lower for SC and non-SC/ST households in rural as well as urban areas. Around two-fifths of the SC households in rural areas lived in houses that had *pucca* walls, whereas over one-half of non-SC/ST households were better off in this regard. The level of both the social groups registered an increase in urban areas where SC and non-SC/ST households stood at 70.1 and 85 percentage points, respectively.

The distribution of SC households in terms of their share of materials used for the construction of roofs and walls could be illuminating. Annexure VI Table 8A.3 shows that the share of SC households that used *kutcha* materials to cover the roofs was disproportionately higher than their share in the total number of households in rural and urban areas. Over one-fourth of all houses with roofs made of grass, thatched or those made of plastic and other such materials belonged to SCs while their share of concrete roof houses was just about 16.3 and 9.5 percentage points in rural and urban areas, respectively. The level of deprivation among SC households was strikingly greater even in urban areas. The use of materials such as asbestos sheets, plastic and polythene to cover roofs of houses may have health implications which have also been reported widely in literature. While both SC and non-SC/ST households are exposed to such hazards, the former are likely to be at a greater risk. The pattern was similar for the materials used for the construction of walls (see Annexure VI Table 8A.4). The inter-state variations in SC houses with *pucca* roofs and walls were perceptibly noticeable with Orissa having the lowest percentage of such houses, followed by Haryana, Assam and Bihar. The gap between non-SC/ST and SC households having *pucca* roofs was observed to be the highest in Jammu and Kashmir, Haryana, West Bengal and Bihar, while in the case of *pucca* walls, the gap between the two social groups was the highest in West Bengal, followed by Kerala, Bihar and Rajasthan. The urban areas indicated a higher magnitude of social disparity with Punjab being the forefront.

LIVING SPACE

The quality of housing is not only a function of how durable the house is, but more significantly, could also be a product of how much living space is available to the inmates. Living space or the number of rooms available to a household is yet another index of quality of housing, as it refers to the extent of crowding and privacy available to an individual for being able to lead a dignified life. Annexure VI Table 8A.5 shows the incidence of households who have no exclusive room to themselves, that is, households who share the living space with other households, which was negligible in 1991, had increased manifold during 2001. Over 4 per cent SC households had no exclusive room to themselves, while the comparable figure for non-SC/ST households was below 3 per cent.

Nearly four-fifths of the SC households lived in houses that had only two or lesser number of rooms, with a significant majority of them living in single rooms. On the other hand, the number of non-SC/ST households who live in houses that had more than two rooms was nearly twice that of SCs. This figure had increased since 1991 for non-SC/ST households, while it had declined in the case of SC households. These figures are indicative of crowding in the house that not only hampers the health of inmates, particularly children, but also simultaneously curbs the freedom of family members and thereby prevents them from organising their personal lives.

HOUSE TENURE

Another important feature of access to housing is revealed by the nature of house tenure, that is, whether the house is owned or has been rented in or is part of any other arrangement such as if it has been provided by the employer of the resident(s) or has been encroached on public or private land as in case of slums. Mostly SC households live in owned houses for economic and social reasons as they have little access to rental housing. During 1990s, the rental housing market did open up a little to include SCs, but it still remains smaller than the proportion of SCs in the total households, in both rural and urban areas. While the availability of rental housing may be a function of affordability, one still should not rule out the possibility of caste-based discrimination or exclusion, particularly when it comes to renting out the room space or a part of the house which constitutes the bulk of housing stock where SC households are observed to be living (see Annexure VI Table 8A.6). Studies have indicated that there is a strong relationship between housing tenure and access to household amenities. It has been observed that access to rental housing has a positive outcome on access to drinking water, electricity and sanitation, as a house equipped with these amenities that may be available within or in close proximity is likely to fetch better economic returns to the owner.

HOUSEHOLD AMENITIES

Access to safe drinking water, sanitation facilities and electricity are the three main household amenities which closely influence human productivity, performance, efficiency and overall quality of life. These amenities are proximately associated with health outcomes. All these three amenities are generally in short supply and available in inadequate quantity. The scarcity of these amenities invariably results in the acquisition of alternative sources that are poor in quality and have serious

Table 8.2
Percentage of Households Who Have Access to Household Amenities by Social Groups, All India, 1991 and 2001

Social Groups		SC			ST			Non-SC/ST		
Amenities	*Year*	*Total*	*Rural*	*Urban*	*Total*	*Rural*	*Urban*	*Total*	*Rural*	*Urban*
Safe drinking water	1991	63.6	59.8	80.6	43.2	41.1	65.7	64.1	56.4	82.0
	2001	81.1	78.5	90.4	61.7	58.7	82.5	79.2	74.1	90.4
Toilet	1991	11.16	5.15	38.28	7.22	4.1	40.68	28.63	11.52	68.38
	2001	23.7	15.1	54.5	17.0	11.1	57.7	42.3	25.8	78.0
Electricity	1991	28.1	21.8	56.3	22.8	19.7	55.9	48.1	34.6	79.3
	2001	44.3	35.1	77.4	36.5	30.4	78.1	61.4	48.2	89.9

Source: Census of India, 1991 and 2001.

health implications. The story of the dearth of drinking water is well known, but it is no less important to note that the lack of sanitation facilities leads to defecation in open spaces which not only posits serious sanitation problems, but also contains serious elements of social conflict, especially in urban areas where open spaces have been shrinking rapidly. The problem is no less acute in rural areas, as common village lands have been appropriated by influential households, while SCs who have little agricultural land to themselves have nowhere to go to ease themselves. The source of drinking water has for long remained the area of conflict between SCs and non-SCs/STs though the state of access to sources of drinking water has improved over the years (see Table 8.2; Annexure VI Table 8A.7).

Drinking Water

According to the Census of India, if a household has access to drinking water supplied from a tap, handpump or tube well situated within or outside the premises, the household is considered to have access to safe drinking water. In 2001, over 90 per cent urban SC households were reported to have access to safe drinking water which registered an improvement of about 10 percentage points since 1991. There was hardly any difference between SC and non-SC/ST households in urban areas though in rural areas, SC households were reported to have better access to drinking water in comparison with their non-SC/ST counterparts. Over 40 per cent households who belonged to the two social groups had no access to drinking water in rural areas. However, when the issue of access to various sources of safe drinking water is examined, one may find that SC households had lower access to tapwater, in both rural and urban areas. The dependence on handpumps and tube wells was greater for SCs as compared to non-SC/ST households. Similarly, SC households had to depend more on public taps or handpumps provided outside the premises. Insofar as the inter-state variations are concerned, Kerala and Bihar stand out as two contrasting cases. Kerala has a tradition of dependence on wells which are usually located within the premises of the house. This results in lower dependence of households on public water supply, especially in rural areas. Bihar, on the other hand, is the only state that shows a significant level of inequality between SC and non-SC/ST households with regard to access to drinking water.

Toilet

Access to toilet facilities was abysmally poor for both SC and non-SC/ST households, especially in rural areas. According to the Census of India 2001, about 85 per cent SC households and 75 per cent non-SC/ST households did not have access to toilet facilities at all. This has serious implications, especially for women who have to use open spaces that invariably result in security threats and sexual exploitation. SC women are particularly prone to greater risks in this context. Among the states that have done relatively better during the last decade in terms of providing toilets to households are Assam, Kerala and Delhi where over one-half of SC households have access to toilet facilities. Orissa, Bihar and Tamil Nadu, on the other hand, have not performed well in terms to ensure access to sanitation for SC households. The rural–urban divide is very large insofar as access to toilet facilities is concerned. Similarly, the gap between SC and non-SC/ST households was significantly large in both rural and urban areas. Although there have been reports of success stories of several such sanitation movements like Sulabh, these movements are significantly urban and based on user fee. Thereby they restrict access to those who cannot afford to pay in order to use the facilities. In many urban slums of Delhi, some such facilities face the problems of water supply and poor maintenance, and hence have been shut down.

Electricity

At all-India level (2001), despite the achievement of 80 per cent electrification of the villages, about 65 per cent SC and 52 per cent non-SC/ST rural households do not have access to electricity. In several states such as Andhra Pradesh, Kerala, Madhya Pradesh, Maharashtra and Rajasthan, about one-third to two-thirds of the rural households were without electricity. In several other states which include

West Bengal, Uttar Pradesh, Orissa and Assam, about 80 per cent households in rural areas still do not have access to electricity. The situation is particularly grim in Bihar, where 94 per cent rural households do not have electricity. The inter-social group analysis indicates that disparities (against SCs) were profound in several states which include Andhra Pradesh, Haryana, Karnataka, Kerala, Maharashtra, Orissa, Punjab, Rajasthan, Tamil Nadu, Uttar Pradesh and West Bengal. In urban areas, the households had greater access to electricity but the gap between the two social groups is quite wide both at all-India level (at about 13 percentage points) as well as in most of the states.

SUMMARY

The access to civic amenities among rural SC households is very poor. A substantially higher proportion of SC households (8.1 per cent) reside in dilapidated houses as compared to non-SC/ST households (4.8 per cent). The building materials used in the construction of houses are far from satisfactory. In rural areas, about 65 per cent SC households used *pucca* materials for roofs while the corresponding figure for non-SC/ST households was about 75 per cent. The percentage of houses having *pucca* walls was even lower for both SC and non-SC/ST households. The size of SC houses was also quite small. Nearly four-fifths of SC households lived in houses that had two or less number of rooms, with a significant majority of them living in single rooms. On the other hand, the number of non-SC/ST households who lived in houses that had more than two rooms was nearly twice that of SCs. The access to safe drinking water was more or less same for SCs (78 per cent) and non-SCs/STs (74 per cent) in rural areas. The rural areas in Kerala fared the worst in terms to provide the households access to safe drinking water, followed by Assam and Rajasthan where less than 25 per cent, 60 per cent and 65 per cent households, respectively, had access to safe drinking water. The state of access to toilet facilities was deplorable for both SC and non-SC/ST households, especially in rural areas. According to the Census of India 2001, about 85 per cent SC households and 75 per cent non-SC/ST households did not have access to toilet facilities at all. Similarly, access was also poor in case of electricity. Despite the achievement of 80 per cent electrification of the villages, in 2001, about 65 per cent SC and 52 per cent non-SC/ST rural households did not have access to electricity. Although access to electricity was better in urban areas, the gap between the two social groups was quite wide at both all-India level (at about 13 percentage points) as well as in most of the states.

ANNEXURE VI

Table 8A.1
Condition of Housing by Social Groups, 2001

Social Groups	Areas	Total			Residence			Residence-cum-Other Use		
		Good	Livable	Dilapidated	Good	Livable	Dilapidated	Good	Livable	Dilapidated
All	Total	50.2	44.3	5.5	50.4	44.1	5.6	46.7	49.1	4.2
	Rural	44.8	48.9	6.2	45.0	48.7	6.3	42.0	53.4	4.6
	Urban	64.2	32.2	3.6	64.2	32.2	3.6	62.1	34.8	3.1
SC	Total	42.2	49.7	8.1	42.4	49.5	8.1	36.8	55.9	7.3
	Rural	39.7	51.8	8.5	39.9	51.6	8.6	33.9	58.4	7.8
	Urban	51.3	42.3	6.4	51.3	42.2	6.5	49.6	45.0	5.3
ST	Total	35.8	58.3	5.9	36.2	57.8	6.0	30.4	66.1	3.6
	Rural	33.8	60.3	5.9	34.1	59.8	6.0	29.5	67.0	3.5
	Urban	49.5	44.8	5.7	49.5	44.7	5.8	48.5	47.2	4.3
Non-SC/ST	Total	54.2	41.0	4.8	54.3	40.8	4.8	51.3	44.8	3.9
	Rural	48.2	46.2	5.6	48.3	46.0	5.7	46.6	49.1	4.2
	Urban	67.2	29.8	3.0	67.4	29.6	3.0	63.9	33.3	2.9

Source: Census of India, 2001.

Table 8A.2
Percentage of Households Living in Houses with Pucca Roofs and Walls by Social Groups, 2001

Aspects	Areas	Social Groups			
		All	SC	ST	Non-SC/ST
Roofs	Total	78.0	70.2	74.4	80.5
	Rural	72.3	65.5	72.3	74.4
	Urban	92.2	86.5	88.9	93.4
Walls	Total	55.5	47.0	25.6	61.8
	Rural	45.1	40.2	20.0	51.0
	Urban	81.8	70.7	63.1	84.8

Source: Census of India, 2001.

Table 8A.3
Materials Used for Roofs in SC Houses, All India, 2001

Particulars/Materials	Total	Rural	Urban
Total number of households	18.7	20.3	14.7
Materials used for roofs			
Grass, thatch, bamboo, wood and mud	25.5	25.5	26.1
Plastic and polythene	27.5	26.7	28.5
Tiles	18.0	18.0	18.2
Slate	22.8	23.6	19.3
GI, metal and asbestos sheets	18.2	18.8	17.1
Brick	19.2	21.0	14.4
Stone	19.2	19.7	18.3
Concrete	12.1	16.3	9.5
Any other material	15.6	15.8	15.0

Source: Census of India, 2001.

Table 8A.4
Materials Used for Walls—Share of SC Households, All India, 2001

Materials	Total	Rural	Urban
Grass, thatch and bamboo	21.2	20.7	26.1
Plastic and polythene	23.7	23.5	24.1
Mud and sunburnt bricks	22.9	22.8	23.7
Wood	12.9	11.9	15.3
GI, metal and asbestos sheets	19.0	19.5	12.9
Burnt bricks	16.1	18.8	12.9
Stone	19.0	20.2	16.0
Concrete	11.9	14.3	10.7
Any other material	19.0	20.2	16.0

Source: Census of India, 2001.

Table 8A.5
Distribution of Households by Number of Dwelling Units, All India, 1991 and 2001

Total/ Rural/ Urban	Social Groups	Households Having Number of Dwelling Rooms							
		No Exclusive Room	1	2	3	4	5	6+	More than Two Rooms
2001									
Total	SC	4.1	47.7	30.0	10.5	4.6	1.5	1.8	18.3
	ST	4.0	47.6	30.2	10.8	4.2	1.4	1.8	18.2
	Non-SC/ST	2.7	34.9	30.0	15.8	8.7	3.5	4.4	32.4
Rural	SC	4.3	48.1	30.1	10.0	4.4	1.4	1.7	17.5
	ST	4.2	48.2	30.2	10.4	4.0	1.3	1.7	17.4
	Non-SC/ST	3.0	35.9	30.2	14.7	8.3	3.4	4.4	30.9
Urban	SC	3.2	46.3	29.5	12.1	5.2	1.7	2.1	21.1
	ST	3.0	43.4	30.1	13.3	5.6	2.0	2.6	23.5
	Non-SC/ST	2.1	32.7	29.5	18.2	9.5	3.6	4.4	35.7
1991									
Total	SC	0.1	48.4	30.9	10.7	4.7	1.8	2.4	19.7
	ST	0.0	50.8	30.8	10.4	3.9	1.4	1.8	17.4
	Non-SC/ST	0.0	37.4	30.5	15.0	8.1	3.7	4.4	31.2
Rural	SC	0.0	48.1	31.0	10.8	4.7	1.8	2.4	19.8
	ST	0.0	51.3	30.8	10.3	3.8	1.4	1.6	17.1
	Non-SC/ST	0.0	37.2	30.5	14.7	8.0	3.8	4.6	31.2
Urban	SC	0.1	49.8	30.3	10.4	4.7	1.6	2.7	19.3
	ST	0.3	46.2	31.8	11.5	4.7	1.7	3.3	21.2
	Non-SC/ST	0.0	37.8	30.3	15.6	8.3	3.4	4.0	31.3

Source: Census of India, 1991 and 2001.

Table 8A.6
Distribution of Households by House Tenure and Share by Social Groups, 1991 and 2001

State	T/R/U	SC			ST			Non-SC/ST		
		Owned	Rented	Others	Owned	Rented	Others	Owned	Rented	Others
House	Total	92.0	5.8	2.2	92.4	5.4	2.1	84.3	14.1	1.7
Tenure	Rural	96.1	2.2	1.7	95.2	3.0	1.8	94.0	4.6	1.3
1991	Urban	73.6	22.1	4.3	63.0	31.4	5.6	61.5	36.0	2.5

(Table 8A.6 Contd.)

(Table 8A.6 Contd.)

State	T/R/U	SC			ST			Non-SC/ST		
		Owned	Rented	Others	Owned	Rented	Others	Owned	Rented	Others
House	Total	89.1	7.4	3.5	90.8	5.9	3.3	83.7	13.4	2.9
Tenure	Rural	94.9	2.7	2.4	94.9	2.5	2.6	93.1	4.7	2.2
2001	Urban	70.5	22.5	7.0	61.7	30.3	8.0	64.7	31.1	4.2
Share of	Total	19.4	8.9	21.8	8.8	3.7	9.6	71.9	87.4	68.6
Tenure	Rural	20.5	11.1	23.3	10.2	7.7	12.6	69.3	81.3	64.1
1991	Urban	14.7	8.2	19.5	2.7	2.5	5.3	82.6	89.4	75.2
Share of	Total	18.4	11.3	20.4	11.4	5.5	11.6	70.2	83.2	68.0
Tenure	Rural	19.2	12.5	19.8	13.5	8.2	15.1	·67.3	79.2	65.1
2001	Urban	15.5	10.9	21.1	4.3	4.6	7.6	80.2	84.5	71.3

Source: Census of India, 1991 and 2001.

Table 8A.7
SC and Non-SC/ST Households by Sources of Drinking Water, 2001

Total/ Rural/ Urban	Location	SC								
		Source of Drinking Water								
		Tap	Hand pump	Tube Well	Safe Water	Well	Tank, Pond, Lake	River, Canal	Spring	Any Other
Total	Total	32.2	43.6	5.3	81.1	15.5	0.9	0.8	0.4	1.2
	Within premises	47.5	38.8	3.2	89.5	10.0	0.3	0.0	0.0	0.2
	Near premises	29.5	48.0	5.2	82.6	14.8	0.8	0.6	0.3	0.8
	Away from premises	18.3	38.2	8.8	65.4	25.1	2.2	2.4	1.1	3.8
Rural	Total	23.5	49.4	5.6	78.5	18.0	1.1	0.9	0.4	1.0
	Within premises	31.0	52.0	3.1	86.2	13.2	0.5	0.0	0.0	0.2
	Near premises	24.3	51.7	5.2	81.2	16.3	0.9	0.7	0.3	0.6
	Away from premises	13.7	40.7	8.9	63.3	27.6	2.4	2.7	1.2	2.8
Urban	Total	63.1	22.7	4.6	90.4	6.6	0.4	0.3	0.2	2.2
	Within premises	73.1	18.5	3.2	94.7	5.0	0.1	0.0	0.0	0.2
	Near premises	58.6	27.1	4.7	90.5	6.4	0.4	0.3	0.3	2.1
	Away from premises	41.4	25.6	8.6	75.6	12.3	1.3	1.0	0.8	8.9

(Table 8A.7 Contd.)

(Table 8A.7 Contd.)

Total/ Rural/ Urban	Location	SC								
		Source of Drinking Water								
		Tap	Hand pump	Tube Well	Safe Water	Well	Tank, Pond, Lake	River, Canal	Spring	Any Other
		Non-SC/ST								
Total	Total	40.1	33.6	5.6	79.2	17.5	1.0	0.8	0.4	1.1
	Within premises	54.4	27.4	4.4	86.1	13.4	0.4	0.0	0.0	0.2
	Near premises	31.6	41.1	5.7	78.4	18.2	1.1	0.9	0.5	0.9
	Away from premises	18.9	32.0	8.9	59.8	28.7	2.6	3.0	1.4	4.4
Rural	Total	26.3	42.1	5.7	74.1	22.0	1.3	1.1	0.5	1.0
	Within premises	33.8	41.8	4.1	79.7	19.5	0.6	0.0	0.0	0.2
	Near premises	25.4	45.1	5.8	76.3	20.3	1.2	1.0	0.5	0.7
	Away from premises	13.9	34.2	8.8	57.0	31.8	2.9	3.4	1.6	3.3
Urban	Total	70.0	15.1	5.2	90.4	7.7	0.3	0.2	0.2	1.4
	Within premises	76.3	12.1	4.6	92.9	6.8	0.1	0.0	0.0	0.2
	Near premises	60.4	22.4	5.6	88.4	8.3	0.4	0.4	0.4	2.1
	Away from premises	42.5	21.4	9.4	73.4	13.9	1.4	0.9	0.8	9.7

Source: Census of India, 2001.

Chapter 9

HEALTH AND NUTRITIONAL STATUS

Vijay Kumar Baraik and P. M. Kulkarni

The objective of this chapter is to present the health conditions of Scheduled Castes (SCs) and Scheduled Tribes (STs), and to compare the same with that of non-SCs/STs in terms of available meaningful indicators of health conditions, health status and healthcare utilisation. These have been examined for India as a whole and for the various states to the extent permitted by the availability of data.

The broad concept of health as a state of complete physical, mental and social well-being and not merely the absence of disease or infirmity has been widely accepted, but assessing this in its entirety for a population is not feasible. Therefore, health conditions are assessed by using a set of measurable indicators that cover most aspects of health even if it not encompasses overall health. The indicators used in the present study that reflect various dimensions of health and for which reasonably reliable data are available include mortality, morbidity and nutritional status which are broadly called 'health outcomes'; and access to and utilisation of preventive, promotive and curative services which are broadly called 'healthcare'.

Due to poor coverage of the civil registration system and non-availability of mortality data by social groups in the sample registration system (SRS) in India, this study relies on surveys to procure relevant information. The National Family Health Surveys (NFHS) collected information on a large number of aspects related to health conditions such as child and infant mortality, healthcare and health service utilisation, especially for women and children (IIPS, 1995; IIPS and ORC Macro, 2000). The first survey (NFHS 1) conducted during 1992–1993 covered 25 states, including Delhi, while the second survey (NFHS 2) conducted in 1998–1999 covered all the states of India.

HEALTH STATUS

Mortality has been an important, universally accepted and widely used indicator of health status of any population. It is also a clearly understood health outcome. Life expectancy, that is, expectation of life at birth, is the preferred measure of survival that can be computed from age-specific death rates. However, in the absence of a good civil registration system, as mentioned earlier, such rates are not available for various social groups. Hence, in order to examine the differentials in mortality across social groups, the estimates of infant and early childhood mortality for sub-populations provided by NFHS have been used.

Infant mortality rate (IMR) and child mortality rate (CMR) are generally highly correlated since broadly the same set of factors (socio-economic, environmental and health service related factors) influence both. However, endogenous factors play a greater role in influencing mortality rates during infancy, especially early infancy (called neonatal mortality), whereas exogenous factors are more crucial during late infancy and early childhood. Although the pattern of differentials in these two indicators are likely to be similar, they need not be the same, and hence the estimates of all the three indicators, such as IMR, CMR and under five mortality rate (U-5MR) by social groups in India have been utilised for discussion in this section.

Infant Mortality Rate

IMR is conventionally computed as the number of infant deaths per 1,000 live births in one year. However, when data on cohorts are available, as in the case of NFHS, it can be obtained as the proportion of newborns who die before the completion of the first year of life.

In India, IMR was very high in the past. Over the years it has shown a declining trend. According to SRS series, IMR has halved from about 130 per 1,000 live births in early 1970s to 64 per 1,000 live births in 2002. The estimates by social groups show that for SCs the level has always been higher than the average. A special survey by SRS conducted in 1984 showed a very high IMR for SCs (127 per 1,000 live births), with the overall average being 104 per 1,000 live births. The IMR for STs, on the other hand, was 101 per 1000 live births and was closer to the average (India, Registrar General, 1989). According to NFHS 1, IMR for India as a whole was 86 per 1,000 live births (this refers to the 10-year period preceding the survey. Since the survey was conducted during 1992–1993, the period concerned would be from 1982–1983 to 1992–1993), but the level for SCs was much higher at 107 per 1,000 live births; whereas for ST, it was 91 per 1,000 live births which was just above the average (see Table 9.1). The estimate from NFHS 2 (corresponding to the period 1988–1999) was lower at 73 per 1,000 live births, but for SCs and STs the levels were still higher at 83 and 84 per 1,000 live births, respectively. Indirect estimates based on the Census of India 1991 also indicate higher than average levels for both SCs and STs. Besides, there were large regional variations in mortality and in some states the mortality was quite high even during in the recent periods. In particular, NFHS

Table 9.1
Infant and Childhood Mortality Indicators for the Social Groups, All India

| | | Social Groups | | | Gap | | |
| | | | | | | | |
Indicators	Sources	SC	ST	Non-SC/ST	All	SC versus Non-SC/ST	ST versus Non-SC/ST
IMR	SRS survey	127	101	99	104	28	2
	NFHS 1	107	91	82	86	25	9
	NFHS 2	83	84	68	73	15	16
CMR	NFHS 1	47	49	35	36	15	17
	NFHS 2	40	46	25	31	15	21
U-5MR	NFHS 1	149	135	112	119	37	23
	NFHS 2	119	127	92	101	27	35

Sources: SRS Survey: India, Registrar General (1989); NFHS 1: IIPS (1995); NFHS 2: IIPS; and ORC Macro (2000).
Note: The SRS survey estimates refer to 1984; NFHS 1 to the 10-year period preceding 1992–1993, and NFHS 2 to the 10-year period preceding 1998–1999.

2 also shows the IMR to be over 100 per 1,000 for SCs in Madhya Pradesh and Uttar Pradesh.

Child Mortality Rate

CMR is the proportion of infants who are alive at the age of one year but die before the completion of five years of age. NFHS 1 estimated CMR as 36 per 1,000 live births for all India, but the rate was much higher for SCs (47 per 1,000 live births), and STs (49 per 1,000 live births) as compared to non-SCs/STs (32 per 1,000 live births). The corresponding NFHS 2 estimates was lower at 31 per 1,000 live births but SCs (40 per 1,000 live births) and STs (46 per 1,000 live births) continued to suffer from higher mortality than non-SCs/STs (25 per 1,000 live births). The CMR for SCs continued to be high, at over 50 per 1,000 live births in a few states such as Madhya Pradesh, Uttar Pradesh and Bihar.

Under-five Mortality Rate

U-5MR incorporates both infant and child mortality, that is, it gives the proportion of newborns who die before the completion of five years of age. Its level was just over 100 per 1,000 births in India (with NFHS 1 estimate being 119 per 1,000 live births and NFHS 2 estimate being 102 per 1,000 live births) which implies that one in every 10 newborns does not survive beyond the fifth year of her/his birth. For SCs, the risk of mortality before the completion of five years of age was much higher than non-SCs/STs as it was close to or higher than 125 per 1,000 live births. It was well above 125 per 1,000 live births for SCs in many states such as Uttar Pradesh, Madhya Pradesh, Rajasthan and Bihar.

NUTRITIONAL STATUS

Nutrition is a prerequisite to ensure good health and well-being of any population, and for children it plays an important role in their physical and mental growth. Chronic illnesses are often associated with poor nutrition, especially among children. Moreover, mother's nutritional status affects both her own health as well as the health of her children. Among many populations, food intakes are inadequate to provide them the required calories, proteins and other nutrients; the deficiency is especially acute among the poor. Nutritional status can be measured in a number of ways, including anthropometric measurements and laboratory tests. These include measures such as weights and heights of children and can be compared to the standards used to ascertain the nutritional status of children. For adults, the body mass index (BMI) which is the ratio of the weight (in kilograms) to the square of height (in square metres) is the most commonly used measure to assess energy deficiency and obesity. Haemoglobin levels obtained from blood samples can also be used to detect protein-deficiency anaemia, which is one of the major health problems in India. It is also a consequence of poor dietary intake.

Nutritional Status among Women

About one-third of women of child-bearing age in India have very low BMI (less than 18.5 kg/m²) which indicate chronic energy deficiency (see Annexure VII Table 9A.1). This proportion is even higher, from 42 to 46 per cent, for women who belong to scheduled groups. The problem is acute for SCs in Orissa with over 50 per cent of them being severely malnourished. In India, 52 per cent women in the reproductive age group are anaemic,[1] 35 per cent are mild anaemic and 17 per cent are moderate or severe anaemic (below 10.0 g/dL). It is the moderate or severe degree of anaemia that causes concern, though its overall prevalence or prevalence among SCs is not very high.

---

[1] Those with haemoglobin level below 12.0 grams per decilitre are considered 'anaemic'. Three degrees of anaemia are specified. They are: mild (10.0–11.9), moderate (7.0–9.9) and severe (below 7.0). For pregnant women, the range 10.0–10.9 is classified as mild anaemia.

Nutritional Status among Children

Undernutrition is a major factor responsible for high morbidity and mortality rates among children in India. The anthropometric measurements in the two NFHS surveys show that nearly half of the children have weights and heights too low for their age as compared to international standards. These children are classified as 'undernourished' and 'stunted'[2] (see Annexure VII Table 9A.2). The degree of undernutrition was higher among SCs as compared to non-SCs/STs. In large number of states such as Uttar Pradesh, Orissa, Bihar, Madhya Pradesh, Rajasthan, West Bengal, Jammu and Kashmir, Karnataka, Himachal Pradesh and Maharashtra, a majority of SC children were undernourished. A similar picture was evident for the indicator 'stunting'. Nearly half of the children were 'stunted', that is, they were too short for their age. However, the incidence of 'wasting' was much less common, at 16–18 per cent overall and at around 20 per cent for SCs, than the incidences of 'undernourishment' and 'stunting'. However, in Karnataka, over 25 per cent SC children were 'wasted', that is, they were underweight for their heights.

A majority of the Indian children also suffer from some form of anaemia. At the national level, the percentage of children (in the age group of 6–35 months) who suffer from moderate and severe forms of anaemia was quite high (51 per cent), that is, half of the children suffered from moderate and severe anaemia. The conditions of SC children were worse off with the prevalence of anaemia among them being higher by 7–8 percentage points than for children from other social groups. In few states like Haryana, Punjab and Rajasthan, the deprivation among SCs was even more acute with over 60 per cent children being moderately or severely anaemic.

HEALTHCARE

Healthcare (preventive, promotive and curative) plays an important role to determine the health status. Public health services in India provide immunisation services, especially for children and pregnant women. Besides, certain nutritional

---

[2] An individual child's nutritional status is reckoned on the basis of the 'z-score' on the international reference for the child's age and sex. Low weight for a particular age suggests undernutrition which results from lack of food, continuous persistence of diarrhea and of other diseases during the period just before measurement. Children with weight more than 2SD below the reference median for that age (weight < reference median –2) are considered to be undernourished and those with weight more than 3SD below the median as severely undernourished. Low height relative to age, called stunting, indicates chronic undernutrition which results from long deprivation in nutrition and long persistence in some disease which causes growth retardation. Children with heights more than 2SD below the reference median for that age are classified as stunted, and those with heights more than 3SD below the median as severely stunted. Low weight at a given height, called wasting, indicates acute undernutrition. Children with weights more than 2SD below the reference median for that height are categorised as wasted while those with heights more than 3SD below the median as severely wasted.

supplements are also given under various child development programmes. Maternal health services which include care during pregnancy, delivery and post-partum period are provided free by a network of primary health centres, government maternity homes and hospitals. Treatment for various illnesses can also be accessed from public sector health outlets, primary health centres (PHC) and government clinics and hospitals, free or at a nominal cost. In addition, the private sector provides maternal as well as general healthcare at a fee. The utilisation of healthcare depends on various factors such as availability, awareness, access and affordability. The economically weaker sections may not be able to afford private sector services and the socially weaker sections may thus face barriers when they enter the private sector services. Therefore, it is important to explore if the utilisation of healthcare services varies by social class and further, whether the nature of the service accessed also varies. For this purpose, child immunisation, maternal care and treatment-seeking behaviour in case of specific illnesses need to be examined. This section, therefore, focuses on child and maternal healthcare.

Child Healthcare

Infancy and early childhood are the periods of life during which a person is highly vulnerable to morbidity. Besides, health during early period of life has long-term implications for the physical as well as the cognitive development of a child. This section highlights the level and gaps in preventive care, nutritional supplements and curative care for common childhood diseases.

Child Immunisation: Child immunisation has been in vogue in India for quite some time. The Universal Immunisation Programme (UIP) was introduced in mid-1980s in all the districts of the country. Later the Child Survival and Safe Motherhood (CSSM) Programme and then the Reproductive and Child Health (RCH) Programme continued to provide immunisation services. At present, PHCs provide vaccination against six preventable diseases free of cost. The recommended set of immunisations includes three doses each of DPT antigen and polio vaccine and one dose of BCG (against tuberculosis) and measles vaccine before the completion of one year of age.

The NFHS surveys asked women to provide details pertaining to immunisation of their children in the age group of 12–23 months. The immunisation coverage was far from universal. Only about 40 per cent children (see Table 9.2) received all the recommended doses (BCG, measles, three doses each of DPT and polio). In a few states, less than one-fifth of the children had received all the doses by 1998–1999 (as given by NFHS 2). In particular, SCs in Bihar, Rajasthan and Madhya Pradesh had an extremely low coverage.

Table 9.2
Preventive and Curative Care for Children by Social Groups

Indicators	Sources	SC	ST	Non-SC/ST	All	SC versus Non-SC/ST	ST versus Non-SC/ST
		Social Groups				*Gap*	
Percentage of children (aged 12–23 months) who received immunisation							
All recommended doses of vaccination	NFHS 1	27	25	38	35	–11	–13
All recommended doses of vaccination	NFHS 2	40	26	45	42	–5	–19
Vitamin A supplement	NFHS 2	27	26	31	30	–4	–5
Percentage of children (under three years of age) with							
Diarrhoea taken to health provider	NFHS 1	61	52	62	61	–1	–10
Diarrhoea taken to health provider	NFHS 2	65	52	65	63	0	–13
Acute respiratory infection (ARI) taken to health provider	NFHS 1	64	59	68	66	–4	–9
ARI taken to health provider	NFHS-2	60	50	68	64	–8	–18

Sources: NFHS 1: IIPS (1995); NFHS 2: IIPS; and ORC Macro (2000).

Vitamin A Supplementation: The deficiency of Vitamin A is a common nutritional disorder and the principal factor responsible for blindness at early age. The PHC in India provide Vitamin A supplementation in the form of oral doses for children below the age of five years. NFHS 2 collected information on this for children in the age group of 12–35 months. The picture was quite dismal in the sense that only 30 per cent children received at least one dose (Table 9.2). The coverage was poorer for SCs (27 per cent); it was below 20 per cent for SCs in Bihar, Uttar Pradesh, Tamil Nadu and Rajasthan.

Curative Care: Treatment in case of an illness depends on various factors which include realisation of illness, recognition of the need for treatment, awareness of source and access to treatment (the latter may, in turn, depend on physical location and affordability). At the cost of repetition, it must be noted here that we are not looking at levels of and differentials in the prevalence of a disease, since self-reported prevalence is often not comparable across social groups, but whether treatment was taken or not in case a disease was perceived to have occurred. For children, information about treatment for two common childhood diseases, that is, diarrhoea and ARI were obtained from mothers.

Worldwide diarrhoea is a major killer disease for children under the age of five years. The two NFHS surveys show that the family took diarrhoea quite seriously, and nearly 60 per cent children were taken to health facilities or providers for treatment. However, the tendency to seek treatment was slightly lower among ST (52 per cent) than others.

ARI, primarily pneumonia, is a major cause of illness among infants and children. Early diagnosis and treatment with antibiotics can prevent a large proportion of ARI/pneumonia-related deaths. Generally, a majority of children who reported symptoms of ARI were taken to a health centre or care providers (Table 9.2). Children who belong to SC families, however, did not get as much care as non-SC/ST children.

Maternal Healthcare

Women in India face a high risk of poor health and mortality during pregnancies and deliveries, with the result that the incidence of maternal mortality rate is very high in India. The NFHS 2 estimates maternal mortality ratio (MMR) at 540 per 100,000 live births. In order to address this issue, the Government Maternal Health Programmes (GMHPs) in India (now a part of the RCHP) provide Antenatal Care (ANC), delivery care and Post Natal Care (PNC) through a network of primary health centres and urban health posts. Most of the services in the public sector are provided free of cost so that even the poor are not deprived of professional maternal healthcare. Besides, the network of health centres makes access to services easy. Thus, in principle, the coverage should be close to universal. However, various surveys indicate that a large proportion of women do not get adequate healthcare during pregnancies and deliveries.

Antenatal Care: A majority of women have received ANC in India in the recent past. The NFHS 2 estimates that during late 1990s, an antenatal check-up was conducted by qualified professionals in case of 65 per cent births (see Annexure VII Table 9A.2). Overall, the coverage was lower for SC population as compared to non-SCs/STs. In spite of discrimination faced, SCs dwell in villages along with others and are more successful than ST in obtaining maternal healthcare services. Yet, a majority of SC women in Bihar, Uttar Pradesh and Rajasthan did not receive any professional ANC.

Delivery Care: In India, a majority of deliveries, especially in rural areas, continue to take place at home. Only a small proportion of deliveries take place in health institutions such as hospitals, maternity homes, public or private, primary health centres and sub-centres. The NFHS 1 and NFHS 2 estimate of the percentage of deliveries in health institutions are 26 per cent and 34 per cent, respectively. The incidence of institutional care was much less among SC women than other women at 27 per cent as estimated by NFHS 2 (see Annexure VII Table 9A.2). Public health services are expected to meet the requirements of the weaker sections that would find it difficult to pay for the services provided by the private sector. However, overall, the public sector meets very little of the said demand, as only 16 per cent deliveries were in public sector institutions, that is, the government health centres and hospitals (NFHS 2 estimate). In Bihar, Haryana, Uttar Pradesh and Punjab, less than 10 per cent SC women were successful in obtaining public sector institutional delivery care.

Medical Assistance at Birth/Delivery: Lack of professional assistance at the time of delivery is a major cause of maternal and neonatal mortality. Traditionally, village midwives and women at home assist at delivery. Over time, many women have begun to seek the help of doctors, or at least trained midwives at the time of delivery. It has been observed that 34 per cent, as per NFHS 1, and 42 per cent as per NFHS 2, of all deliveries were assisted by a professional, that is, a doctor or a trained midwife (see Annexure VII Table 9A.2). As seen in many other indicators, SCs fare poorly (37 per cent deliveries among SC women received professional assistance as evident from NFHS 2). There are large inter-state variations. In Kerala most of the women including SC women got professional assistance at the time of delivery. On the other hand, less than one-fifth of the deliveries got such care among SCs in Bihar and Uttar Pradesh.

DISPARITIES AMONG THE SOCIAL GROUPS

The preceding description clearly shows that the health conditions for SCs and STs are quite poor. This section examines the inter-social group disparities, particularly in comparison to non-SCs/STs in order to bring out the degree of deprivation of the scheduled groups in terms of access to health services. The disparity has been measured as simple gap between the indicator for a social group (SCs or STs) and the reference group, or as the ratio, that is, the ratio of the indicator for a social group to the reference group (non-SCs/STs).

Early Childhood Mortality

Although SCs show higher early childhood mortality than the rest of the population, the level of disparity is not identical across states. In many states, the differences among social groups are large. The IMR for SCs is higher than non-SCs/STs in Andhra Pradesh, Bihar, Madhya Pradesh and Uttar Pradesh. Karnataka, Maharashtra, Orissa, Punjab and Tamil Nadu also show large disparities in one of the surveys. On the other hand, in Gujarat, Haryana, Himachal Pradesh and Jammu and Kashmir, IMR for SCs was not notably higher than that for non-SCs/STs.

In case of child mortality, the level for SCs was well above non-SCs/STs in Gujarat and Uttar Pradesh, and also in Haryana, Maharashtra, Karnataka, Orissa and Tamil Nadu, in one of the surveys. However, the pattern of disparity for SCs is not consistent over the two surveys. Overall, SCs face a higher risk of U-5MR as compared to other sections of the Indian population in most of the states. Only a few states, notably Assam, Haryana, Himachal Pradesh and Jammu and Kashmir show low disparity. The nature and degree of disparity among the social groups varies. The SCs are more vulnerable than STs in Bihar and Gujarat. A generally low level of mortality in a region does not necessarily ensure a low level of mortality for SCs in that particular region. In Maharashtra and Tamil Nadu, though the overall level of U-5MR was not high (relative to the national average), SCs had unusually high U-5MR as estimated by NFHS 1. This was also observed in Andhra Pradesh, Karnataka, Gujarat and Punjab in the second survey (it was not possible to examine the disparities in Kerala, which has very low U-5MR, since the sample sizes for SCs were too small to permit the estimation of infant and childhood mortality). The existence of large disparities in states with relatively low mortality is a matter of great concern. Clearly, the weaker sections have been deprived of recent advances and improvements in child survival.

Nutritional Status

Although SC women are more undernourished than their non-SC/ST counterparts, the deprivation is greater among STs. This is markedly so in Maharashtra (where STs are worse off than non-SCs/STs and SCs), and in Tamil Nadu and West Bengal (where both SCs and STs were disadvantaged but the latter were more so). Assam was an exception where both SCs and STs were not disadvantaged as compared to non-SCs/STs.

In case of protein deficiency anaemia, the gap between SCs and non-SCs/STs was quite narrow. However, in a few states like Punjab, Karnataka, West Bengal, Orissa and Bihar, there was a large gap of over 5 percentage points which shows poorer conditions for SCs as compared to non-SCs/STs.

At the national level, the degree of malnourishment among children does not vary much by social groups; the gap was only 5 to 10 points (the NFHS 2 shows wider gaps than the NFHS 1). But in many states, the condition of the SCs was much worse than that of the non-SCs/STs. In particular, in quite a few states (Gujarat, Haryana, Himachal Pradesh, Jammu and Kashmir, Orissa, Punjab, Karnataka, Kerala, Uttar Pradesh and West Bengal), a gap of over 10 points was seen between the SCs and the non-SCs/STs in at least one of the surveys.

Child Healthcare

In NFHS 1, the immunisation coverage among SCs was much below non-SCs/STs, but NFHS 2 shows a relatively narrower gap. In most of the states, the gap was close to 10 points in NFHS 1, but had narrowed down by the time of the NFHS 2. Punjab was an exception; the gap widened substantially there primarily because of the larger rise in the coverage for non-SCs/STs, but not for SCs. Madhya Pradesh also continued to show wide gaps. Overall though, one can say that as far as immunisation is concerned, SCs get nearly as much coverage as non-SCs/STs. The public immunisation programmes, thus, seem to have been able to cater to SCs nearly as successfully as to non-SCs/STs.

There is hardly any difference in the level of treatment-seeking for common childhood illnesses between SCs and non-SCs/STs. In both the groups, treatment was sought in about 60–65 per cent cases at the national level. Further, the gap was narrow in most of the states. On the other hand, STs were not successful in obtaining treatment in diarrhoea. The gap was about 10 points nationally and very high in Bihar and Orissa, according to NFHS 2. A plausible reason for lack of difference between SCs and non-SCs/STs was that the risk associated with diarrhoea was well-recognised by parents and an affected child was taken to a service provider in most cases. It is, however, not clear as to why this was not done by ST to the same extent as by non-SCs/STs. Perhaps lack of access to a provider posed a problem, or the severity of the illness was not realised, or possibly home remedies were resorted to.

Maternal Healthcare

SC women do not get as much ANC as other women. The relative deprivation of SCs in this regard was seen in almost all the states. Assam was a notable exception but this was not due to good coverage for SCs in the state, but was rather on account of poor coverage for all the communities. Since Kerala has reached near-universal coverage, obviously hardly any difference was seen among the social groups. A few states exhibited large disparities between SCs and non-SCs/STs (Rajasthan, Karnataka, Haryana and Uttar Pradesh in two surveys, and Bihar, West Bengal and Punjab in at least one round of NFHS).

Overall, SCs are not able to access as much institutional delivery care as non-SCs/STs, but the differences are primarily on account of delivery care from the private sector. Obviously, women from the non-scheduled groups, who are financially better off than their SC and ST counterparts, utilise private sector health services substantially more than the scheduled women. In contrast, the gaps are narrower for delivery care from the public sector; the percentage of deliveries which take place in government institutions was almost the same for SC and non-SC/ST women, and were only marginally lower for ST women, according to NFHS 2. In a few states, a higher proportion of SCs utilised delivery services from the public sector than non-SCs/STs. This was notably so in Kerala, and to some extent, in Gujarat, as well as in Maharashtra and West Bengal, as evident from NFHS 2. This does not, however, imply that the government sector seeks to cater more to SCs, but quite plausibly non-SCs/STs, who have greater financial resources, prefer to access private sector services for delivery care. Thus, SCs are not able to obtain private delivery care to the extent that non-SCs/STs are, with affordability being the main obstacle. Assam and Bihar showed narrow gaps because the coverage was low among all the social groups; the high-level equity in Kerala contrasted with the low-level equity in the latter two states. The quality of medical assistance offered was appreciable in Tamil Nadu, though there was a visible gap between the assistance received by the two communities, such as the non-SCs/STs and the SCs.

SUMMARY

The above discussion clearly brings out the fact that the health conditions of SCs and STs are quite poor in India, and that they are more deprived in terms of access to health services than the other sections of the population. This is particularly true of childhood survival, nutritional status, child healthcare and maternal healthcare. In spite of an improvement in survival levels, IMR of 83 and 84 per 1,000 live births, and CMR of 40 and 46 per 1,000 live births among SCs and STs, respectively, are unacceptably high for the contemporary period. Besides, over two-fifths of the SC/ST women suffer from chronic energy deficiency as seen from their BMI figures. The anthropometric measures used for data analysis show that nearly half of the young children are undernourished or stunted, and that over half the children are moderately or severely anaemic. However, as per the recent evidence, the immunisation coverage among SC and ST children has nearly caught up with that among the general population. This is true both at the national level as well as in most of the states. The campaign type approach followed in immunisation programmes ensures that all sections within an area are covered. In addition, another aspect wherein the deprivation level for SCs is not very high is the degree of treatment-seeking in case of common childhood illnesses such as diarrhoea and ARI, though this situation is not seen in a few states. Since the issue of quality of treatment has not been addressed here, it could be possible that despite the narrow gap in terms of coverage, probably children from weaker sections cannot easily access high quality services and hence do not get the same level of treatment that non-SC/ST children do. The provision of maternal healthcare has been given a high degree of importance in PHCs in India, but the goal to provide professional health-care during pregnancy and delivery is far from being achieved. A few states, notably Kerala and Tamil Nadu, are nearing complete coverage in many aspects of maternal care, while the situation is still quite poor in Uttar Pradesh, Bihar and Rajasthan. Orissa seems to have improved recently and risen above the latter states in this regard. Since maternal healthcare is provided free of cost by primary healthcare network which involves community health centres, PHCs and sub-centres, all sections should be able to access this care. Yet, the coverage is lower for scheduled groups and the deprivation is worse for ST women than their SC counterparts, probably due to the locational disadvantages that STs face. Institutional delivery is not as easily obtainable as ANC. Nationally, only about one-third of the deliveries are conducted in health institutions. Again, there are large inter-state variations in this regard with Kerala and Tamil Nadu being at the high end and the north-central states at the low end. In most of the states, the public maternity facilities have not attracted a large proportion of expectant mothers. Since reliance on private delivery care is high and professional care, obviously, entails a substantial cost, the weaker sections are not able to obtain much delivery care. A similar picture is seen in the case of professional assistance at delivery. It is, in fact, possible that the poor coverage of the scheduled groups by modern delivery care might also be attributable, in part, to their faith in the traditional systems, in addition to, inaccessibility to modern health providers.

Overall, SCs and STs seem to suffer nearly equally in terms of health outcomes such as mortality and nutritional status. The health outcomes are influenced substantially by household endowments like food intake, housing conditions and ability to secure paid healthcare. Both the scheduled groups are at a disadvantage here and seem to suffer equally. The broad pattern of inter-social group disparities can be summarised as follows: in health outcomes, large SC versus non-SC/ST, as well as ST versus non-SC/ST disparities and in services, large ST versus non-SC/ST but smaller SC versus non-SC/ST disparities.

The social gaps in health outcomes could possibly be a consequence of differences in household endowments. Public services try to facilitate reduce mortality and improve nutrition, yet differences among social groups persist. However, the case of health services is quite different. It must be noted here that most of the services listed in this chapter, such as immunisation, maternal care and even some curative care are amply provided by public healthcare network and that the poor coverage points to the failure of the public healthcare service system to reach STs in particular.

ANNEXURE VII

Table 9A.1
Nutritional Status of Women and Children for Social Groups

Indicators	Sources	Social Groups				Gap	
		SC	ST	Non-SC/ST	All	SC versus Non-SC/ST	ST versus Non-SC/ST
Percentage of women of age 15–49 years with							
Body mass index < 18.5 kg/m²	NFHS 2	42	46	33	36	9	13
Moderate or severe anaemia	NFHS 2	19	24	15	17	4	9
Percentage of children under three years of age who are							
Undernourished	NFHS 1	58	57	52	53	6	5
Undernourished	NFHS 2	54	56	44	47	10	12
Stunted	NFHS 1	58	53	51	52	7	2
Stunted	NFHS 2	52	53	43	46	9	10
Wasted	NFHS 1	19	22	17	18	2	5
Wasted	NFHS 2	16	22	15	16	1	7
Per cent of children aged six to 35 months with moderate or severe anaemia	NFHS 2	56	57	49	51	7	8

Sources: NFHS 1: IIPS (1995); NFHS 2: IIPS; and ORC Macro (2000).

Table 9A.2
Maternal Healthcare by Social Groups

Indicators	Sources	Social Groups				Gap	
		SC	ST	Non-SC/ST	All	SC versus Non-SC/ST	ST versus Non-SC/ST
Percentage of women who received antenatal check-ups	NFHS 1	58	48	66	53	–8	–18
Percentage of women who received antenatal check-ups	NFHS 2	62	57	69	65	–7	–12
Percentage of deliveries							
In health institutions	NFHS 1	16	9	29	26	–13	–20
In health institutions	NFHS 2	27	17	38	34	–11	–21
In public health institutions	NFHS 1	11	7	16	15	–5	–9
In public health institutions	NFHS 2	16	11	17	16	–1	–6
Assisted by health professionals	NFHS 1	25	18	38	34	–13	–20
Assisted by health professionals	NFHS 2	37	23	47	42	–10	–24

Sources: NFHS 1: IIPS (1995); NFHS 2: IIPS; and ORC Macro (2000).
Note: For deliveries, the data is for the four- and three-year period before NFHS 1 and NFHS 2, respectively.

Chapter 10

OCCUPATIONAL PATTERN

M. Thangaraj

Agriculture continues to be the mainstay of the Indian population, though some trends towards occupational diversification of rural workers from agricultural sector toward non-agricultural sector have been observed in the recent decades. Traditionally, Scheduled Castes (SCs) have been denied property rights. Caste system as a system of occupational assignment and social milieu has relegated them to the peripheral occupations and hence, economic mobility. Several welfare programmes aimed to promote the emancipation and economic mobility among the scheduled groups have been conceived and implemented by the government. It is worthwhile to evaluate the changes that such policy interventions have brought about in the occupational status of SCs and Scheduled Tribes (STs).

The main objective of this chapter is to analyse the changes in the livelihood patterns among social groups in India. Specifically, the analysis examines three major aspects of occupational diversification; namely shift from agricultural to non-agricultural occupations in rural areas, pattern of diversification within agriculture sector and changes in occupation pattern in urban areas.

The study uses two data sources for delineating the occupational pattern across social groups: Population Census that is conducted decennially and National Sample Survey (NSS) employment surveys that are carried out quinquennially. The decennial Population Census of India provides information on the working population or labour force. The workers are categorised into main workers and marginal workers on the basis of the duration of work, and further classified on the basis of ninefold industrial classification of workforce. This study takes into consideration the data on main workers only for the periods 1981, 1991 and 2001. The typology of National Sample Survey Organisation (NSSO) data is different. In the rural areas, workers are categorised as self-employed in agriculture (SEA), agricultural labourers, self-employed in non-agriculture (SENA), other labourers and other workers. In urban areas, there is a fourfold classification of workers into urban self-employed, wage and salaried workers, urban casual workers, and other households. NSS data for periods, 1993–1994 and 1999–2000 is employed to conduct an analysis in this chapter.

SECTORAL DISTRIBUTION OF RURAL WORKFORCE

This section examines the pattern and trends in the distribution of rural workforce in agriculture and non-agriculture sectors. The all-India and state level analyses are presented on the basis of the Census and NSS data.

The Census of India

The rural workforce in India is predominantly employed in agriculture sector but in case of the scheduled groups, the dependence on this traditional sector is more prominent than non-SCs/STs (Table 10.1).

Over the years, this proportion has shown a gradual decline. The occupational diversification of rural main workers from agricultural to non-agricultural sector which was negligible during the 1980s, sharpened during the decade of the 1990s for all the social groups. The percentage of rural SC main workers engaged in the agricultural sector declined by more than 11 percentage points from 84.49 per cent in 1991 to 72.93 per cent in 2001, while for the STs, the corresponding decline was of a somewhat lesser magnitude. Although the share of the agricultural workforce came down during the 1980s, yet in absolute terms, the number of main workers in the agricultural sector increased at a compound annual growth rate of about 2.5 per cent per annum for the SCs and STs, and at a slightly lower rate of 2 per cent for the non-SCs/STs. It was only during the period 1991–2001 that the agricultural workforce declined in both relative and absolute terms for all the social groups.

At the state level, the observed all-India trend is discernible in all the states in varying magnitudes (see Annexure VIII Table 10A.1). The diversification trend

Table 10.1
Share and Growth of Rural Main Workers in Agriculture Sector, All India (Per Cent)

Social Groups	Percentage of Rural Main Workers in Agricultural Sector			Compound Annual Growth Rate of Rural Agricultural Workforce		
	1981	*1991*	*2001*	*1981–1991*	*1991–2001*	*1981–2001*
SC	85.12	84.49	72.93	2.50	−2.02	0.21
ST	90.19	90.72	84.20	2.61	−0.87	0.86
Non-SC/ST	78.31	76.93	67.85	2.06	−0.65	0.70
Total	80.99	80.03	70.63	2.22	−0.94	0.63

Sources: (1) Union Primary Census Abstract General Population, Census of India, 1981, Series I, Parts i, ii and iii; (2) Office of the Registrar General of India, Census of India 1991 and 2001, Compact Disk.

among SCs is particularly sharp in the smaller states of Assam, Haryana, Kerala and Punjab. In the larger states of Andhra Pradesh, Bihar (including Jharkhand), Madhya Pradesh (including Chhattisgarh), Maharashtra, Tamil Nadu and Uttar Pradesh, where the concentration of SC population is higher, the decline in agricultural workforce during the period 1991–2001 has been lower, ranging between 3 and 11 per cent. In two of the states, such as Madhya Pradesh and Maharashtra, this marginal decline came about after an increase in the same during 1981–1991. Therefore, the net change in percentage share of rural SC workers engaged in agricultural sector to total number of SC main workers was quite low in these states.

Among STs, the diversification trend was observed for all the states during the 1990s, and more prominently so in the eastern and north-eastern parts of the country as compared to the central tribal belt (see Annexure VIII Table 10A.2). Interestingly, in the north-east and the two other states Kerala and Uttar Pradesh, a distinct decline was discernible in the share of ST agricultural workforce in the total rural ST main workers, was discernible even during the 1980s.

This trend towards the shifting of workforce away from agricultural sector occurred across all social groups, and its pace among SCs and non-SCs/STs was nearly at par. As a result, during 1981–2001, the disparity index of workers engaged in agricultural sector was more or less unchanged for SCs in comparison to non-SCs/STs (Figure 10.1). However, the disparities were higher in the case of STs versus non-SCs/STs and the same got accentuated over the years due to slower diversification among the former compared to latter.

Across the states, in 2001, the disparity ratio of SCs versus non-SCs/STs was greater than 1 in nearly all the states except Punjab (0.87) and Haryana (0.80). This indicates that the pattern of a higher proportion of SC workers being engaged in the agricultural sector than their non-SC/ST counterparts is nearly

Figure 10.1
Disparities in Share of Agricultural Workers to Total Main Workers in Rural India

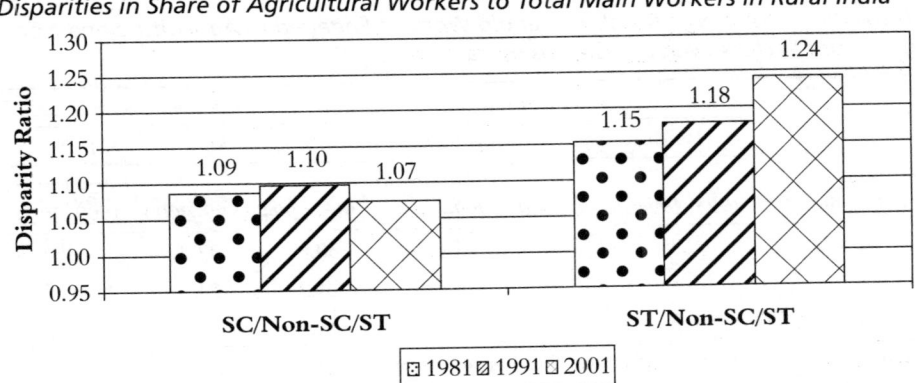

Source: Census of India: 1981, 1991 and 2001.

universal across states (see Annexure VIII Table 10A.3). In consonance with all-India trend, the disparity levels have remained more or less unchanged during 1981–2001 except in a few states like Punjab where the disparity ratio declined. The inter-state variations in the disparity ratio were quite prominent in case of STs versus non-SCs/STs, ranging from 1.07 in Uttar Pradesh to 3.35 in Mizoram. The disparity ratio has increased over time in the north-eastern states (except Mizoram) and other important states, namely Kerala, Gujarat, Andhra Pradesh, Orissa and West Bengal.

The NSS Employment–Unemployment Survey

The NSS data substantiates the pattern of occupational shift from agricultural to non-agricultural sector among SCs and non-SCs/STs during the past decade (Table 10.2). The magnitude of the shift was reported to be more prominent among non-SCs/STs households, and hence the inter-social group disparity among them was accentuated marginally during 1993–1994 to 1999–2000 (see Table 10.3).

At the state level, the NSS household data for SCs and non-SCs/STs broadly conforms to the direction of the observed changes from the Census data on the main workers (see Annexure VIII Tables 10A.4 and 10A.5). Both data sources distinctly indicate heavy dependence of SC workforce on agriculture sector and persistence of disparities among SCs and non-SCs/STs, as a larger proportion of SC rural workers are engaged in the traditional sector in comparison to the proportion of non-SC/ST rural workforce.

The inter-social group disparities are higher for ST as compared to non-SC/ST households and the same have got accentuated over time at all-India level in

Table 10.2

Distribution of All-India Rural Household Workers Engaged in Agriculture and Non-agriculture Sectors by Social Groups (Rural) (Per Cent)

		Agriculture Sector			Non-agriculture Sector		
		Percentage Share		*Net Change*	*Percentage Share*		*Net Change*
S. No.	Social Groups	*1993–1994*	*1999–2000*	*1993–1994 to 1999–2000*	*1993–1994*	*1999–2000*	*1993–1994 to 1999–2000*
1.	SC	59.4	67.8	–1.6	30.6	32.2	1.6
2.	ST	75.8	75.9	0.1	24.2	24.2	0
3.	Non-SC/ST	66.5	62.0	–4.5	33.4	37.9	4.5

Source: Employment and Unemployment Situation among Social Groups in India, 1993–1994 and 1999–2000, Department of Statistics, Government of India, New Delhi.

Table 10.3
Disparity Ratio for All-India Workers Engaged in Agriculture and Non-agriculture Sectors

		Agriculture Sector		Non-agriculture Sector	
S. No.		1993–1994	1999–2000	1993–1994	1999–2000
1.	SC/ST	0.92	0.89	1.26	1.33
2.	SC versus Non-SC/ST	1.04	1.09	0.92	0.85
3.	ST versus Non-SC/ST	1.14	1.22	0.72	0.64

Source: Employment and Unemployment Situation among Social Groups in India, 1993–1994 and 1999–2000, Department of Statistics, Government of India, New Delhi.

most of the states (see Annexure VIII Table 10A.5). However, all-India trend of the unchanged proportion of the STs engaged in agriculture during 1993–1994 to 1999–2000 varied widely across states. In the states of Assam, Gujarat, Himachal Pradesh, Kerala, Madhya Pradesh, Maharashtra, Mizoram, Sikkim, Tamil Nadu and Uttar Pradesh occupational diversification was observed among STs, as the percentage of the ST workers engaged in agricultural sector declined by 2–28 percentage points (see Annexure VIII Table 10A.6). On the other hand, this percentage increased sharply in Andhra Pradesh, Karnataka, Manipur, Orissa, Rajasthan and West Bengal.

RURAL OCCUPATIONAL PATTERN IN AGRICULTURE SECTOR

The Census of India classifies the rural workers engaged in agricultural sector as cultivators and agricultural labourers. NSS categorises the rural agricultural households as SEA and agricultural labourers. The former category in either classification signifies access of rural households to their own asset, such as land, while the latter category shows dependence on wage labour. The percentage distribution of workforce employed as cultivators to the total number of main workers by social groups (Table 10.4) highlights the fact that cultivation is the major economic activity of STs and non-SCs/STs while rural SC workers in agriculture sector predominantly work as labourers. In 2001, only about 27 per cent SC rural workers were cultivators as against 54 per cent ST rural workers and 47 per cent non-SC/ST rural workers. A majority of SC workers in rural areas have traditionally served as agricultural labourers, as their engagement in this occupation has been rather favoured by the upper castes. Moreover, due to their lack of education and technical skill, their absorption in other jobs has been difficult. As agricultural labourers, they are unorganised and have neither social nor economic security.

Table 10.4

Percentage of All-India Rural Cultivators and Agricultural Labourer Main Workers by Social Groups

S. No.	Social Groups	Cultivators			Agricultural Labourers		
		1981	1991	2001	1981	1991	2001
1.	SC	31.94	29.37	26.78	53.20	55.12	46.15
2.	ST	56.80	57.19	54.32	33.39	33.52	29.88
3.	Non-SC/ST	55.26	52.09	46.85	23.05	24.84	21.00
4.	Total	51.12	48.39	44.22	29.98	31.64	26.41

Sources: (1) Union Primary Census Abstract General Population, Census of India, 1981, Series I, Parts i, ii and iii; (2) Office of the Registrar General of India, Census of India, 1991 and 2001, Compact Disk.

During the decade 1991–2001, the occupational diversification of workers from agriculture to non-agriculture sector was reflected in declining proportion of both cultivators and agricultural labourers among all the social groups. However, the fall in the proportion of agricultural labourers was more prominent (by 9 percentage points) among SCs as compared to STs and non-SCs/STs. The inter-social group disparities in the nature of agricultural occupations were also evident from the NSS household data (Table 10.5). The proportion of self-employed rural agricultural households is more than twice that of agricultural labourer households and about half among the non-SCs/STs than SCs. Among the STs and non-SCs/STs, the percentage of self-employed households in agriculture was about the same during 1999–2000, but the incidence of persons engaged in agricultural labour was much higher among STs. Between 1993–1994 and 1999–2000, the outreach of rural households to land resources worsened, as indicated by the declining proportion of SEA and rise in the percentage of agricultural labour households.

At the state level, there are large inter-state variations in the occupational pattern of SC rural workers in agricultural sector. In the states of Himachal

Table 10.5

All-India Rural Households, SEA and Agricultural Labourers (Per Cent)

S. No.	Social Groups	SEA		Agricultural Labourers	
		1993–1994	1999–2000	1993–1994	1999–2000
1.	SC	20.1	16.4	49.3	51.4
2.	ST	38	36.2	37.8	39.7
3.	Non-SC/ST	43.3	37.9	23.2	24.1

Source: Employment and Unemployment Situation among Social Groups in India, 1993—1994 and 1999–2000, Department of Statistics, Government of India, New Delhi.

Pradesh, Jammu and Kashmir and Rajasthan, more than half of the SC main workers in rural areas were cultivators (see Annexure VIII Table 10A.7), while in Andhra Pradesh, Bihar, Haryana, Kerala and Punjab, less than 15 per cent SC workers were cultivating land. The proportion of cultivators went down during 1981–2001 in nearly all the states, though the percentage point change during this period was negligible in Kerala and Maharashtra. The state with the highest concentration of SC population, such as Uttar Pradesh, witnessed a very steep fall of 7 percentage points in the proportion of rural SC cultivators among main workers from about 52 per cent in 1981 to 45 per cent in 2001. The percentage of ST cultivators in rural main workers (during 2001) was high (more than 50 per cent) in Madhya Pradesh, Uttar Pradesh, Himachal Pradesh, Rajasthan, Bihar and the north-eastern states (see Annexure VIII Table 10A.8), while in Andhra Pradesh, Gujarat, Karnataka, Kerala, Maharashtra, Orissa, Tamil Nadu and West Bengal, it ranged from 25 per cent in West Bengal to 48 per cent in Orissa. The inter-social group disparity ratio of workers engaged as rural cultivators (Annexure VIII Table 10A.9) (10.9) clearly indicates a higher proportion of rural cultivators among non-SCs/STs than SCs, and hence better access of the former social group to agricultural land as compared to latter. These disparities have remained more or less unchanged during the past two decades at all-India level and have, in fact, worsened in Andhra Pradesh and Tamil Nadu.

Contrary to the observed disparities among SCs and non-SCs/STs in 2001, the disparity ratio between STs and non-SCs/STs was greater than unity at all-India level (1.16) and in most of the states except Karnataka, Maharashtra and West Bengal. At all-India level, the ratio increased marginally during 1981–1991, with several states conforming to all-India trend.

RURAL OCCUPATIONAL STRUCTURE IN NON-AGRICULTURAL SECTOR

The sectoral occupational diversification trends brought out earlier indicated the same shift in rural workforce from agricultural to non-agricultural sector. The Census of India classifies non-agricultural workforce into two groups. They are: (a) those engaged in household industry, and (b) other workers. The household industry is defined as 'an industry conducted by the head of the household herself/himself and/or by the members of the household at home or within the village in rural areas....' Household industry relates to the production, processing, servicing, repairing or making and selling (but not merely selling) of goods. The concept of household industry, thus, in a way signifies that the workers engaged in this industry have some access to capital. In contrast, non-agricultural workers classified as 'other workers' are those who are engaged in factory, plantation, trade, commerce, business transport, mining, construction, political or social work, pavement service, etc., and have negligible access to capital.

The Census data indicates that household industry accounts for a very small proportion of rural non-agricultural workers, engaging less than 4 per cent of the total main workers (Table 10.6). The rural labour force shifting out of agricultural occupation has been absorbed in non-agricultural sector as 'other workers' rather than in the household industry, as is evident from the rising proportion of other workers during the past two decades and near-stagnation in share of household industry during this period. In fact, the percentage of workers in household industry actually declined during 1981–1991, but regained ground during the subsequent decade to reach marginally above the 1981 level.

Across social groups, during both the decades, the proportion of rural workers in household industry was more or less the same for SCs and non-SCs/STs, but lower for STs. During 1981–2001, the increase in percentage of other workers was much higher among SCs (11.70 percentage points) than among non-SCs/STs (9.89 percentage points) and STs (5.54 percentage points).

The absorption of SC rural labour in household industry is low (less than 2.5 per cent) and hence the access of this group to capital is particularly low in Andhra Pradesh, Haryana, Jammu and Kashmir, Karnataka and Tamil Nadu (see Annexure VIII Table 10A.10). Over the years, the proportion of SC workers in household industry has increased markedly in Assam and Orissa, while a perceptible decline has occurred in the corresponding figures in Gujarat and Maharashtra. The proportion of ST rural workforce in household industry ranges from 0.54 per cent in Rajasthan to 4.11 per cent in Uttar Pradesh (see Annexure VIII Table 10A.11). During 1981–2001, there was some increase in the absorption of ST rural main workers in household industry in most of the states except four. In Rajasthan and Uttar Pradesh, the proportion remained nearly stagnant while in Andhra Pradesh and Maharashtra it declined. The state level pattern of disparity between rural SCs

Table 10.6

Percentage Distribution of Workers Engaged in Non-agricultural Sector to Total Rural Main Workers by Social Groups

S. No.	Social Groups	Household Industry			Other Workers		
		1981	1991	2001	1981	1991	2001
1.	SC	3.08	2.24	3.57	11.80	13.27	23.50
2.	ST	1.26	0.95	1.71	8.55	8.33	14.09
3.	Non-SC/ST	3.39	2.36	3.96	18.30	20.71	28.19
4.	Total	3.08	2.16	3.63	15.93	17.81	25.74

Sources: (1) Union Primary Census Abstract General Population, Census of India, 1981, Series I, Parts i, ii and iii; (2) Office of the Registrar General of India, Census of India, 1991 and 2001, Compact Disk.

and non-SCs/STs in terms of their access to capital brings out some interesting results (see Annexure VIII Table 10A.12). The all-India trend indicated that SCs have poorer access to both land and capital resources, but the inter-social group disparity in terms of access to capital was less pronounced. However, in Assam, Gujarat, Haryana, Himachal Pradesh, Madhya Pradesh, Maharashtra, Orissa and Rajasthan, the disparity index of greater than 1 indicates that SC rural workers had somewhat better access to capital than their non-SC/ST counterparts (as captured by the proportion of workers in household industry). However, in Bihar, Kerala, Punjab and Uttar Pradesh, rural SC workers were relatively worse off in this aspect. The inter-social group disparities among STs and non-SCs/STs were very high with a disparity ratio of less than 0.5 at all-India level (0.43) and in 10 states which include Andhra Pradesh, Gujarat, Jammu and Kashmir, Madhya Pradesh, Maharashtra, Manipur, Rajasthan, Tamil Nadu, Tripura and West Bengal. Other than Mizoram and Himachal Pradesh, the disparity ratio was less than unity in rest of the states as well. The trends indicate a worsening of disparities to the disadvantage of ST in most of the states during 1981–2001.

The NSS classification of non-agricultural workers as SENA, non-agricultural labourers and other workers provides additional insight into the limited access of SC households to capital resources (Table 10.7). In 1993–1994, 10.7 per cent of SC households were SENA and about the same proportion were non-agricultural labourers. By 1999–2000, though the proportion of self-employed SC households in non-agricultural activities increased marginally to 12 per cent, yet it was about 3 percentage points lower than non-SC/ST households that were SENA. The relatively disadvantageous position of ST with respect to SENA occupations is strikingly evident in Table 10.7.

Across the states, the access of SC rural households to capital was quite poor in the southern states of Andhra Pradesh, Karnataka, Kerala, Tamil Nadu and also in Maharashtra (see Annexure VIII Table 10A.13), while it was better than all-India average in West Bengal, Punjab, Rajasthan, Himachal Pradesh, Haryana and

Table 10.7
Distribution of Rural Non-agricultural Households According to Household Type

S. No.	Social Groups	Self-employed in Non-agriculture		Labourers	
		1993–1994	*1999–2000*	*1993–1994*	*1999–2000*
1.	SC	10.7	12.0	10.2	10.0
2.	ST	5.9	5.2	10.1	8.9
3.	Non-SC/ST	14.4	15.2	6.9	7.1

Source: Employment and Unemployment Situation among Social Groups in India, 1993–1994, 5th Quinquennial Survey, NSS 50th round, July 1993–June 1994, Department of Statistics, Government of India, New Delhi, November 1997.

Orissa. In case of ST, the engagement of rural households as SENA was relatively high in Uttar Pradesh (17.6 per cent), Himachal Pradesh (15.3 per cent), Punjab (11.8 per cent), Kerala (10.8 per cent) and Karnataka (10.5 per cent), while this proportion was below 5 per cent in Bihar, Gujarat, Madhya Pradesh, Maharashtra, Manipur, Nagaland and West Bengal.

URBAN OCCUPATIONAL PATTERN

Given the limited availability of cultivable land in urban areas, the urban work-force is predominantly engaged in non-agricultural activities. The NSS's categorisation of the urban workforce into self-employed, regular wage earners/salaried class and casual labourers brings out very interesting features of urban occupational patterns across social groups. As expected, the percentage of self-employed SC and ST workers was much lower while that of casual labourers was much higher than non-SCs/STs (Table 10.8) during both the years under study. The inter-social group variations in the percentage of regular wage earners/salaried households were of a very low magnitude which indicates the positive role of reservation policy for the scheduled groups. However, the brunt of slackening public employment during the economic reform period has fallen heavily on SCs, as the proportion of regular wage/salaried SC households declined from 44.4 per cent in 1993–1994 to 37.6 per cent in 1999–2000, while the corresponding decline was only to the tune of 0.8 and 2.8 percentage points for ST and non-SC/ST households, respectively.

The state level analysis (1999–2000) indicates that at least one-third of the urban SC households comprised casual labourers in Andhra Pradesh, Gujarat, Haryana, Jammu and Kashmir, Karnataka, Kerala, Madhya Pradesh, Orissa and Tamil Nadu (see Annexure VIII Table 10A.14). In Karnataka, Orissa and Tamil Nadu, together with high incidence of casual labour, the percentage of regular

Table 10.8
Percentage Distribution of Urban Households in Non-agricultural Occupations

		Self-employed		Regular Wage/Salaried		Casual Labour	
S. No.	Social Groups	1993–1994	1999–2000	1993–1994	1999–2000	1993–1994	1999–2000
1.	SC	21.6	27.3	44.4	37.6	20.1	26.5
2.	ST	24.9	21.6	39.2	38.0	27.6	25.6
3.	Non-SC/ST	35.5	36.6	43.9	41.4	10.8	12.4

Source: Employment and Unemployment Situation among Social Groups in India, 1993–1994, 5th Quinquennial Survey, NSS 50th round, July 1993–June 1994, Department of Statistics, Government of India, New Delhi, November 1997.

wage/salaried households was quite low (about 30 per cent) in comparison to all-India average (38 per cent) which indicates the poor status of urban SCs. The regular wage earners/salaried SC households were even lower in Assam (26 per cent) and Jammu and Kashmir (19 per cent). In most of the states, except a few like Maharashtra, there was a steep fall in the proportion of this category of SC households during 1993–1994 to 1999–2000. The decline was particularly notable in Tamil Nadu (33 percentage points), Gujarat (23 percentage points) and Assam (22 percentage points). Contrary to all-India trend, in Maharashtra, the number of regular wage earners increased among urban SCs during the 1990s. In general, SCs in urban areas appeared to be in a relatively better position in Maharashtra and West Bengal, as nearly 54 per cent of them were regular wage earners in the former state while over 40 per cent were self-employed in the latter. The wage/salaried households were the most prevalent types of households among STs at all-India level and in a majority of the states (see Annexure VIII Table 10A.15). However, in Gujarat, Karnataka, Kerala and Orissa, the percentage of casual labour households was higher, while in Uttar Pradesh, urban STs were mostly self-employed. During 1993–1994 to 1999–2000, the proportion of casual labour households declined in several states, though Gujarat and West Bengal were the exceptions, where the number of urban ST casual labour households increased by 14 and 12 per cent, respectively. The number of wage/salaried households declined sharply in these two states as also in Andhra Pradesh, Karnataka and Meghalaya.

SUMMARY

Despite the trend towards occupational diversification of rural workforce across all social groups observed during previous decade, 73 per cent and 84 per cent of SC and ST rural workforce, respectively, continues to be employed in agricultural sector and their dependence on this traditional sector is more prominent than among non-SCs/STs (68 per cent). The diversification trend among SCs is particularly sharp in Assam, Haryana, Kerala and Punjab. In Andhra Pradesh, Bihar (including Jharkhand), Madhya Pradesh (including Chhattisgarh), Maharashtra, Tamil Nadu and Uttar Pradesh, where the concentration of SC population is higher than in the other states, the decline in the number of SC agricultural workers during 1991–2001 was lower than in the other states, ranging between 3 and 11 percentage points. Except for a few states (Assam, Haryana, Punjab, Rajasthan, Madhya Pradesh and Maharashtra) the disparity index of SC as compared to non-SC/ST workers engaged in agricultural sector remained above 1 which indicates a higher percentage of SC workforce as opposed to non-SC/ST workforce. Among STs, the diversification trend was observed for all the states during the 1990s, and more prominently so in the eastern and north-eastern parts of the country as compared to the central tribal belt.

A majority of SC workers (46 per cent) in rural areas serve as agricultural labourers. Traditionally, SCs have been discriminated against in the possession of land and cultivation is the major economic activity of both STs and non-SCs/STs. In 1981, only about 32 per cent SC rural workers were cultivators as against corresponding figures of 57 per cent for ST and 55 per cent for non-SC/ST rural workers. By 2001, this proportion declined to 27 per cent, 55 per cent and 47 per cent for SCs, STs and non-SCs/STs, respectively. The NSS household data also substantiates the inter-social group disparities in rural occupation pattern. The proportion of self-employed rural agricultural households is more than twice that of agricultural labourer households and about half among non-SCs/STs than among SCs.

The non-agricultural rural workforce has limited access to capital as only 3.6 per cent (2001) is employed in household industry, and 26 per cent are other workers, mostly non-agricultural labourers. Across social groups and over time (1981–2001), the proportion of rural workers in household industry was more or less the same for SCs and non-SCs/STs (about 3 to 4 per cent), and below 2 per cent for ST. However, during the period 1981–2001, the percentage of 'other workers' increased sharply among SCs (11.70 percentage points) than among non-SCs/STs (9.89 percentage points) and STs (5.54 percentage points) which implies that the labour force displaced from agricultural sector is not absorbed in rural household industry but are engaged as other workers with limited access to capital. The absorption of SC rural labour in household industry is particularly low (less than 2.5 per cent) in Andhra Pradesh, Haryana, Jammu and Kashmir, Karnataka and Tamil Nadu. The proportion of ST rural workforce in household industry ranges from 0.54 per cent in Rajasthan to 4.11 per cent in Uttar Pradesh.

The scheduled groups in urban India also occupy a relatively disadvantageous position as compared to non-SCs/STs as the percentage of self-employed SC and ST workers is lower (about 9–15 percentage points in 1999–2000) while that of casual labourers is higher (14 percentage points) than the corresponding figures for non-SCs/STs. The inter-social group variations in the percentage of regular wage earners/salaried households is much lower which indicate the positive role of the reservation policy for the scheduled groups. However, the proportion of regular wage/salaried SC households declined from 44.4 per cent in 1993–1994 to 37.6 per cent in 1999–2000, while the corresponding decline was only by 2.8 per cent points for non-SC/ST households. This implies that the brunt of slackening public employment during the economic reform period has fallen more heavily upon SCs.

ANNEXURE VIII

Table 10A.1
Percentage Share of Rural SC Workers Engaged in Agriculture Sector to Total Rural SC Main Workers

States	1981	1991	2001
Andhra Pradesh	91.74	91.66	84.33
Arunachal Pradesh	22.67	23.03	28.85
Assam	N.A.	69.09	48.48
Bihar (including Jharkhand)	90.91	92.12	84.72
Gujarat	77.29	76.12	66.02
Haryana	72.05	72.49	50.76
Himachal Pradesh	79.88	77.01	65.79
Jammu and Kashmir	78.29	N.A.	58.97
Karnataka	83.43	84.27	73.93
Kerala	63.40	61.10	35.45
Madhya Pradesh (including Chhattisgarh)	85.10	86.12	80.47
Maharashtra	78.36	81.57	78.60
Manipur (excluding three subdivisions in 2001)	82.33	74.04	57.49
Meghalaya	24.39	37.43	18.43
Mizoram	4.82	9.59	1.72
Nagaland	N.A.	N.A.	N.A.
Orissa	81.38	80.29	64.09
Punjab	77.24	75.18	48.60
Rajasthan	79.64	82.26	70.71
Sikkim	70.65	67.40	52.59
Tamil Nadu	89.57	88.42	78.19
Tripura	68.86	66.83	45.64
Uttar Pradesh (including Uttarakhand)	89.01	88.00	77.00
West Bengal	80.66	77.32	61.30
All India	**85.12**	**84.49**	**72.93**

Sources: (1) Union Primary Census Abstract General Population, Census of India, 1981, Series I, Parts i, ii and iii; (2) Office of the Registrar General of India, Census of India, 1991 and 2001, Compact Disk.
Note: N.A. means not available. (1) The Census was not held in Assam in 1981 and in Jammu and Kashmir in 1991. (2) No SC has been scheduled by the President of India for Nagaland, Andaman and Nicobar Islands, and Lakshadweep.

Table 10A.2
Percentage Share of Rural ST Workers Engaged in Agriculture Sector to Total Rural ST Main Workers

States	1981	1991	2001
Andhra Pradesh	89.72	90.80	86.62
Arunachal Pradesh	93.03	88.83	83.45
Assam	N.A.	90.17	79.90
Bihar (including Jharkhand)	89.57	92.12	85.21
Gujarat	90.26	89.36	83.45
Haryana	N.A.	N.A.	N.A.
Himachal Pradesh	80.35	75.80	71.16
Jammu and Kashmir	N.A.	N.A.	61.69
Karnataka	86.13	85.49	78.86
Kerala	78.88	73.76	56.73
Madhya Pradesh (including Chhattisgarh)	93.95	94.90	90.97
Maharashtra	89.56	90.81	86.97
Manipur (excluding three subdivisions in 2001)	91.54	89.15	76.55
Meghalaya	85.86	81.18	78.15
Mizoram	91.22	88.32	87.00
Nagaland	88.09	87.24	80.69
Orissa	90.89	91.52	80.87
Punjab	N.A.	N.A.	N.A.
Rajasthan	90.22	92.19	84.65
Sikkim	77.20	72.86	63.16
Tamil Nadu	86.22	86.56	79.88
Tripura	93.69	88.59	77.63
Uttar Pradesh (including Uttarakhand)	89.10	85.88	80.38
West Bengal	81.54	82.48	71.96
All India	**90.19**	**90.72**	**84.20**

Source: (1) Union Primary Census Abstract General Population, Census of India, 1981, Series I, Parts i, ii and iii; (2) Office of the Registrar General of India, Census of India, 1991 and 2001, Compact Disk.
Notes: N.A. means not available. (1) The Census was not held in Assam in 1981 and in Jammu and Kashmir in 1991. (2) No SC has been scheduled by the President of India for Nagaland, Andaman and Nicobar Islands and Lakshadweep.

Table 10A.3
Disparity Ratio of Workers Engaged in Agriculture Sector

States/Union Territories	SC and Non-SC/ST			ST and Non-SC/ST		
	1981	*1991*	*2001*	*1981*	*1991*	*2001*
Andhra Pradesh	1.20	1.19	1.23	1.17	1.18	1.26
Arunachal Pradesh	0.67	0.62	0.64	2.75	2.40	1.85
Assam	N.A.	1.04	0.97	N.A.	1.36	1.59
Bihar (including Jharkhand)	1.07	1.07	1.10	1.05	1.07	1.10
Gujarat	1.01	1.05	1.05	1.17	1.23	1.32
Haryana	0.94	0.99	0.80	N.A.	N.A.	N.A.
Himachal Pradesh	1.08	1.10	1.05	1.08	1.08	1.14
Jammu and Kashmir	1.08	N.A.	1.11	N.A.	N.A.	1.16
Karnataka	1.06	1.08	1.07	1.09	1.09	1.14
Kerala	1.43	1.44	1.54	1.78	1.74	2.46
Madhya Pradesh (including Chhattisgarh)	1.01	1.02	0.99	1.12	1.12	1.12
Maharashtra	0.95	1.00	1.01	1.09	1.11	1.12
Manipur (excluding three subdivisions in 2001)	1.22	1.16	1.25	1.35	1.40	1.67
Meghalaya	0.40	0.84	0.46	1.40	1.82	1.94
Mizoram	0.52	0.72	0.07	9.84	6.60	3.35
Nagaland	N.A.	N.A.	N.A.	2.94	2.08	3.02
Orissa	1.05	1.07	1.03	1.18	1.22	1.30
Punjab	1.02	1.03	0.87	N.A.	N.A.	N.A.
Rajasthan	1.00	1.03	0.97	1.13	1.15	1.16
Sikkim	0.97	0.94	0.93	1.06	1.02	1.11
Tamil Nadu	1.20	1.20	1.23	1.15	1.18	1.26
Tripura	1.15	1.19	1.12	1.57	1.58	1.91
Uttar Pradesh (including Uttarakhand)	1.04	1.06	1.02	1.04	1.03	1.07
West Bengal	1.16	1.19	1.20	1.18	1.27	1.41
All India	**1.09**	**1.10**	**1.07**	**1.15**	**1.18**	**1.24**

Sources: (1) Union Primary Census Abstract General Population, Census of India, 1981, Series I, Parts i, ii and iii; (2) Office of the Registrar General of India, Census of India, 1991 and 2001, Compact Disk.
Notes: N.A. means not available. (1) The Census was not held in Assam in 1981 and in Jammu and Kashmir in 1991. (2) No SC has been scheduled by the President of India for Nagaland, Andaman and Nicobar Islands, and Lakshadweep. (3) No ST has been scheduled by the President of India for Haryana, Jammu and Kashmir, Punjab, Chandigarh, Delhi and Pondicherry.

Table 10A.4

Percentage Distribution of SC Rural Households Engaged in Agriculture Sector

| | Agriculture Sector | | |
| | Percentage Share | | Net Change |
States	*1993–1994*	*1999–2000*	*1993–1994 to 1999–2000*
Andhra Pradesh	80.4	74.4	–6
Arunachal Pradesh	0	0	0
Assam	48.9	48.1	–0.8
Bihar	83.6	76.5	–7.1
Gujarat	65.8	66.1	0.3
Haryana	42.3	47.5	5.2
Himachal Pradesh	54.6	37.8	–16.8
Jammu and Kashmir	47.7	47.6	–0.1
Karnataka	78.6	79.7	1.1
Kerala	67.4	62.1	–5.3
Madhya Pradesh	80.9	78	–2.9
Maharashtra	66.6	72.2	5.6
Manipur	N.A.	82.2	N.A.
Meghalaya	N.A.	0	N.A.
Mizoram	N.A.	0	N.A.
Nagaland	N.A.	100	N.A.
Orissa	54.6	63.8	9.2
Punjab	55.5	47.8	–7.7
Rajasthan	56.1	53.2	–2.9
Sikkim	30.3	33.8	3.5
Tamil Nadu	77.1	72.8	–4.3
Tripura	42.7	36.2	–6.5
Uttar Pradesh	66.3	67	0.7
West Bengal	65.6	63.2	–2.4
All India	**69.4**	**67.8**	**–1.6**

Source: 'Employment and Unemployment Situation among Social Groups in India, 1993–1994 and 1999–2000', NSS 50th and 55th rounds, Department of Statistics, Government of India, New Delhi.

Table 10A.5
Disparity Ratio of Rural Agricultural Workers

States	SC and Non-SC/ST		ST and Non-SC/ST	
	1993–1994	*1999–2000*	*1993–1994*	*1999–2000*
Andhra Pradesh	1.24	1.18	1.21	1.31
Arunachal Pradesh	0.00	0.00	0.85	1.36
Assam	0.76	0.97	1.24	1.52
Bihar	1.15	1.16	1.09	1.20
Gujarat	0.97	1.01	1.16	1.15
Haryana	0.72	0.90	1.15	1.32
Himachal Pradesh	0.82	0.86	1.12	1.07
Jammu and Kashmir	0.74	0.87	1.20	1.05
Karnataka	1.06	1.11	0.98	1.07
Kerala	1.37	1.66	1.46	1.58
Madhya Pradesh	1.01	1.04	1.11	1.10
Maharashtra	0.92	1.10	1.15	1.12
Manipur	N.A.	1.55	1.57	1.55
Meghalaya	N.A.	0.00	1.11	1.50
Mizoram	N.A.	0.00	0.73	0.83
Nagaland	N.A.	9.09	2.82	5.50
Orissa	0.90	1.03	1.07	1.36
Punjab	0.87	0.90	1.26	0.70
Rajasthan	0.79	0.86	0.66	0.87
Sikkim	0.65	0.66	1.19	1.03
Tamil Nadu	1.35	1.49	1.35	1.43
Tripura	1.07	0.97	1.26	1.40
Uttar Pradesh	0.94	1.01	0.84	0.87
West Bengal	1.18	1.23	1.23	1.65
All India	**1.04**	**1.09**	**1.14**	**1.22**

Source: 'Employment and Unemployment Situation among Social Groups in India, 1993–1994 and 1999–2000', NSS 50th and 55th rounds, Department of Statistics, Government of India, New Delhi.

Table 10A.6
Percentage Distribution of ST Rural Households Engaged in Agriculture Sector

| | Agriculture Sector | | |
| | Percentage Share | | Net Change |
States	*1993–1994*	*1999–2000*	*1993–1994 to 1999–2000*
Andhra Pradesh	78.4	83.1	4.7
Arunachal Pradesh	58.9	60	1.1
Assam	79.6	75.1	–4.5
Bihar	79.3	78.8	–0.5
Gujarat	78.9	75.9	–3
Haryana	67.4	70.1	2.7
Himachal Pradesh	74.5	46.8	–27.7
Jammu and Kashmir	76.9	57.5	–19.4
Karnataka	72.4	76.8	4.4
Kerala	71.8	59.2	–12.6
Madhya Pradesh	89.4	82.4	–7
Maharashtra	83	73.6	–9.4
Manipur	76.2	82.2	6
Meghalaya	76.8	79.5	2.7
Mizoram	69.7	67.5	–2.2
Nagaland	61.3	60.5	–0.8
Orissa	65	84	19
Punjab	80.3	37.1	–43.2
Rajasthan	47	54.1	7.1
Sikkim	55.4	53.1	–2.3
Tamil Nadu	76.9	69.7	–7.2
Tripura	50.1	52.2	2.1
Uttar Pradesh	59.4	57.3	–2.1
West Bengal	68.5	84.6	16.1
All India	**75.8**	**75.9**	**0.1**

Source: 'Employment and Unemployment Situation among Social Groups in India, 1993–1994 and 1999–2000', NSS 50th and 55th rounds, Department of Statistics, Government of India, New Delhi.

Table 10A.7
Per Cent of SC Cultivators among Rural Main Workers

States/Union Territories	1981	1991	2001
Andhra Pradesh	19.07	14.18	13.07
Arunachal Pradesh	21.17	19.62	26.90
Assam	N.A.	53.93	38.90
Bihar (including Jharkhand)	14.40	16.48	11.62
Gujarat	22.12	18.24	16.85
Haryana	13.60	9.31	11.20
Himachal Pradesh	74.86	71.36	63.26
Jammu and Kashmir	68.40	N.A.	52.80
Karnataka	31.71	27.57	29.65
Kerala	2.45	3.30	1.89
Madhya Pradesh (including Chhattisgarh)	42.08	42.55	39.74
Maharashtra	20.05	19.27	19.47
Manipur (excluding three subdivisions in 2001)	77.48	62.30	48.07
Meghalaya	8.76	14.24	6.54
Mizoram	4.82	5.75	1.72
Nagaland	N.A.	N.A.	N.A.
Orissa	31.10	30.84	25.40
Punjab	7.75	5.47	5.19
Rajasthan	60.38	57.93	54.47
Sikkim	64.77	57.88	45.34
Tamil Nadu	20.70	16.65	15.25
Tripura	36.28	35.23	24.35
Uttar Pradesh (including Uttarakhand)	51.92	46.66	44.75
West Bengal	33.72	31.27	23.94
All India	**31.94**	**29.37**	**26.78**

Sources: (1) Union Primary Census Abstract General Population, Census of India, 1981, Series I, Parts i, ii and iii; (2) Office of the Registrar General of India, Census of India, 1991 and 2001, Compact Disk.
Notes: N.A. means not available. (1) The Census was not held in Assam in 1981 and in Jammu and Kashmir in 1991. (2) No SC has been scheduled by the President of India for Nagaland, Andaman and Nicobar Islands and Lakshadweep.

Table 10A.8

Per Cent of ST Cultivators among Rural Main Workers

States/Union Territories	1981	1991	2001
Andhra Pradesh	45.23	43.40	43.21
Arunachal Pradesh	92.32	87.44	82.27
Assam	N.A.	79.67	73.53
Bihar (including Jharkhand)	65.71	65.93	61.50
Gujarat	48.94	48.88	45.27
Haryana	N.A.	N.A.	N.A.
Himachal Pradesh	77.75	73.49	70.38
Jammu and Kashmir	N.A.	N.A.	57.28
Karnataka	43.84	40.19	40.87
Kerala	20.80	17.14	14.22
Madhya Pradesh (including Chhattisgarh)	62.33	65.26	62.11
Maharashtra	42.31	41.01	37.89
Manipur (excluding three subdivisions in 2001)	89.66	86.90	72.06
Meghalaya	75.38	67.25	63.67
Mizoram	90.00	86.75	85.08
Nagaland	87.83	86.77	79.09
Orissa	53.99	52.59	48.37
Punjab	N.A.	N.A.	N.A.
Rajasthan	80.26	78.47	77.55
Sikkim	75.07	67.72	59.07
Tamil Nadu	50.79	40.61	47.41
Tripura	64.70	58.27	47.14
Uttar Pradesh (including Uttarakhand)	81.70	72.53	68.11
West Bengal	31.90	30.72	24.89
All India	**56.80**	**57.19**	**54.32**

Sources: (1) Union Primary Census Abstract General Population, Census of India, 1981, Series I, Parts i, ii and iii; (2) Office of the Registrar General of India, Census of India, 1991 and 2001, Compact Disk.
Notes: N.A. means not available. (1) The Census was not held in Assam in 1981 and in Jammu and Kashmir in 1991. (2) No SC has been scheduled by the President of India for Nagaland, Andaman and Nicobar Islands and Lakshadweep.

Table 10A.9
Disparity Index of Workers Engaged as Rural Cultivators

States/Union Territories	SC and Non-SC/ST			ST and Non-SC/ST		
	1981	*1991*	*2001*	*1981*	*1991*	*2001*
Andhra Pradesh	0.45	0.38	0.37	1.06	1.15	1.22
Arunachal Pradesh	0.82	0.87	0.70	3.56	3.88	2.14
Assam	N.A.	1.03	1.00	N.A.	1.52	1.89
Bihar (including Jharkhand)	0.27	0.31	0.28	1.22	1.24	1.47
Gujarat	0.41	0.38	0.40	0.91	1.02	1.06
Haryana	0.20	0.15	0.20	N.A.	N.A.	N.A.
Himachal Pradesh	1.04	1.06	1.05	1.08	1.09	1.16
Jammu and Kashmir	0.99	N.A.	1.10	N.A.	N.A.	1.19
Karnataka	0.61	0.57	0.61	0.84	0.83	0.84
Kerala	0.14	0.19	0.18	1.19	1.00	1.37
Madhya Pradesh (including Chhattisgarh)	0.66	0.67	0.65	0.98	1.02	1.02
Maharashtra	0.39	0.37	0.38	0.82	0.79	0.75
Manipur (excluding three subdivisions in 2001)	1.27	1.17	1.29	1.47	1.63	1.94
Meghalaya	0.19	0.50	0.27	1.66	2.35	2.66
Mizoram	0.69	0.54	0.08	12.97	8.15	3.79
Nagaland	N.A.	N.A.	N.A.	3.50	2.91	3.76
Orissa	0.55	0.57	0.58	0.95	0.98	1.10
Punjab	0.12	0.09	0.11	N.A.	N.A.	N.A.
Rajasthan	0.80	0.80	0.80	1.07	1.08	1.14
Sikkim	0.94	0.93	0.87	1.09	1.09	1.14
Tamil Nadu	0.47	0.44	0.43	1.16	1.07	1.34
Tripura	0.97	1.02	0.97	1.72	1.68	1.88
Uttar Pradesh (including Uttarakhand)	0.70	0.68	0.72	1.11	1.06	1.10
West Bengal	0.76	0.74	0.80	0.71	0.73	0.83
All India	**0.58**	**0.56**	**0.57**	**1.03**	**1.10**	**1.16**

Sources: (1) Union Primary Census Abstract General Population, Census of India, 1981, Series I, Parts i, ii and iii; (2) Office of the Registrar General of India, Census of India, 1991 and 2001, Compact Disk.

Notes: N.A. means not available. (1) The Census was not held in Assam in 1981 and in Jammu and Kashmir in 1991. (2) No SC has been scheduled by the President of India for Nagaland, Andaman and Nicobar Islands and Lakshadweep. (3)No ST has been scheduled by the President of India for Haryana, Jammu and Kashmir, Punjab, Chandigarh, Delhi and Pondicherry.

Table 10A.10

Percentage Distribution of SC Main Rural Workers in Household Industry

States/Union Territories	1981	1991	2001
Andhra Pradesh	1.29	0.91	1.68
Arunachal Pradesh	1.37	0.30	1.27
Assam	N.A.	2.32	5.06
Bihar (including Jharkhand)	2.11	1.61	3.58
Gujarat	6.27	4.35	3.30
Haryana	3.43	1.35	2.20
Himachal Pradesh	4.13	2.89	3.08
Jammu and Kashmir	2.10	N.A.	1.79
Karnataka	2.55	1.58	2.40
Kerala	3.55	2.49	2.69
Madhya Pradesh (including Chhattisgarh)	6.24	4.47	5.99
Maharashtra	6.51	3.56	3.38
Manipur (excluding three subdivisions in 2001)	6.34	6.34	9.93
Meghalaya	12.99	2.52	5.35
Mizoram	0.00	2.74	0.00
Nagaland	N.A.	N.A.	N.A.
Orissa	4.92	4.70	6.00
Punjab	3.02	1.41	2.62
Rajasthan	5.17	2.67	2.97
Sikkim	5.57	3.56	6.57
Tamil Nadu	1.21	0.99	2.07
Tripura	1.75	2.23	3.72
Uttar Pradesh (including Uttarakhand)	2.62	1.78	4.08
West Bengal	2.83	3.18	5.21
All India	**3.08**	**2.24**	**3.57**

Sources: (1) Union Primary Census Abstract General Population, Census of India, 1981, Series I, Parts i, ii and iii; (2) Office of the Registrar General of India, Census of India, 1991 and 2001, Compact Disk.
Notes: N.A. means not available. (1) The Census was not held in Assam in 1981 and in Jammu and Kashmir in 1991. (2) No SC has been scheduled by the President of India for Nagaland, Andaman and Nicobar Islands and Lakshadweep.

Table 10A.11
Percentage Distribution of ST Main Rural Workers in Household Industry

States/Union Territories	1981	1991	2001
Andhra Pradesh	3.54	2.43	2.67
Arunachal Pradesh	0.10	0.11	0.94
Assam	N.A.	0.36	2.17
Bihar (including Jharkhand)	1.84	1.37	3.26
Gujarat	0.81	0.64	0.80
Haryana	N.A.	N.A.	N.A.
Himachal Pradesh	1.17	1.26	1.49
Jammu and Kashmir	N.A.	N.A.	1.77
Karnataka	2.10	1.13	2.21
Kerala	0.73	0.40	2.59
Madhya Pradesh (including Chhattisgarh)	0.89	0.60	1.06
Maharashtra	1.26	0.71	0.95
Manipur (excluding three subdivisions in 2001)	0.56	0.75	3.09
Meghalaya	0.56	0.29	1.82
Mizoram	0.44	0.41	0.74
Nagaland	0.17	0.26	1.57
Orissa	1.39	1.66	3.48
Punjab	N.A.	N.A.	N.A.
Rajasthan	0.21	0.09	0.54
Sikkim	0.54	0.54	1.18
Tamil Nadu	1.36	1.33	1.98
Tripura	0.24	0.34	1.13
Uttar Pradesh (including Uttarakhand)	4.08	2.99	4.11
West Bengal	1.03	1.29	2.24
All India	**1.26**	**0.95**	**1.71**

Sources: (1) Union Primary Census Abstract General Population, Census of India, 1981, Series I, Parts i, ii and iii; (2) Office of the Registrar General of India, Census of India, 1991 and 2001, Compact Disk.
Notes: N.A. means not available. (1) The Census was not held in Assam in 1981 and in Jammu and Kashmir in 1991. (2) No SC has been scheduled by the President of India for Nagaland, Andaman and Nicobar Islands, and Lakshadweep.

Table 10A.12
Disparity Index of Workers Engaged in Household Industry

States/Union Territories	ST and Non-SC/ST			SC and Non-SC/ST		
	1981	*1991*	*2001*	*1981*	*1991*	*2001*
Andhra Pradesh	0.65	0.61	0.50	0.24	0.23	0.31
Arunachal Pradesh	0.17	0.33	0.93	2.22	0.93	1.25
Assam	N.A.	0.46	0.88	N.A.	3.04	2.04
Bihar (including Jharkhand)	0.77	0.87	0.88	0.88	1.02	0.97
Gujarat	0.34	0.45	0.44	2.59	3.10	1.83
Haryana	N.A.	N.A.	N.A.	1.47	1.07	1.08
Himachal Pradesh	1.19	1.39	1.05	4.19	3.21	2.18
Jammu and Kashmir	N.A.	N.A.	0.28	0.45	N.A.	0.28
Karnataka	0.54	0.68	0.55	0.66	0.95	0.59
Kerala	0.18	0.16	0.75	0.89	0.98	0.77
Madhya Pradesh (including Chhattisgarh)	0.26	0.26	0.35	1.82	1.94	1.96
Maharashtra	0.64	0.55	0.47	3.32	2.77	1.68
Manipur (excluding three subdivisions in 2001)	0.04	0.08	0.40	0.47	0.67	1.28
Meghalaya	0.31	0.24	0.64	7.28	2.08	1.88
Mizoram	1.18	1.65	1.40	0.00	11.02	0.00
Nagaland	0.28	0.23	0.95	N.A.	N.A.	N.A.
Orissa	0.37	0.47	0.78	1.31	1.32	1.35
Punjab	N.A.	N.A.	N.A.	1.55	1.34	0.90
Rajasthan	0.08	0.05	0.22	1.96	1.54	1.19
Sikkim	0.99	1.18	0.88	10.15	7.82	4.91
Tamil Nadu	0.29	0.35	0.35	0.25	0.26	0.36
Tripura	0.10	0.16	0.39	0.75	1.02	1.27
Uttar Pradesh (including Uttarakhand)	1.41	1.65	0.91	0.91	0.98	0.91
West Bengal	0.24	0.25	0.28	0.66	0.61	0.65
All India	**0.37**	**0.41**	**0.43**	**0.91**	**0.95**	**0.90**

Sources: (1) Union Primary Census Abstract General Population, Census of India, 1981, Series I, Parts i, ii and iii; (2) Office of the Registrar General of India, Census of India, 1991 and 2001, Compact Disk.
Notes: N.A. means not available. (1) The Census was not held in Assam in 1981 and in Jammu and Kashmir in 1991. (2) No SC has been scheduled by the President of India for Nagaland, Andaman and Nicobar Islands and Lakshadweep. (3) No ST has been scheduled by the President of India for Haryana, Jammu and Kashmir, Punjab, Chandigarh, Delhi and Pondicherry.

Table 10A.13
Proportion of Rural Households Engaged as Self-employed in Non-agriculture

States	SC		ST	
	1993–1994	*1999–2000*	*1993–1994*	*1999–2000*
Andhra Pradesh	5.5	6.2	10.2	7.4
Arunachal Pradesh	36.5	0	2.6	8.6
Assam	20.8	23.8	4.2	7.1
Bihar	6.1	11	4.7	4
Gujarat	9.6	12.4	2.3	3.2
Haryana	15.4	15.6	0	0
Himachal Pradesh	14.6	16.9	7.4	15.3
Jammu and Kashmir	10.8	8.4	0	0.5
Karnataka	9.2	5.6	11.6	10.5
Kerala	5.3	4.1	5.6	10.9
Madhya Pradesh	6	10.1	3.6	3.3
Maharashtra	10.8	6.1	4.6	4.9
Manipur	N.A.	3.7	11.2	3.7
Meghalaya	N.A.	100	7.2	5.6
Mizoram	N.A.	0	8.8	5.5
Nagaland	N.A.	0	7.9	2.5
Orissa	20.4	15.5	11.8	5.5
Punjab	16.7	18.2	3.3	11.8
Rajasthan	12.8	16.5	4.5	5.1
Sikkim	24.8	19	2.6	1.9
Tamil Nadu	4.3	6	4.7	7
Tripura	18.3	18.8	6	8.3
Uttar Pradesh	11.2	13.1	10.5	17.6
West Bengal	17.4	21.6	4.1	4.3
All India	**10.7**	**12**	**5.9**	**5.2**

Source: 'Employment and Unemployment Situation among Social Groups in India, 1993–1994 and 1999–2000', NSS 50th and 55th rounds, Department of Statistics, Government of India, New Delhi.

Table 10A.14

Percentage Distribution of Urban SC Households by Household Type, 1999–2000

States	Household Types			
	Self-employed	*Regular Wage/Salaried*	*Casual Labour*	*Others*
Andhra Pradesh	17.0	37.4	32.7	12.9
Arunachal Pradesh	45.6	41.2	13.2	0.0
Assam	42.5	25.8	18.6	12.9
Bihar	29.7	34.8	25.8	9.7
Gujarat	18.7	38.6	33.4	9.3
Haryana	30.4	35.5	32.3	1.8
Himachal Pradesh	26.9	47.0	18.1	8.1
Jammu and Kashmir	38.6	19.3	35.2	7.0
Karnataka	22.0	29.9	38.0	10.1
Kerala	14.2	34.1	44.5	7.3
Madhya Pradesh	24.1	34.1	33.1	8.8
Maharashtra	20.3	54.1	16.9	8.6
Manipur	31.5	6.1	12.1	50.4
Meghalaya	6.1	57.9	36.0	0.0
Mizoram	17.7	70.1	12.2	0.0
Nagaland	45.8	33.1	7.0	14.1
Orissa	30.7	29.0	35.0	4.8
Punjab	31.4	40.6	23.1	4.8
Rajasthan	33.7	33.3	26.4	6.5
Sikkim	29.9	51.6	16.8	1.8
Tamil Nadu	14.6	29.6	36.4	18.3
Tripura	24.5	38.0	24.7	12.8
Uttar Pradesh	35.6	34.5	23.2	6.4
West Bengal	43.0	34.2	18.7	4.0
All India	**27.3**	**37.6**	**26.5**	**8.5**

Source: 'Employment and Unemployment Situation among Social Groups in 1999–2000', NSS 55th rounds, Department of Statistics, Government of India, New Delhi.

Table 10A.15
Distribution of Urban ST Households by Household Type, 1999–2000

| States | Household Types | | | |
	Self-employed	Regular Wage/Salaried	Casual Labour	Others
Andhra Pradesh	27.40	26.20	20.60	25.80
Arunachal Pradesh	9.10	37.60	39.30	13.90
Assam	11.50	53.40	3.60	31.50
Bihar	20.00	40.70	5.20	34.10
Gujarat	22.40	35.80	18.00	22.20
Haryana	55.20	44.80	0.00	0.00
Himachal Pradesh	18.40	33.20	43.30	5.20
Jammu and Kashmir	4.20	0.00	0.60	95.10
Karnataka	3.60	33.80	0.00	62.60
Kerala	11.00	77.20	0.00	11.80
Madhya Pradesh	31.40	25.80	36.40	6.40
Maharashtra	26.20	26.30	41.70	5.80
Manipur	21.20	43.50	19.90	15.50
Meghalaya	18.40	58.00	6.30	17.40
Mizoram	11.80	34.10	42.60	11.40
Nagaland	4.70	80.30	0.00	15.00
Orissa	15.30	38.30	33.60	12.80
Punjab	20.20	52.80	19.80	7.10
Rajasthan	29.30	20.70	7.50	42.50
Sikkim	46.10	26.60	0.90	26.40
Tamil Nadu	17.30	48.70	13.50	20.00
Tripura	22.60	35.30	28.70	13.30
Uttar Pradesh	36.80	42.50	12.20	8.20
West Bengal	7.00	67.10	0.40	25.50
All India	**21.60**	**38.00**	**25.60**	**14.70**

Source: 'Employment and Unemployment Situation among Social Groups in 1999–2000', NSS 55th rounds, Department of Statistics, Government of India, New Delhi.

Chapter 11

ACCESS TO AGRICULTURAL LAND AND CAPITAL ASSETS

R. S. Deshpande and Motilal Mahamallik

Asset holdings indicate the economic position of a household or group which is determined partially by the current economic activities and largely by a derivative from cumulative operations in the labour, product and factor markets. The current asset-holding position of Dalit households has its roots in the economic discrimination faced by them. It has been well-documented that a Dalit household cannot acquire land very easily and further cannot retain the land even if it succeeds to acquire it. Over the years, the trends in ownership and operational holding of land by Scheduled Castes (SCs) and Scheduled Tribes (STs) need to be viewed in a comprehensive manner in order to understand the operation of this process.

This chapter explores the changes in access to land and capital assets of Dalits as reflected in the wide surveys of land and asset holdings conducted by the National Sample Survey Organisation (NSSO). First, the disparities in land assets are examined, followed by an analysis of non-farm asset holdings and disparities in aggregate capital assets. The study also assesses the data on household assets which reflect the clear divide between SCs and STs on one hand, and non-SCs/STs on the other hand.

LAND ASSETS

Land is the basic productive asset for Dalits and it not only supports the production sector but also has a strong linkage with the labour market. At all-India level, 10 per cent SCs are landless, whereas about 7 per cent STs have no land (see Table 11.1). More than 75 per cent SCs have a very thin or negligible land base which indicates their frugal means of livelihood. The situation is not very different for STs.

It is seen that even within the group, there is a significant level of inequality in landholding. Across the states, this inequality is the highest in Punjab,

Table 11.1
Percentage Distribution of All-India Rural Households by Size of Land Owned, 1999

Social Groups	Size of Landholding (Hectares)					
	0	*0.99*	*1.00–2.49*	*2.5–4.99*	*5.00–10.00*	*10.00 and Above*
SC	10	65.00	14.70	6.5	2.8	1.1
ST	7.2	39.1	24.3	16.5	9.9	3
Non-SC/ST	5.8	46.3	19.1	12.8	9.3	6.7

Source: NSS Employment-Unemployment Survey, 1999.

Haryana, Kerala, Tamil Nadu, Bihar and West Bengal. However, Madhya Pradesh, Rajasthan, Maharashtra and Karnataka show relatively less dispersion among the groups by size of landholdings (see Figures 11.1 and 11.2).

The distribution of land is fairer in case of STs than SCs. Almost 30 per cent STs have landholdings of size above 2.5 hectares as against only about 11 per cent among SCs (see Annexure IX Table 11A.1). There is better distribution of land among STs that provides credence to the hypothesis that SCs usually opt to stay within the village and depend on upper-caste population for their livelihood, which eventually causes the loss of land resources. This does not happen with ST as a group as they have always been away from the villages and thus did not depend exclusively on upper castes.

The contrast between Dalits and non-Dalits becomes very clear when we look at the distribution of land in non-SC/ST social groups which represents 'non-Dalit' group. Almost 30 per cent non-Dalits hold land above 2.5 hectares, whereas only 6 per cent among them are landless. The lowest size group of landholding is also smaller in case of non-SCs/STs than Dalits (see Figure 11.3).

The disparities in land assets between scheduled and non-scheduled groups are brought out further in the tenancy situation among them and inter-group variations in the value of land assets. The SCs largely do not have a high proportion of leased land (see Annexure IX Table 11A.2), which probably indicates non-preference of SC tenants among landlords. There are a large number of farmers who partly owned land. This indicates lower control of scheduled groups on owned land resources. The area under irrigated landholdings is also lower among SCs when compared to non-SCs/STs (see Annexure IX Table 11A.3). The quality of land as captured through the area under irrigated landholdings underscores the weak resource base of SCs as only 29 per cent gross cropped area cultivated by SCs was irrigated.

The inter-social group variations in the value of land assets are also indicators of the differences in the quality of land owned by them. The SCs own land assets worth ₹28,900, whereas per-household land assets owned by other castes are worth ₹87,700, which is more than three times the land held by SCs (see Table 11.2). The discrimination suffered by SCs in rural and urban areas is

Figure 11.1
Per Cent Distribution of Rural SC Household Size of Land Owned

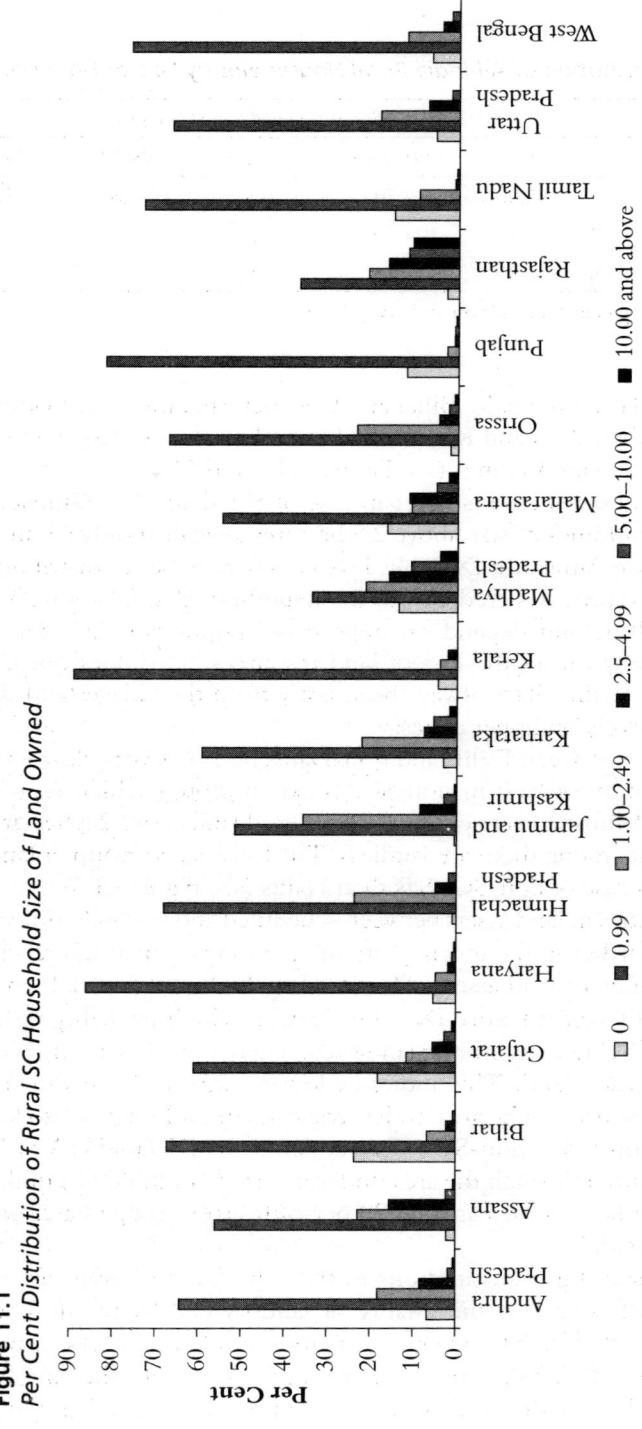

Source: NSSO, 55th round, Employment and Unemployment Survey, 1999–2000.

Figure 11.2
Per Cent Distribution of Rural ST Household Size of Land Owned

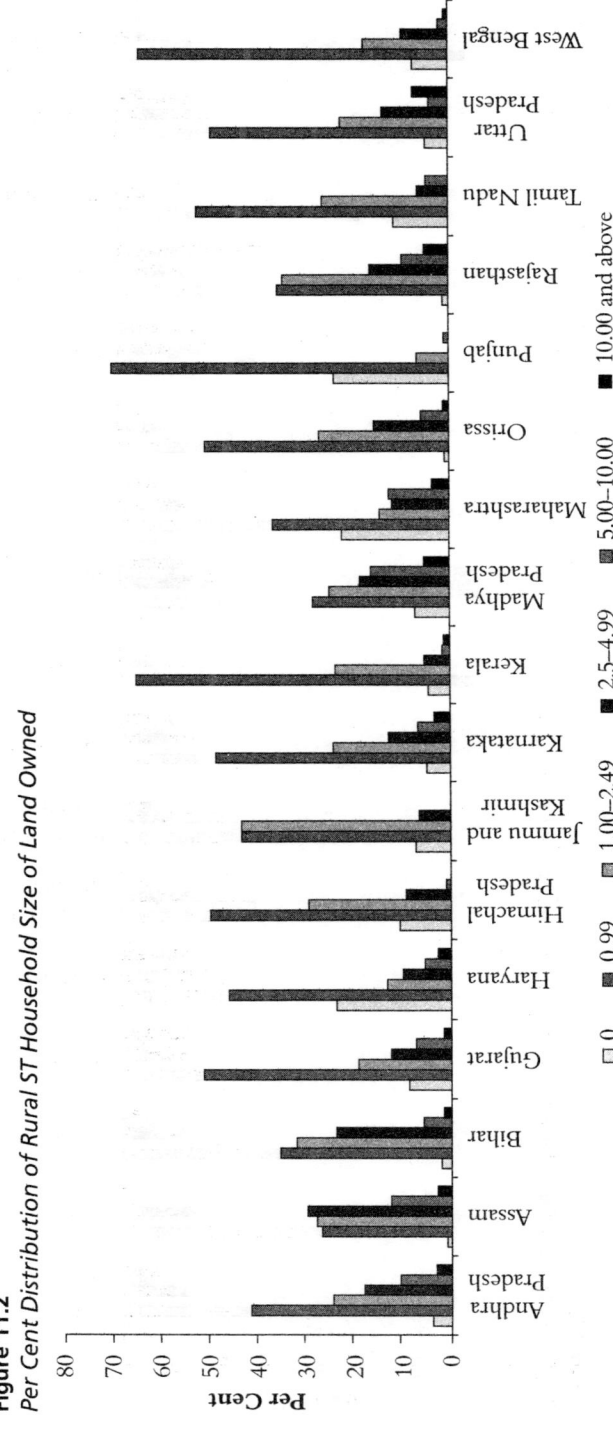

Source: NSSO, 55th round, Employment and Unemployment Survey, 1999–2000.

Figure 11.3

Per Cent Distribution of Rural Other Household Size of Land Owned

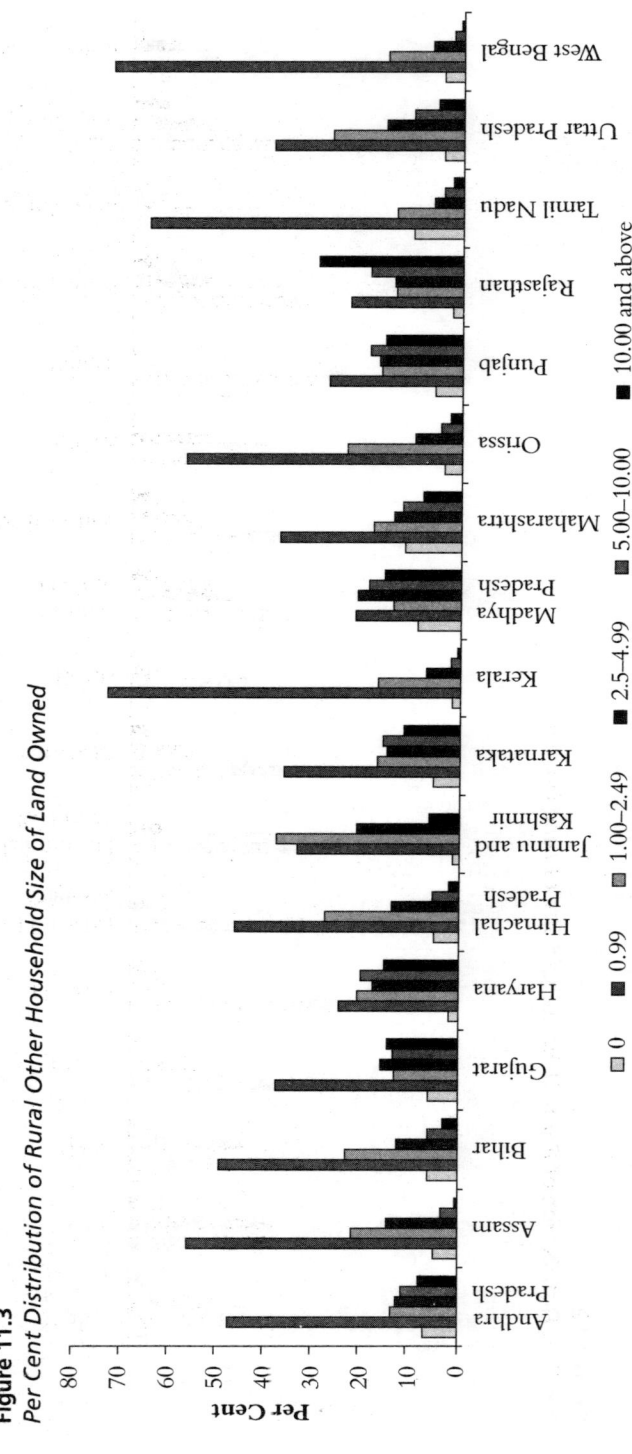

Source: NSSO, 55th round, Employment and Unemployment Survey, 1999–2000.

Table 11.2
Level of Capital Assets at All-India Level by Categories of Assets, 1992

Types of Assets	Rural				Urban			
	ST	SC	Non-SC/ST	All	ST	SC	Non-SC/ST	All
Land assets	31,025	28,927	87,743	68,749	28,668	20,554	56,575	51,279
Agricultural machinery	796	649	3214	2391	269	83	419	372
Livestock and poultry	3391	2132	4134	3618	720	371	643	611
Non-farm business equipment	76	120	454	340	306	448	2442	2126
Buildings	12,186	13,417	27,698	22,899	24,428	21,658	63,083	56,779
Aggregate capital assets	52,660	49,189	1,34,500	1,07,007	68,763	57,908	1,59,745	1,44,330

Source: NSS, 'Debt and Investment Survey, Household Assets and Indebtedness of Social Groups', 48th round, 1992.

almost similar. However, the differences between SCs and the other castes are much sharper in rural areas. This argument has been emphasised in the literature several times, particularly by Ambedkar (1946), Gail Omvedt (1996) and Thorat (1996).

Across the states, the rural areas of Gujarat, Maharashtra, Bihar, West Bengal, Assam, Kerala and Orissa have lower average land assets owned by SCs (see Annexure IX Table 11A.4). If we take the ratio of assets held by Dalits along with those held by non-Dalits, we observe that the disparity among land assets is quite high, particularly in Punjab, Haryana, Bihar, Gujarat and Tamil Nadu (see Annexure IX Table 11A.1). It is interesting to note that the same states do not necessarily feature in the process of discrimination in urban areas, and therefore, one can easily see the differences in discrimination between urban and rural areas. The observed pattern leads to two important postulates. One, the states which have higher disparity than all-India average are also the high-income states of the country, and this observation leads to the hypothesis that Dalits suffer higher deprivation in the states that generate a higher state income. Hence, the deprivation is rather acutely felt as it is compounded by high inequality. Second, the process of discrimination is significantly different between rural and urban areas as far as land assets are concerned. It also points to the fact that better quality land is owned by different elite groups in urban areas as against rural areas.

NON-LAND FARM ASSETS

The average value of agricultural machinery owned by all households is ₹2,391 (see Table 11.2). In rural areas, the households which belong to other castes have, on an average, machinery worth ₹3,214, which is about five times higher than the value of machines owned by SCs. In urban areas, the difference is almost the same. Interestingly, STs are in a better position as compared to SCs in both urban and rural areas. The differences across the states are, however, quite visible and expectedly well-defined. Punjab and Haryana have the highest value of agricultural machinery owned by households. The eastern and north-eastern states have a lower value of agricultural machinery owned by households. The cross-classification of states, according to the level of agricultural machines owned by different social groups, indicates that SC households in rural areas of Maharashtra, Karnataka and West Bengal have a significantly low holding of agricultural machinery (see Annexure IX Table 11A.5). This is certainly not an unexpected result. As the size of landholding is quite low among SCs, therefore, it would certainly mean that they do not have better means of production even in terms of agricultural machinery. It must be made clear that agricultural machinery here does not necessarily focus on the hind machinery like tractors or powered tillers but also include all other machines.

Another important non-land farm asset is livestock that works as an insurance for the poor farmers in the event of exigencies. It is quite well known that animal husbandry is an allied agricultural activity which protects the poor households at times when their farm income fails due to droughts, floods or other climatic and non-climatic factors. The average value of livestock and poultry held by all households comes to ₹3,618 in rural areas, and is quite low in urban areas. In rural areas, average SC households have assets worth ₹2,132 as against assets worth ₹4,134 owned by other castes (see Table 11.2). The situation varies across states. The differentials are not as large as those visible among states in case of agricultural machinery. However, these are also quite significant as they reflect the assets of better-off among the poor across states. The cross-classification of states indicates that SCs in Maharashtra, West Bengal, Bihar, Orissa and Tamil Nadu have relatively poor holdings of these assets (see Annexure IX Table 11A.6).

NON-FARM BUSINESS ASSETS

The value of non-farm business equipment indicates non-farm activity being undertaken by a household in order to supplement the farm income, especially to protect a farm household when the farm income dips. The SC households have slightly better holdings as compared to the ST households. The differential between SCs and STs is not significant in urban areas. However, it is quite high between these caste groups and other castes. Moreover, non-farm business activities which predominate in rural areas do not lead to as many restrictions on SCs as they do in urban areas (see Annexure IX Table 11A.7).

HOUSEHOLD ASSETS

The weaker sections, specifically SCs and STs, are deprived of land assets, farm and non-farm equipment and machinery, and other capital assets. This deprivation has been perpetuated and built over generations through institutionalised social practices. The result is severe poverty which in turn has further led to significantly low household assets. While an average household that belong to other castes has household assets worth ₹27,000 in rural areas, SC households have assets worth only ₹12,000. The disparities are almost similar in rural and urban areas, but certainly different across states. Here again, the developed regions (with few exceptions) show the prevalence of greater discrimination as against underdeveloped regions. The cross-classification across states depicts a very different picture which would lead one to question the meaning of development when a sizeable group is rather deliberately kept out of its ambit in terms of average value of household assets (see Figure 11.4).

AGGREGATE CAPITAL ASSETS

While we accept the fact that it is difficult for SCs and STs to acquire any capital assets under a situation of perpetual discrimination, it is essential to highlight the differences between various social groups to emphasise that perpetual discrimination not only causes social misery, but also leads to fewer economic opportunities for SCs and STs. The aggregate capital asset holdings per household at the national level clearly indicate that SCs have significantly low capital asset holdings as compared to other social groups. The per-household capital assets of SCs are worth about ₹49,000, whereas the corresponding figure for all households is ₹1.07 lakhs. This difference between the two figures is quite large when compared to other castes with SCs and STs. The households which belong to other castes have, on an average, ₹1.35 lakhs as average household capital assets.

Punjab, Haryana, Jammu and Kashmir, Rajasthan, Uttar Pradesh and Himachal Pradesh have large capital asset holdings in rural areas. Some of these states also dominate in terms of higher asset holdings in urban areas (see Annexure IX Table 11A.8). The SCs are well-placed in Jammu and Kashmir, Punjab, Haryana, Himachal Pradesh and Uttar Pradesh. The cross-classification of the states on the basis of higher asset holdings and lower holding groups of states across different social groups reveals an interesting picture. Kerala, West Bengal, Maharashtra,

Figure 11.4
Disparity of Households Having Buildings (in Value Terms) among Social Groups, 1991

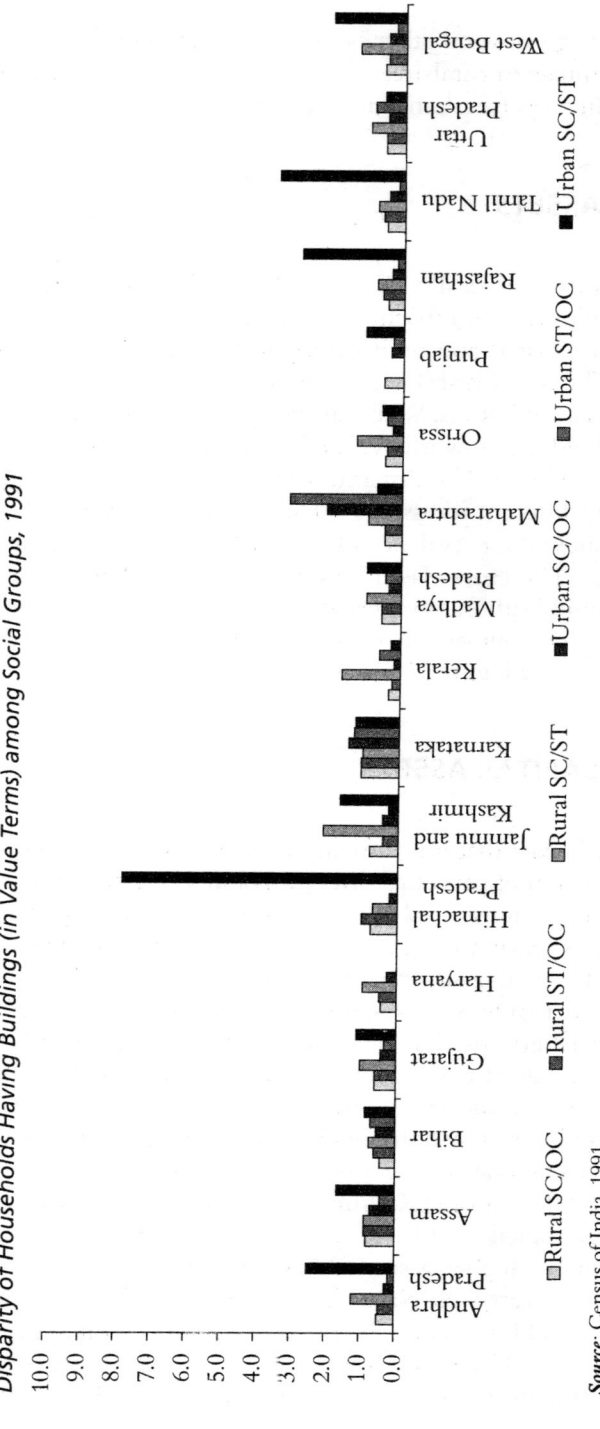

Source: Census of India, 1991.

Bihar, Tamil Nadu and Andhra Pradesh have low capital formation among SCs. The components of different types of assets held by social groups show that the differential largely originates from buildings, non-farm business equipments, and agricultural machinery. It is commonly observed in both rural and urban areas that SCs and STs are largely asset-poor almost at equally relative terms. The asset-holding across these components also reflects their capacity to reach higher income levels (see Annexure IX Tables 11A.9 and 11A.10).

CONCLUSION

The SCs and STs are placed at the lowest rung of the ladder of development. These groups have lower holdings in most of the assets, be it land; and farm, non-farm, other productive assets; or most importantly, capital assets. The exasperating fact is not the lower asset holdings of the weaker sections but the fact that this process has continued unabated, even through the 1990s. Not much has changed during the eventful decade of the 1990s, for the opening up of the markets has, in fact, led to larger discrimination against SCs and STs than earlier. The asset positions very clearly indicate that the relative economic strength (or weakness) of the weaker sections has been worsening over the years. An interesting observation that emerges from the study is that there is a positive relationship between development and discrimination, especially since larger disparities in asset holdings are seen between SCs and STs, and non-SCs/STs in the developed states.

ANNEXURE IX

Table 11A.1
Disparity of Land Assets Owned by Households (in Value Terms) among Social Groups, 1991

	Rural			Urban		
	SC versus Non-SC/ST	*ST versus Non-SC/ST*	*SC/ST*	*SC versus Non-SC/ST*	*ST versus Non-SC/ST*	*SC/ST*
States						
Andhra Pradesh	0.3	0.5	1.7	0.3	0.1	2.7
Assam	0.7	1.1	1.5	0.6	1.7	0.4
Bihar	0.2	0.7	2.7	0.6	1.4	0.4
Gujarat	0.5	0.4	0.8	0.4	0.1	3.2
Haryana	0.2	0.1	0.7	0.4	0.2	1.8

(Table 11A.1 Contd.)

(Table 11A.1 Contd.)

States	Rural			Urban		
	SC versus Non-SC/ST	*ST versus Non-SC/ST*	*SC/ST*	*SC versus Non-SC/ST*	*ST versus Non-SC/ST*	*SC/ST*
Himachal Pradesh	0.5	1.0	1.9	0.2	0.0	34.1
Jammu and Kashmir	0.7	0.4	0.6	0.4	0.6	0.7
Karnataka	0.4	0.5	1.1	0.4	0.5	0.8
Kerala	0.2	0.3	1.8	0.1	1.4	0.1
Madhya Pradesh	0.4	0.4	0.9	0.4	0.5	0.7
Maharashtra	0.3	0.4	1.4	0.4	1.1	0.4
Orissa	0.4	0.4	1.1	0.3	0.1	3.8
Punjab	0.1	N.A.	N.A.	0.3	0.3	0.7
Rajasthan	0.5	0.4	0.8	0.3	0.1	2.9
Tamil Nadu	0.3	0.6	2.0	0.3	0.0	14.4
Uttar Pradesh	0.4	0.5	1.3	0.4	1.5	0.3
West Bengal	0.6	0.5	0.8	0.7	0.1	4.7
All India	**0.3**	**0.4**	**1.1**	**0.4**	**0.5**	**0.7**

Source: Calculated from the 'Debt and Investment Survey, Household Assets and Indebtedness of Social Groups', NSS, 48th round, 1992.

Table 11A.2
Tenancy Status for SCs in India, 1985–1986

S. No.	Major Size Classes	Wholly Owned and Self-operated	Partly Owned	Wholly Leased-in	Wholly Otherwise Operated	Partly Leased-in	Partly Otherwise Operated
1.	Marginal	2,845 (23.7)	47 (16.2)	28 (30.1)	28 (37.3)	33 (28.9)	13 (22.8)
2.	Small	2,552 (21.3)	65 (22.4)	25 (26.9)	21 (28.0)	35 (30.7)	15 (26.3)
3.	Medium	2,503 (20.8)	78 (27.0)	18 (19.4)	10 (13.3)	17 (14.9)	11 (19.3)
4.	Large	1,371 (11.4)	28 (9.6)	3 (3.2)	2 (2.7)	5 (4.4)	3 (5.3)
5.	All classes	12,005 (100.0)	289 (100.0)	92 (100.0)	75 (100.0)	113 (100.0)	57 (100.0)

Source: Agricultural Census, 1985–1986, Government of India, New Delhi.
Note: Figures in brackets indicate percentages.

Table 11A.3
Percentage Distribution of Size and Class-wise Irrigated and Unirrigated Area—
Scheduled Castes, 1985–1986 and 1990–1991

S. No.	Size/Class of Holding	Gross Cropped Area			
		Irrigated		Unirrigated	
		1985–1986	*1990–1991*	*1985–1986*	*1990–1991*
1.	Marginal	39.0	41.8	61.0	58.2
2.	Small	29.5	30.4	70.5	69.6
3.	Semi-medium	24.4	25.9	75.6	71.4
4.	Medium	19.6	22.2	80.4	77.8
5.	Large	9.7	11.5	90.3	88.5
6.	All classes	27.3	29.2	72.7	70.8

Source: Agricultural Census, 1980–1981 and 1985–1986, Government of India, New Delhi.
Notes: (1) Landholding sizes are: Marginal—up to 1 hectare, Small—1.0 to 2.0 hectares, Semi-medium—2.0 hectares, Medium—4.0 to 10.0 hectares, Large—Above 10 hectares.

Table 11A.4
States Classified According to Level of Average Land Assets Owned by Different
Social Groups

Social Groups	Rural		Urban	
	High	*Low*	*High*	*Low*
SC	Jammu and Kashmir, Haryana, Rajasthan, Punjab, Uttar Pradesh, Madhya Pradesh, Himachal Pradesh, Karnataka	Gujarat, Assam, West Bengal, Maharashtra, Bihar, Kerala, Orissa, Andhra Pradesh, Tamil Nadu	Jammu and Kashmir, Uttar Pradesh, Assam, Punjab, Bihar, Haryana, West Bengal	Madhya Pradesh, Rajasthan, Himachal Pradesh, Karnataka, Gujarat, Kerala, Tamil Nadu, Maharashtra, Andhra Pradesh, Orissa
ST	Himachal Pradesh, Bihar, Uttar Pradesh, Rajasthan, Jammu and Kashmir, Haryana, Assam, Karnataka, Kerala, Madhya Pradesh	Maharashtra, Andhra Pradesh, Tamil Nadu, Gujarat, West Bengal, Orissa, Punjab	Kerala, Uttar Pradesh, Assam, Bihar, Jammu and Kashmir, Punjab, Maharashtra	Madhya Pradesh, Karnataka, Haryana, Rajasthan, Gujarat, West Bengal, Andhra Pradesh, Orissa, Tamil Nadu, Himachal Pradesh

(Table 11A.4 Contd.)

(Table 11A.4 Contd.)

Social Groups	Rural		Urban	
	High	Low	High	Low
Non-SC/ST	Punjab, Haryana, Rajasthan, Uttar Pradesh, Kerala, Jammu and Kashmir, Madhya Pradesh	Bihar, Maharashtra, Karnataka, Himachal Pradesh, Gujarat, Andhra Pradesh, West Bengal, Tamil Nadu, Orissa, Assam	Punjab, Kerala, Himachal Pradesh, Jammu and Kashmir, Uttar Pradesh, Haryana, Rajasthan	Tamil Nadu, Madhya Pradesh, Assam, Bihar, Karnataka, Gujarat, Andhra Pradesh, West Bengal, Maharashtra, Orissa

Source: 'Debt and Investment Survey, Household Assets and Indebtedness of Social Groups', NSS, 48th round, 1992.
Note: High: Above all-India average, Low: Below all-India average.

Table 11A.5
States Classified According to Level of Average Agricultural Machinery Owned by Different Social Groups

Social Group	Rural		Urban	
	High	Low	High	Low
SC	Haryana, Punjab, Rajasthan, Uttar Pradesh, Gujarat, Jammu and Kashmir	Tamil Nadu, Orissa, Madhya Pradesh, Himachal Pradesh, Maharashtra, Karnataka, West Bengal, Andhra Pradesh, Bihar, Assam, Kerala	Karnataka, Uttar Pradesh, Bihar, Jammu and Kashmir, Madhya Pradesh, Assam	Tamil Nadu, Himachal Pradesh, West Bengal, Punjab, Rajasthan, Kerala, Maharashtra, Haryana, Gujarat, Andhra Pradesh, Orissa
ST	Jammu and Kashmir, Tamil Nadu, Rajasthan, Uttar Pradesh, Gujarat, Karnataka	Maharashtra, Andhra Pradesh, Madhya Pradesh, Himachal Pradesh, Haryana, Assam, West Bengal, Bihar, Orissa, Kerala, Punjab	Uttar Pradesh, Punjab	Maharashtra, Bihar, Karnataka, Kerala, Jammu and Kashmir, Gujarat, Orissa, West Bengal, Madhya Pradesh, Assam, Rajasthan, Andhra Pradesh, Tamil Nadu, Himachal Pradesh, Haryana

(Table 11A.5 Contd.)

(Table 11A.5 Contd.)

Social	Rural		Urban	
Group	High	Low	High	Low
Non-SC/ST	Haryana, Punjab, Rajasthan, Uttar Pradesh, Gujarat, Madhya Pradesh	Maharashtra, Karnataka, Tamil Nadu, Bihar, Andhra Pradesh, Jammu andKashmir, West Bengal, Himachal Pradesh, Orissa, Assam, Kerala	Punjab, Rajasthan, Madhya Pradesh, Himachal Pradesh, Kerala, Haryana, Uttar Pradesh, Karnataka, Andhra Pradesh	Maharashtra, Bihar, Gujarat, Tamil Nadu, Jammu and Kashmir, West Bengal, Orissa, Assam

Source: NSS, 'Debt and Investment Survey, Household Assets and Indebtedness of Social Groups', NSS, 48th round, 1992.
Note: High: Above all-India average; Low: Below all-India average.

Table 11A.6
States Classified According to Level of Average Livestock, Poultry and Birds Owned by Different Social Groups

Social	Rural		Urban	
Groups	High	Low	High	Low
SC	Jammu and Kashmir, Gujarat, Haryana, Rajasthan, Himachal Pradesh, Punjab, Assam, Uttar Pradesh, Madhya Pradesh, Karnataka	Maharashtra, West Bengal, Bihar, Andhra Pradesh, Orissa, Tamil Nadu, Kerala	Jammu and Kashmir, Assam, Himachal Pradesh, Punjab, Bihar, Uttar Pradesh, Haryana, Rajasthan, Karnataka	Tamil Nadu, West Bengal, Madhya Pradesh, Kerala, Andhra Pradesh, Maharashtra, Orissa, Gujarat
ST	Haryana, Himachal Pradesh, Jammu and Kashmir, Assam, Rajasthan, Gujarat, Madhya Pradesh	Bihar, Maharashtra, Uttar Pradesh, Karnataka, West Bengal, Andhra Pradesh, Orissa, Tamil Nadu, Kerala, Punjab	Uttar Pradesh, Punjab, Kerala, Bihar, Orissa, Gujarat, Karnataka	Madhya Pradesh, Jammu and Kashmir, West Bengal, Assam, Andhra Pradesh, Maharashtra, Rajasthan, Tamil Nadu, Himachal Pradesh, Haryana
Non-SC/ST	Haryana, Jammu and Kashmir, Punjab, Rajasthan, Gujarat, Madhya	Bihar, Maharashtra, Assam, Andhra Pradesh, Orissa,	Rajasthan, Uttar Pradesh, Punjab, Himachal Pradesh,	Gujarat, Jammu and Kashmir, Orissa, Karnataka, Tamil Nadu,

(Table 11A.6 Contd.)

(Table 11A.6 Contd.)

Social Groups	Rural		Urban	
	High	Low	High	Low
	Pradesh, Himachal Pradesh, Uttar Pradesh, Karnataka	West Bengal, Tamil Nadu, Kerala	Haryana, Kerala, Assam, Madhya Pradesh, Bihar, Maharashtra	Andhra Pradesh, West Bengal

Source: 'Debt and Investment Survey, Household Assets and Indebtedness of Social Groups', NSS, 48th round, 1992.

Note: High: Above all-India average; Low: Below all-India average.

Table 11A.7

States Classified According to Level of Average Non-farm Business Equipment Owned by Different Social Groups

Social Groups	Rural		Urban	
	High	Low	High	Low
SC	Jammu and Kashmir, Gujarat, Punjab, Assam, Maharashtra, Himachal Pradesh, West Bengal	Tamil Nadu, Andhra Pradesh, Uttar Pradesh, Rajasthan, Madhya Pradesh, Kerala, Haryana, Orissa, Karnataka, Bihar	Punjab, Assam, Maharashtra	Uttar Pradesh, Gujarat, Madhya Pradesh, Rajasthan, Jammu and Kashmir, West Bengal, Haryana, Orissa, Himachal Pradesh, Karnataka, Bihar, Andhra Pradesh, Tamil Nadu, Kerala
ST	Jammu and Kashmir, Assam, West Bengal, Himachal Pradesh, Maharashtra, Karnataka	Gujarat, Orissa, Bihar, Rajasthan, Madhya Pradesh, Andhra Pradesh, Haryana, Tamil Nadu, Uttar Pradesh	Uttar Pradesh, Gujarat, Punjab	Tamil Nadu, Madhya Pradesh, Maharashtra, Assam, Andhra Pradesh, Bihar, Himachal Pradesh, Karnataka, Orissa, Kerala, Rajasthan, West Bengal
Non-SC/ST	Himachal Pradesh, Maharashtra, Rajasthan, Kerala, Tamil Nadu, Karnataka, Gujarat, West Bengal	Madhya Pradesh, Orissa, Haryana, Jammu and Kashmir, Andhra Pradesh, Punjab, Uttar Pradesh, Assam, Bihar	Gujarat, Punjab, Haryana, Tamil Nadu	Madhya Pradesh, Maharashtra, Jammu and Kashmir, Karnataka, Andhra Pradesh, Uttar Pradesh, West Bengal, Rajasthan, Assam, Orissa, Bihar, Kerala, Himachal Pradesh

Source: 'Debt and Investment Survey, Household Assets and Indebtedness of Social Groups', NSS, 48th round, 1992.

Note: High: Above all-India average; Low: Below all-India average.

Table 11A.8
States Classified According to Level of Average Buildings, etc. Owned by Different Social Groups

Social Groups	Rural		Urban	
	High	*Low*	*High*	*Low*
SC	Jammu and Kashmir, Himachal Pradesh, Uttar Pradesh, Gujarat, Haryana, Kerala, Orissa, West Bengal	Punjab, Assam, Madhya Pradesh, Bihar, Maharashtra, Tamil Nadu, Andhra Pradesh, Rajasthan, Karnataka	Punjab, Jammu and Kashmir, Uttar Pradesh, Gujarat, West Bengal, Maharashtra	Assam, Haryana, Madhya Pradesh, Bihar, Himachal Pradesh, Rajasthan, Andhra Pradesh, Kerala, Tamil Nadu, Orissa, Karnataka
ST	Himachal Pradesh, Rajasthan, West Bengal, Gujarat, Haryana, Jammu and Kashmir, Orissa, Punjab, Bihar	Assam, Madhya Pradesh, Kerala, Maharashtra, Tamil Nadu, Andhra Pradesh, Karnataka	Punjab, Rajasthan, Maharashtra, Kerala, Uttar Pradesh, Gujarat, Orissa	Jammu and Kashmir, Bihar, Madhya Pradesh, Assam, Tamil Nadu, West Bengal, Andhra Pradesh, Himachal Pradesh, Karnataka
Non-SC/ST	Uttar Pradesh, Kerala, Himachal Pradesh, Haryana, Jammu and Kashmir, West Bengal, Orissa, Gujarat	Bihar, Maharashtra, Madhya Pradesh, Tamil Nadu, Andhra Pradesh, Assam, Rajasthan, Punjab, Karnataka	Uttar Pradesh, Jammu and Kashmir, Gujarat, West Bengal, Himachal Pradesh, Haryana	Kerala, Madhya Pradesh, Andhra Pradesh, Orissa, Bihar, Assam, Tamil Nadu, Maharashtra, Punjab, Rajasthan, Karnataka

Source: 'Debt and Investment Survey, Household Assets and Indebtedness of Social Groups', NSS, 48th round, 1992.
Note: High: Above all-India average; Low: Below all-India average.

Table 11A.9
Level of Aggregate Capital Assets (Per Household) among Social Groups at State Level, 1992 (Value in ₹)

States	Rural				Urban			
	ST	SC	Non-SC/ST	All	ST	SC	Non-SC/ST	All
Andhra Pradesh	34,649	24,586	72,744	58,175	10,060	27,936	105,015	94,806
Assam	60,895	44,515	61,490	60,087	106,169	63,377	115,325	112,206
Bihar	73,335	34,100	119,327	97,900	96,101	58,943	1,047,000	98,966
Gujarat	54,849	59,121	123,955	102,942	52,582	73,689	174,590	160,016
Haryana	76,938	90,232	425,234	337,619	15,131	59,124	166,138	151,221
Himachal Pradesh	142,085	86,837	148,042	134,261	20,743	44,175	200,628	160,612
Jammu and Kashmir	79,105	126,882	177,745	162,749	73,781	88,928	224,633	201,967
Karnataka	64,405	55,650	123,539	107,150	48,906	58,411	134,954	125,116
Kerala	48,056	44,791	198,759	181,534	195,531	36,850	198,759	221,516
Madhya Pradesh	51,292	55,080	129,415	93,062	5,426	46,254	139,946	117,338
Maharashtra	48,172	36,508	115,769	92,890	87,061	58,940	181,580	165,149
Orissa	33,003	25,551	63,380	45,733	20,553	24,080	92,858	72,314
Punjab	–	90,386	474,892	328,671	90,386	84,412	292,394	255,694
Rajasthan	90,521	87,201	198,903	158,809	28,973	55,755	185,275	161,046
Tamil Nadu	42,579	27,178	78,548	61,978	8,163	4,356	132,138	119,619
Uttar Pradesh	84,781	65,662	166,055	139,233	211,824	82,574	170,746	157,539
West Bengal	36,717	41,274	74,772	61,881	19,304	58,943	109,675	101,113
All India	**52,660**	**49,189**	**134,500**	**107,007**	**68,763**	**57,908**	**159,745**	**144,330**

Source: 'Debt and Investment Survey, Household Assets and Indebtedness of Social Groups', NSS, 48th round, 1992.

Table 11A.10

Disparity of Aggregate Capital Assets (in Value Terms) among Social Groups, 1992

States	Rural			Urban		
	SC and Non-SC/ST	*ST and Non-SC/ST*	*SC and ST*	*SC and Non-SC/ST*	*ST and Non-SC/ST*	*SC and ST*
Andhra Pradesh	0.3	0.5	0.7	0.3	0.1	2.8
Assam	0.7	1.0	0.7	0.5	0.9	0.6
Bihar	0.3	0.6	0.5	0.1	0.1	0.6
Gujarat	0.5	0.4	1.1	0.4	0.3	1.4
Haryana	0.2	0.2	1.2	0.4	0.1	3.9
Himachal Pradesh	0.6	1.0	0.6	0.2	0.1	2.1
Jammu and Kashmir	0.7	0.4	1.6	0.4	0.3	1.2
Karnataka	0.5	0.5	0.9	0.4	0.4	1.2
Kerala	0.2	0.2	0.9	0.2	1.0	0.2
Madhya Pradesh	0.4	0.4	1.1	0.3	0.0	8.5
Maharashtra	0.3	0.4	0.8	0.3	0.5	0.7
Orissa	0.4	0.5	0.8	0.3	0.2	1.2
Punjab	0.2			0.3	0.3	0.9
Rajasthan	0.4	0.5	1.0	0.3	0.2	1.9
Tamil Nadu	0.3	0.5	0.6	0.0	0.1	0.5
Uttar Pradesh	0.4	0.5	0.8	0.5	1.2	0.4
West Bengal	0.6	0.5	1.1	0.5	0.2	3.1
All India	**0.4**	**0.4**	**0.9**	**0.4**	**0.4**	**0.8**

Source: Calculated from the 'Debt and Investment Survey, Household Assets and Indebtedness of Social Groups', NSS, 48th round, 1992.

Chapter 12

EMPLOYMENT AND UNEMPLOYMENT SITUATION: RURAL AND URBAN

Sukhadeo Thorat and Chittaranjan Senapati

The importance of high employment rate to eradicate poverty and elevate socio-economic standards of any social groups needs no emphasis. This chapter provides an overview of the present scenario of Scheduled Castes (SCs) and Scheduled Tribes (STs) employed in the labour markets and a comparison of their relative status vis-à-vis non-SCs/STs in India. To ascertain the employment and unemployment rate of different social groups in rural and urban areas, a state-wise analysis based on the Current Daily Status (CDS) has been undertaken. This analysis is based on *National Sample Survey* (NSS) reports for the years 1983 and 1999 on employment and unemployment situation across social groups. For the year 1999–2000, the two categories, namely Other Backward Classes (OBCs) and Others, have been clubbed together to create a single category called non-SCs/STs. The chapter discusses gender-wise estimates of employment and unemployment levels and disparities in the same across social groups. The changes in the levels of employment and unemployment, and changes in the disparity therein among various social groups are also presented.

EMPLOYMENT LEVEL—RURAL (1999–2000)

The CDS employment rates for SCs, STs and non-SCs/STs in rural areas are discussed at all-India level, followed by a discussion on inter-state variations in the level of employment.

The data at all-India level shows that in 1999–2000, the rural male employment rate was the lowest for SCs (46.2 per cent), followed by non-SCs/STs and STs (Figure 12.1), while the female employment rate was the lowest among non-SCs/STs and again the highest for STs (Figure 12.2).

Across states, the level of employment for SC males was the highest in Jammu and Kashmir (55.4 per cent), Assam (51.6 per cent) and Himachal Pradesh (50.8

Figure 12.1
Level of Male Employment (CDS) in Rural India, 1999–2000

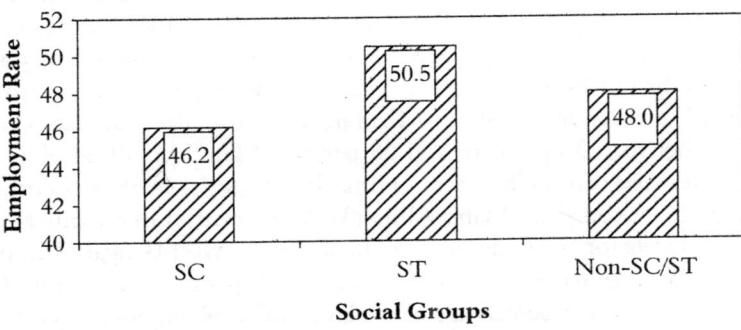

Source: NSSO, 55th round, Employment and Unemployment Survey, 1999–2000.

Figure 12.2
Level of Female Employment (CDS) in Rural India, 1999–2000

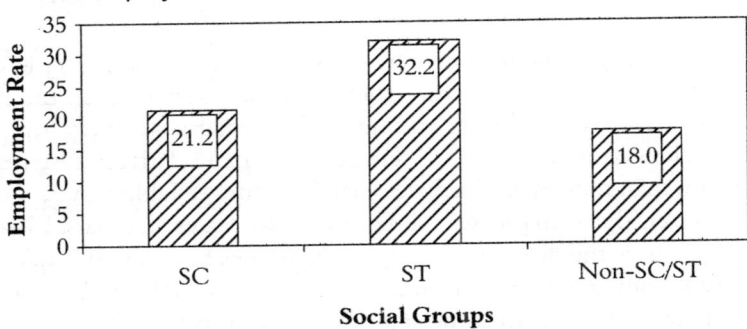

Source: NSSO, 55th round, Employment and Unemployment Survey, 1999–2000.

per cent), respectively (see Annexure X Table 12A.1). Conversely, the level of employment for SC males was the lowest for Kerala (41.50 per cent), Maharashtra (41.9 per cent) and Uttar Pradesh (43.2 per cent).

Among ST males, the level of employment in the central tribal belt was higher than all-India average in all the states except Maharashtra and West Bengal. The employment rate was relatively much lower in the north-eastern states, especially in Arunachal Pradesh, Manipur, Sikkim and Tripura. The level of employment for non-SC/ST males was the highest in Karnataka (55.8 per cent), Andhra Pradesh (54.75 per cent) and Gujarat (53.45 per cent). On the other hand, the employment levels for non-SC/ST males were the lowest in Kerala (42.95 per cent), Bihar (43.65 per cent) and Haryana (44.65 per cent).

The female employment rate for SCs was the highest in Andhra Pradesh (36.8 per cent), Karnataka (31.7 per cent), Tamil Nadu (30.6 per cent) and Gujarat (30.5 per cent). Conversely, the level of unemployment was the lowest in West Bengal (10.6 per cent), Haryana (11.3 per cent) and Assam (12.2 per cent). The rate of female employment among STs was the maximum in Andhra Pradesh (41.3 per cent), followed by Rajasthan (39.4 per cent) and Maharashtra (36.8 per cent). The employment rate was very low in Bihar (20.9 per cent) and West Bengal (20.4 per cent). As compared to the central belt, the level of female employment was somewhat lower in the north-eastern states. It was less than 20 per cent in Assam, Sikkim and Tripura. However, in Nagaland, Mizoram and Meghalaya, the rate of employment varied between 33 per cent and 38 per cent. The level of employment for non-SC/ST females was the highest in Himachal Pradesh (34.55 per cent), Andhra Pradesh (33.75 per cent) and Maharashtra (31.85 per cent). On the other hand, the employment levels for SC females were the lowest in West Bengal (7.15 per cent) and Bihar (8.35 per cent). The states of Haryana (11.1 per cent) and Assam (12.2 per cent) also recorded a low percentage in the levels of employment for SC females.

DISPARITY IN THE LEVELS OF RURAL EMPLOYMENT ACROSS SOCIAL GROUPS, 1999–2000

The disparity in employment levels across social groups using the ratio of CDS levels of employment (disparity ratio) shows that at all-India level, the disparity in employment rates between SC and non-SC/ST males was very low (disparity ratio was close to unity). The SC females were in a relatively better employment situation than non-SC/ST females (see Annexure X Table 12A.2). However, at the state level, the scenario was different in the states like Tamil Nadu and Maharashtra, where the disparity in employment rates between SC and non-SC/ST males was high, and a higher employment rate existed for the non-SC/ST males as compared to SCs. In some states like Assam, Bihar, Himachal Pradesh, Jammu and Kashmir and West Bengal, SC males had some advantage in terms of CDS employment rates as compared to non-SCs/STs. In case of females, the disparities were the highest in Himachal Pradesh, Punjab and Rajasthan, which placed SC females at a disadvantage, while in most other states, the SC female employment rate was much higher than non-SC/ST females.

A comparison of employment disparity ratio of STs and non-SCs/STs revealed that for both males and females, the disparity ratio was greater than or equal to unity in most of the states. This indicates nearly equal or greater employment rate for the former social group, except in case of male employment rates in West Bengal and Nagaland, where the disparity ratio was below unity.

CHANGES IN RURAL EMPLOYMENT LEVEL AND SOCIAL GROUP DISPARITY, 1983 TO 1999–2000

During 1983 to 1999–2000, at all-India level, the employment rates declined in case of all three social groups for either sex (Table 12.1). The decline was higher

Table 12.1

Changes in Rural Employment Level and Social Group Disparity during 1983 to 1999–2000, All India

Social Groups	Percentage Point Change in Level of Employment	
	Male	*Female*
SC	−6.90	−3.00
ST	−11.10	−6.20
Non-SC/ST	−7.80	−2.30
	Difference in Employment Disparity Ratio	
	Male	*Female*
SC and Non-SC/ST	0.01	−0.01
ST and Non-SC/ST	−0.05	−0.10

Source: 'Employment and Unemployment Situation among Social Groups in India, 1993–94 and 1999–2000', Department of Statistics, Government of India, New Delhi.

for STs than other social groups. The female employment rates declined by a lower magnitude than the male employment rates.

Contrary to all-India trend, in a few states, namely Gujarat, Haryana and Kerala, the employment rates for SC males increased—marginally in Gujarat, moderately in Haryana and sharply in Kerala (see Annexure X Table 12A.3). Kerala was the only state that recorded an increase in male employment rate for both STs and non-SCs/STs. The ST male employment rate also showed an increase in Karnataka. In all other states, there was a fall in employment and the percentage point decline was, in general, the sharpest for STs followed by non-SCs/STs and SCs.

The female employment rates for SCs increased in Assam, Jammu and Kashmir and Punjab. The change at 11 percentage points was particularly high in Jammu and Kashmir. The other states which indicate a marginal increase in SC female employment rate were Gujarat, Karnataka, Kerala, Tamil Nadu and West Bengal. The rest of the states recorded a declining trend in employment rates for SC females. The condition of ST females was favourable in Assam, Karnataka, Kerala, Madhya Pradesh, Tripura and Uttar Pradesh, except Kerala, where percentage point change was 16.10. In rest of the states, it was less than 5.00. The decline in ST female employment rate was very sharp in Bihar (−21.80), Rajasthan (−20.90) and the north-eastern state of Manipur (−16.6). The non-SC/ST female employment rate declined in 15 states. Haryana, Rajasthan and Mizoram recorded a very high percentage point decline. The six states which showed an increase in non-SC/ST female employment rate include Assam, Jammu and Kashmir, Karnataka, Punjab, Tripura and West Bengal. The increase was notable in Punjab.

The trends in employment rate during 1983 to 1999–2000 indicated that at all-India level the decline in SC male employment rate was lower than that in non-SCs/STs. Hence, the disparity ratio improved in favour of SC males. However, at the state level, some states that have substantial SC population, namely Andhra Pradesh, Himachal Pradesh, Maharashtra, Orissa, Rajasthan, Tamil Nadu and Uttar Pradesh recorded worsening male disparities (see Annexure X Table 12A.4). In three of these seven states, the female disparity ratio also moved against SCs. The other states where inter-social group disparities between SCs and non-SCs/STs with regard to female employment went up were Punjab, West Bengal and Karnataka. Similarly, at all-India and state levels, the disparity ratio of ST and non-SC/ST male and female employment rate either worsened for the former social group or remained more or less unchanged during the 16-year period of the study.

EMPLOYMENT LEVEL—URBAN, 1999–2000

The urban employment pattern across social groups is different from the related scenario prevalent in rural India. The all-India CDS male employment level for non-SCs/STs was about 50 per cent, which was the maximum among all the social groups (Figure 12.3). The employment levels of SCs and STs were more or less equal.

The all-India analysis of CDS female employment rate indicates that the rate of employment for ST females was the highest, followed by SC and non-SC/ST social groups (Figure 12.4).

The state level data shows that West Bengal, Himachal Pradesh and Punjab had a high rate of SC male employment (more than 50 per cent), while in Kerala, Madhya Pradesh, Assam and Andhra Pradesh, about 41–42 per cent SC males were employed (see Annexure X Table 12A.5). Among STs, the male employment rate was high in Andhra Pradesh, Gujarat, West Bengal, Maharashtra and Karnataka, while it was low in the north-eastern states. In case of non-SCs/STs, more than

Figure 12.3
Level of Male Employment (CDS) in Urban India, 1999–2000

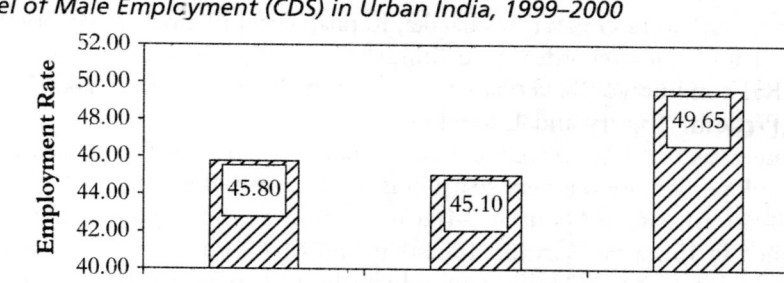

Source: NSSO, 55th round, Employment and Unemployment Survey, 1999–2000.

Figure 12.4
Level of Female Employment (CDS) in Urban India, 1999–2000

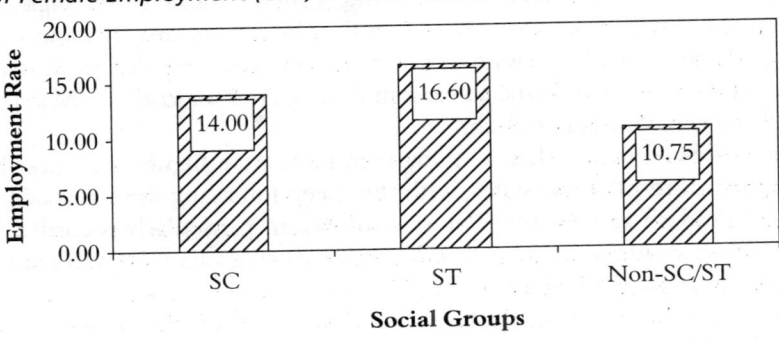

Source: NSSO, 55th round, Employment and Unemployment Survey, 1999–2000.

50 per cent males were employed in 10 states, among which West Bengal, Punjab and Karnataka indicated a high rate of employment. The states of Bihar, Orissa and Kerala had the lowest rates of employment for non-SC/ST males.

The female employment rate in urban areas is lower than the corresponding rate in rural areas. The states where female employment rate for SCs was greater than the all-India average were Karnataka, Kerala, Orissa, Tamil Nadu, Andhra Pradesh, Maharashtra, Gujarat and Madhya Pradesh. In the first four states, the rate was higher than 20 per cent, which was substantially greater than the all-India average, while in the last two states, it was marginally higher than the all-India figures. The ST female employment rate in urban areas was more than the corresponding rate for SC and non-SC/ST females in most states. Of these, Kerala, Karnataka, Gujarat, Sikkim, Tamil Nadu, Meghalaya and Mizoram had particularly notable rates of urban female employment for STs. In most of these states, except Gujarat, Meghalaya and Mizoram, female employment rate is high (more than 10 per cent) for non-SCs/STs too. In most of the states, non-SC/ST female employment rate was lower than all-India average.

DISPARITY IN LEVELS OF URBAN EMPLOYMENT ACROSS SOCIAL GROUPS, 1999–2000

The analysis for the period 1999–2000 brought to the fore the existence of a narrow disparity (disparity ratio 0.92) in employment rates between SC and non-SC/ST males in urban areas (see Annexure X Table 12A.6). An analysis of the figures for SC and non-SC/ST females highlights that more SC females were employed than non-SC/ST females in urban areas. The disparity pattern for STs and non-SCs/STs was similar, with near equality in male employment rate and higher ST female employment rate. At the state level, in four out of 17 states, SC male disparity ratio was more than unity which indicates their slight advantage in employment rate over non-SCs/STs. The lowest disparity between SC and non-SC/ST males was found in Uttar Pradesh and West Bengal. Conversely, the highest disparity was found to exist in Assam, Andhra Pradesh, Maharashtra, Tamil Nadu and Madhya Pradesh.

In case of SC females, their employment rates were higher than non-SC/ST counterparts in most of the states, with the exception being the states of Punjab, Himachal Pradesh and Assam. The state of Assam particularly recorded a high degree of discrimination as far as female employment under CDS was concerned. The disparity ratio of ST and non-SC/ST employment level was below unity for males except in Andhra Pradesh, Gujarat and Kerala, while the converse was true for females. The disparities in case of males were quite profound (disparity ratio less than 0.9) in Andhra Pradesh, Assam, Bihar, Meghalaya, Mizoram, Nagaland, Sikkim, Tamil Nadu, Tripura and West Bengal. Interestingly, in all these states, the disparity ratio was substantially higher than unity for females.

CHANGES IN URBAN EMPLOYMENT LEVEL AND SOCIAL GROUP DISPARITY, 1983 TO 1999–2000

The CDS employment rates for SC, ST and non-SC/ST males and females were found to have declined from 1983 to 1999 (see Annexure X Table 12A.7). The decline was sharper in case of males than females (Table 12.2). The declining trend

Table 12.2

Changes in Urban Employment Level and Social Group Disparity during 1983 to 1999–2000, All India

Social Groups	Percentage Point Change in Level of Employment	
	Male	*Female*
SC	−4.34	−2.77
ST	−7.61	−3.89
Non-SC/ST	−4.32	−0.51
	Difference in Employment Disparity Ratio	
	Male	*Female*
SC and Non-SC/ST	−0.01	−0.19
ST and Non-SC/ST	−0.07	−0.28

Source: 'Employment and Unemployment Situation among Social Groups in India, 1993–94 and 1999–2000', Department of Statistics, Government of India, New Delhi.

in the employment rate for SC males was observed in all the states except Kerala and Karnataka. The employment rate for SC females remained unchanged in Gujarat and increased in about seven states, among which Haryana, Orissa and Jammu and Kashmir recorded a sharp increase. The male ST employment rate showed an increase by about 2 percentage points in the two states, namely Andhra Pradesh and Gujarat in the central tribal belt, while it remained stagnant in Maharashtra, and declined in the remaining states. The female ST employment rates in several states were not quite in consonance with the declining all-India trend. During the period 1983 to 1999–2000, this rate increased substantially in Gujarat, Karnataka, Tamil Nadu and West Bengal, as also in some north-eastern states. The employment rates for non-SC/ST males increased in Kerala and West Bengal. A higher rate of decline was seen to exist in Bihar and Orissa, with Bihar recording the highest decline.

The disparity ratio declined at all-India level for either gender in case of both SC and ST social groups as compared to non-SCs/STs. Across states, the dispari-ties between SC males and their non-SC/ST counterparts increased in Andhra Pradesh, Bihar, Himachal Pradesh, Karnataka, Kerala, Orissa and Rajasthan (see Annexure X Table 12A.8). The SC females, on the other hand, faced a disadvan-tage in terms of an increase in disparities, which were substantial in Haryana, Karnataka and Orissa, and moderate in Andhra Pradesh, Jammu and Kashmir, Tamil Nadu and West Bengal. The disparities between STs and non-SCs/STs declined in most of the states in case of males but increased for females in several north-eastern states that have sizeable tribal populations.

RURAL UNEMPLOYMENT: LEVEL AND CHANGES

The male and female unemployment levels (1999–2000) were the highest among SC (Figure 12.5) which indicate that this social group has limited employment opportunities.

The highest percentages of unemployed SC males (14.09 per cent) and females (9.0 per cent) were found in Kerala. Meanwhile, a low employment rate for SC males (2–2.5 per cent) was found in Assam, Himachal Pradesh and Rajasthan, and for SC females (less than 1 per cent) was found in Assam, Haryana, Himachal Pradesh, Jammu and Kashmir, Punjab, Rajasthan and Uttar Pradesh (see Annexure X Table 12A.9). Among STs, the rural unemployment rate for males was over 5 per cent in Tamil Nadu (11.1 per cent), Kerala (9.6 per cent), West Bengal (8.9 per cent) and Bihar (5.8 per cent). Except for the north-eastern states and Rajasthan, in most other states, the unemployment rate was well over 1 per cent. The ST female unemployment was high in Kerala (5.8 per cent), Tamil Nadu (4.6 per cent), West Bengal (4.6 per cent) and Andhra Pradesh (4.5 per cent), while it was lower in the rest of the states. The highest unemployment rates of 9.7 per cent and 7.4 per cent for non-SC/ST males were observed in the states like Kerala and West

Figure 12.5
Level of Rural Unemployment (CDS) in India, 1999–2000

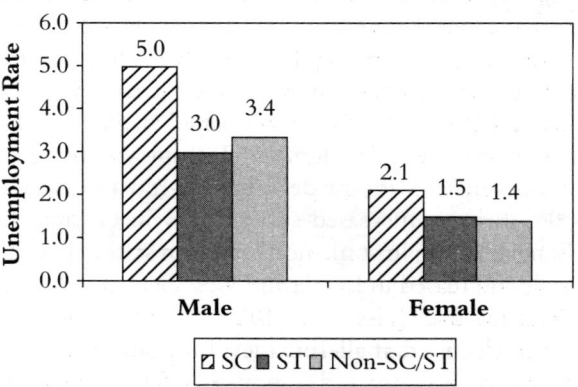

Source: NSSO, 55th round, Employment and Unemployment Survey, 1999–2000.

Bengal, respectively. In the case of non-SC/ST females, these figures were close to 5 per cent in Kerala and below 2 per cent in most other states.

Between 1983 and 1999–2000, the CDS unemployment rate for SCs declined by more than 2 percentage points for both males and females, whereas the decline in unemployment rate for ST males and their non-SC/ST counterparts was marginal (Figure 12.6). The all-India trend of a declining SC unemployment rate was observed in nearly all the states except Assam, Haryana, Jammu and Kashmir, Himachal Pradesh and Madhya Pradesh in the case of males, and Assam, Jammu and Kashmir and Karnataka in the case of females (see Annexure X Table 12A.10). The unemployment rates for STs also declined or remained unchanged in a majority of the states except Bihar and Tamil Nadu, where a sharp increase in male unemployment rates was observed.

Figure 12.6
Changes in Level of Rural Unemployment in India, 1983–1999/2000

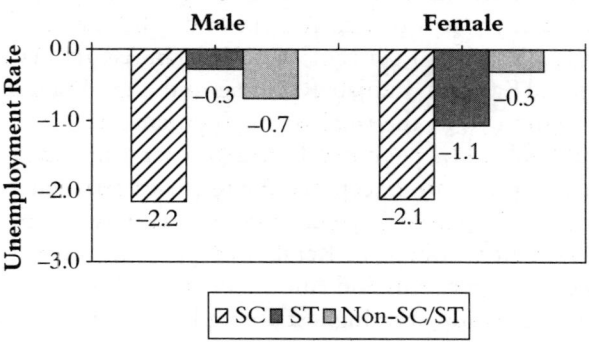

Source: NSSO, 55th round, Employment and Unemployment Survey, 1999–2000.

DISPARITIES IN RURAL UNEMPLOYMENT: LEVEL AND CHANGES

A high level of inter-social group disparities to the disadvantages of SCs was observed at all-India level (Table 12.3) which were not uniform across all states. The unemployment rate for SC males was found to be higher than non-SC/ST males in all the states except Assam, Himachal Pradesh, Jammu and Kashmir, Orissa and West Bengal (see Annexure X Table 12A.11). The unemployment rate for SC females was also lower than non-SC/ST counterparts in Assam, Orissa, West Bengal, Punjab and Gujarat.

Table 12.3
Inter-social Group Disparities in Rural Employment Level, All India

Social Groups	*Unemployment Disparity Ratio: 1999–2000*	
	Male	*Female*
SC and Non-SC/ST	1.49	1.50
ST and Non-SC/ST	0.90	1.07
	Difference in Unemployment Disparity Ratio: 1983 to 1999–2000	
	Male	*Female*
SC and Non-SC/ST	−0.28	−0.96
ST and Non-SC/ST	0.08	−0.42

Source: 'Employment and Unemployment Situation among Social Groups in India, 1993–94 and 1999–2000', Department of Statistics, Government of India, New Delhi.

As regards disparity ratio between STs and non-SCs/STs, Nagaland had the highest disparity ratio for male unemployment rate, followed by Tamil Nadu, while in case of females, the disparities were maximum in Bihar (disparity ratio 3.33). During the course of the period under study (1983 to 1999–2000), the disparity in unemployment rate between scheduled and non-scheduled social groups declined. Across states, a decrease in disparities was observed in most of the states. However, Haryana showed a sharp increase in both male and female disparity ratios for SCs. The disparities in SC female unemployment rate also got sharply accentuated in Karnataka and Uttar Pradesh. The ST and non-SC/ST disparity for male unemployment increased sharply in Tamil Nadu and Bihar, and marginally in Gujarat, Sikkim and Uttar Pradesh, while it declined in the rest of the states. The states where decline occurred in the disparity ratio for females include Gujarat, Kerala, Madhya Pradesh, Maharashtra, Orissa, Rajasthan, Sikkim and West Bengal (see Annexure X Table 12A.12).

URBAN UNEMPLOYMENT: LEVEL AND CHANGES

The unemployment rate for SC males was the highest among all social groups, while it was the same for STs and non-SCs/STs (Figure 12.7). The female unemployment rates in urban areas were more or less equal for all the social groups.

The urban unemployment rate for SC males was very high in Kerala, Tamil Nadu and West Bengal (more than 7.5 per cent) but was lower (less than 3.5 per cent) in Punjab, Rajasthan and Gujarat (see Annexure X Table 12A.13). According to CDS, the unemployment rate for females was lower than that for males. The unemployment rate for SC females was the highest in Kerala (more than 8 per cent) and lowest in Uttar Pradesh.

Among STs, the male unemployment rate was higher than all-India average in Bihar, Gujarat, Kerala, Nagaland, Tamil Nadu, Tripura and West Bengal. In most of these states, the female unemployment rates were also more than all-India average of 1.1 per cent.

During the course of the period under study (1983 to 1999–2000), the CDS unemployment rate for SC, ST and non-SC/ST males declined by about 2–1.5 percentage points. A marginal decline occurred in the unemployment rate for females belonging to all three social groups (Figure 12.8).

Across the states, a declining trend was registered for SC male unemployment rate except in the three states of Assam, Bihar and Madhya Pradesh. The reduction was notably drastic in Andhra Pradesh, Rajasthan and Gujarat, at 6.27, 4.87, and 3.6 percentage points, respectively (see Annexure X Table 12A.14). The unemployment rate for SC females reduced substantially in Rajasthan (2.04 percentage points) and by a lower magnitude in most of the states, except Assam, Karnataka and Kerala. The urban unemployment rates among ST males increased substantially (by about 2 percentage points) in Bihar and Gujarat, while it registered a

Figure 12.7
Level of Urban Unemployment (CDS) in India, 1999–2000

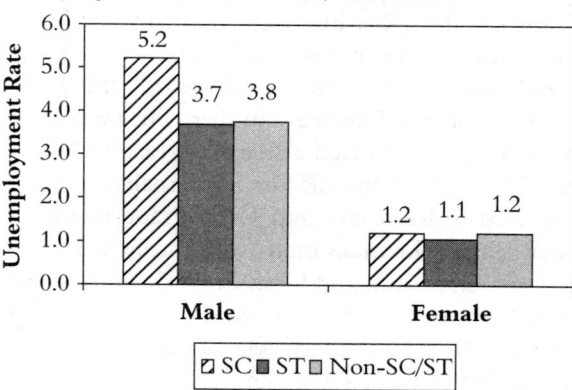

Source: NSSO, 55th round, Employment and Unemployment Survey, 1999–2000.

Figure 12.8
Changes in Level of Urban Unemployment in India, 1983–1999/2000

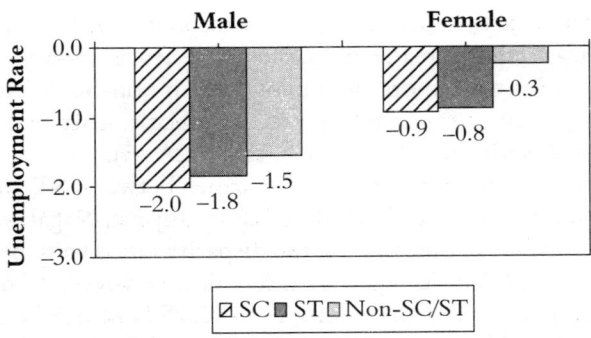

Source: NSSO, 38th and 55th rounds, Employment and Unemployment Survey, 1983 and 1999–2000.

sharp fall in several important states, namely Andhra Pradesh, Karnataka, Madhya Pradesh, Maharashtra, Orissa, Sikkim, Tamil Nadu and Uttar Pradesh. Except in Bihar, ST female urban unemployment also fell during the period under study. The direction of change in almost all the states for non-SC/ST workers was more or less similar to the trends observed for SC workers.

DISPARITIES IN URBAN UNEMPLOYMENT: LEVEL AND CHANGES

The all-India disparity ratio shows that SC males were more unemployed than non-SC/ST males (Table 12.4) while for SC females and ST males and females, the unemployment levels were more or less equal to those observed for

Table 12.4
Inter-social Group Disparities in Urban Employment Level, All India

Social Groups	Unemployment Disparity Ratio: 1999–2000	
	Male	*Female*
SC and Non-SC/ST	1.39	1.00
ST and Non-SC/ST	0.99	0.92
	Difference in Unemployment Disparity Ratio: 1983 to 1999–2000	
	Male	*Female*
SC and Non-SC/ST	0.02	–0.48
ST and Non-SC/ST	–0.05	–0.45

Source: 'Employment and Unemployment Situation among Social Groups in India, 1993–94 and 1999–2000', Department of Statistics, Government of India, New Delhi.

non-SCs/STs. The disparities have either come down or remained unchanged during the period 1983 to 1999–2000.

In all the states except Orissa, SC male disparity ratios were greater than one which indicates their greater unemployment levels vis-à-vis non-SCs/STs. Similarly, SC females were more unemployed than non-SC/ST females in nine states. The inter-social group disparity was particularly sharp in Kerala, Madhya Pradesh and Tamil Nadu (see Annexure X Table 12A.15).

In contrast to the above trends, the disparities between ST and non-SC/ST males existed only in few states, including Bihar, Gujarat, Nagaland, Tamil Nadu and West Bengal, while in other states, the disparity ratios were below unity (see Annexure X Table 12A.16). As regards the females, however, the unemployment rate was higher among STs than among non-SCs/STs in nearly all the states of the central tribal belt. The magnitude of increase in SC male disparity ratios was small across the states. The disparity between SC and non-SC/ST females either remained more or less unchanged or decreased during the study period in all the states except Madhya Pradesh. In case of STs, a notable accentuation in disparities occurred for males in Bihar, while the female disparity ratio came down substantially in the state. In most other states, there was a clear trend towards a decrease in inter-social group disparities.

SUMMARY

The SC male employment rates were lower than the employment rates for non-SC/ST males in both rural (46.2 per cent and 48 per cent, respectively) and urban areas (45.8 per cent and 49.6 per cent, respectively), but the female employment rate was higher for the former social group as compared to the latter by about 3 percentage points. The rural employment rate was the highest among ST. This social group also had the highest female employment rate in urban areas. In Maharashtra, Tamil Nadu and Uttar Pradesh, SC rural male employment rate was 3–4 percentage points lower than all-India average of 46.2 per cent in 1999–2000, while urban male employment rate was low in Kerala (41.1 per cent), Madhya Pradesh (41.9 per cent), Assam (41.9 per cent) and Andhra Pradesh (42.5 per cent). The SC rural female employment rate was very low, and stood at about 11–12 per cent in West Bengal, Haryana and Assam. In urban Assam, Himachal Pradesh, Punjab and Uttar Pradesh also, the SC female employment rate was much lower than the national average of 14 per cent. During the period 1983 to 1999–2000, except in few states, the rural and urban employment rates for SCs declined for either sex, with the decline being higher for males than females. The male and female employment rates declined by 6.9 and 3.2 percentage points, respectively, in rural areas and by 4.3 and 2.8 percentage points, respectively, in urban areas. The rural employment rates for SC males increased marginally in Gujarat, moderately in Haryana and sharply in Kerala, while urban employment rates increased in Karnataka and Kerala.

At all-India level, the disparity ratios between SC and non-SC/ST employment rates were near unity for males, while in case of females, SC females were in a relatively better position. However, there was a substantial disparity in rural employment rates between SC and non-SC/ST males in Tamil Nadu, Maharashtra and Punjab, and in Himachal Pradesh, Punjab and Rajasthan for females, placing SCs at a disadvantage. The disparity in urban male employment was high in Assam, Andhra Pradesh, Maharashtra, Tamil Nadu and Madhya Pradesh. The rural unemployment level of SC males (5.0 per cent) and females (2.1 per cent) was higher than that for non-SC/ST males (3.4 per cent) and females (1.9 per cent), respectively, which indicate the availability of relatively limited employment for SCs. Despite a large decline in CDS unemployment rate of SCs (for the period 1983 to 1999–2000) relative to that of their non-SC/ST counterparts, the former social group registered a higher level of unemployment. This trend was widespread in most of the states except Assam, Himachal Pradesh, Jammu and Kashmir, Orissa and West Bengal, where a greater proportion of non-SC/ST males were unemployed. The unemployment situation in urban areas was no better. The unemployment rate for SC males was 5.2 percentage points (1999–2000), which was about 2 percentage points lower than the corresponding figure in 1983. Similarly, the unemployment rate for non-SC/ST males was 3.5 per cent in 1999 and 5.28 per cent in 1983. The SC males faced a greater degree of unemployment than their non-SC/ST males in all the states, except Orissa. The female unemployment rate (1999–2000) was about 1 per cent for both the social groups, which was marginally lower in comparison to the corresponding figure in 1983. However, in about nine states, the inter-social group disparity in female unemployment existed to the disadvantage of SC females. The male and female unemployment rates for ST in both rural and urban areas were close to the corresponding rates for non-SCs/STs. Over the years, the level of unemployment has declined among ST. The trend was near-universal in most of the states, except Bihar and Tamil Nadu, where a sharp increase was observed in rural male unemployment rates. In Bihar, the urban unemployment rates among ST males and females also increased substantially during the study period.

ANNEXURE X

Table 12A.1
Percentage of Employed Persons Aged Five Years and Above According to Current Daily Status: Rural

States	1999–2000						1983–1984					
	ST		SC		Non-SC/ST		ST		SC		Non-SC/ST	
	Male	Female	Male	Female	Male	Female	Male	Female	Male	Female	Male	Female
Andhra Pradesh	54.4	41.3	50.3	36.8	54.8	32.8	63.4	42.9	56.7	36.9	61.3	34.1
Arunachal Pradesh	29.4	22.2			50.1	28.3						
Assam	48.0	11.2	51.6	12.2	48.5	9.9	55.9	6.6	57.1	7.9	53.6	8.4
Bihar	50.7	20.9	46.4	16.7	43.7	8.4	62.8	42.7	52.3	20.5	53.1	11.3
Gujarat	53.3	31.6	48.6	30.5	53.5	26.2	62.5	35.4	48.5	27.9	56.3	26.2
Haryana	26.7	13.4	44.4	11.3	44.7	10.1	*	*	43.6	21.1	53.9	35.2
Himachal Pradesh	50.2	27.4	50.8	29.4	49.9	34.6	71.4	46.9	59.8	30.4	55.9	35.2
Jammu and Kashmir	58.3	13.2	55.4	16.6	51.7	9.1	*	*	56.8	5.1	55.3	5.5
Karnataka	58.3	34.9	50.6	31.7	55.8	28.5	56.4	31.2	54.3	31.5	60.3	20.0
Kerala	59.8	27.0	41.5	21.0	43.0	12.7	53.8	10.9	36.5	20.4	40.8	12.9
Madhya Pradesh	52.2	36.8	46.7	25.7	49.1	19.5	63.9	43.7	56.7	37.2	59.8	28.8
Maharashtra	47.7	36.8	41.9	29.5	49.1	31.9	58.4	41.6	51.8	35.8	56.5	33.2
Manipur	48.0	22.0			43.4	14.7	50.1	38.6	*	*	47.0	20.6
Meghalaya	51.9	38.2			30.5	21.1	62.2	47.6	*	*	67.6	23.8
Mizoram	50.8	35.9			39.2	13.5	63.4	32.1	*	*	73.4	31.4

State												
Nagaland	51.5	33.7			61.0	10.4						
Orissa	50.6	31.5	46.5	18.6	48.1	11.0	62.6	32.4	59.5	21.7	57.6	13.9
Punjab	50.4	4.9	48.5	14.1	50.4	16.3	61.3	5.3	55.2	11.6	60.6	5.4
Rajasthan	51.3	39.4	46.6	22.2	47.4	25.3	66.4	60.3	58.3	37.9	58.4	37.1
Sikkim	45.8	16.7			49.8	18.6	53.2	28.7	★	★	54.4	19.7
Tamil Nadu	50.8	35.8	43.3	30.6	53.1	23.8	64.0	42.3	49.1	30.4	54.4	28.2
Tripura	46.0	12.7			50.0	6.5	62.2	10.1	59.2	3.0	54.2	4.6
Uttar Pradesh	41.6	15.0	43.2	16.1	44.8	11.3	60.0	14.6	55.2	20.0	56.2	14.9
West Bengal	40.1	20.4	48.4	10.6	46.5	7.2	54.9	25.0	49.6	10.3	50.7	6.1
All India	**50.5**	**32.2**	**46.2**	**21.2**	**48.0**	**18.0**	**61.6**	**38.4**	**53.1**	**24.2**	**55.8**	**20.3**

Source: 'Employment and Unemployment Situation in India', 38th and 55th rounds, NSS, Ministry of Statistics and Programme Implementation, Government of India, New Delhi.

Note: ★ is for not available.

Table 12A.2

Disparities in Rural Employment Rate (CDS) across Social Groups, 1999–2000

States	ST and Non-SC/ST		SC and Non-SC/ST	
	Male	*Female*	*Male*	*Female*
Andhra Pradesh	0.99	1.26	0.92	1.12
Arunachal Pradesh	0.59	0.78	–	–
Assam	0.99	1.14	1.07	1.24
Bihar	1.16	2.50	1.06	2.00
Gujarat	1.00	1.21	0.91	1.16
Haryana	0.60	1.33	0.99	1.12
Himachal Pradesh	1.01	0.79	1.02	0.85
Jammu and Kashmir	1.13	1.45	1.07	1.82
Karnataka	1.04	1.23	0.91	1.11
Kerala	1.39	2.13	0.97	1.65
Madhya Pradesh	1.06	1.89	0.95	1.32
Maharashtra	0.97	1.16	0.85	0.93
Manipur	1.11	1.50	–	–
Meghalaya	1.70	1.81	–	–
Mizoram	1.30	2.66	–	–
Nagaland	0.84	3.26	–	–
Orissa	1.05	2.86	0.97	1.69
Punjab	1.00	0.30	0.96	0.87
Rajasthan	1.08	1.56	0.98	0.88
Sikkim	0.92	0.90	–	–
Tamil Nadu	0.96	1.51	0.82	1.29
Tripura	0.92	1.95	–	–
Uttar Pradesh	0.93	1.33	0.97	1.42
West Bengal	0.86	2.85	1.04	1.48
All India	**1.05**	**1.79**	**0.96**	**1.18**

Source: 55th round of Employment and Unemployment Report, NSS.

Table 12A.3
Percentage Point Change in Rural Employment Level (CDS), 1983 to 1999–2000

States	ST		SC		Non-SC/ST	
	Male	*Female*	*Male*	*Female*	*Male*	*Female*
Andhra Pradesh	−9.00	−1.60	−6.40	−0.10	−6.55	−1.35
Arunachal Pradesh	−	−	−	−	−	−
Assam	−7.90	4.60	−5.50	4.30	−5.15	1.45
Bihar	−12.10	−21.80	−5.90	−3.80	−9.45	−2.95
Gujarat	−9.20	−3.80	0.10	2.60	−2.85	0.00
Haryana	−	−	0.80	−9.80	−9.25	−25.15
Himachal Pradesh	−21.20	−19.50	−9.00	−1.00	−6.05	−0.65
Jammu and Kashmir	−	−	−1.40	11.50	−3.60	3.60
Karnataka	1.90	3.70	−3.70	0.20	−4.50	8.45
Kerala	6.00	16.10	5.00	0.60	2.15	−0.20
Madhya Pradesh	−11.70	−6.90	−10.00	−11.50	−10.70	−9.35
Maharashtra	−10.70	−4.80	−9.90	−6.30	−7.45	−1.35
Manipur	−2.10	−16.60	−	−	−3.60	−5.90
Meghalaya	−10.30	−9.40	−	−	−37.15	−2.70
Mizoram	−12.60	3.80	−	−	−34.25	−17.90
Nagaland	−	−	−	−	−	−
Orissa	−12.00	−0.90	−13.00	−3.10	−9.55	−2.90
Punjab	−10.90	−0.40	−6.70	2.50	−10.20	10.85
Rajasthan	−15.10	−20.90	−11.70	−15.70	−11.00	−11.80
Sikkim	−7.40	−12.00	−	−	−4.65	−1.10
Tamil Nadu	−13.20	−6.50	−5.80	0.20	−1.35	−4.45
Tripura	−16.20	2.60	−	−	−4.20	1.90
Uttar Pradesh	−18.40	0.40	−12.00	−3.90	−11.45	−3.60
West Bengal	−14.80	−4.60	−1.20	0.30	−4.20	1.05
All India	**−11.10**	**−6.20**	**−6.90**	**−3.00**	**−7.80**	**−2.30**

Source: 38th and 55th rounds of Employment and Unemployment Report, NSS.

Table 12A.4

Change in Rural Employment Disparity Ratio, 1983 to 1999–2000

States	ST and Non-SC/ST		SC and Non-SC/ST	
	Male	Female	Male	Female
Andhra Pradesh	−0.04	0.00	−0.01	0.04
Arunachal Pradesh				
Assam	−0.05	0.35	0.00	0.30
Bihar	−0.02	−1.28	0.08	0.19
Gujarat	−0.11	−0.15	0.05	0.10
Haryana			0.19	0.52
Himachal Pradesh	−0.27	−0.54	−0.05	−0.01
Jammu and Kashmir			0.04	0.90
Karnataka	0.11	−0.33	0.01	−0.46
Kerala	0.07	1.28	0.07	0.07
Madhya Pradesh	−0.01	0.37	0.00	0.03
Maharashtra	−0.06	−0.10	−0.06	−0.15
Manipur	0.04	−0.38		
Meghalaya	0.78	−0.19		
Mizoram	0.43	1.64		
Nagaland				
Orissa	−0.03	0.53	−0.07	0.13
Punjab	−0.01	−0.68	0.05	−1.28
Rajasthan	−0.05	−0.07	−0.02	−0.14
Sikkim	−0.06	−0.56		
Tamil Nadu	−0.22	0.01	−0.09	0.21
Tripura	−0.23	−0.24		
Uttar Pradesh	−0.14	0.35	−0.02	0.08
West Bengal	−0.22	−1.25	0.06	−0.21
All India	**−0.05**	**−0.10**	**0.01**	**−0.01**

Source: 'Employment and Unemployment Situation among Social Groups in India, 1993–94 and 1999–2000', Department of Statistics, Government of India, New Delhi.

Table 12A.5

Percentage of Employed Persons Aged Five Years and Above According to Current Daily Status: Urban

| | 1999–2000 | | | | | | 1983–1984 | | | | | |
| | ST | | SC | | Non-SC/ST | | ST | | SC | | Non-SC/ST | |
States	Male	Female	Male	Female	Male	Female	Male	Female	Male	Female	Male	Female
Andhra Pradesh	52.10	17.30	42.50	17.40	49.00	13.95	49.88	27.50	44.97	16.46	54.77	13.71
Arunachal Pradesh	26.40	10.30			30.25	9.25						
Assam	41.70	19.00	41.90	7.70	50.10	9.35	*	*	49.21	8.07	53.16	6.96
Bihar	35.50	11.00	43.70	11.70	42.30	5.25	55.11	20.57	48.71	18.25	51.90	7.33
Gujarat	55.40	28.40	46.70	14.90	50.90	9.50	53.52	20.98	50.51	14.91	54.22	9.36
Haryana	18.90	4.50	44.30	14.20	51.25	6.95	*	*	56.40	9.43	60.00	9.17
Himachal Pradesh	37.40	0.00	52.40	8.60	51.35	13.60	*	*	53.57	18.45	58.53	13.74
Jammu and Kashmir	66.00	10.20	49.90	10.60	50.10	4.20	*	*	58.43	6.97	57.50	16.21
Karnataka	49.10	22.70	49.20	20.70	52.30	14.65	53.17	16.73	45.78	16.94	54.16	16.79
Kerala	46.10	36.50	41.10	22.90	45.40	13.45	*	*	33.11	22.45	43.97	11.42
Madhya Pradesh	41.70	15.20	41.90	14.90	46.50	9.80	50.30	16.06	49.64	21.27	52.19	10.23
Maharashtra	49.10	13.80	44.20	16.00	51.55	11.10	48.93	26.25	47.21	17.49	54.79	11.19
Manipur	42.50	11.50			43.40	17.45	42.18	20.47	*	*	45.90	26.92
Meghalaya	35.70	22.70			48.25	4.20	44.75	24.64	*	*	59.19	15.07
Mizoram	43.80	23.30			52.05	6.10	50.63	21.12	*	*	*	*
Nagaland	35.40	17.50			65.40	18.90	52.28	17.40	*	*	81.84	1.6
Orissa	41.10	17.90	47.00	20.00	44.65	7.30	55.53	20.61	54.84	15.35	53.93	6.65
Punjab	56.70	13.30	49.90	7.50	53.70	8.20	*	*	56.29	12.56	59.81	8.18

(Table 12A.5 Contd.)

(Table 12A.5 Contd.)

States	1999–2000						1983–1984					
	ST		SC		Non-SC/ST		ST		SC		Non-SC/ST	
	Male	Female	Male	Female	Male	Female	Male	Female	Male	Female	Male	Female
Rajasthan	47.90	7.20	43.50	12.50	48.20	9.10	60.71	46.78	45.45	19.11	53.02	13.26
Sikkim	43.00	25.40			53.20	17.95	64.42	16.40	*	*	59.82	18.28
Tamil Nadu	41.90	25.20	43.00	21.90	51.90	16.20	55.61	22.62	49.16	19.10	53.90	16.42
Tripura	42.70	11.00			50.95	7.20	*	*	46.16	5.28	52.47	10.56
Uttar Pradesh	43.40	11.10	45.90	9.50	47.00	6.25	56.80	10.21	53.13	16.43	53.55	6.33
West Bengal	49.20	17.90	52.80	12.40	55.70	8.55	54.93	15.19	55.01	13.46	54.86	10.12
All India	**45.10**	**16.60**	**45.80**	**14.00**	**49.65**	**10.75**	**52.71**	**20.49**	**50.14**	**16.77**	**53.97**	**11.26**

Source: 'Employment and Unemployment Situation among Social Groups in India, 1993–94 and 1999–2000', Department of Statistics, Government of India, New Delhi.
Note: ★ is for not available.

Table 12A.6
Disparities in Urban Employment Rate (CDS) across Social Groups, 1999–2000

States	ST and Non-SC/ST		SC and Non-SC/ST	
	Male	*Female*	*Male*	*Female*
Andhra Pradesh	1.06	1.24	0.87	1.25
Arunachal Pradesh	0.87	1.11	–	–
Assam	0.83	2.03	0.84	0.82
Bihar	0.84	2.10	1.03	2.23
Gujarat	1.09	2.99	0.92	1.57
Haryana	0.37	0.65	0.86	2.04
Himachal Pradesh	0.73	0.00	1.02	0.63
Jammu and Kashmir	1.32	2.43	1.00	2.52
Karnataka	0.94	1.55	0.94	1.41
Kerala	1.02	2.71	0.91	1.70
Madhya Pradesh	0.90	1.55	0.90	1.52
Maharashtra	0.95	1.24	0.86	1.44
Manipur	0.98	0.66	–	–
Meghalaya	0.74	5.40	–	–
Mizoram	0.84	3.82	–	–
Nagaland	0.54	0.93	–	–
Orissa	0.92	2.45	1.05	2.74
Punjab	1.06	1.62	0.93	0.91
Rajasthan	0.99	0.79	0.90	1.37
Sikkim	0.81	1.42	–	–
Tamil Nadu	0.81	1.56	0.83	1.35
Tripura	0.84	1.53	–	–
Uttar Pradesh	0.92	1.78	0.98	1.52
West Bengal	0.88	2.09	0.95	1.45
All India	**0.91**	**1.54**	**0.92**	**1.30**

Source: 'Employment and Unemployment Situation among Social Groups in India 1993–94 and 1999–2000', Department of Statistics, Government of India, New Delhi.

Table 12A.7

Percentage Point Change in Urban Employment Level (CDS), 1983 to 1999–2000

	ST		SC		Non-SC/ST	
States	Male	Female	Male	Female	Male	Female
Andhra Pradesh	2.22	−10.20	−2.47	0.94	−5.77	0.24
Arunachal Pradesh	–	–	–	–	–	–
Assam	–	–	−7.31	−0.37	−3.06	2.39
Bihar	−19.61	−9.57	−5.01	−6.55	−9.60	−2.08
Gujarat	1.88	7.42	−3.81	−0.01	−3.32	0.14
Haryana	–	–	−12.10	4.77	−8.75	−2.22
Himachal Pradesh	–	–	−1.17	−9.85	−7.18	−0.14
Jammu and Kashmir	–	–	−8.53	3.63	−7.40	−12.01
Karnataka	−4.07	5.97	3.42	3.76	−1.86	−2.14
Kerala	–	–	7.99	0.45	1.43	2.03
Madhya Pradesh	−8.60	−0.86	−7.74	−6.37	−5.69	−0.43
Maharashtra	0.17	−12.45	−3.01	−1.49	−3.24	−0.09
Manipur	0.32	−8.97	–	–	−2.50	−9.47
Meghalaya	−9.05	−1.94	–	–	−10.94	−10.87
Mizoram	−6.83	2.18	–	–	–	–
Nagaland	−16.88	0.10	–	–	−16.44	17.30
Orissa	−14.43	−2.71	−7.84	4.65	−9.28	0.65
Punjab	–	–	−6.39	−5.06	−6.11	0.02
Rajasthan	−12.81	−39.58	−1.95	−6.61	−4.82	−4.16
Sikkim	−21.42	9.00	–	–	−6.62	−0.33
Tamil Nadu	−13.71	2.58	−6.16	2.80	−2.00	−0.22
Tripura	−3.46	5.72	–	–	−1.52	−3.36
Uttar Pradesh	−13.40	0.89	−7.23	−6.93	−6.55	−0.08
West Bengal	−5.73	2.71	−2.21	−1.06	0.84	−1.57
All India	**−7.61**	**−3.89**	**−4.34**	**−2.77**	**−4.32**	**−0.51**

Source: 'Employment and Unemployment Situation among Social Groups in India 1993–94 and 1999–2000', Department of Statistics, Government of India, New Delhi.

Table 12A.8

Change in Urban Employment Disparity Ratio, 1983 to 1999–2000

States	ST and Non-SC/ST		SC and Non-SC/ST	
	Male	*Female*	*Male*	*Female*
Andhra Pradesh	0.15	−0.77	0.05	0.05
Arunachal Pradesh	–	–	–	–
Assam	0.83	2.03	−0.09	−0.34
Bihar	−0.22	−0.71	0.09	−0.26
Gujarat	0.10	0.75	−0.01	−0.02
Haryana	–	–	−0.08	1.01
Himachal Pradesh	–	–	0.11	−0.71
Jammu and Kashmir	–	–	−0.02	2.09
Karnataka	−0.04	0.55	0.10	0.40
Kerala	–	–	0.15	−0.26
Madhya Pradesh	−0.07	−0.02	−0.05	−0.56
Maharashtra	0.06	−1.10	–	–
Manipur	0.06	−0.10	–	–
Meghalaya	−0.02	3.77	–	–
Mizoram	0.84	3.82	–	–
Nagaland	−0.10	−9.95	–	–
Orissa	−0.11	−0.65	0.04	0.43
Punjab	1.06	1.62	−0.01	−0.62
Rajasthan	−0.15	−2.74	0.05	−0.07
Sikkim	−0.27	0.52	–	–
Tamil Nadu	−0.22	0.18	−0.08	0.19
Tripura	−0.04	1.03	–	–
Uttar Pradesh	−0.14	0.16	−0.02	−1.08
West Bengal	−0.12	0.59	−0.05	0.12
All India	**−0.07**	**−0.28**	**−0.01**	**−0.19**

Source: 'Employment and Unemployment Situation among Social Groups in India, 1993–94 and 1999–2000', Department of Statistics, Government of India, New Delhi.

Table 12A.9

Percentage of Unemployed Persons Aged Five Years and Above According to Current Daily Status: Rural

States	1999–2000						1983					
	ST		SC		Non-SC/ST		ST		SC		Non-SC/ST	
	Male	Female	Male	Female	Male	Female	Male	Female	Male	Female	Male	Female
Andhra Pradesh	3.0	4.5	7.2	5.1	4.1	2.3	4.0	3.8	7.5	8.3	4.7	3.1
Arunachal Pradesh	0.5	0.0	–	–	1.3	0.0	–	–	–	–	–	–
Assam	3.2	0.5	2.5	0.7	3.8	1.8	7.3	0.1	2.4	0.4	2.1	0.6
Bihar	5.8	1.5	5.0	1.8	3.2	0.5	2.2	1.4	7.5	4.9	3.5	1.2
Gujarat	3.6	1.5	5.4	0.3	2.3	0.8	3.6	3.1	5.6	2.9	2.6	0.7
Haryana	12.0	0.0	6.1	0.4	1.5	0.1	★	★	5.8	0.7	3.0	0.3
Himachal Pradesh	1.6	0.9	2.0	0.4	2.4	0.3	–	–	1.4	–	1.4	0.4
Jammu and Kashmir	0.7	0.0	2.8	0.2	3.7	0.2	★	★	1.8	0.1	5.6	0.2
Karnataka	1.7	2.6	4.9	2.1	1.9	1.0	6.1	2.6	7.6	1.6	3.5	2.3
Kerala	9.6	5.8	14.9	9.0	9.7	4.6	16.1	7.1	19.8	12.0	12.0	5.4
Madhya Pradesh	1.5	0.6	2.8	1.4	1.8	0.8	1.2	0.6	2.2	1.5	1.1	0.5
Maharashtra	2.8	2.5	5.1	3.8	3.1	2.2	4.3	4.3	6.4	4.3	3.3	2.2
Manipur	0.9	0.6	–	–	0.8	0.2	1.0	0.4	★	★	0.2	–
Meghalaya	0.3	0.3	–	–	0.0	0.0	2.1	1.9	★	★	2.0	2.6
Mizoram	0.9	0.1	–	–	0.0	0.0	0.2	0.1	★	★	–	–
Nagaland	1.4	0.7	–	–	0.1	4.0						
Orissa	3.5	1.0	4.1	1.1	4.6	1.3	5.4	4.4	6.6	3.4	4.4	1.7

Punjab	3.6	2.6	3.8	0.2	1.7	0.5	6.1	–	8.1	1.3	2.9	0.5
Rajasthan	1.0	0.0	2.5	0.9	1.5	0.6	1.7	0.5	3.4	1.6	1.9	0.4
Sikkim	2.6	0.2	–	–	1.4	0.8	1.7	0.9	*	*	1.5	0.3
Tamil Nadu	11.1	4.6	10.9	5.5	4.8	2.7	7.7	6.4	17.2	13.4	9.8	5.7
Tripura	0.0	0.0	–	–	1.1	0.3	3.9	0.4	1.3	0.0	2.2	2.1
Uttar Pradesh	2.2	0.0	2.8	0.8	1.5	0.1	2.0	–	3.9	1.1	1.6	0.2
West Bengal	8.9	4.6	6.3	1.2	7.4	2.1	9.8	10.5	9.7	3.9	7.8	1.4
All India	**3.0**	**1.5**	**5.0**	**2.1**	**3.4**	**1.4**	**3.3**	**2.6**	**7.2**	**4.2**	**4.0**	**1.7**

Source: 'Employment and Unemployment Situation among Social Groups in India, 1993–1994 and 1999–2000', Department of Statistics, Government of India, New Delhi.

Note: * is for not available.

Table 12A.10

Percentage Point Change in Rural Unemployment Level (CDS), 1983 to 1999–2000

States	ST		SC		Non-SC/ST	
	Male	*Female*	*Male*	*Female*	*Male*	*Female*
Andhra Pradesh	−1.0	0.7	−0.3	−3.2	−0.6	−0.9
Arunachal Pradesh	0.5	0.0	0.0	0.0	1.3	0.0
Assam	−4.1	0.4	0.1	0.3	1.7	1.1
Bihar	3.6	0.1	−2.5	−3.1	−0.3	−0.8
Gujarat	0.1	−1.6	−0.2	−2.6	−0.3	0.1
Haryana	−	−	0.3	−0.3	−1.5	−0.2
Himachal Pradesh	−	−	0.7	−	1.0	−0.1
Jammu and Kashmir	−	−	1.0	0.1	−1.9	0.0
Karnataka	−4.4	0.0	−2.7	0.5	−1.6	−1.3
Kerala	−6.5	−1.3	−4.9	−3.0	−2.3	−0.8
Madhya Pradesh	0.3	0.0	0.6	−0.1	0.7	0.3
Maharashtra	−1.5	−1.8	−1.3	−0.5	−0.2	−0.1
Manipur	−0.1	0.2	−	−	0.6	
Meghalaya	−1.8	−1.6	−	−	−2.0	−2.6
Mizoram	0.7	0.0	−	−	−	−
Nagaland	−	−	−	−	−	−
Orissa	−1.9	−3.4	−2.5	−2.3	0.2	−0.4
Punjab	−2.5	−	−4.3	−1.1	−1.2	0.0
Rajasthan	−0.7	−0.5	−0.9	−0.7	−0.5	0.1
Sikkim	0.9	−0.7	−	−	−0.2	0.5
Tamil Nadu	3.4	−1.8	−6.3	−7.9	−5.0	−3.0
Tripura	−3.9	−0.4	−1.3	0.0	−1.1	−1.8
Uttar Pradesh	0.3	−	−1.1	−0.3	−0.1	−0.1
West Bengal	−0.9	−5.9	−3.4	−2.7	−0.5	0.7
All India	**−0.3**	**−1.1**	**−2.2**	**−2.1**	**−0.7**	**−0.3**

Source: 'Employment and Unemployment Situation among Social Groups in India, 1993–94 and 1999–2000', Department of Statistics, Government of India, New Delhi.

Table 12A.11

Disparities in Rural Unemployment Rate (CDS) across Social Groups, 1999–2000

States	ST and Non-SC/ST		SC and Non-SC/ST	
	Male	*Female*	*Male*	*Female*
Andhra Pradesh	0.74	2.00	1.78	2.27
Arunachal Pradesh	0.38	–	–	–
Assam	0.85	0.29	0.67	0.40
Bihar	1.81	3.33	1.56	4.00
Gujarat	1.57	1.88	2.35	0.38
Haryana	8.00	–	4.07	4.00
Himachal Pradesh	0.68	3.00	0.85	1.33
Jammu and Kashmir	0.19	–	0.76	1.00
Karnataka	0.92	2.74	2.65	2.21
Kerala	0.99	1.26	1.54	1.96
Madhya Pradesh	0.83	0.75	1.56	1.75
Maharashtra	0.92	1.16	1.67	1.77
Manipur	1.20	3.00	–	–
Meghalaya	–	–	–	–
Mizoram	–	–	–	–
Nagaland	14.00	0.18	–	–
Orissa	0.76	0.80	0.89	0.88
Punjab	2.12	5.20	2.24	0.40
Rajasthan	0.69	0.00	1.72	1.64
Sikkim	1.93	0.25	–	–
Tamil Nadu	2.34	1.70	2.29	2.04
Tripura	–	–	–	–
Uttar Pradesh	1.47	0.00	1.87	8.00
West Bengal	1.21	2.24	0.86	0.59
All India	**0.90**	**1.07**	**1.49**	**1.50**

Source: 'Employment and Unemployment Situation among Social Groups in India, 1993–94 and 1999–2000', Department of Statistics, Government of India, New Delhi.

Table 12A.12

Change in Rural Unemployment Disparity Ratio, 1983 to 1999–2000

States	ST and Non-SC/ST		SC and Non-SC/ST	
	Male	Female	Male	Female
Andhra Pradesh	−0.13	0.78	0.17	−0.41
Arunachal Pradesh	−	−	−	−
Assam	−2.64	0.12	−0.48	−0.26
Bihar	1.19	2.18	−0.59	−0.04
Gujarat	0.17	−2.53	0.17	−3.74
Haryana	−	−	2.13	1.68
Himachal Pradesh	−	−	−0.14	−
Jammu and Kashmir	−	−	0.44	0.13
Karnataka	−0.86	1.59	0.46	1.52
Kerala	−0.35	−0.05	−0.11	−0.26
Madhya Pradesh	−0.30	−0.35	−0.55	−1.21
Maharashtra	−0.39	−0.76	−0.29	−0.19
Manipur	−4.45	−	−	−
Meghalaya	−	−	−	−
Mizoram	−	−	−	−
Nagaland	−	−	−	−
Orissa	−0.45	−1.83	−0.60	−1.16
Punjab	−0.01	−	−0.59	−1.98
Rajasthan	−0.21	−1.32	−0.06	−2.19
Sikkim	0.82	−3.06	0.00	0.00
Tamil Nadu	1.55	0.59	0.53	−0.30
Tripura	−	−	−	−
Uttar Pradesh	0.28	−	−0.50	2.05
West Bengal	−0.04	−5.45	−0.38	−2.24
All India	**0.08**	**−0.42**	**−0.28**	**−0.96**

Source: 'Employment and Unemployment Situation among Social Groups in India, 1993–94 and 1999–2000', Department of Statistics, Government of India, New Delhi.

Table 12A.13

Percentage of Unemployed Persons Aged Five Years and Above, According to Current Daily Status: Urban

States	1999–2000 ST Male	ST Female	SC Male	SC Female	Non–SC/ST Male	Non–SC/ST Female	1983 ST Male	ST Female	SC Male	SC Female	Non–SC/ST Male	Non–SC/ST Female
Andhra Pradesh	3.4	2.0	4.5	1.7	4.3	1.4	6.10	1.62	10.77	3.28	4.99	1.82
Arunachal Pradesh	0.9	1.4	0.0	0.0	0.5	1.2	–	–	–	–	–	–
Assam	3	0.0	6.3	1.9	4.2	2.4	★	★	5.80	1.54	3.34	0.64
Bihar	6.5	1.8	4.9	0.9	3.9	1.0	4.36	0.42	3.85	2.43	3.73	0.31
Gujarat	4.7	0.6	3.4	1.3	1.7	0.6	2.61	2.52	6.56	1.49	4.39	0.38
Haryana	0.0	0.0	4.5	1.2	2.0	0.3	★	★	6.19	2.92	4.54	0.52
Himachal Pradesh	0.0	0.0	5.9	0.9	2.8	1.9	★	★	6.06	–	4.96	2.06
Jammu and Kashmir	0.0	0.0	5.2	0.9	2.1	0.4	★	★	6.53	–	2.75	0.90
Karnataka	2.4	1.1	3.9	1.1	3.4	0.9	4.97	3.60	5.70	2.55	5.19	1.58
Kerala	6.4	7.9	14.0	8.7	8.1	5.1	★	★	22.23	6.10	11.86	4.90
Madhya Pradesh	3.3	0.5	5.4	1.7	3.6	0.5	6.92	1.90	3.14	0.88	2.77	0.44
Maharashtra	3.8	1.8	6.4	1.5	4.2	1.2	6.63	1.42	8.62	2.36	5.02	1.32
Manipur	0.5	0.0	3.9	0.0	2.5	1.4	–	–	★	★	0.22	0.05
Meghalaya	1.6	1.1	1.5	3.9	4.8	0.8	2.50	2.86	★	★	7.36	3.71
Mizoram	1.6	0.8	7.7	1.8	0.0	2.0	0.71	0.26	★	★	★	★
Nagaland	5.1	2.1	0.2	0.0	0.9	0.0	–	–	★	★	0.53	–
Orissa	3.7	0.4	4.2	0.8	4.8	1.0	8.99	1.51	4.74	1.28	4.47	1.09

(Table 12A.13 Contd.)

(Table 12A.13 Contd.)

States	1999–2000						1983					
	ST		SC		Non–SC/ST		ST		SC		Non–SC/ST	
	Male	Female	Male	Female	Male	Female	Male	Female	Male	Female	Male	Female
Punjab	3.7	0.0	2.9	0.2	3.4	0.7	★	★	4.87	0.66	4.44	1.10
Rajasthan	1.1	0.3	2.9	0.0	1.9	0.5	0.33	–	7.77	1.39	4.89	0.50
Sikkim	3.3	1.9	5.9	4.9	4.2	2.2	7.71	3.03	★	★	8.08	1.39
Tamil Nadu	7.8	1.0	10.2	3.2	4.0	1.5	10.09	6.66	14.63	5.24	8.90	2.93
Tripura	6.8	0.0	1.5	0.1	2.8	1.0	★	★	–	1.70	4.28	4.37
Uttar Pradesh	2.2	0.0	3.7	0.2	3.1	0.4	3.85	0.52	5.58	0.68	4.13	0.42
West Bengal	6.9	3.6	7.6	0.6	5.7	2.2	6.95	3.91	8.51	1.65	7.94	2.36
All India	**3.7**	**1.1**	**5.2**	**1.2**	**3.8**	**1.2**	**5.49**	**1.94**	**7.20**	**2.10**	**5.28**	**1.42**

Source: 'Employment and Unemployment Situation among Social Groups in India, 1993–94 and 1999–2000', Department of Statistics, Government of India, New Delhi.
Note: ★ is for not available.

Table 12A.14

Percentage Point Change in Urban Unemployment Level (CDS), 1983 to 1999–2000

States	ST		SC		Non-SC/ST	
	Male	*Female*	*Male*	*Female*	*Male*	*Female*
Andhra Pradesh	−2.7	0.4	−6.3	−1.6	−0.7	−0.5
Arunachal Pradesh	0.9	1.4	0.0	0.0	0.5	1.2
Assam	–	–	0.5	0.4	0.8	1.8
Bihar	2.1	1.4	1.1	−1.5	0.2	0.6
Gujarat	2.1	−1.9	−3.2	−0.2	−2.7	0.2
Haryana	–	–	−1.7	−1.7	−2.6	−0.2
Himachal Pradesh	–	–	−0.2	–	−2.2	−0.2
Jammu and Kashmir	–	–	−1.3	–	−0.7	−0.6
Karnataka	−2.6	−2.5	−1.8	−1.5	−1.8	−0.7
Kerala	–	–	−8.2	2.6	−3.8	0.2
Madhya Pradesh	−3.6	−1.4	2.3	0.8	0.8	0.0
Maharashtra	−2.8	0.4	−2.2	−0.9	−0.8	−0.2
Manipur	–	–	–	–	2.3	–
Meghalaya	−0.9	−1.8	–	–	−2.6	−3.0
Mizoram	0.9	0.5	–	–	–	–
Nagaland	–	–	–	–	–	–
Orissa	−5.3	−1.1	−0.5	−0.5	0.3	−0.1
Punjab	–	–	−2.0	−0.5	−1.0	−0.5
Rajasthan	0.8	–	−4.9	−1.4	−3.0	−0.1
Sikkim	−4.4	−1.1	–	–	−3.9	0.8
Tamil Nadu	−2.3	−5.7	−4.4	−2.0	−5.0	−1.5
Tripura	–	–	–	−1.6	−1.5	−3.4
Uttar Pradesh	−1.7	–	−1.9	−0.5	−1.0	0.0
West Bengal	0.0	−0.3	−0.9	−1.1	−2.2	−0.2
All India	**−1.8**	**−0.8**	**−2.0**	**−0.9**	**−1.5**	**−0.2**

Source: 'Employment and Unemployment Situation among Social Groups in India, 1993–94 and 1999–2000', Department of Statistics, Government of India, New Delhi.

Table 12A.15
Disparities in Urban Unemployment Rate (CDS) across Social Groups, 1999–2000

States	ST and Non-SC/ST		SC and Non-SC/ST	
	Male	*Female*	*Male*	*Female*
Andhra Pradesh	0.80	1.48	1.06	1.26
Arunachal Pradesh	2.00	–	–	–
Assam	0.72	0.00	1.52	0.79
Bihar	1.67	1.89	1.26	0.95
Gujarat	2.76	1.09	2.00	2.36
Haryana	0.00	–	2.31	4.00
Himachal Pradesh	0.00	0.00	2.11	0.47
Jammu and Kashmir	0.00	–	2.54	2.57
Karnataka	0.72	1.29	1.16	1.29
Kerala	0.80	1.55	1.74	1.71
Madhya Pradesh	0.93	1.11	1.52	3.78
Maharashtra	0.90	1.57	1.52	1.30
Manipur	0.20	0.00	–	–
Meghalaya	–	–	–	–
Mizoram	–	–	–	–
Nagaland	5.67	–	–	–
Orissa	0.78	0.42	0.88	0.84
Punjab	1.09	0.00	0.85	0.31
Rajasthan	0.59	0.67	1.57	0.00
Sikkim	0.80	0.86	–	–
Tamil Nadu	1.97	0.69	2.58	2.21
Tripura	–	–	–	–
Uttar Pradesh	0.71	–	1.19	0.50
West Bengal	1.21	1.64	1.33	0.27
All India	**0.99**	**0.92**	**1.39**	**1.00**

Source: 'Employment and Unemployment Situation among Social Groups in India, 1993–94 and 1999–2000', Department of Statistics, Government of India, New Delhi.

Table 12A.16

Change in Urban Unemployment Disparity Ratio, 1983 to 1999–2000

States	ST and Non-SC/ST		SC and Non-SC/ST	
	Male	*Female*	*Male*	*Female*
Andhra Pradesh	–0.42	0.59	–1.10	–0.54
Arunachal Pradesh	–	–	–	–
Assam	0.72	0.00	–0.22	–1.61
Bihar	0.50	0.54	0.22	–6.89
Gujarat	2.17	–5.54	0.51	–1.56
Haryana	–	–	0.94	–1.62
Himachal Pradesh	–	–	0.89	–
Jammu and Kashmir	–	–	0.16	2.57
Karnataka	–0.24	–0.98	0.07	–0.32
Kerala	0.80	1.55	–0.14	0.46
Madhya Pradesh	–1.57	–3.21	0.39	1.78
Maharashtra	–0.42	0.49	–0.19	–0.48
Manipur	0.20	–	–	–
Meghalaya	–	–	–	–
Mizoram	–	–	–	–
Nagaland	–	–	–	–
Orissa	–1.23	–0.96	–0.18	–0.33
Punjab	1.09	–	–0.24	–0.29
Rajasthan	0.53	0.67	–0.02	–2.78
Sikkim	–0.16	–1.32	0.00	0.00
Tamil Nadu	0.84	–1.58	0.94	0.42
Tripura	–	–	–	–
Uttar Pradesh	–0.22	–	–0.16	–1.12
West Bengal	0.34	–0.02	0.26	–0.43
All India	**–0.05**	**–0.45**	**0.02**	**–0.48**

Source: 'Employment and Unemployment Situation among Social Groups in India, 1993–94 and 1999–2000', Department of Statistics, Government of India.

Chapter 13

RESERVATION AND SHARE IN PUBLIC EMPLOYMENT

Sukhadeo Thorat and Chittaranjan Senapati

The issue of reservations for Scheduled Castes (SCs) and Scheduled Tribes (STs) in government services, educational institutions and political bodies like central and state legislatures falls under the purview of anti-discriminatory and pro-active measures to mainstream the marginalised social groups. Such measures have been used to ensure proportional participation of SCs and STs in various public domains. This chapter outlines the main provisions of reservation policy and examines its impact on the employment and education of SCs and STs and their representation in the legislature.

RESERVATION POLICY

The reservation policy of the government is operative in and limited to mainly three spheres—public sector services, admission to public educational institutions and seats in central, state and local legislatures and other bodies. It must be mentioned that in the case of public services and education, the affirmative action policy is confined to state-run and state-supported sector. The vast private sector, wherein more than 90 per cent SC and ST workers are engaged, is excluded, and they, therefore, remain unprotected from possible discrimination. The services in the private sector and private educational institutions are completely excluded from the purview of the policy. Over a period of time, the government sphere has expanded along with the scope of reservation policy. The new spheres include proportional representation of marginalised sections in government housing, shops and commercial activities, and a number of other small spheres. Such measures not only favourably include the excluded in nation's development process but also relate to the enhancement of their relative economic status.

One of the central aspects of the reservation policy pertains to reservation in government services. Article 16(A) of the Constitution of India permits reservations in favour of marginalised social groups like SCs, STs and Other Backward Classes (OBCs) in pursuance of this provision in proportion to their relative share in the population (Table 13.1). Besides, the promotional aspects of employed persons are also covered by the provisions of reservation policy. The scope and extent of the reservation policy is applicable to public sector which includes civil services, public sector undertakings (PSUs), statutory and semi-government bodies and voluntary agencies. At the central level, some services in defence and judiciary are excluded from the ambit of reservation policy.[1]

Table 13.1
Present Percentages of Reservation for SC, ST and OBC in Government Services

S. No. Mode of Appointment	*Fixed Percentage of Reservation for*		
	SC	*ST*	*OBC*
(1) Direct recruitment on all-India basis by open competition (i.e. through the UPSC, by means of written competitive test held by SSC and any other authority).	15	7.5	27
(2) Direct recruitment on an all-India basis otherwise than (a) above, that is, by SSC exam or any other authority by not conducting a written competitive test.	16.75	7.5	27
(3) Direct recruitment to Class III and IV posts (Group C and D posts), which normally attract candidates from a locality or region	Generally in proportion to the population of SC, ST and OBC in the respective states and Union Territories		
(4) Posts filled by promotion in grades or services in which the element of direct recruitment, if any, does not exceed 75 per cent.	*SC*	*ST*	
Through limited departmental competitive examination in Groups B, C and D.	15	7.5	
By Selection from Group B to the lower rung or category in Group A or Groups B, C and D.	15	7.5	
On the basis of seniority subject to fitness in Groups A, B, C and D.	15	7.5	

Source: Annual Report; Ministry of Personnel, Public Grievances and Pensions; Government of India; 2002–2003, Chapter 5, Paragraph 5.2.

[1] The reservation policy in government jobs was launched in 1931 under the Poona Pact. However, reservation with specific quotas in government services was introduced in 1943 through a government order, which was further formalised later on in 1947 under the provisions of Independent India's Constitution (see Galanter, 1991: 86).

Reservation is accompanied by an array of special provisions, which are designed to facilitate and improve the ability of the marginalised social groups to compete for government jobs. These include relaxation of minimum age for entry to service; relaxation of minimum standards of suitability within a reasonable limit (subject to the fulfilment of the required minimum qualifications); relaxation in fee; and provisions for pre-examination training; separate interviews for SC and ST persons and provision of inclusion of experts from SC/ST background on the selection committees, among others.

The second important sphere of reservation pertains to education. Article 15(4) of the Constitution of India empowers the state to make special provisions for the advancement of SCs and STs. Under this provision, the state has reserved seats for SC and ST students in educational institutions which include colleges and universities (including technical, engineering and medical) run by the central and state governments and in government-aided educational institutions. These provisions are further strengthened by a number of financial schemes which include scholarships, special hostels for SC and ST students, concessions in fee, grants for books and remedial coaching, among others.

The third most important sphere of reservation is representation in central and state legislatures. Reservation in legislative bodies is one of the specific and mandatory Constitutional provisions for SCs and STs. Under Articles 330, 332 and 334 of the Indian Constitution, seats are reserved for SCs and STs in the central and state legislatures in proportion to the population share of marginalised communities. Similar aspects of reservation are also applicable to local level bodies at district, taluk and village levels. The constitutional provision to reserve seats in legislative bodies is complemented by certain statutory provisions for the enhancement of political participation by SCs and STs. For instance, smaller election deposits are required from members of these groups. Political reservations, at present, have a time dimension to their applicability; presently extended up to 2020.

IMPACT OF RESERVATIONS

This section of the chapter examines the impact of reservation policy specifically on employment, education and legislature.

Employment

There has been a substantial increase in the number of SC and ST government employees over the years. In 1956, there were 212,000 SC employees which increased to 641,000 in 1991 and 540,000 in 2003 (see Annexure XI Table 13A.1).

The corresponding increase in the percentages of SC employees to total government employees increased from 00.14 per cent in 1956 to about 17 per cent in 2003 which is fairly close to their share in population (see Annexure XI Table 13A.2). In the case of STs, the numbers increased from 22,000 in 1956 to 211,000 in 2003, with a corresponding increase in percentages from 0.01 per cent in 1956 to 7 per cent in 2003. Similarly, the number of SC employees in PSUs increased from 40,000 in 1970 to 296,000 in 2003, while the corresponding figures for ST stood at 12,000 in 1970 and 138,000 in 2003. In case of nationalised banks, the number of SC employees increased from 4,000 in 1972 to 143,000 in 2000, while for the same period, the actual number of STs increased from 400 to 43,000. The corresponding percentage for SCs stood at 1.89 per cent in 1970 and 13.32 per cent in 2000. Similarly, the percentage increase for STs was 0.19 per cent in 1970 and 4 per cent in 2000. It is pertinent to mention here that the above analysis does not include many government spheres such as educational institutions and others, so it is likely that with the inclusion of these spheres, the figures of employment under reservations might swell up (see Annexure XI Tables 13A.3 and 13A.4).

Thus, during the last 50 years or so, the share of SCs and STs in government services has improved significantly. There are, however, variations between different categories of jobs. Generally, reservations are close to the stipulated quotas in grades C and D jobs, but less so in case of grades A and B jobs. In 2003, grades C and D category of jobs accounted for almost 95 per cent of the total SC and ST posts. An analysis of the quotas stipulated for fulfilment in government services indicates that though the representation of SCs and STs is fairly close to the proportion of their respective populations in grades C and D category of jobs, their representation is far from satisfactory in grades A and B categories of jobs. This analysis also holds true for several other categories of technical jobs which include jobs in universities. This assertion is again indicative of the lack of social mobility that the caste system imposes on marginalised social groups and re-affirms hierarchical and stratified nature of the same, whereby SCs, particularly, are relegated to certain degrading professions (Table 13.2).

Education

The analysis of admissions in educational institutions is hampered by limited estimates, particularly with regard to the impact of reservations in higher education. Nevertheless, the limited evidence indicates that student enrolment has increased proportionally with an increase in reservations. In 1981, one estimate puts the proportion of SC graduates at around 3.3 per cent, and ST graduates at 0.8 per cent, which incidentally, is far below their share in the total population. By the late 1990s, the proportion of SC and ST students to the total students enrolled had risen to 7.8 per cent and 2.7 per cent, respectively. However, compared to

Table 13.2
Employment Share by Job Categories

Social Groups	Job Categories			
	A	B	C	D
Percentage Share to the Total Employees in Government Jobs				
SC	11.93	14.32	16.29	17.98
ST	4.18	4.32	6.54	6.96
Non-SC/ST	83.88	81.36	77.17	75.06
Percentage Share to the Total Employees in PSUs				
SC	7.49	7.60	60.95	29.55
ST	4.75	6.74	62.17	26.76
Non-SC/ST	13.36	12.46	55.55	18.70

Source: Annual Report; Ministry of Personnel, Public Grievances and Pensions; Government of India; 2002–2003.

their respective shares in the total population, which are approximately 16 per cent and 8 per cent for SCs and STs, respectively, the enrolment ratios were very low. Given the lack of data in this regard, it is difficult to obtain the actual estimates of students who benefit from reservations. One estimate indicates that in 1996–1997 roughly 510,000 SC and 180,000 ST students were enrolled in higher education—of these, roughly 200,000 SC and ST students put together may have enrolled in desirable programmes in higher education (where reservation matters). Weisskopf (2005) estimates that about one-third SC and ST students enrolled in universities were pursuing higher education in desirable programmes as a direct outcome of the reservation policy.

Legislature

The constitutional provisions for reservation in government services and educational institutions are merely authorisations which empower the state to make special provisions for the discriminated social groups and are, therefore, not mandatory. However, reservations in the legislatures, at both the central and state levels are specially incorporated in the Constitution of India itself. The seats in the central and state legislatures are reserved for SCs and STs in proportion to their population. It is obligatory and mandatory on the part of the government to extend the scope of reservations to the legislatures. Thus, in 2004, out of a total of 545 seats in the Lok Sabha or the Lower House of the Parliament, 75 (13.81 per cent) seats were reserved for SC candidates and 41 seats (7.55 per cent) for ST candidates, respectively. Of the total number of seats in the Vidhan Sabha

(State Legislative Assembly), more than 2,000 seats were reserved for SC and ST candidates. However, reservations in the legislative houses of the central and state governments align with the population estimates of SC and ST population in 1981, and so far the population estimates of the said social groups have not been updated in accordance with the 2001 census (Table 13.3).

Table 13.3
Members of Parliament by Social Groups from 5th to 14th Lok Sabha

S. No.	Chronology of the Lok Sabha	Election Year	Actual No. of Members of Parliament				Per Cent Share of the Members of Parliament			
			SCs	*STs*	*Non-SCs/STs*	*Total*	*SCs*	*STs*	*Non-SCs/STs*	*Total*
1.	5th Lok Sabha	1971	75	33	440	548	13.69	6.02	80.29	100
2.	6th Lok Sabha	1977	64	33	462	559	11.45	5.90	82.65	100
3.	7th Lok Sabha	1980	81	31	453	565	14.34	5.49	80.18	100
4.	8th Lok Sabha	1984	79	43	449	571	13.84	7.53	78.63	100
5.	9th Lok Sabha	1989	81	37	413	531	15.25	6.97	77.78	100
6.	10th Lok Sabha	1991	78	39	427	544	14.34	7.17	78.49	100
7.	11th Lok Sabha	1996	79	38	428	545	14.50	6.97	78.53	100
8.	12th Lok Sabha	1998	74	39	432	545	13.58	7.16	79.27	100
9.	13th Lok Sabha	1999	83	41	443	567	14.64	7.23	78.13	100
10.	14th Lok Sabha	2004	75	41	427	543	13.81	7.55	78.64	100

Source: http://www.parliamentofindia.nic.in

CONCLUSION

As is apparent from the preceding discussion, the reservation policy in government services, educational institutions, legislative houses at both the central and state levels and other bodies at lower levels, has succeeded, to a considerable extent, in increasing the representation of SC and ST in these spheres. However, the actual reservations stipulated by the Constitution of India fall short of the target in some categories of jobs, particularly grade A and B categories of jobs in government services. With specific regard to reservations in government jobs, the reservation policy tends to cause clustering of SCs in certain services, departments and grades of jobs. The process to achieve reservations is, therefore, marred by certain prejudices, which are possibly caste-based and appear to be operational in various forms. In the sphere of admission to educational institutions, the share of SCs and STs is much less than desired in preferred institutions. In many cases, though reservations are accepted in theory, they are not implemented pragmatically. The extent and scope of the reservation policy is also limited by the fact that it is applicable to a tiny government and government-supported sector and excludes within its purview, the vast private sector, wherein, more than 90 per cent SC and ST workers are engaged.

In the case of political representation, two problems remain at the centre-stage. There has been resistance, even on the part of the government, to update the share of seats for SCs and STs in the central and state legislatures in proportion to their recent population estimates as delineated by the 2001 census, with the present allocation of seats being based on the 1981 population census. It is important to mention that the population share of SCs and STs in 1981 was about 14 per cent and 7.55 per cent, respectively, which increased to 17 per cent for SCs and 8.5 per cent for STs in 2001. Thus, both the social groups continue to suffer from under-representation in central and state legislatures.

ANNEXURE XI

Table 13A.1
Government Employment under Reservation (1956–2003)

As on 1 January	Total	SC	ST	Non-SC/ST
1956	1,420,051	212,754	22,549	1184,748
1957	1,826,424	253,308	29,248	1543,868
1958	1,744,056	215,940	30,518	1497,598
1959	1,839,101	223,124	35,652	1580,325
1960	1,866,729	228,497	37,704	1600,528
1961	1,903,110	235,968	38,510	1628,632
1962	2,119,204	267,000	43,933	1808,271
1963	2,206,955	283,108	47,477	1876,370
1964	2,265,199	298,369	50,989	1915,841
1965	2,344,487	311,425	52,655	1980,407

(Table 13A.1 Contd.)

(Table 13A.1 Contd.)

As on 1 January	Total	SC	ST	Non-SC/ST
1966	2,362,276	316,073	55,178	1,991,025
1967	2,499,283	334,744	57,497	2,107,042
1968	2,587,843	341,010	61,075	2,185,758
1969	2,643,476	359,943	64,315	2,219,218
1970	2,228,925	291,874	60,325	1,876,726
1971	2,698,151	360,042	67,957	2,270,152
1972	2,749,985	370,584	71,569	2,307,832
1973	2,436,063	340,938	418,229	1,676,896
1974	2,893,751	395,453	81,512	2,416,786
1975	2,954,098	408,879	86,897	2,458,322
1976	2,973,278	421,685	90,392	2,461,201
1977	3,020,755	441,463	101,552	2,477,740
1978	3,028,792	448,713	108,052	2,472,027
1979	3,093,123	467,712	120,443	2,504,968
1980	3,137,001	490,592	125,004	2,521,405
1981	3,227,528	490,194	123,314	2,614,020
1982	3,124,860	520,994	149,301	2,454,565
1983	3,278,290	536,037	167,363	2,574,890
1984	3,303,619	529,573	149,391	2,624,655
1985	3,374,021	567,356	156,911	2,649,754
1986	3,455,634	551,161	158,656	2,745,817
1987	3,433,984	555,471	161,012	2,717,501
1988	3,335,997	543,905	164,459	2,627,633
1989	3,464,435	568,600	174,101	2,721,734
1990	3,477,053	590,108	185,245	2,701,700
1991	3,735,017	641,920	203,253	2,889,844
1992	3,659,391	628,709	156,377	2,874,305
1993	3,530,023	604,347	202,068	2,723,608
1994	3,567,112	602,670	195,802	2,768,640
1995	3,557,210	619,986	205,436	2,731,788
1996	3,474,827	590,556	196,137	2,688,134
1997	3,307,984	582,230	203,037	2,522,717
1998	3,431,756	605,206	210,405	2,616,145

(Table 13A.1 Contd.)

(Table 13A.1 Contd.)

As on 1 January	Total	SC	ST	Non-SC/ST
1999	3,544,262	591,740	218,653	2,733,869
2000	3,627,882	593,639	225,917	2,808,326
2001	3,729,557	611,869	237,051	2,880,647
2002	3,381,221	574,033	206,752	2,600,436
2003	3,269,345	540,220	211,345	2,517,780

Source: The Reports of the National Commission for the SCs and the STs and the Annual Report of the Department of Personnel, Public Grievances and Pensions, Government of India (GoI).

Table 13A.2
Percentage Share in Government Employment (1956–2003)

As on 1 January	SC	ST	Non-SC/ST
1956	14.98	1.59	83.43
1957	13.87	1.60	84.53
1958	12.38	1.75	85.87
1959	12.13	1.94	85.93
1960	12.24	2.02	85.74
1961	12.40	2.02	85.58
1962	12.60	2.07	85.33
1963	12.83	2.15	85.02
1964	13.17	2.25	84.58
1965	13.28	2.25	84.47
1966	13.38	2.34	84.28
1967	13.39	2.30	84.31
1968	13.18	2.36	84.46
1969	13.62	2.43	83.95
1970	13.09	2.71	84.20
1971	13.34	2.52	84.14
1972	13.48	2.60	83.92
1973	14.00	17.17	68.84
1974	13.67	2.82	83.52
1975	13.84	2.94	83.22
1976	14.18	3.04	82.78
1977	14.61	3.36	82.02
1978	14.81	3.57	81.62

(Table 13A.2 Contd.)

(Table 13A.2 Contd.)

As on 1 January	SC	ST	Non-SC/ST
1979	15.12	3.89	80.99
1980	15.64	3.98	80.38
1981	15.19	3.82	80.99
1982	16.67	4.78	78.55
1983	16.35	5.11	78.54
1984	16.03	4.52	79.45
1985	16.82	4.65	78.53
1986	15.95	4.59	79.46
1987	16.18	4.69	79.14
1988	16.30	4.93	78.77
1989	16.41	5.03	78.56
1990	16.97	5.33	77.70
1991	17.19	5.44	77.37
1992	17.18	4.27	78.55
1993	17.12	5.72	77.16
1994	16.90	5.49	77.62
1995	17.43	5.78	76.80
1996	17.00	5.64	77.36
1997	17.60	6.14	76.26
1998	17.64	6.13	76.23
1999	16.70	6.17	77.14
2000	16.36	6.23	77.41
2001	16.41	6.36	77.24
2002	16.98	6.11	76.91
2003	16.52	6.46	77.01

Source: The Reports of the National Commission for the SCs and the STs and the Annual Report of the Department of Personnel, Public Grievances and Pensions, Government of India (GoI).

Table 13A.3
Employment under Reservation in Public Sector Undertakings (PSUs) (1970–2003)

As on 1 January	Total	SC	ST	Non-SC/ST
1970	547,629	40,640	12,309	494,680
1971	638,151	59,108	19,412	559,631
1972	814,123	103,416	33,604	677,103

(Table 13A.3 Contd.)

(Table 13A.3 Contd.)

As on 1 January	Total	SC	ST	Non-SC/ST
1973	1,173,680	198,273	89,747	885,660
1974	1,381,279	226,142	99,923	1,055,214
1975	1,372,506	236,810	123,719	1,012,077
1976	1,576,146	275,362	125,364	1,175,420
1977	1,681,360	283,248	128,440	1,269,672
1978	1,737,134	300,405	136,061	1,300,668
1979	1,820,302	317,401	138,364	1,364,537
1980	1,863,204	318,204	144,432	1,400,568
1981	1,946,887	335,441	164,246	1,447,200
1982	1,951,440	338,347	166,876	1,456,217
1983	1,929,990	267,043	179,724	1,483,223
1984	2,053,134	371,625	180,715	1,500,794
1985	2,088,742	395,622	193,381	1,499,739
1986	2,117,179	399,382	195,554	1,522,243
1987	2,134,585	414,539	209,954	1,510,092
1988	2,172,877	423,879	212,460	1,536,538
1989	2,188,835	428,491	216,355	1,543,989
1990	2,215,895	432,890	220,118	1,562,887
1991	2,152,650	365,421	162,819	1,624,410
1992	2,084,914	369,834	162,000	1,553,080
1993	2,084,914	369,834	168,065	1,547,015
1994	2,075,049	371,022	168,065	1,535,962
1995	2,021,500	364,262	160,053	1,497,185
1996	1,973,141	356,366	160,067	1,456,708
1997	1,996,786	362,028	161,917	1,472,841
1998	1,938,094	351,278	155,748	1,431,068
1999	1,926,403	336,140	152,286	1,437,977
2000	1,800,628	324,140	145,581	1,330,907
2001	1,725,656	311,337	141,821	1,272,498
2002	1,636,762	292,677	133,548	1,210,537
2003	1,632,998	296,388	138,504	1,198,106

Source: The Reports of the National Commission for the SCs and the STs and the Annual Report of the Department of Personnel, Public Grievances and Pensions, Government of India (GoI).

Table A13.4
Percentage of SC and ST Employees in Public Sector Undertakings (PSUs) (1970–2003)

As on 1 January	SC	ST	Non-SC/ST
1970	7.42	2.25	90.33
1971	9.26	3.04	87.70
1972	12.70	4.13	83.17
1973	16.89	7.65	75.46
1974	16.37	7.23	76.39
1975	17.25	9.01	73.73
1976	17.47	7.95	74.58
1977	16.85	7.64	75.51
1978	17.29	7.83	74.87
1979	17.44	7.60	74.96
1980	17.08	7.75	75.17
1981	17.23	8.44	74.33
1982	17.25	8.51	74.24
1983	13.84	9.31	76.85
1984	18.10	8.80	73.10
1985	18.94	9.26	71.80
1986	18.86	9.24	71.90
1987	19.42	9.84	70.74
1988	19.51	9.78	70.71
1989	19.58	9.88	70.54
1990	19.54	9.93	70.53
1991	16.98	7.56	75.46
1992	17.74	7.77	74.49
1993	17.74	8.06	74.20
1994	17.88	8.10	74.02
1995	18.02	7.92	74.06
1996	18.06	8.11	73.83
1997	18.13	8.11	73.76
1998	18.12	8.04	73.84
1999	17.45	7.91	74.65
2000	18.00	8.09	73.91
2001	18.04	8.22	73.74
2002	17.88	8.16	73.96
2003	18.15	8.48	73.37

Source: The Reports of the National Commission for the SCs and the STs and the Annual Report of the Department of Personnel, Public Grievances and Pensions, Government of India.

Chapter 14

THE ROAD AHEAD: DALITS IN THE NEW MILLENNIUM

Sukhadeo Thorat and Nidhi Sadana Sabharwal

INTRODUCTION

This book assesses the attainments of Scheduled Castes (SCs), Scheduled Tribes (STs) and the residual category of non-SCs/STs in areas of human development, human poverty and certain other related indicators. These attainments reflect on the access which the concerned social categories enjoy to resources or income-earning assets such as agricultural land and non-land assets, employment, education and social needs like healthcare, water and housing. In addition, they determine the extent and nature of the caste and untouchability-based exclusion and discrimination in the economic, civil, cultural, social and political spheres, as also in terms of various food security programmes and institutions of justice, all of which are useful to identify the factors that contribute towards or curtail human development and support inter-social group disparities. The above-mentioned variables were accessed for the period between 1980 and 2000.

Further, the analysis related to the attainments in human development and human deprivation of the socially marginalised sections, and the changes in the level and disparities in human development index (HDI), human poverty index (HPI) and their individual components during 1983 and 2000 highlight certain trends. The latter enable the book to first segregate the factors responsible for the prevalence of either a high level of human development among certain social groups or states or a low level of attainments and widespread deprivations among these social groups or states. Second, the emerging trends permit the initiation of a policy dialogue to facilitate higher levels of attainment and eliminate deprivation among these groups.

Most significantly, the book observed a positive improvement in HDI and HPI values and other related components of human development and human poverty at the overall levels and for all social groups during 1980–2000. It was found that with some exceptions, the gaps or disparities between SCs and STs, on one hand, and non-SCs/STs, on the other hand, in terms of HDI, HPI and each individual component of these two indices have also reduced during the time period under consideration. However, the rate of decline was more pronounced in case of some indicators than in others. Nevertheless, at overall level, the book submits that disparity between SCs/STs and non-SCs/STs has reduced. Despite the positive improvements in the attainment levels of composite indices of HDI, HPI and related indicators, the rate of improvement among SCs and STs in the HDI and HPI values was not high enough to bridge the gap and bring SCs and STs at par with non-SCs/STs. Albeit, the objective of all government programmes and policies is to facilitate the mainstreaming of marginalised sections. However, despite the composite indices which indicate improvements at the overall levels and for all social groups in 2000, the disparities between the socially marginalised groups comprising SCs and STs, on one hand, and non-SCs/STs, on the other hand, continue to persist to a significant degree.

In case of HDI, the disparity ratio between SCs and non-SCs/STs had improved from 0.57 in 1983 to 0.77 in 2000, thereby approaching the equality value of 1. However, since the base level of HDI for SCs and STs in 1983 was low, the disparity in HDI between them and non-SCs/STs persisted in 2000. The HPI also improved for all the social groups, but at a lower per annum rate for SCs and STs. The net differences between SCs/STs and non-SCs/STs had declined, but the rate of decline was marginal, which is why the disparities between SCs/STs and non-SCs/STs continue to persist over the period 1983–2000. In fact, the gap between SCs/STs and non-SCs/STs seems to have widened during the time period under consideration.

Third, exceptions apart, various individual components of HDI and HPI also indicated trends of persistent disparities between SCs/STs and non-SCs/STs. While the infant mortality ratios were found to have improved for all the social groups during the period 1983–2000, the rate of decline in this indicator was, however, not sufficiently high to significantly reduce the disparity ratios between SCs/STs and non-SCs/STs. Consequently, there was little difference in the disparity ratios for the SCs from 1983 to 2000, while the corresponding disparity for STs actually increased over the given period. The literacy rates also seem to have improved during the time periods under consideration, for all the social groups. The rate of growth for SC and ST population was high enough to reduce inter-social group divide with regard to non-SCs/STs to some extent. However, disparities in this regard too were evident in 2000. The monthly per capita consumption expenditure was also found to have increased for all the social groups. It must be remembered that an increase in the value of monthly per capita consumption expenditure was observed for all social groups and since in the base year, that is, 1983, significant disparities persisted among the social groups, any subsequent increase in the rates for monthly per capita consumption expenditure could not contribute towards decreasing disparities between SCs/STs and non-SCs/STs as the levels of monthly per capita consumption expenditure were increasing from a level that was already higher. The disparity ratios for SCs and STs in 1983 were

0.74 and 0.66, respectively, which remained at 0.73 and 0.66, respectively, in 2000. The incidence of poverty also declined for all the social groups, but again at a lower rate for SCs and STs. The poverty gaps between SCs/STs and non-SCs/STs, in fact, increased during 1983–2000, at least in relative terms, mainly due to a slower decline in poverty for these social groups. Similar trends were also visible for the nutritional levels. Between 1990 and 2000, though the nutritional status of all the three social groups improved, yet it did so by a lower margin for SCs and STs. The access to public health was found to have improved at overall levels and for all social groups. However, the rate of decline was less for SCs and STs and as a result, the gaps between them and non-SCs/STs in terms of the access to public health services continued to persist in 2000.

Fourth, though there have been improvements in the values of HDI, HPI and its other related variables, as was evident from the preceding discussion, the same were lower for SCs and STs as compared to non-SCs/STs or alternatively, at a rate lower than required to bridge the gap between SCs/STs and non-SCs/STs. Therefore, as a direct outcome of the above, the inter-social group disparities seemed to persist in 2000 and the marginalized social groups seemed to lag behind non-SCs/STs in terms of attainment levels. In 2000, as compared to non-SCs/STs, the HDI for SCs and STs was less by a margin of about 23 and 31 percentage points, respectively. Consequently, these groups suffered from a high degree of human deprivation as compared to non-SCs/STs with respect to each of the individual components of HDI and HPI, namely infant mortality ratios, poverty, under nutrition, access to public health services, literacy rates and monthly per capita consumption expenditure in 2000. The disparities between SCs/STs and non-SCs/STs, however, varied for each individual indicator. For instance, in 2000, infant mortality ratio was higher among SCs/STs than non-SCs/STs by about 25 percentage points. In addition, as compared to non-SCs/STs, the literacy rates among SCs and STs were lower by 14 and 21 percentage points, respectively. The monthly per capita consumption expenditure for SCs and STs was also less by about 25 and 34 percentage points, respectively as compared to non-SCs/STs. The incidence of aggregate poverty among SCs and STs was higher by about 70 and 100 percentage points, respectively, as compared to non-SCs/STs. Further, the percentage of undernourished children among SCs and STs was higher by 23 and 27 percentage points, respectively, and access to public health services was less by 23 and 44 percentage points for SCs and STs, respectively, as compared to non-SCs/STs.

Despite an improvement in the levels of HDI and HPI and their individual components among all social groups and subsequent reduction in disparities in HDI and HPI (and also in most of their components, if not all) between all the social groups during 1983–2000, the level of HDI in 2000 among SCs and STs was relatively lower. Hence, the incidence of human poverty among these marginalised groups was relatively high. Similar disparities also prevailed in different components of HDI and HPI.

Fifth, the analysis indicates that the disparities in the achievement levels in HDI and HPI, and their individual components between SCs and STs, on one hand, and non-SCs/STs, on the other hand, are intrinsically linked with the lower access of marginalised groups to sources of income and human resource capabilities. The sources of income and human resource capabilities include capital assets such as agricultural land and non-land assets and/or low productivity of those assets, low urbanisation and employment diversification, exceptionally high dependence on casual wage labour, high incidence of underemployment, low daily wages particularly in non-farm sector, and low level of attainment in literacy rates and educational levels.

Sixth, empirical evidence also shows that lower access for the marginalised groups to resources is linked with the processes of exclusion and discrimination, partly carried forward as the residual impact of the denial of right to property and education in the past, but also in the form of exclusion and discrimination faced by the marginalised social groups in the present. In the economic spheres, the empirical evidence indicates the prevalence of exclusion and differential treatment of the marginalised social groups in various markets, namely agricultural land, capital, employment and consumer goods, as well as in transactions conducted through non-market channels. Discrimination was also evidently experienced by Dalits in terms of access to public services related to education, healthcare, public water sources, post offices and participation in village-level political institutions. In addition, Dalits face violence and atrocities when they make attempts to secure human rights and lawful entitlements. The restrictions assume various covert and overt forms which range from social and economic boycott to incidences of physical violence. In addition, there are ample evidences to suggest that exclusionary and discriminatory treatments persist in the functioning of public institutions specifically with regard to the operation of food security schemes such as the Mid-Day Meal Scheme and the enforcement of anti-discrimination laws by the police, judiciary and other organs of the state. Insofar as the enforcement of anti-discrimination laws is incumbent on the state and its related organs, the same were not found to be independent of caste prejudice. Further, the monitoring mechanisms of the state show that they have certain inherent inadequacies that impede both the enforcement of equal opportunities and punishment of perpetrators of discrimination. Even more worrisome are the discriminatory or the prejudiced attitudes of certain organs of the state like the police and others.

Societal discrimination and exclusion in multiple spheres coupled with violent opposition of higher castes and some organs of the state have drastically reduced the space for SCs and STs to utilise the civil, political and economic rights, and equal opportunities guaranteed to them by the Constitution of India. The failure of entitlements due to caste-based exclusion assumes significant proportions. It becomes apparent that among other reasons, caste- and untouchability-based exclusion and discrimination against SCs and isolation and exclusion of STs in the past and the persistence of these practices in the present (through residual traditional attributes) continue to posit challenges in terms of low level of human development and high level of deprivation among SCs and STs.

The strategy of the Indian policy makers to overcome the adverse effects of discrimination and to address the issue of social exclusion include interventions in the form of legal enforcement of anti-discriminatory laws, group targeting through reservations and other financial schemes such as the Scheduled Castes Sub-Plan and the Tribal Sub-Plan, and preferential and general empowering measures intertwined with anti-poverty programme. These polices have brought about significant and positive changes in the relative positioning of the marginalised social groups, but unfortunately, the rate of improvement in relative condition of the marginalised social groups has not been sufficient to reduce the absolute level of deprivation between them and non-SCs/STs among the Indian population. The continuing incidence of a high degree of 'exclusion-induced deprivation' of the disadvantaged social groups indicates that to address the problem of social exclusion is an even more difficult challenge than to deal with material poverty. The social and cultural sources of exclusion in economic, civil and political spheres, the prevalence of stigmas, dogmas, discrimination and denial of citizenship are rooted in an informal social structure and the institution of caste and untouchability the influence of which not only covers the private domain but also spills over into the public domain governed by the state. In this context, the inclusion of excluded groups, therefore, becomes a somewhat more complex goal in comparison with the objective to ensure the social inclusion of materially deprived people. Poverty, even when broadly defined as exclusion from the means necessary for full participation in normal activities of society, is largely a question of denial of access to resources and services. The exclusion of groups or individuals within that group, on the other hand, is foremost a denial of equal opportunity and thereby, of the recognition of their right to development. Group exclusion is 'horizontal' and in its outcome, may affect even relatively the better-off members within the excluded groups. Fighting discrimination, therefore, necessitates additional policies to complement anti-poverty and economic development programmes. However, since a considerable overlap already exists within the policy measures, there is a need to combine and compliment rather than to divert the programmes.

Developing socially inclusive policies, however, requires informed efforts to deal with the forms, nature and mechanisms of exclusion in the social, political and economic spheres, and their consequences on human development. Facilitated by legal provisions, the issue of discrimination in the social spheres on the basis of caste and untouchability has been well-researched, but studies on exclusion in the political and economic spheres have received less attention and, therefore, require concerted efforts to deal with the problem. This would not only enable various processes to address the nature and forms of economic and political exclusion, but would also be useful to draft and implement policies to tackle the challenges which confront the marginalised social groups.

BIBLIOGRAPHY

ActionAid. 2001. *Untouchability in Rural India* by Ghanshyam Shah, Harsh Mander, Sukhadeo Thorat, Satish Deshpande and Amita Baviskar. New Delhi: SAGE Publications.

Adhav, Vilas. 2005. 'Maharashtratil Durbal Ghatakatil Shetivipanachya Samasya'. Unpublished Ph.D. Thesis submitted to the University of Pune, Pune.

Ambedkar, B. R. 1936. 'Annihilation of Caste', in Basant Moon (ed.), *Dr. Babasaheb Ambedkar: Writings and Speeches*, vol. 1, pp. 3–22. Department of Education, Bombay: Government of Maharashtra.

———. 1945. 'What Congress and Gandhi Have Done to Untouchables', in Vasant Moon (ed.), *Dr. Babasaheb Ambedkar Writings and Speeches*, vol. 9. Department of Education, Bombay: Government of Maharashtra.

———. 1948. *The Untouchables: Who Were They and Why They Became Untouchables?* New Delhi: Amrit Book Co.

———. 1987. 'Philosophy of Hinduism', in Vasant Moon (ed.), *Dr. Babasaheb Ambedkar: Writings and Speeches*, vol. 3, p. 194. Department of Education, Government of Maharashtra.

———. 1987. 'The Hindu Social Order—Its Unique Features', in Vasant Moon (ed.), *Dr. Babasaheb Ambedkar: Writings and Speeches*, vol. 3, pp. 95–115. Department of Education, Government of Maharashtra.

———. 1999. *The Fractured Civilisation: Caste Society in the Throes of Change*. Mumbai: Bhartiya-JanawadiAghadi.

Anitha, B. K. 2000. *Village, Caste and Education*. Jaipur: Rawat Publications.

Banerjee, Biswajit and J. B. Knight. 1985. 'Caste Discrimination in Indian Urban Labour Market', *Journal of Developing Economics*, 17: 277–307.

Birdsall, Nancy and Richard Sabot. 1991. 'Unfair Advantage—Labour Market Discrimination in Developing Countries', World Bank Studies. Washington DC: The World Bank.

Bhalla, A. and F. Lapeyre. 1997. 'Social Exclusion: Towards an Analytical and Operational Framework', *Development and Change*, 28(3): 413–433.

Buvinic, Mayra. 2005. 'Social Exclusion in Latin America', in Mayra Buvinic, Jacqueline Mazza and Ruthanne Deutsch (eds), *Social Inclusion and Economic Development in Latin America*. New York: John Hopkins University Press.

Corbridge, Staurat. 2000. 'Competing Inequalities: The Scheduled Tribes and the Reservation Systems in India's Jharkhand', *The Journal of Asian Studies*, 59(1): 62–85.

Darity, Jr., William. 1995. *Economics and Discrimination*, vols I and II. Elgar Reference Collection, USA.

———. 1997. "Reparations", in Samuel L. Myers, Jr. (ed.), *Civil Rights and Race Relations in the Post Reagan-Bush Era*. London: Praeger.

Darity, Jr. William and Steven Shulman. 1989. *Question of Discrimination—Racial Inequality in the US Labour Market*. Middletown, Connecticut: Wesleyan University Press.

de Haan, Arjan. 1997. 'Poverty and Social Exclusion: A Comparison of Debates on Deprivation', *Working Paper No. 2*, Poverty Research Unit, University of Sussex, Brighton.

de Haan, Arjan and Amaresh Dubey. 2003. Draft paper for Manchester conference on Chronic Poverty, April 2003, session 'Social Exclusion, Rights and Chronic Poverty'.

Dreze, Jean and Haris Gazdar. 1996. 'Uttar Pradesh: The burden of inertia', in Jean Dreze and Amartya Sen (eds), *Indian Development: Selected Regional Perspectives*, pp. 33–128. New Delhi: Oxford University Press.

Galanter, Mark. 1984. *Competing Equalities—Law and the Backward Classes in India*. Berkeley: University of California Press.

Ghanekar-Kajale, Jayanti. 1998. 'An Analysis of Wages of Agricultural Labourers in Maharashtra: 1961–1994'. Unpublished Ph.D. Thesis submitted to Gokhale Institute of Politics and Economics, Pune: University of Pune.

Government of Assam. 2003. *Assam Human Development Report 2003*. Dispur: Planning and Development Department, Government of Assam.

Government of Himachal Pradesh. 2002. *Himachal Pradesh Human Development Report 2002*. Shimla: Government of Himachal Pradesh.

Government of India. 1990. *Agricultural Census—1985–86*. Census Commissioner, New Delhi: Ministry of Agriculture.

———. 1998. *All India Report on Agricultural Census 1990–91*. New Delhi: Ministry of Agriculture.

———. 2005. *Agricultural Statistics at a Glance*. Directorate of Economics and Statistics, New Delhi: Ministry of Agriculture.

———. 2005. *Annual Report 2004–05*. New Delhi: Ministry of Tribal Affairs.

———. 2008. *Annual Report 2007–08*. New Delhi: Ministry of Social Justice and Empowerment.

Government of Karnataka. 2005. *Karnataka Human Development Report 2005: Investing in Human Development*. Bangalore: Planning and Statistics Department, Government of Karnataka.

Government of Madhya Pradesh. 2002. *The Madhya Pradesh Human Development Report 2002: Using the Power of Democracy for Development*. Bhopal: Government of Madhya Pradesh.

Government of Maharashtra. 2002. *Human Development Report Maharashtra 2002*. Mumbai: Government of Maharashtra.

Government of Punjab. 2004. *Human Development Report 2004: Punjab*. New Delhi: Government of Punjab.

Government of Rajasthan. 2002. *Rajasthan Human Development Report 2002*. Jaipur: Government of Rajasthan.

Government of Sikkim. 2001. *Sikkim Human Development Report 2001*. Delhi: Government of Sikkim and Social Science Press.

Government of Tamil Nadu. 2003. *Tamil Nadu Human Development Report*. Delhi: Government of Tamil Nadu and Social Science Press.

Government of West Bengal. 2004. *West Bengal Human Development Report 2004*, Development and Planning Department: Government of West Bengal.

Gupta, Dipankar. 2000. *Interrogating Caste: Understanding Hierarchy and Difference in Indian Society*. New Delhi: Penguin Books India.

Halis, Akder. 1994. 'A Means to Closing Gaps: Disaggregated Human Development Index', UNDP Occasional Paper 18. New York: United Nations Development Programme.

Haq, Mahbub-Ul. 1995. *Reflections on Human Development*. New York: Oxford University Press.

Hooda, Sagar Preet. 2001. *Contesting Reservations*. Jaipur and New Delhi: Rawat Publications.

International Institute for Population Sciences (IIPS). 1995. *National Family Health Survey (MCH and Family Planning), India 1992–93*. Bombay: IIPS.

International Institute for Population Sciences (IIPS) and OCR Macro. 2000. *National Family Health Survey (NFHS-2), 1998–99: India*. Mumbai: IIPS.

Jomo, K. S. 2003. 'Ethnic Discrimination: A Critical Survey of Economic Explanations', Department of Applied Economics, University of Malaya, Kuala Lumpur, Malaysia.

Kamble, B. N. 1985. 'Effectiveness of Developmental Programmes for Scheduled Castes and Scheduled Tribes in Maharashtra'. Unpublished Ph.D. Thesis submitted to Gokhale Institute of Politics and Economics, Pune: University of Pune.

Khan, Mumtaz Ali. 1995. *Human Rights and the Dalits*. Delhi: Uppal Publishers.

Kirpal, V. and M. Gupta. 1999. *Equality through Reservations*. Jaipur and New Delhi: Rawat Publications.

Lal, Deepak. 1988. *Hindu Equilibrium, Cultural Stability and Economic Stagnation*, vol. 1. Oxford: Clarendon Press.

Mishra, Narayan. 2001. *Scheduled Castes Education: Issues and Aspects*. New Delhi: Kalpaz Publications.

Nabhi's Brochure. 2003. *Reservation and Concessions for Scheduled Castes, Scheduled Tribes, Other Backward Classes*, 3rd revised edition. New Delhi: Nabhi Publication.

Nalwade, M. D. 2003. *Chhatrapati Shahu and His Reservation Policy*. Jaipur: Mahatma Publishers.

Nambissan, Geetha B. 2001. 'Social diversity and regional disparities in schooling: A study of rural Rajasthan', in A. Vaidyanathan and P.R. Gopinathan (eds), *Elementary Education in Rural India*. New Delhi: SAGE Publications.

National Crime Records Bureau. 1999, 2000 and 2001. *Crime in India*. Ministry of Home Affairs, New Delhi: Government of India.

Nayak, Vijay and Shailaja Prasad. 1984. 'On Levels of Living of Scheduled Castes and Scheduled Tribes', *Economic and Political Weekly*, 19(30): 1205–1213.

Omvedt, Gail. 1996. 'Economic Policy, Poverty and Dalits'. Paper presented at the Seminar on 'Impact of NEP on Dalits'. Department of Sociology, Pune: University of Pune.

Panandiker, V. A. Pai (ed.). 1997. *The Politics of Backwardness: Reservation Policy in India*. Delhi: Konark Publishers Pvt. Ltd.

Planning Commission. 2002. *National Human Development Report 2001*. New Delhi: Government of India.

Radhakrishnan, P. 2002. 'Sensitising Officials on Dalits and Reservations', *Economic and Political Weekly*, 37(7): 653–659.

Rao, S. S. 2001. 'Equality in Higher Education: Impact of Affirmative Action Policies in India', in E. F. Beckham (ed.), *Global Collaborations: The Role of Higher Education in Diverse Democracies*. Washington, DC: Association of American Colleges and Universities.

Scoville, James G. L. 1996. "Labour Market Underpinnings of a Caste Economy—Failing the Caste Theorem", *The American Journal of Economics and Sociology*, 55(4 October): 385–394.

Sen, Abhijit. 1996. 'Economic Reforms, Employment and Poverty: Trends and Options', *Economic and Political Weekly*, 31(31–33): 2459–2477.

Sen, Abhijit, and Himanshu. 2004. 'Poverty and Inequality in India: I', *Economic and Political Weekly*, XXXIX(38): 4247–4263.

Sen, A. 2000. 'Social Exclusion: Concept, Application, and Scrutiny', Social Development paper no. 1, Asian Development Bank.

Sridevi, G. 2005. 'Food Security in the Context of Liberalisation: A Case of Andhra Pradesh', Unpublished Ph.D. Thesis. Bangalore: Institute for Social and Economic Change.

Thorat, S. K. 1996. 'Ambedkar on Economics of Hindu Social Order: Understanding its Orthodoxy and Legacy', in Walter Fernandes (ed.), *The Emerging Dalit Identity*. New Delhi: Indian Social Institute.

Thorat, S. K. and R. S. Deshpande. 1999. 'Caste and Labour Market Discrimination', *Indian Journal of Labour Economics*, 42(4): 25–35.

Thorat, Sukhadeo. 2000. 'Isolation and Deprivations: Economic Situation of Tribals in India', in Department of Economics, Dr. Babashaheeb Marathwada University (ed.), *Development Issue in India*. Aurangabad, Maharashtra.

Thorat, Sukhadeo. 2001. 'Caste and Untouchability-based Economic and market Discrimination—Theory, Concept and Consequences', *ArthaVidhyan*, XLIII(1–2).

———. 2002. 'Oppression and Denial—Dalit Discrimination in the 1990s', *Economic and Political Weekly*, 37(6): 572–578.

———. 2003. 'Caste, Ethnicity, and Religion: An Overview Paper on Exclusion/Discrimination and Deprivation', Concept Paper for DFID, Delhi, May.

———. 2004a. 'On Reservation Policy for the Private Sector', *Economic and Political Weekly*, 39(25): 717–726.

———. 2004b. 'Remedies against Economic Discrimination—International Experience of Reservation Policy in the Private Sector', in Bibek Debroy and Shyam Babu (eds), *The Dalit Question—Reforms and Social Justice*. Delhi: Globus.

Thorat, S. K. and Umakant. 2004. *Caste, Race and Discrimination*. New Delhi and Jaipur: Indian Institute of Dalit Studies, and Rawat Publications.

Thorat, Sukhadeo, Aryama and Prashant Negi (eds). 2005. *Reservation and Private Sector—Quest for Equal Opportunity and Growth*. New Delhi: Rawat Publications.

Tilak, Jandhyala BG. 2002. 'Education and poverty', *Journal of Human Development* 3(2): 191–207.

Tripathy, R. B. 1994. *Dalits: A Sub-human Society*. Delhi: Ashish Publishing House.

United Nations Development Programme. 2000. *Human Development Report 2000: Human Rights and Human Development*. New York: Oxford University Press.

United Nations Development Programme. 2004. *Human Development Report 2004: Cultural Liberty in Today's Diverse World*. New York: Hoechstetter Printing Co.

Venkateswarlu, D. 1990. *Harijan–Upper Class Conflict*. New Delhi: Discovery Publishing House Private Limited.

Weisskopf, Thomas E. 2004. *Affirmative Action in the United States and India: A Comparative Perspective*. London: Routledge.

Zoninsein, Jonas. 2001. 'GDP Gains and Long Term Discrimination against Blacks: The Inverse Relationship', in Charles V. Hamilton, Lynn Huntley, Neville Alexander, Antonio Sergio Alfredo Guimaraes and Wilmot James (eds), *Beyond Racism: Race and Inequality in Brazil, South Africa and the United States*. Colorado and London: Lynne Rienner Publishers, Inc.

ABOUT THE EDITORS AND CONTRIBUTORS

EDITORS

Sukhadeo Thorat is Chairman, Indian Council of Social Science Research (ICSSR); former Chairman of University Grants Commission (UGC); and Professor of Economics, Jawaharlal Nehru University, New Delhi. He has a BA (Milind College of Arts, Aurangabad, Maharashtra), MA in Economics (Dr Babasaheb Ambedkar Marathwada University, Aurangabad), MPhil/PhD in Economics (Jawaharlal Nehru University) and Diploma in Economic Planning (Main School of Planning, Warsaw, Poland). His research areas include agricultural development, rural poverty, institution and economic growth, problems of marginalised groups, economics of caste system, caste discrimination and poverty. He was the Director of the Indian Institute of Dalit Studies, New Delhi from 2003 to 2006 and the Research Associate of International Food Policy Research Institute, Washington DC, USA, since 1992.

Nidhi Sadana Sabharwal is currently the Director at the Indian Institute of Dalit Studies (IIDS), New Delhi. She is also in charge of the Gender and Social Exclusion Studies Unit at IIDS. She has a PhD from Jawaharlal Nehru University, New Delhi, with specialisation in economic geography, and has significant experience in human development research. She has published articles on caste, ethnicity and economic discrimination, caste and religion links to malnutrition and child labour. She has extensive experience in data collection and analysis and policy advocacy. She has actively worked on key issues affecting the poor and vulnerable in India, through organisations based in India and the United Kingdom.

CONTRIBUTORS

Vijay Kumar Baraik is the Reader in Geography in the School of Sciences at Indira Gandhi National Open University, New Delhi. His areas of interests are regional development and planning especially in the tribal areas of India and applications of geoinformatics in research and development. He has succefully applied geoinformatics in development planning and eGovernance.

Ashwini Deshpande is the Professor in the Department of Economics at Delhi School of Economics, University of Delhi. Her areas of specialisation include economics of discrimination with a focus on caste and gender in India, inequalities and group disparities; aspects of the Chinese economy; and International debt.

R. S. Deshpande is the Director, Institute for Social and Economic Change, Bengaluru. His specialisations include agricultural development policy, watershed development, agriculture and trade, rural policy and poverty, economics of drought-prone areas and rainfed regions, economics of irrigation, policy analysis and applied econometrics.

Amaresh Dubey is Professor of Economics in the Centre for the Study of Regional Development, School of Social Sciences, Jawaharlal Nehru University, New Delhi. His research interest includes poverty assessment, education and labour markets.

Arjan de Haan leads the International Development Research Centre's (Canada) programme supporting inclusive growth, social and economic policy. He is a development expert who focuses on public policy and poverty in Asia. His expertise is on social policy, social exclusion, poverty measurement and migration.

P. M. Kulkarni is Professor in Population Studies, in the Centre for the Study of Regional Development, School of Social Sciences, Jawaharlal Nehru University, New Delhi. His areas of specialisation include health, health policies and demographic techniques.

Motilal Mahamallik is Assistant Professor at the Institute of Development Studies, Jaipur. His areas of specialisation include poverty and human development with a focus on marginalised groups, rural agrarian institutions, social exclusion and economics of discrimination.

Prashant Negi is Assistant Professor in Dr K. R. Narayanan Centre for Dalit and Minorities Studies and Programme for Social Exclusion and Inclusive Policy, Jamia Millia Islamia, New Delhi. He is a sociologist whose areas of specialisation are theoretical approaches to social exclusion, development theory, challenges of transformation and change, and topical issues pertaining to Tribals/Dalits, marginality and deprivation. He is particularly interested in the psychology of discrimination and exclusion, and the pedagogy of oppression.

Chittaranjan Senapati is Asssistant Professor of Politics and International Relations at the Pandit Deendayal Petroleum University, Gandhinagar. His areas of specialisation include industrial development, marginalised groups, ethnicity, poverty, exclusion and inclusive policy.

Sachidanand Sinha is Associate Professor, Centre for the Study of Regional Development, School of Social Sciences, Jawaharlal Nehru University, New Delhi. His areas of specialisation include education, health and study of marginalised groups.

M. Thangaraj is Professor in the Department of Economics at the University of Madras. His areas of specialisation include economic development, marginalised groups and discrimination.

S. Venkatesan is currently working as the Programme Administrator with DanChurch Aid, South Asia Regional Office, New Delhi. His areas of specialisation include caste, social exclusion, power relations, human development, Dalit development, public policy, civil society and social justice.

INDEX